The Pro-slavery Argument

THE
PRO-SLAVERY ARGUMENT,

AS MAINTAINED BY THE MOST

DISTINGUISHED WRITERS OF THE SOUTHERN STATES:

CONTAINING THE

SEVERAL ESSAYS, ON THE SUBJECT,

OF

CHANCELLOR HARPER, GOVERNOR HAMMOND,
DR. SIMMS, AND PROFESSOR DEW.

PHILADELPHIA:
LIPPINCOTT, GRAMBO, & CO.
1853.

B33.8.10
KD 40076

HARVARD
UNIVERSITY
LIBRARY

HARPER ON SLAVERY.

THE institution of domestic slavery exists over far the greater portion of the inhabited earth. Until within a very few centuries, it may be said to have existed over the whole earth—at least in all those portions of it which had made any advances towards civilization. We might safely conclude then, that it is deeply founded in the nature of man and the exigencies of human society. Yet, in the few countries in which it has been abolished—claiming, perhaps justly, to be farthest advanced in civilization and intelligence, but which have had the smallest opportunity of observing its true character and effects—it is denounced as the most intolerable of social and political evils. Its existence, and every hour of its continuance, is regarded as the crime of the communities in which it is found. Even by those in the countries alluded to, who regard it with the most indulgence or the least abhorrence—who attribute no criminality to the present generation—who found it in existence, and have not yet been able to devise the means of abolishing it,—it is pronounced a misfortune and a curse injurious and dangerous always, and which must be finally fatal to the societies which admit it. This is no longer regarded as a subject of argument and investigation. The opinions referred to are assumed as settled, or the truth of them as self-evident. If any voice is raised among ourselves to extenuate or to vindicate, it is unheard. The judgment is made up. We can have no hearing before the tribunal of the civilized world. Yet, on this very account, it is more important that we, the inhabitants of the slaveholding States of America, insulated as we are, by this institution, and cut off, in some degree, from the communion and sympathies of the world by which we are surrounded, or with which we have intercourse, and exposed continually to their animadversions and attacks, should thoroughly understand this subject, and our strength and weakness in relation to it. If it be thus criminal, dangerous, and fatal; and if it be possible to devise means of freeing ourselves from it, we ought at once to set about the employing of those means. It would be the most wretched and imbecile fatuity, to shut our eyes to the impending dangers and horrors, and "drive darkling down the current of our fate," till we are overwhelmed in the final destruction. If we are tyrants, cruel, unjust, oppressive, let us humble ourselves and repent in the sight of heaven, that the foul stain may be cleansed, and we enabled to stand erect as having common claims to humanity with our fellow-men.

But if we are nothing of all this; if we commit no injustice or cruelty; if the maintenance of our institutions be essential to our prosperity, our character, our safety, and the safety of all that is dear to us, let us enlighten our minds and fortify our hearts to defend them.

It is a somewhat singular evidence of the indisposition of the rest of the world to hear anything more on this subject, that perhaps the most profound, original, and truly philosophical treatise, which has appeared within the time of my recollection,* seems not to have attracted the slightest attention out of the limits of the slaveholding States themselves. If truth, reason, and conclusive argument, propounded with admirable temper and perfect candor, might be supposed to

* President Dew's Review of the Virginia Debates on the subject of Slavery.

have an effect on the minds of men, we should think this work would have put an end to agitation on the subject. The author has rendered inappreciable service to the South in enlightening them on the subject of their own institutions, and turning back that monstrous tide of folly and madness which, if it had rolled on, would have involved his own great State along with the rest of the slaveholding States in a common ruin. But beyond these, he seems to have produced no effect whatever. The denouncers of Slavery, with whose productions the press groans, seems to be unaware of his existence—unaware that there is reason to be encountered or argument to be answered. They assume that the truth is known and settled, and only requires to be enforced by denunciation.

Another vindicator of the South has appeared in an individual who is among those that have done honor to American literature.* With conclusive argument, and great force of expression, he has defended Slavery from the charge of injustice or immorality, and shewn clearly the unspeakable cruelty and mischief which must result from any scheme of abolition. He does not live among slaveholders, and it cannot be said of him, as of others, that his mind is warped by interest, or his moral sense blunted by habit and familiarity with abuse. These circumstances, it might be supposed, would have secured him hearing and consideration. He seems to be equally unheeded, and the work of denunciation disdaining argument, still goes on.

President Dew has shewn that the institution of Slavery is a principal cause of civilization. Perhaps nothing can be more evident than that it is the sole cause. If anything can be predicated as universally true of uncultivated man, it is that he will not labor beyond what is absolutely necessary to maintain his existence. Labor is pain to those who are unac-

* Paulding on Slavery.

customed to it, and the nature of man is averse to pain. Even with all the training, the helps and motives of civilization, we find that this aversion cannot be overcome in many individuals of the most cultivated societies. The coercion of Slavery alone is adequate to form man to habits of labor. Without it, there can be no accumulation of property, no providence for the future, no tastes for comfort or elegancies, which are the characteristics and essentials of civilization. He who has obtained the command of another's labor, first begins to accumulate and provide for the future, and the foundations of civilization are laid. We find confirmed by experience that which is so evident in theory. Since the existence of man upon the earth, with no exception whatever, either of ancient or modern times, every society which has attained civilization, has advanced to it through this process.

Will those who regard Slavery as immoral, or crime in itself, tell us that man was not intended for civilization, but to roam the earth as a biped brute? That he was not to raise his eyes to heaven, or be conformed in his nobler faculties to the image of his Maker? Or will they say that the Judge of all the earth has done wrong in ordaining the means by which alone that end can be obtained? It is true that the Creator can make the wickedness as well as the wrath of man to praise him, and bring forth the most benevolent results from the most atrocious actions. But in such cases, it is the motive of the actor alone which condemns the action. The act itself is good, if it promotes the good purposes of God, and would be approved by him, if that result only were intended. Do they not blaspheme the providence of God who denounce as wickedness and outrage, that which is rendered indispensable to his purposes in the government of the world? Or at what stage of the progress of society will they say that Slavery ceases to be necessary, and its very existence becomes sin and crime? I am aware that such argument would have little effect on those with whom it would be degrading to contend—who pervert the inspired writings—which in some parts expressly sanction Slavery, and throughout indicate most clearly that it is a civil institution, with which religion has no concern—with a shallowness and presumption not less flagrant and shameless than his, who would justify murder from the text, "and Phineas arose and executed judgment."

There seems to be something in this subject which blunts the perceptions, and darkens and confuses the understandings and moral feelings of men. Tell them that, of necessity, in every civilized society, there must be an infinite variety of conditions and employments, from the most eminent and intellectual, to the most servile and laborious; that the negro race, from their temperament and capacity, are peculiarly suited to the situation which they occupy, and not less happy in it than any corresponding class to be found in the world; prove incontestibly that no scheme of emancipation could be carried into effect without the most intolerable mischiefs and calamities to both master and slave, or without probably throwing a large and fertile portion of the earth's surface out of the pale of civilization—and you have done nothing. They reply, that whatever may be the consequence, you are bound to do *right*; that man has a right to himself, and man cannot have property in man; that if the negro race be naturally inferior in mind and character, they are not less entitled to the rights of humanity; that if they are happy in their condition, it affords but the stronger evidence of their degradation, and renders them still more objects of commiseration. They repeat, as the fundamental maxim of our civil policy, that all men are born free and equal, and quote from our Declaration of Independence, "that men are endowed by their Creator with certain inalienable *rights*, among which are life, liberty, and the pursuit of happiness."

It is not the first time that I have had occasion to observe that men may repeat with the utmost confidence, some maxim or sentimental phrase, as self-evident or admitted truth, which is either palpably false, or to which, upon examination, it will be found that they attach no definite idea. Notwithstanding our respect for the important document which declared our independence, yet if any thing be found in it, and especially in what may be regarded rather as its ornament than its substance—false, sophistical or unmeaning, that respect should not screen it from the freest examination.

All men are born free and equal. Is it not palpably nearer the truth to say that no man was ever born free, and that no two men were ever born equal? Man is born in a state of the most helpless dependence on others. He continues subject to the absolute control of others, and remains without many of the civil and all of the political privileges of his society, until the period which the laws have fixed as that at which he is supposed to have attained the maturity of his faculties. Then inequality is further developed, and becomes infinite in every society, and under whatever form of government. Wealth and poverty, fame or obscurity, strength or weakness, knowledge or ignorance, ease or labor, power or subjection, mark the endless diversity in the condition of men.

But we have not arrived at the profundity of the maxim. This inequality is, in a great measure, the result of abuses in the institutions of society. They do not speak of what exists, but of what ought to exist. Every one should be left at liberty to obtain all the advantages of society which he can compass, by the free exertion of his faculties, unimpeded by civil restraints. It may be said that this would not remedy the evils of society which are complained of. The inequalities to which I have referred, with the misery resulting from them, would exist in fact under the freest and most popular form of government that man could devise. But what is the foundation of the bold dogma so confidently announced? Females are human and rational beings. They may be found of better faculties, and better qualified to exercise political privileges, and to attain the distinctions of society, than many men; yet who complains of the order of society by which they are excluded from them? For I do not speak of the few who would desecrate them; do violence to the nature which their Creator has impressed upon them; drag them from the position which they necessarily occupy for the existence of civilized society, and in which they constitute its blessing and ornament—the only position which they have ever occupied in any human society—to place them in a situation in which they would be alike miserable and degraded. Low as we descend in combating the theories of presumptuous dogmatists, it cannot be necessary to stoop to this. A youth of eighteen may have powers which cast into the shade those of any of his more advanced cotemporaries. He may be capable of serving or saving his country, and if not permitted to do so now, the occasion may have been lost forever. But he can exercise no political privilege, or aspire to any political distinction. It is said that, of necessity, society must exclude from some civil and political privileges those who are unfitted to exercise them, by infirmity, unsuitableness of character, or defect of discretion; that of necessity there must be some general rule on the subject, and that any rule which can be devised will operate with hardship and injustice on individuals. This is all that can be said, and all that need be said. It is saying, in other words, that the privileges in question are no matter of natural right, but to be settled by convention, as the good and safety of society may require. If society should disfranchise individuals convicted of infamous crimes, would this be an invasion of natural right? Yet this would not be justified on the score of their moral guilt, but that the good of society required or would be promoted by it. We admit the existence of a moral law, binding on societies as on individuals. Society must act in good faith. No man, or body of men, has a right to inflict pain or privation on others, unless with a view, after full and impartial deliberation, to prevent a greater evil. If this deliberation be had, and the decision made in good faith, there can be no imputation of moral guilt. Has any politician contended that the very existence of governments in which there are orders privileged by law, constitutes a violation of morality; that their continuance is a crime, which men are bound to put an end to, without any consideration of the good or evil to result from the change? Yet this is the natural inference from the dogma of the natural equality of men as applied to our institution of Slavery—an equality not to be invaded without injustice and wrong, and requiring to be restored instantly, unqualifiedly, and without reference to consequences.

This is sufficiently common-place, but we are sometimes driven to common-place. It is no less a false and shallow, than a presumptuous philosophy, which theorizes on the affairs of men as of a problem to be solved by some unerring rule of human reason, without reference to the designs of a superior intelligence, so far as he has been pleased to indicate them, in their creation and destiny. Man is born to subjection. Not only during infancy is he dependent, and under the control of others; at all ages, it is the very bias of his nature, that the strong and the wise should control the weak and the ignorant. So it has been since the days of Nimrod. The existence of some form of slavery in all ages and countries, is proof enough of this. He is born to subjection as he is born in sin and ignorance. To make any considerable progress in knowledge, the continued efforts of successive generations, and the diligent training and unwearied exertions of the individual, are requisite. To make progress in moral virtue, not less time and effort, aided by superior help, are necessary; and it is only by the matured exercise of his knowledge and his virtue, that he can attain to civil freedom. Of all things, the existence of civil liberty is most the result of artificial institution. The proclivity of the natural man is to domineer or to be subservient. A noble result, indeed, but in the attaining of which, as in the instances of knowledge and virtue, the Creator, for his own purposes, has set a limit beyond which we cannot go.

But he who is most advanced in knowledge, is most sensible of his own ignorance, and how much must forever be unknown to man in his present condition. As I have heard it expressed, the further you extend the circle of light, the wider is the horizon of darkness. He who has made the greatest progress in moral purity, is most sensible of the depravity, not only of the world around him, but of his own heart, and the imperfection of his best motives; and this he knows that men must feel and lament so long as they continue men. So when the greatest progress in civil liberty has been made, the enlightened lover of liberty will know that there must remain much inequality, much injustice, much *slavery*, which no human wisdom or virtue will ever be able wholly to prevent or redress. As I have before had the honor to say to this Society, the condition of our whole existence is but to struggle with evils—to compare them—to choose between them, and, so far as we can, to mitigate them. To say that there is evil in any institution, is only to say that it is human.

And can we doubt but that this long discipline and laborious process, by which men are required to work out the elevation and improvement of their individual nature and their social condition, is imposed for a great and benevolent end? Our faculties are not adequate to the solution of the mystery, why it should be so; but the truth is clear, that the world was not intended for the seat of universal knowledge, or goodness, or happiness, or freedom.

Man has been endowed by his Creator with certain inalienable rights, among which are life, liberty, and the pursuit of happiness. What is meant by the *inalienable* right of liberty? Has any one who has used the words ever asked himself this question? Does it mean that a man has no right to alienate his own liberty—to sell himself and his posterity for slaves? This would seem to be the more obvious meaning. When the word *right* is used, it has reference to some law which sanctions it, and would be violated by its invasion. It must refer either to the general law of morality, or the law of the country—the law of God or the law of man. If the law of any country permitted it, it would of course be absurd to say that the law of that country was violated by such alienation. If it have any meaning in this respect, it must mean that though the law of the country permitted it, the man would be guilty of an immoral act who should thus alienate his liberty. A fit question for schoolmen to discuss, and the consequences resulting from its decision as important as from any of theirs. Yet who will say that the man pressed by famine, and in prospect of death, would be criminal for such an act? Self-preservation, as is truly said, is the first law of nature. High and peculiar characters, by elaborate cultivation, may be taught to prefer death to slavery, but it would be folly to prescribe this as a duty to the mass of mankind.

If any rational meaning can be attributed to the sentence I have quoted, it is this:—That the society, or the individuals who exercise the powers of government, are guilty of a violation of the law of God or of morality, when, by any law or public act, they deprive men of life or liberty, or restrain them in the pursuit of happiness. Yet every government does, and of necessity must, deprive men of life and liberty for offences against society. Restrain them in the pursuit of happiness ! Why all the laws of society are intended for nothing else but to restrain men from the pursuit of happiness, according to their own ideas of happiness or advantage—which the phrase must mean if it means any thing. And by what right does society punish by the loss of life or liberty? Not on account of the moral guilt of the criminal—not by impiously and arrogantly assuming the prerogative of the Almighty, to dispense justice or suffering, according to moral desert. It is for its own protection—it is the right of self-defence. If there existed the blackest moral turpitude, which by its example or consequences, could be of no evil to society, government would have nothing to do with that. If an action, the most harmless in its moral character, could be dangerous to the security of society, society would have the perfect right to punish it. If the possession of a black skin would be otherwise dangerous to society, society has the same right to protect itself by disfranchising the possessor of civil privileges, and to continue the disability to his posterity, if the same danger would be incurred by its removal. Society inflicts these forfeitures for the security of the lives of its members; it inflicts them for the security of their property, the great essential of civilization; it inflicts them also for the protection of its political institutions, the forcible attempt to overturn which, has always been justly regarded as the greatest crime; and who has questioned its right so to inflict? "Man cannot have property in man"—a phrase as full of meaning as, " who slays fat oxen should himself be fat."

Certainly he may, if the laws of society allow it, and if it be on sufficient grounds, neither he nor society do wrong.

And is it by this—as we must call it, however recommended to our higher feelings by its associations—well-sounding, but unmeaning verbiage of natural equality and inalienable rights, that our lives are to be put in jeopardy, our property destroyed, and our political institutions overturned or endangered? If a people had on its borders a tribe of barbarians, whom no treaties or faith could bind, and by whose attacks they were constantly endangered, against whom they could devise no security, but that they should be exterminated or enslaved; would they not have the right to enslave them, and keep them in slavery so long as the same danger would be incurred by their manumission? If a civilized man and a savage were by chance placed together on a desolate island, and the former, by the superior power of civilization, would reduce the latter to subjection, would he not have the same right? Would this not be the strictest self-defence? I do not now consider, how far we can make out a similar case to justify our enslaving of the negroes. I speak to those who contend for inalienable rights, and that the existence of slavery always, and under all circumstances, involves injustice and crime.

As I have said, we acknowledge the existence of a moral law. It is not necessary for us to resort to the theory which resolves all right into force. The existence of such a law is imprinted on the hearts of all human beings. But though its existence be acknowledged, the mind of man has hitherto been tasked in vain to discover an unerring standard of morality. It is a common and undoubted maxim of morality, that you shall not do evil that good may come. You shall not do injustice or commit an invasion of the rights of others, for the sake of a greater ulterior good. But what is injustice, and what are the rights of others? And why are we not to commit the one or invade the others? It is because it inflicts pain or suffering, present or prospective, or cuts them off from enjoyment which they might otherwise attain. The Creator has sufficiently revealed to us that *happiness* is the great end of existence, the sole object of all animated and sentient beings. To this he has directed their aspirations and efforts, and we feel that we thwart his benevolent purposes when we destroy or impede that happiness. This is the only *natural* right of man. All other rights result from the conventions of society, and these, to be sure, we are not to invade, whatever good may appear to us likely to follow. Yet are we in no instance to inflict pain or suffering, or disturb enjoyment, for the sake of producing a greater good? Is the madman not to be restrained who would bring destruction on himself or others? Is pain not to be inflicted on the child, when it is the only means by which he can be effectually instructed to provide for his own future happiness? Is the surgeon guilty of wrong who amputates a limb to preserve life? Is not the object of all penal legislation, to inflict suffering for the sake of greater good to be secured to society?

By what right is it that man exercises dominion over the beasts of the field; subdues them to painful labor, or deprives them of life for his sustenance or enjoyment? They are not rational beings. No, but they are the creatures of God, sentient beings, capable of suffering and enjoyment, and entitled to enjoy according to the measure of their capacities. Does not the voice of nature inform every one, that he is guilty of wrong when he inflicts on them pain without necessity or object? If their existence be limited to the present life, it affords the stronger argument for affording them the brief enjoyment of which it is capable. · It is because the greater good is effected; not only to man but to the inferior animals themselves. The care of man gives the boon of existence to myriads who would never otherwise have enjoyed it, and the enjoyment of their existence is better provided for while it lasts. It belongs to the being of superior faculties to judge of the relations which shall subsist between himself and inferior animals, and the use he shall make of them; and he may justly consider himself, who has the greater capacity of enjoyment, in the first instance. Yet he must do this conscientiously, and no doubt, moral guilt has been incurred by the infliction of pain on these animals, with no adequate benefit to be expected. I do no disparagement to the dignity of human nature, even in its humblest form, when I say that on the very same foundation, with the difference only of circumstance and degree, rests the right of the civilized and cultivated man, over the savage and ignorant. It is the order of nature and of God, that the being of superior faculties and knowledge, and therefore of superior power, should control and dispose of those who are inferior. It is as much in the order of nature, that men should enslave each other, as that other animals should prey upon each other. I admit that he does this under the highest moral responsibility, and is most guilty if he wantonly inflicts misery or privation on beings more capable of enjoyment or suffering than brutes, without necessity or any view to the greater good which is to result. If we conceive of society existing without government, and that one man by his superior strength, courage or wisdom, could obtain the mastery of his fellows, he would have a perfect right to do so. He would be morally responsible for the use of his power, and guilty if he failed to direct them so as to promote their happiness as well as his own. Moralists have denounced the injustice and cruelty which have been practised towards our aboriginal Indians, by which they have been driven from their native seats and exterminated, and no doubt with much justice. No doubt, much fraud and injustice has been practised in the circumstances and the manner of their removal. Yet who has contended that civilized man had no moral right to possess himself of the country? That he was bound to leave this wide and fertile continent, which is capable of sustaining uncounted myriads of a civilized race, to a few roving and ignorant barbarians? Yet if any thing is certain, it is certain that there were no means by which he could possess the country, without exterminating or enslaving them. Savage and civilized man cannot live together, and the savage can only be tamed by being enslaved or by having slaves. By enslaving alone could he have preserved them.* And who shall take upon himself to decide that the more benevolent course, and more pleasing to God, was pursued towards them, or that it would not have been better that they had been enslaved generally, as they were in particular instances? It is a refined philosophy, and utterly false in its application to general nature, or the mass of human kind, which teaches that existence is not the greatest of all boons, and worthy of being preserved even under the most adverse circumstances. The strongest instinct of all animated beings sufficiently proclaims this. When the last red man shall have vanished from our forests, the sole remaining traces of his blood will be found among our enslaved population.† The African slave trade has given, and will give, the boon of existence to millions and millions in our country, who would otherwise never have enjoyed it, and the enjoyment of their existence is better provided for while it lasts. Or if, for the rights of man over inferior animals, we are referred to reve-

* I refer to President Dew on this subject.
† It is not uncommon, especially in Charleston, to see slaves, after many descents and having mingled their blood with the Africans, possessing Indian hair and features.

lation, which pronounces—" ye shall have dominion over the beasts of the field, and over the fowls of the air," we refer to the same, which declares not the less explicitly—

" Both the bondmen and bondmaids which thou shalt have, shall be of the heathen that are among you. Of them shall you buy bondmen and bondmaids."

" Moreover of the children of strangers that do sojourn among you, of them shall ye buy, and of their families that are with you, which they begot in your land, and they shall be your possession. And ye shall take them as an inheritance for your children after you, to inherit them by possession. They shall be your bondmen forever."

In moral investigations, ambiguity is often occasioned by confounding the intrinsic nature of an action, as determined by its consequence, with the motives of the actor, involving moral guilt or innocence. If poison be given with a view to destroy another, and it cures him of disease, the poisoner is guilty, but the act is beneficent in its results. If medicine be given with a view to heal, and it happens to kill, he who administered it is innocent, but the act is a noxious one. If they who begun and prosecuted the slave trade, practised horrible cruelties and inflicted much suffering—as no doubt they did, though these have been much exaggerated—for merely selfish purposes, and with no view to future good, they were morally most guilty. So far as unnecessary cruelty was practised, the motive and the act were alike bad. But if we could be sure that the entire effect of the trade has been to produce more happiness than would otherwise have existed, we must pronounce it good, and that it has happened in the ordering of God's providence, to whom evil cannot be imputed. Moral guilt has not been imputed to Las Casas, and if the importation of African slaves into America, had the effect of preventing more suffering than it inflicted, it was good, both in the motive and the result. I freely admit that, it is hardly possible to justify morally, those who begun and carried on the slave trade. No speculation of future good to be brought about, could compensate the enormous amount of evil it occasioned.

If we should refer to the common moral sense of mankind, as determined by their conduct in all ages and countries, for a standard of morality, it would seem to be in favor of Slavery. The will of God, as determined by utility, would be an infallible standard, if we had an unerring measure of utility. The utilitarian philosophy, as it is commonly understood, referring only to the animal wants and employments, and physical condition of man, is utterly false and degrading. If a sufficiently extended definition be given to utility, so as to include every thing that may be a source of enjoyment or suffering, it is for the most part useless. How can you compare the pleasures resulting from the exercise of the understanding, the taste and the imagination, with the animal enjoyments of the senses—the gratification derived from a fine poem with that from a rich banquet? How are we to weigh the pains and enjoyments of one man highly cultivated and of great sensibility, against those of many men of blunter capacity for enjoyment or suffering? And if we could determine with certainty in what utility consists, we are so short-sighted with respect to consequences—the remote results of our best considered actions are so often wide of our anticipations, or contrary to them, that we should still be very much in the dark. But though we cannot arrive at absolute certainty with respect to the utility of actions, it is always fairly matter of argument. Though an imperfect standard, it is the best we have, and perhaps the Creator did not intend that we should arrive at perfect certainty with regard to the morality of many actions. If, after the most careful examination of consequences that we are able to make, with due distrust of ourselves, we impartially, and in good faith, decide for that which appears likely to produce the greatest good, we are free from moral guilt. And I would impress most earnestly, that with our imperfect and limited faculties, and short-sighted as we are to the future, we can rarely, very rarely indeed, be justified in producing considerable present evil or suffering, in the expectation of remote future good—if indeed this can ever be justified.

In considering this subject, I shall not regard it in the first instance in reference to the present position of the slaveholding States, or the difficulties which lie in the way of their emancipating their slaves, but as a naked, abstract question—whether it is better that the institution of praedial and domestic Slavery should, or should not, exist in civilized society. And though some of my remarks may seem to have such a tendency, let me not be understood as taking upon myself to determine that it is better that it should exist. God forbid that the responsibility of deciding such a question should ever be thrown on me or my countrymen. But this I will say, and not without confidence, that it is in the power of no human intellect to establish the contrary proposition—that it is better it should not exist. This is probably known but to one being, and concealed from human sagacity.

There have existed in various ages, and we now see existing in the world, people in every stage of civilization, from the most barbarous to the most refined. Man, as I have said, is not born to civilization. He is born rude and ignorant. But it will be, I suppose, admitted that it is the design of his Creator that he should attain to civilization: that religion should be known, that the comforts and elegancies of life should be enjoyed, that letters and arts should be cultivated; in short, that there should be the greatest possible development of moral and intellectual excellence. It can hardly be necessary to say any thing of those who have extolled the superior virtues and enjoyments of savage life—a life of physical wants and sufferings, of continual insecurity, of furious passions and depraved vices. Those who have praised savage life, are those who have known nothing of it, or who have become savages themselves. But as I have said, so far as reason or universal experience instruct us, the institution of Slavery is an essential process in emerging from savage life. It must then produce good, and promote the designs of the Creator.

I add further, *that Slavery anticipates the benefits of civilization, and retards the evils of civilization.* The former part of this proposition has been so fully established by a writer of great power of thought—though I fear his practical conclusions will be found of little value—that it is hardly necessary to urge it.* Property—the accumulation of capital, as it is commonly called—is the first element of civilization. But to accumulate, or to use capital to any considerable extent, the combination of labor is necessary. In early stages of society, when people are thinly scattered over an extensive territory, the labor necessary to extensive works cannot be commanded. Men are independent of each other. Having the command of abundance of land, no one will submit to be employed in the service of his neighbor. No one, therefore, can employ more capital than he can use with his own hands, or those of his family, nor have an income much beyond the necessaries of life. There can, therefore, be little leisure

---

* The author of "England and America." We do, however, most indignantly repudiate his conclusion, that we are bound to submit to a tariff of protection, as an expedient for retaining our slaves, "the force of the whole Union being required to preserve Slavery, to keep down the slaves."

for intellectual pursuits, or means of acquiring the comforts or elegancies of life. It is hardly necessary to say, however, that if a man has the command of slaves, he may combine labor, and use capital to any required extent, and therefore accumulate wealth. He shows that no colonies have been successfully planted without some sort of Slavery. So we find the fact to be. It is only in the slaveholding States of our Confederacy, that wealth can be acquired by agriculture—which is the general employment of our whole country. Among us, we know that there is no one, however humble his beginning, who, with persevering industry, intelligence, and orderly and virtuous habits, may not attain to considerable opulence. So far as wealth has been accumulated in the States which do not possess slaves, it has been in cities by the pursuits of commerce, or lately, by manufactures. But the products of slave labor furnish more than two-thirds of the materials of our foreign commerce, which the industry of those States is employed in transporting and exchanging; and among the slaveholding States is to be found the great market for all the productions of their industry, of whatever kind. The prosperity of those States, therefore, and the civilization of their cities, have been for the most part created by the existence of Slavery. Even in the cities, but for a class of population, which our institutions have marked as servile, it would be scarcely possible to preserve the ordinary habitudes of civilized life, by commanding the necessary menial and domestic service.

Every stage of human society, from the most barbarous to the most refined, has its own peculiar evils to mark it as the condition of mortality; and perhaps there is none but omnipotence who can say in which the scale of good or evil most preponderates. We need say nothing of the evils of savage life. There is a state of society elevated somewhat above it, which is to be found in some of the more thinly peopled portions of our own country—the rudest agricultural state—which is thus characterized by the author to whom I have referred: "The American of the back woods has often been described to the English as grossly ignorant, dirty, unsocial, delighting in rum and tobacco, attached to nothing but his rifle, adventurous, restless, more than half savage. Deprived of social enjoyments or excitements, he has recourse to those of savage life, and becomes (for in this respect the Americans degenerate) unfit for society." This is no very inviting picture, which, though exaggerated, we know not to be without likeness. The evils of such a state, I suppose, will hardly be thought compensated by unbounded freedom, perfect equality, and ample means of subsistence.

But let us take another stage in the progress—which to many will appear to offer all that is desirable in existence, and realize another Utopia. Let us suppose a state of society in which all shall have property, and there shall be no great inequality of property—in which society shall be so much condensed as to afford the means of social intercourse, without being crowded, so as to create difficulty in obtaining the means of subsistence—in which every family that chooses may have as much land as will employ its own hands, while others may employ their industry in forming such products as it may be desirable to exchange with them. Schools are generally established, and the rudiments of education universally diffused. Religion is taught, and every village has its church, neat, though humble, lifting its spire to heaven. Here is a situation apparently the most favorable to happiness. I say *apparently*, for the greatest source of human misery is not in external circumstances, but in men themselves—in their depraved inclinations, their wayward passions and perverse wills. Here is room for all the petty competition, the envy, hatred, malice and dissimulation, that torture the heart in what may be supposed the most sophisticated states of society; and though less marked and offensive, there may be much of the licentiousness.

But apart from this, in such a condition of society, if there is little suffering, there is little high enjoyment. The even flow of life forbids the high excitement which is necessary for it. If there is little vice, there is little place for the eminent virtues, which employ themselves in controlling the disorders and remedying the evils of society, which, like war and revolution, call forth the highest powers of man, whether for good or for evil. If there is little misery, there is little room for benevolence. Useful public institutions we may suppose to be created, but not such as are merely ornamental. Elegant arts can be little cultivated, for there are no means to reward the artists; nor the higher literature, for no one will have leisure or means to cultivate it for its own sake. Those who acquire what may be called liberal education, will do so in order to employ it as the means of their own subsistence or advancement in a profession, and literature itself will partake of the sordidness of trade. In short, it is plain that in such a state of society, the moral and intellectual faculties cannot be cultivated to their highest perfection.

But whether that which I have described be the most desirable state of society or no, it is certain that it cannot continue. Mutation and progress is the condition of human affairs. Though retarded for a time by extraneous or accidental circumstances, the wheel must roll on. The tendency of population is to become crowded, increasing the difficulty of obtaining subsistence. There will be some without any property except the capacity for labor. This they must sell to those who have the means of employing them, thereby swelling the amount of their capital, and increasing inequality. The process still goes on. The number of laborers increases until there is a difficulty in obtaining employment. Then competition is established. The remuneration of the laborer becomes gradually less and less; a larger and larger proportion of the product of his labor goes to swell the fortune of the capitalist; inequality becomes still greater and more invidious, until the process ends in the establishment of just such a state of things, as the same author describes as now existing in England. After a most imposing picture of her greatness and resources; of her superabounding capital, and all-pervading industry and enterprise; of her public institutions for purposes of art, learning and benevolence; her public improvements, by which intercourse is facilitated, and the convenience of man subserved; the conveniences and luxuries of life enjoyed by those who are in possession of fortune, or have profitable employments; of all, in short, that places her at the head of modern civilization, he proceeds to give the reverse of the picture. And here I shall use his own words: "The laboring class compose the bulk of the people; the great body of the people; the vast majority of the people—these are the terms by which English writers and speakers usually describe those whose only property is their labor."

"Of comprehensive words, the two most frequently used in English politics, are distress and pauperism. After these, of expressions applied to the state of the poor, the most common are vice and misery, wretchedness, sufferings, ignorance, degradation, discontent, depravity, drunkenness, and the increase of crime; with many more of the like nature."

He goes on to give the details of this inequality and wretchedness, in terms calculated to sicken and appal one to whom the picture is new. That he has painted strongly we may suppose; but there is ample corroborating testimony, if such were needed, that the representation is substantially just.

Where so much misery exists, there must of course be much discontent, and many have been disposed to trace the sources of the former in vicious legislation, or the structure of government; and the author gives the various schemes, sometimes contradictory, sometimes ludicrous, which projectors have devised as a remedy for all this evil to which flesh is heir. That ill judged legislation may have sometimes aggravated the general suffering, or that its extremity may be mitigated by the well directed efforts of the wise and virtuous, there can be no doubt. One purpose for which it has been permitted to exist is, that it may call forth such efforts, and awaken powers and virtues which would otherwise have slumbered for want of object. But remedy there is none, unless it be to abandon their civilization. This inequality, this vice, this misery, this *Slavery*, is the price of England's civilization. They suffer the lot of humanity. But perhaps we may be permitted humbly to hope, that great, intense and widely spread as this misery undoubtedly is in reality, it may yet be less so than in appearance. We can estimate but very, very imperfectly the good and evil of individual condition, as of different states of society. Some unexpected solace arises to alleviate the severest calamity. Wonderful is the power of custom, in making the hardest condition tolerable; the most generally wretched life has circumstances of mitigation, and moments of vivid enjoyment, of which the more seemingly happy can scarcely conceive; though the lives of individuals be shortened, the aggregate of existence is increased; even the various forms of death accelerated by want, familiarized to the contemplation, like death to the soldier on the field of battle, may become scarcely more formidable than what we are accustomed to regard as nature's ordinary outlets of existence. If we could perfectly analyze the enjoyments and sufferings of the most happy, and the most miserable man, we should perhaps be startled to find the difference so much less than our previous impressions had led us to conceive. But it is not for us to assume the province of omniscience. The particular theory of the author quoted, seems to be founded on an assumption of this sort—that there is a certain stage in the progress, when there is a certain balance between the demand for labor, and the supply of it, which is more desirable than any other—when the territory is so thickly peopled that all cannot own land and cultivate the soil for themselves, but a portion will be compelled to sell their labor to others; still leaving, however, the wages of labor high, and the laborer independent. It is plain, however, that this would in like manner partake of the good and the evil of other states of society. There would be less of equality and less rudeness, than in the early stages; less civilization, and less suffering, than in the latter.

It is the competition for employment, which is the source of this misery of society, that gives rise to all excellence in art and knowledge. When the demand for labor exceeds the supply, the services of the most ordinarily qualified laborer will be eagerly retained. When the supply begins to exceed, and competition is established, higher and higher qualifications will be required, until at length when it becomes very intense, none but the most consummately skilful can be sure to be employed. Nothing but necessity can drive men to the exertions which are necessary so to qualify themselves.' But it is not in arts, merely mechanical alone, that this superior excellence will be required. It will be extended to every intellectual employment; and though this may not be the effect in the instance of every individual, yet it will fix the habits and character of the society, and prescribe every where, and in every department, the highest possible standard of attainment.

But how is it that the existence of Slavery, as with us, will retard the evils of civilization? Very obviously. It is the intense competition of civilized life, that gives rise to the excessive cheapness of labor, and the excessive cheapness of labor is the cause of the evils in question. Slave labor can never be so cheap as what is called free labor. Political economists have established as the natural standard of wages in a fully peopled country, the value of the laborer's existence. I shall not stop to inquire into the precise truth of this proposition. It certainly approximates the truth. Where competition is intense, men will labor for a bare subsistence, and less than a competent subsistence. The employer of free laborers obtains their services during the time of their health and vigor, without the charge of rearing them from infancy, or supporting them in sickness or old age. This charge is imposed on the employer of slave labor, who, therefore, pays higher wages, and cuts off the principal source of misery—the wants and sufferings of infancy, sickness, and old age. Laborers too will be less skilful, and perform less work—enhancing the price of that sort of labor. The poor laws of England are an attempt—but an awkward and empirical attempt—to supply the place of that which we should suppose the feelings of every human heart would declare to be a natural obligation—that he who has received the benefit of the laborer's services during his health and vigor, should maintain him when he becomes unable to provide for his own support. They answer their purpose, however, very imperfectly, and are unjustly and unequally imposed. There is no attempt to apportion the burden according to the benefit received—and perhaps there could be none. This is one of the evils of their condition.

In periods of commercial revulsion and distress, like the present, the distress, in countries of free labor, falls principally on the laborers. In those of slave labor, it falls almost exclusively on the employer. In the former, when a business becomes unprofitable, the employer dismisses his laborers or lowers their wages. But with us, it is the very period at which we are least able to dismiss our laborers; and if we would not suffer a further loss, we cannot reduce their wages. To receive the benefit of the services of which they are capable, we must provide for maintaining their health and vigor. In point of fact, we know that this is accounted among the necessary expenses of management. If the income of every planter of the Southern States were permanently reduced one-half, or even much more than that, it would not take one jot from the support and comforts of the slaves. And this can never be materially altered, until they shall become so unprofitable that Slavery must be of necessity abandoned. It is probable that the accumulation of individual wealth will never be carried to quite so great an extent in a slaveholding country, as in one of free labor; but a consequence will be, that there will be less inequality and less suffering.

Servitude is the condition of civilization. It was decreed, when the command was given, " be fruitful, and multiply and replenish the earth, and subdue it," and when it was added, "in the sweat of thy face shalt thou eat bread." And what human being shall arrogate to himself the authority to pronounce that our form of it is worse in itself, or more displeasing to God, than that which exists elsewhere? Shall it be said that the servitude of other countries grows out of the exigency of their circumstances, and therefore society is not responsible for it? But if we know that in the progress of things it is to come, would it not seem the part of wisdom and foresight, to make provision for it, and thereby, if we can, mitigate the severity of its evils? But the fact is not so. Let any one who doubts, read the book to which I have several times referred, and he may be satisfied that it was forced upon us by the extremest exigency of circumstances, in a struggle for very existence. Without it, it is doubtful whether a white man would be now existing on this continent—certain, that if there were, they would be in a state of the utmost destitution, weakness, and misery. It was forced on us by necessity, and further fastened upon us by the superior authority of the mother country. I, for one, neither deprecate nor resent the gift. Nor did we institute Slavery. The Africans brought to us had been, speaking in the general, slaves in their own country, and only underwent a change of masters. In the countries of Europe, and the States of our Confederacy, in which Slavery has ceased to exist, it was abolished by positive legislation. If the order of nature has been departed from, and a forced and artificial state of things introduced, it has been, as the experience of all the world declares, by them and not by us.

That there are great evils in a society where Slavery exists, and that the institution is liable to great abuse, I have already said. To say otherwise, would be to say that they were not human. But the whole of human life is a system of evils and compensations. We have no reason to believe that the compensations with us are fewer, or smaller in proportion to the evils, than those of any other condition of society. Tell me of an evil or abuse; of an instance of cruelty, oppression, licentiousness, crime or suffering, and I will point out, and often in five fold degree, an equivalent evil or abuse in countries where Slavery does not exist.

Let us examine without blenching, the actual and alleged evils of Slavery, and the array of horrors which many suppose to be its universal concomitants. It is said that the slave is out of the protection of the law; that if the law purports to protect him in life and limb, it is but imperfectly executed; that he is still subject to excessive labor, degrading blows, or any other sort of torture, which a master pampered and brutalized by the exercise of arbitrary power, may think proper to inflict; he is cut off from the opportunity of intellectual, moral, or religious improvement, and even positive enactments are directed against his acquiring the rudiments of knowledge; he is cut off forever from the hope of raising his condition in society, whatever may be his merit, talents, or virtues, and therefore deprived of the strongest incentive to useful and praiseworthy exertion; his physical degradation begets a corresponding moral degradation: he is without moral principle, and addicted to the lowest vices, particularly theft and falsehood; if marriage be not disallowed, it is little better than a state of concubinage, from which results general licentiousness, and the want of chastity among females—this indeed is not protected by law, but is subject to the outrages of brutal lust; both sexes are liable to have their dearest affections violated; to be sold like brutes; husbands to be torn from wives, children from parents;—this is the picture commonly presented by the denouncers of Slavery.

It is a somewhat singular fact that when there existed in our State no law for punishing the murder of a slave, other than a pecuniary fine, there were, I will venture to say, at least ten murders of freemen, for one murder of a slave. Yet it is supposed they are less protected, or less secure than their masters. Why they are protected by their very situation in society, and therefore less need the protection of law. With any other person than their master, it is hardly possible for them to come into such sort of collision as usually gives rise to furious and revengeful passions; they offer no temptation to the murderer for gain; against the master himself, they have the security of his own interest, and by his superintendence and authority, they are protected from the revengeful passions of each other. I am by no means sure that the cause of humanity has been served by the change in jurisprudence, which has placed their murder on the same footing with that of a freemen. The change was made in subserviency to the opinions and clamor of others who were utterly incompetent to form an opinion on the subject; and a wise act is seldom the result of legislation in this spirit. From the fact which I have stated, it is plain that they less need protection. Juries are, therefore, less willing to convict, and it may sometimes happen that the guilty will escape all punishment. *Security* is one of the compensations of their humble position. We challenge the comparison, that with us there have been fewer murders of slaves, than of parents, children, apprentices, and other murders, cruel and unnatural, in society where slavery does not exist.

But short of life or limb, various cruelties may be practised as the passions of the master may dictate. To this the same reply has been often given—that they are secured by the master's interest. If the state of Slavery is to exist at all, the master must have, and ought to have, such power of punishment as will compel them to perform the duties of their station. And is not this for their advantage as well as his? No human being can be contented, who does not perform the duties of his station. Has the master any temptation to go beyond this? If he inflicts on him such punishment as will permanently impair his strength, he inflicts a loss on himself, and so if he requires of him excessive labor. Compare the labor required of the slave, with those of the free agricultural or manufacturing laborer in Europe, or even in the more thickly peopled portions of the non-slaveholding States of our Confederacy—though these last are no fair subjects of comparison—they enjoying, as I have said, in a great degree, the advantages of Slavery along with those of an early and simple state of society. Read the English Parliamentary reports, on the condition of the manufacturing operatives, and the children employed in factories. And such is the impotence of man to remedy the evils which the condition of his existence has imposed on him, that it is much to be doubted whether the attempts by legislation to improve their situation, will not aggravate its evils. They resort to this excessive labor as a choice of evils. If so, the amount of their compensation will be lessened also with the diminished labor; for this is a matter which legislation cannot regulate. Is it the part of benevolence then to cut them off even from this miserable liberty of choice? Yet would these evils exist in the same degree, if the laborers were the *property* of the master—having a direct interest in preserving their lives, their health and strength? Who but a drivelling fanatic has thought of the necessity of protecting domestic animals from the cruelty of their owners? And yet are not great and wanton cruelties practised on these animals? Compare the whole of the cruelties inflicted on slaves throughout our Southern country, with those elsewhere, inflicted by ignorant and depraved portions of the community, on those whom the relations of society put into their power—of brutal husbands on their wives; of brutal parents—subdued against the strongest instincts of nature to that brutality by the extremity of their misery—on their children; of brutal masters on apprentices. And if it should be asked, are not similar cruelties inflicted, and miseries endured, in your society? I answer, in no comparable degree. The class in question are placed under the control of others, who are interested to restrain their excesses of cruelty or rage. Wives are protected from their husbands, and children from their parents. And this is no inconsiderable compensation of the evils of our system; and would so appear, if we could form any conception of the immense amount of misery which is elsewhere thus inflicted. The other class of society, more elevated in their position, are also (speaking of course in the general) more elevated in character, and more responsible to public opinion.

But besides the interest of their master, there is another security against cruelty. The relation of master and slave, when there is no mischievous interference between them, is, as the experience of all the world declares, naturally one of kindness. As to the fact, we should be held interested witnesses, but we appeal to universal nature. Is it not natural that a man should be attached to that which is *his own*, and which has contributed to his convenience, his enjoyment, or his vanity? This is felt even towards animals and inanimate objects. How much more towards a being of superior intelligence and usefulness, who can appreciate our feelings towards him, and return them? Is it not natural that we should be interested in that which is dependent on us for protection and support? Do not men everywhere contract kind feelings towards their dependants? Is it not natural that men should be more attached to those whom they have long known—whom, perhaps, they have reared or been associated with from infancy—than to one with whom their connexion has been casual and temporary? What is there in our atmosphere or institutions, to produce a perversion of the general feelings of nature? To be sure, in this as in all other relations, there is frequent cause of offence or excitement—on one side, for some omission of duty, on the other, on account of reproof or punishment inflicted. But this is common to the relation of parent and child; and I will venture to say, that if punishment be justly inflicted—and there is no temptation to inflict it unjustly—it is as little likely to occasion permanent estrangement or resentment as in that case. Slaves are perpetual children. It is not the common nature of man, unless it be depraved by his own misery, to delight in witnessing pain. It is more grateful to behold contented and cheerful beings, than sullen and wretched ones. That men are sometimes wayward, depraved and brutal, we know. That atrocious and brutal cruelties have been perpetrated on slaves, and on those who were not slaves, by such wretches, we also know. But that the institution of Slavery has a natural tendency to form such a character, that such crimes are more common, or more aggravated than in other states of society, or produce among us less surprise and horror, we utterly deny, and challenge the comparison. Indeed, I have little hesitation in saying, that if full evidence could be obtained, the comparison would result in our favor, and that the tendency of Slavery is rather to humanize than to brutalize.

The accounts of travellers in oriental countries, give a very favorable representation of the kindly relations which exist between the master and slave; the latter being often the friend, and sometimes the heir of the former. Generally, however, especially if they be English travellers—if they say any thing which may seem to give a favorable complexion to Slavery, they think it necessary to enter their protest, that they shall not be taken to give any sanction to Slavery as it exists in America. Yet human nature is the same in all countries. There are very obvious reasons why in those countries there should be a nearer approach to equality in their manners. The master and slave are often of cognate races, and therefore tend more to assimilate. There is, in fact, less inequality in mind and character, where the master is but imperfectly civilized. Less labor is exacted, because the master has fewer motives to accumulate. But is it an injury to a human being, that regular, if not excessive labor, should be required of him? The primeval curse, with the usual benignity of providential contrivance, has been turned into the solace of an existence that would be much more intolerable without it. If they labor less, they are much more subject to the outrages of capricious passion. If it were put to the choice of any human being, would he prefer to be the slave of a civilized man, or of a barbarian or semi-barbarian? But if the general tendency of the institution in those countries is to create kindly relations, can it be imagined why it should operate differently in this? It is true, as suggested by President Dew—with the exception of the ties of close consanguinity, it forms one of the most intimate relations of society. And it will be more and more so, the longer it continues to exist. The harshest features of Slavery were created by those who were strangers to Slavery—who supposed that it consisted in keeping savages in subjection by violence and terror. The severest laws to be found on our statute book, were enacted by such, and such are still found to be the severest masters. As society becomes settled, and the wandering habits of our countrymen altered, there will be a larger and larger proportion of those who were reared by the owner, or derived to him from his ancestors, and who therefore will be more and more intimately regarded, as forming a portion of his family.

It is true that the slave is driven to labor by stripes ; and if the object of punishment be to produce obedience or reformation, with the least permanent injury, it is the best method of punishment. But is it not intolerable, that a being formed in the image of his Maker, should be degraded by *blows?* This is one of the perversions of mind and feeling, to which I shall have occasion again to refer. Such punishment would be degrading to a freeman, who had the thoughts and aspirations of a freeman. In general, it is not degrading to a slave, nor is it felt to be so. The evil is the bodily pain. Is it degrading to a child? Or if in any particular instance it would be so felt, it is sure not to be inflicted—unless in those rare cases which constitute the startling and eccentric evils, from which no society is exempt, and against which no institutions of society can provide.

The slave is cut off from the means of intellectual, moral, and religious improvement, and in consequence his moral character becomes depraved, and he addicted to degrading vices. The slave receives such instruction as qualifies him to discharge the duties of his particular station. The Creator did not intend that every individual human being should be highly cultivated, morally and intellectually, for, as we have seen, he has imposed conditions on society which would render this impossible. There must be general mediocrity, or the highest cultivation must exist along with ignorance, vice, and degradation. But is there in the aggregate of society, less opportunity for intellectual and moral cultivation, on account of the existence of Slavery? We must estimate institutions from their aggregate of good or evil. I refer to the views which I have before expressed to this society. It is by the existence of Slavery, exempting so large a portion of our citizens from the necessity of bodily labor, that we have a greater proportion than any other people, who have leisure for intellectual pursuits, and the means of attaining a liberal education. If we throw away this opportunity, we shall be morally responsible for the neglect or abuse of our advantages, and shall most unquestionably pay the penalty. But the blame will rest on ourselves, and not on the character of our institutions.

I add further, notwithstanding that *equality* seems to be the passion of the day, if, as Providence has evidently decreed, there can be but a certain portion of intellectual excellence in any community, it is better that it should be *unequally* divided. It is better that a part should be fully and highly cultivated, and the rest utterly ignorant. To constitute a society, a variety of offices must be discharged, from those requiring but the lowest degree of intellectual power, to those requiring the very highest, and it should seem that the endowments ought to be apportioned according to the exigencies of the situation. In the course of human affairs, there arise difficulties which can only be comprehended or surmounted by the strongest native power of intellect, strengthened by the most assiduous exercise, and enriched with the most extended knowledge—and even these are sometimes found inadequate to the exigency. The first want of society is—leaders. Who shall estimate the value to Athens, of Solon, Aristides, Themistocles, Cymon, or Pericles? If society have not leaders qualified, as I have said, they will have those who will lead them blindly to their loss and ruin. Men of no great native power of intellect, and of imperfect and superficial knowledge, are the most mischievous of all—none are so busy, meddling, confident, presumptuous, and intolerant. The whole of society receives the benefit of the exertions of a mind of extraordinary endowments. Of all communities, one of the least desirable, would be that in which imperfect, superficial, half-education should be universal. The first care of a state which regards its own safety, prosperity and honor, should be, that when minds of extraordinary power appear, to whatever department of knowledge, art or science, their exertions may be directed, the means should be provided of their most consummate cultivation. Next to this, that education should be as widely extended as possible.

Odium has been cast upon our legislation, on account of its forbidding the elements of education to be communicated to slaves. But, in truth, what injury is done to them by this? He who works during the day with his hands, does not read in intervals of leisure for his amusement, or the improvement of his mind—or the exceptions are so very rare, as scarcely to need the being provided for. Of the many slaves whom I have known capable of reading, I have never known one to read any thing but the Bible, and this task they impose on themselves as matter of duty. Of all methods of religious instruction, however, this, of reading for themselves, would be the most inefficient—their comprehension is defective, and the employment is to them an unusual and laborious one. There are but very few who do not enjoy other means more effectual for religious instruction. There is no place of worship opened for the white population, from which they are excluded. I believe it a mistake, to say that the instructions there given are not adapted to their comprehension, or calculated to improve them. If they are given as they ought to be—practically, and without pretension, and are such as are generally intelligible to the free part of the audience, comprehending all grades of intellectual capacity,—they will not be unintelligible to slaves. I doubt whether this be not better than instruction, addressed specially to themselves—which they might look upon as a device of the master's, to make them more obedient and profitable to himself. Their minds, generally, show a strong religious tendency, and they are fond of assuming the office of religious instructors to each other; and perhaps their religious notions are not much more extravagant than those of a large portion of the free population of our country. I am not sure that there is a much smaller proportion of them, than of the free population, who make some sort of religious profession. It is certainly the master's *interest* that they should have proper religious sentiments, and if he fails in his duty towards them, we may be sure that the consequences will be visited not upon them, but upon him.

If there were any chance of their elevating their rank and condition in society, it might be matter of hardship, that they should be debarred those rudiments of knowledge which open the way to further attainments. But this they know cannot be, and that further attainments would be useless to them.

Of the evil of this, I shall speak hereafter. A knowledge of reading, writing, and the elements of arithmetic, is convenient and important to the free laborer, who is the transactor of his own affairs, and the guardian of his own interests—but of what use would they be to the slave? These alone do not elevate the mind or character, if such elevation were desirable.

If we estimate their morals according to that which should be the standard of a free man's morality, then I grant they are degraded in morals—though by no means to the extent which those who are unacquainted with the institution seem to suppose. We justly suppose, that the Creator will require of man the performance of the duties of the station in which his providence has placed him, and the cultivation of the virtues which are adapted to their performance; that he will make allowance for all imperfection of knowledge, and the absence of the usual helps and motives which lead to self-correction and improvement. The degradation of morals relate principally to loose notions of honesty, leading to petty thefts; to falsehood and to licentious intercourse between the sexes. Though with respect even to these, I protest against the opinion which seems to be elsewhere entertained, that they are universal, or that slaves, in respect to them, might not well bear a comparison with the lowest laborious class of other countries. But certainly there is much dishonesty leading to petty thefts. It leads, however, to nothing else. They have no contracts or dealings which might be a temptation to fraud, nor do I know that their characters have any tendency that way. They are restrained by the constant, vigilant, and interested superintendence which is exercised over them, from the commission of offences of greater magnitude—even if they were disposed to them—which I am satisfied they are not. Nothing is so rarely heard of, as an atrocious crime committed by a slave; especially since they have worn off the savage character which their progenitors brought with them from Africa. Their offences are confined to petty depredations, principally for the gratification of their appetites, and these for reasons already given, are chiefly confined to the property of their owner, which is most exposed to them. They could make no use of a considerable booty, if they should obtain it. It is plain that this is a less evil to society in its consequences and example, than if committed by a freeman, who is master of his own time and actions. With reference to society then, the offence is less in itself—and may we not hope that it is less in the sight of God? A slave has no hope that by a course of integrity, he can materially elevate his condition in society, nor can his offence materially depress it, or affect his means of support, or that of his family. Compared to the freeman, he has no character to establish or to lose. He has not been exercised to self-government, and being without intellectual resources, can less resist the solicitations of appetite. Theft in a freeman is a crime; in a slave, it is a vice. I recollect to have heard it said, in reference to some question of a slave's theft which was agitated in a Court, "Courts of Justice have no more to do with a slave's stealing, than with his lying—that is a matter for the domestic forum." It was truly said—the theft of a slave is no offence against society. Compare all the evils resulting from this, with the enormous amount of vice, crime, and depravity, which in an European, or one of our Northern cities, disgusts the moral feelings, and render life and property insecure. So with respect to his falsehood. I have never heard or observed, that slaves have any peculiar proclivity to falsehood, unless it be in denying or concealing their own offences, or those of their fellows. I have never heard of falsehood told by a slave for a malicious purpose. Lies of vanity are sometimes told, as among the weak and ignorant of other conditions. Falsehood is not attributed to an individual charged with an offence before a Court of Justice, who pleads *not guilty*—and certainly the strong temptation to escape punishment, in the highest degree extenuates, if it does not excuse, falsehood told by a *slave*. If the object be to screen a fellow slave, the act bears some semblance of fidelity, and perhaps truth could not be told without breach of confidence. I know not how to characterize the falsehood of a slave.

It has often been said by the denouncers of Slavery, that marriage does not exist among slaves. It is difficult to understand this, unless wilful falsehood were intended. We know that marriages are contracted; may be, and often are, solemnized with the forms usual among other classes of society, and often faithfully adhered to during life. The law has not provided for making those marriages indissoluble, nor could it do so. If a man abandons his wife, being without property, and being both property themselves, he cannot be required to maintain her. If he abandons his wife, and lives in a state of concubinage with another, the law cannot punish him for bigamy. It may perhaps be meant that the chastity of wives is not protected by law from the outrages of violence—I answer, as with respect to their lives, that they are protected by manners, and their position. Who ever heard of such outrages being offered? At least as seldom, I will venture to say, as in other communities of different forms of polity. One reason doubtless may be, that often there is no disposition to resist. Another reason also may be, that there is little temptation to such violence, as there is so large a proportion of this class of females who set little value on chastity, and afford easy gratification to the hot passions of men. It might be supposed, from the representations of some writers, that a slaveholding country was one wide stew for the indulgence of unbridled lust. Particular instances of intemperate and shameless debauchery are related, which may perhaps be true, and it is left to be inferred that this is the universal state of manners. Brutes and shameless debauchees there are in every country; we know that if such things are related as general or characteristic, the representation is false. Who would argue from the existence of a Col. Chartres in England, or of some individuals who might, perhaps, be named in other portions of this country, of the horrid dissoluteness of manners occasioned by the want of the institution of Slavery? Yet the argument might be urged quite as fairly, and really it seems to me with a little more justice—for there such depravity is attended with much more pernicious consequences. Yet let us not deny or extenuate the truth. It is true that in this respect the morals of this class are very loose, (by no means so universally so as is often supposed,) and that the passions of men of the superior caste, tempt and find gratification in the easy chastity of the females. This is evil, and to be remedied, if we can do so, without the introduction of greater evil. But evil is incident to every condition of society, and as I have said, we have only to consider in which institution it most predominates.

Compare these prostitutes of our country, (if it is not injustice to call them so,) and their condition with those of other countries—the seventy thousand prostitutes of London, or of Paris, or the ten thousand of New-York, or our other Northern cities. Take the picture given of the first from the author whom I have before quoted. "The laws and customs of England conspire to sink this class of English women into a state of vice and misery below that which necessarily belongs to their condition. Hence their extreme degradation, their troopers' oaths, their love of gin, their desperate recklessness, and the shortness of their miserable lives."

"English women of this class, or rather girls, for few of

them live to be women, die like sheep with the rot; so fast that soon there would be none left, if a fresh supply were not obtained equal to the number of deaths. But a fresh supply is always obtained without the least trouble; seduction easily keeps pace with prostitution or mortality. Those that die are, like factory children that die, instantly succeeded by new competitors for misery and death." There is no hour of a summer's or a winter's night, in which there may not be found in the streets a ghastly wretch, expiring under the double tortures of disease and famine. Though less aggravated in its features, the picture of prostitution in New-York or Philadelphia would be of like character.

In such communities, the unmarried woman who becomes a mother, is an outcast from society—and though sentimentalists lament the hardship of the case, it is justly and necessarily so. She is cut off from the hope of useful and profitable employment, and driven by necessity to further vice. Her misery, and the hopelessness of retrieving, render her desperate, until she sinks into every depth of depravity, and is prepared for every crime that can contaminate and infest society. She has given birth to a human being, who, if it be so unfortunate as to survive its miserable infancy, is commonly educated to a like course of vice, depravity, and crime.

Compare with this the female slave under similar circumstances. She is not a less useful member of society than before. If shame be attached to her conduct, it is such shame as would be elsewhere felt for a venial impropriety. She has not impaired her means of support, nor materially impaired her character, or lowered her station in society; she has done no great injury to herself, or any other human being. Her offspring is not a burden but an acquisition to her owner; his support is provided for, and he is brought up to usefulness; if the fruit of intercourse with a freeman, his condition is, perhaps, raised somewhat above that of his mother. Under these circumstances, with imperfect knowledge, tempted by the strongest of human passions—unrestrained by the motives which operate to restrain, but are so often found insufficient to restrain the conduct of females elsewhere, can it be matter of surprise that she should so often yield to the temptation? Is not the evil less in itself, and in reference to society—much less in the sight of God and man? As was said of theft—the want of chastity, which among females of other countries is sometimes vice, sometimes crime—among the free of our own, much more aggravated; among slaves, hardly deserves a harsher term than that of weakness. I have heard of complaint made by a free prostitute, of the greater countenance and indulgence shown by society towards colored persons of her profession, (always regarded as of an inferior and servile class, though individually free,) than to those of her own complexion. The former readily obtain employment; are even admitted into families, and treated with some degree of kindness and familiarity, while any approach to intercourse with the latter is shunned as contamination. The distinction is habitually made, and it is founded on the unerring instinct of nature. The colored prostitute is, in fact, a far less contaminated and depraved being. Still many, in spite of temptation, do preserve a perfectly virtuous conduct, and I imagine it hardly ever entered into the mind of one of these, that she was likely to be forced from it by authority or violence.

It may be asked, if we have no prostitutes from the free class of society among ourselves. I answer, in no assignable proportion. With general truth, it might be said, that there are none. When such a case occurs, it is among the rare evils of society. And apart from other and better reasons, which we believe to exist, it is plain that it must be so, from the comparative absence of temptation. Our brothels, comparatively very few—and these should not be permitted to exist at all—are filled, for the most part, by importations from the cities of our confederate States, where Slavery does not exist. In return for the benefits which they receive from our Slavery, along with tariffs, libels, opinions moral, religious, or political—they furnish us also with a supply of thieves and prostitutes. Never, but in a single instance, have I heard of an imputation on the general purity of manners, among the free females of the slaveholding States. Such an imputation, however, and made in coarse terms, we have never heard here—*here* where divorce was never known—where no Court was ever polluted by an action for criminal conversation with a wife—where it is related rather as matter of tradition, not unmingled with wonder, that a Carolinian woman of education and family, proved false to her conjugal faith—an imputation deserving only of such reply as self-respect would forbid us to give, if respect for the author of it did not. And can it be doubted, that this purity is caused by, and is a compensation for the evils resulting from the existence of an enslaved class of more relaxed morals?

It is mostly the warm passions of youth, which give rise to licentious intercourse. But I do not hesitate to say, that the intercourse which takes place with enslaved females, is less depraving in its effects, than when it is carried on with females of their own caste. In the first place, as like attracts like, that which is unlike repels; and though the strength of passion be sufficient to overcome the repulsion, still the attraction is less. He feels that he is connecting himself with one of an inferior and servile caste, and that there is something of degradation in the act. The intercourse is generally casual; he does not make her habitually an associate, and is less likely to receive any taint from her habits and manners.

He is less liable to those extraordinary fascinations, with which worthless women sometimes entangle their victims, to the utter destruction of all principle, worth and vigor of character. The female of his own race offers greater allurements. The haunts of vice often present a show of elegance, and various luxury tempts the senses. They are made an habitual resort, and their inmates associates, till the general character receives a taint from the corrupted atmosphere. Not only the practice is licentious, but the understanding is sophisticated; the moral feelings are bewildered, and the boundaries of virtue and vice are confused. Where such licentiousness very extensively prevails, society is rotten to the heart.

But is it a small compensation for the evils attending the relation of the sexes among the enslaved class, that they have universally the opportunity of indulging the first instinct of nature, by forming matrimonial connexions? What painful restraint—what constant effort to struggle against the strongest impulses, are habitually practised elsewhere, and by other classes? And they must be practised, unless greater evils would be encountered. On the one side, all the evils of vice, with the miseries to which it leads—on the other, a marriage cursed and made hateful by want—the sufferings of children, and agonizing apprehensions concerning their future fate. Is it a small good that the slave is free from all this? He knows that his own subsistence is secure, and that his children will be in as good a condition as himself. To a refined and intellectual nature, it may not be difficult to practise the restraint of which I have spoken. But the reasoning from such to the great mass of mankind, is most fallacious. To these, the supply of their natural and physical wants, and the indulgence of the natural domestic affections, must, for the most part, afford the greatest good of which they are capable. To the evils which sometimes attend their matrimonial connexions, arising from their looser morality, slaves, for obvious reasons, are comparatively insensible. I am no apologist of vice, nor would I extenuate the conduct of the profligate and unfeeling, who would violate the sanctity of even these engagements, and occasion the pain which such violations no doubt do often inflict. Yet such is the truth, and we cannot make it otherwise. We know that a woman's having been before a mother, is very seldom indeed an objection to her being made a wife. I know perfectly well how this will be regarded by a class of reasoners or declaimers, as imposing a character of deeper horror on the whole system; but still, I will say, that if they are to be exposed to the evil, it is mercy that the sensibility to it should be blunted. Is it no compensation also for the vices incident to Slavery, that they are, to a great degree, secured against the temptation to greater crimes, and more atrocious vices, and the miseries which attend them; against their own disposition to indolence, and the profligacy which is its common result?

But if they are subject to the vices, they have also the virtues of slaves. Fidelity—often proof against all temptation—even death itself—an eminently cheerful and social temper—what the Bible imposes as a duty, but which might seem an equivocal virtue in the code of modern morality—submission to constituted authority, and a disposition to be attached to, as well as to respect those, whom they are taught to regard as superiors. They may have all the knowledge which will make them useful in the station in which God has been pleased to place them, and may cultivate the virtues which will render them acceptable to him. But what has the slave of any country to do with heroic virtues, liberal knowledge, or elegant accomplishments? It is for the master; arising out of his situation—imposed on him as duty—dangerous and disgraceful if neglected—to compensate for this, by his own more assiduous cultivation, of the more generous virtues, and liberal attainments.

It has been supposed one of the great evils of Slavery, that it affords the slave no opportunity of raising himself to a higher rank in society, and that he has, therefore, no inducement to meritorious exertion, or the cultivation of his faculties. The indolence and carelessness of the slave, and the less productive quality of his labor, are traced to the want of such excitement. The first compensation for this disadvantage, is his security. If he can rise no higher, he is just in the same degree secured against the chances of falling lower. It has been sometimes made a question whether it were better for man to be freed from the perturbations of hope and fear, or to be exposed to their vicissitudes. But I suppose there could be little question with respect to a situation, in which the fears must greatly predominate over the hopes. And such, I apprehend, to be the condition of the laboring poor in countries where Slavery does not exist. If not exposed to present suffering, there is continual apprehension for the future—for themselves—for their children—of sickness and want, if not of actual starvation. They expect to improve their circumstances! Would any person of ordinary candor, say that there is one in a hundred of them, who does not well know, that with all the exertion he can make, it is out of his power materially to improve his circumstances? I speak not so much of menial servants, who are generally of a superior class, as of the agricultural and manufacturing laborers. They labor with no such view. It is the instinctive struggle to preserve existence, and when the superior efficiency of their labor over that of our slaves is pointed out, as being animated by a free man's hopes, might it not well be replied—it is because they labor under a sterner compulsion. The laws interpose no obstacles to their raising their condition in society. 'Tis a great boon—but as to the great mass, they know that they never will be able to raise it—and it should seem not very important in effect, whether it be the interdict of law, or imposed by the circumstances of the society. One in a thousand is successful. But does his success compensate for the sufferings of the many who are tantalized, baffled, and tortured in vain attempts to attain a like result? If the individual be conscious of intellectual power, the suffering is greater. Even where success is apparently attained, he sometimes gains it but to die—or with all capacity to enjoy it exhausted—worn out in the struggle with fortune. If it be true that the African is an inferior variety of the human race, of less elevated character, and more limited intellect, is it not desirable that the inferior laboring class should be made up of such, who will conform to their condition without painful aspirations and vain struggles?

The slave is certainly liable to be sold. But, perhaps, it may be questioned, whether this is a greater evil than the liability of the laborer, in fully peopled countries, to be dismissed by his employer, with the uncertainty of being able to obtain employment, or the means of subsistence elsewhere. With us, the employer cannot dismiss his laborer without providing him with another employer. His means of subsistence are secure, and this is a compensation for much. He is also liable to be separated from wife and child—though not more frequently, that I am aware of, than the exigency of their condition compels the separation of families among the laboring poor elsewhere—but from native character and temperament, the separation is much less severely felt. And it is one of the compensations, that he may sustain these relations without suffering a still severer penalty for the indulgence.

The love of liberty is a noble passion—to have the free, uncontrolled disposition of ourselves, our words and actions.

But alas! it is one in which we know that a large portion of the human race can never be gratified. It is mockery, to say that the laborer any where has such disposition of himself—though there may be an approach to it in some peculiar, and those, perhaps, not the most desirable, states of society. But unless he be properly disciplined and prepared for its enjoyment, it is the most fatal boon that could be conferred—fatal to himself and others. If slaves have less freedom of action than other laborers, which I by no means admit, they are saved in a great degree from the responsibility of self-government, and the evils springing from their own perverse wills. Those who have looked most closely into life, and know how great a portion of human misery is derived from these sources —the undecided and wavering purpose—producing ineffectual exertion, or indolence with its thousand attendant evils—the wayward conduct—intemperance or profligacy—will most appreciate this benefit. The line of a slave's duty is marked out with precision, and he has no choice but to follow it. He is saved the double difficulty, first of determining the proper course for himself, and then of summoning up the energy which will sustain him in pursuing it.

If some superior power should impose on the laborious poor of any other country—this as their unalterable condition—you shall be saved from the torturing anxiety concerning your own future support, and that of your children, which now pursues you through life, and haunts you in death—you shall be under the necessity of regular and healthful, though not excessive labor—in return, you shall have the ample supply of your natural wants—you may follow the instinct of nature in becoming parents, without apprehending that this supply will fail yourselves or your children—you shall be supported and relieved in sickness, and in old age, wear out the remains of existence among familiar scenes and accustomed associates, without being driven to beg, or to resort to the hard and miserable charity of a work-house—you shall of necessity be temperate, and shall have neither the temptation nor opportunity to commit great crimes, or practice the more destructive vices—how inappreciable would the boon be thought! And is not this a very near approach to the condition of our slaves? The evils of their situation they but lightly feel, and would hardly feel at all, if they were not seduously instructed into sensibility. Certain it is, that if their fate were at the absolute disposal of a council of the most enlightened philanthropists in Christendom, with unlimited resources, they could place them in no situation so favorable to themselves, as that which they at present occupy. But whatever good there may be, or whatever mitigation of evil, it is worse than valueless, because it is the result of *Slavery*.

I am aware, that however often answered, it is likely to be repeated again and again—how can that institution be tolerable, by which a large class of society is cut off from the hope of improvement in knowledge; to whom blows are not degrading; theft no more than a fault; falsehood and the want of chastity almost venial, and in which a husband or parent looks with comparative indifference, on that which, to a freeman, would be the dishonor of a wife or child?

But why not, if it produces the greatest aggregate of good? Sin and ignorance are only evils, because they lead to misery. It is not our institution, but the institution of nature, that in the progress of society a portion of it should be exposed to want, and the misery which it brings, and therefore involved in ignorance, vice, and depravity. In anticipating some of the good, we also anticipate a portion of the evil of civilization. But we have it in a mitigated form. The want and the misery are unknown; the ignorance is less a misfortune, because the being is not the guardian of himself, and partly on account of that involuntary ignorance, the vice is less vice—less hurtful to man, and less displeasing to God.

There is something in this word *Slavery* which seems to partake of the qualities of the insane root, and distempers the minds of men. That which would be true in relation to one predicament, they misapply to another, to which it has no application at all. Some of the virtues of a freeman would be the vices of slaves. To submit to a blow, would be degrading to a freeman, because he is the protector of himself. It is not degrading to a slave—neither is it to a priest or woman. And is it a misfortune that it should be so? The freeman of other countries is compelled to submit to indignities hardly more endurable than blows—indignities to make the sensitive feelings shrink, and the proud heart swell; and this very name of freeman gives them double rancor. If when a man is born in Europe, it were certainly foreseen that he was destined to a life of painful labor—to obscurity, contempt, and privation—would it not be mercy that he should be reared in ignorance and apathy, and trained to the endurance of the evils he must encounter? It is not certainly foreseen as to any individual, but it is foreseen as to the great mass of those born of the laboring poor; and it is for the mass, not for the exception, that the institutions of society are to provide. Is it not better that the character and intellect of the individual should be suited to the station which he is to occupy? Would you do a benefit to the horse or the ox, by giving him a cultivated understanding or fine feelings? So far as the mere laborer has the pride, the knowledge, or the aspirations of a freeman, he is unfitted for his situation, and must doubly feel its infelicity. If there are sordid, servile, and laborious offices to be performed, is it not better that there should be sordid, servile, and laborious beings to perform them? If there were infallible marks by which individuals of inferior intellect, and inferior character, could be selected at their birth—would not the interests of society be served, and would not some sort of fitness seem to require, that they should be selected for the inferior and servile offices? And if this race be generally marked by such inferiority, is it not fit that they should fill them?

I am well aware that those whose aspirations are after a state of society from which evil shall be banished, and who look in life for that which life will never afford, contemplate that all the offices of life may be performed without contempt or degradation—all be regarded as equally liberal, or equally respected. But theorists cannot control nature and bend her to their views, and the inequality of which I have before spoken is deeply founded in nature. The offices which employ knowledge and intellect, will always be regarded as more liberal than those which require the labor of the hands. When there is competition for employment, he who gives it bestows a favor, and it will be so received. He will assume superiority from the power of dismissing his laborers, and from fear of this, the latter will practise deference, often amounting to servility. Such in time will become the established relation between the employer and the employed, the rich and the poor. If want be accompanied with sordidness and squalor, though it be pitied, the pity will be mixed with some degree of contempt. If it lead to misery, and misery to vice, there will be disgust and aversion.

What is the essential character of *Slavery*, and in what does it differ from the *servitude* of other countries? If I should venture on a definition, I should say that where a man is compelled to labor at the will of another, and to give him much the greater portion of the product of his labor, there *Slavery* exists; and it is immaterial by what sort of compulsion the will of the laborer is subdued. It is what no human being would do without some sort of compulsion. He cannot be compelled to labor by blows. No—but what difference does it make, if you can inflict any other sort of torture which will be equally effectual in subduing the will? if you can starve him, or alarm him for the subsistence of himself or his family? And is it not under this compulsion that the *freeman* labors? I do not mean in every particular case, but in the general. Will any one be hardy enough to say that he is at his own disposal, or has the government of himself? True, he may change his employer if he is dissatisfied with his conduct towards him; but this is a privilege he would in the majority of cases gladly abandon, and render the connexion between them indissoluble. There is far less of the interest and attachment in his relation to his employer, which so often exists between the master and the slave, and mitigates the condition of the latter. An intelligent English traveller has characterized as the most miserable and degraded of all beings, "a masterless slave." And is not the condition of the laboring poor of other countries too often that of masterless slaves? Take the following description of a *free* laborer, no doubt highly colored, quoted by the author to whom I have before referred.

"What is that defective being, with calfless legs and stooping shoulders, weak in body and mind, inert, pusillanimous and stupid, whose premature wrinkles and furtive glance, tell of misery and degradation? That is an English peasant or pauper, for the words are synonimous. His sire was a pauper, and his mother's milk wanted nourishment. From infancy his food has been bad, as well as insufficient; and he now feels the pains of unsatisfied hunger nearly whenever he is awake. But half clothed, and never supplied with more warmth than suffices to cook his scanty meals, cold and wet come to him, and stay by him with the weather. He is married, of course;

for to this he would have been driven by the poor laws, even if he had been, as he never was, sufficiently comfortable and prudent to dread the burden of a family. But though instinct and the overseer have given him a wife, he has not tasted the highest joys of husband and father. His partner and his little ones being like himself, often hungry, seldom warm, sometimes sick without aid, and always sorrowful without hope, are greedy, selfish, and vexing; so, to use his own expression, he hates the sight of them, and resorts to his hovel, only because a hedge affords less shelter from the wind and rain. Compelled by parish law to support his family, which means to join them in consuming an allowance from the parish, he frequently conspires with his wife to get that allowance increased, or prevent its being diminished. This brings beggary, trickery, and quarrelling, and ends in settled craft. Though he have the inclination, he wants the courage to become, like more energetic men of his class, a poacher or smuggler on a large scale, but he pilfers occasionally, and teaches his children to lie and steal. His subdued and slavish manner towards his great neighbors, shews that they treat him with suspicion and harshness. Consequently, he at once dreads and hates them; but he will never harm them by violent means. Too degraded to be desperate, he is only thoroughly depraved. His miserable career will be short; rheumatism and asthma are conducting him to the workhouse; where he will breathe his last without one pleasant recollection, and so make room for another wretch, who may live and die in the same way." And this description, or some other not much less revolting, is applied to "the bulk of the people, the great body of the people." Take the following description of the condition of childhood, which has justly been called eloquent.*

* Essays of Elia.

"The children of the very poor have no young times; it makes the very heart bleed, to over-hear the casual street talk between a poor woman and her little girl, a woman of the better sort of poor, in a condition rather above the squalid beings we have been contemplating. It is not of toys, of nursery books, of summer holidays, (fitting that age,) of the promised sight or play; of praised sufficiency at school. It is of mangling and clear starching; of the price of coals, or of potatoes. The questions of the child, that should be the very outpourings of curiosity in idleness, are marked with forecast and melancholy providence. It has come to be a woman, before it was a child. It has learnt to go to market; it chaffers, it haggles, it envies, it murmurs; it is knowing, acute, sharpened; it never prattles." Imagine such a description applied to the children of negro slaves, the most vacant of human beings, whose life is a holiday.

And this people, to whom these horrors are familiar, are those who fill the world with clamor, concerning the injustice and cruelty of Slavery. I speak in no invidious spirit. Neither the laws nor the government of England are to be reproached with the evils which are inseparable from the state of their society—as little, undoubtedly, are we to be reproached with the existence of our Slavery. Including the whole of the United States—and for reasons already given, the whole ought to be included, as receiving in no unequal degree the benefit—may we not say justly that we have less Slavery, and more mitigated Slavery, than any other country in the civilized world?

That they are called free, undoubtedly aggravates the sufferings of the slaves of other regions. They see the enormous inequality which exists, and feel their own misery, and can hardly conceive otherwise, than that there is some injustice in the institutions of society to occasion these. They regard the apparently more fortunate class as oppressors, and it adds bitterness that they should be of the same name and race. They feel indignity more acutely, and more of discontent and evil passion is excited; they feel that it is mockery that calls them free. Men do not so much hate and envy those who are separated from them by a wide distance, and some apparently impassable barrier, as those who approach nearer to their own condition, and with whom they habitually bring themselves into comparison. The slave with us is not tantalized with the name of freedom, to which his whole condition gives the lie, and would do so if he were emancipated to-morrow. The African slave sees that nature herself has marked him as a separate—and if left to himself, I have no doubt he would feel it to be an inferior—race, and interposed a barrier almost insuperable to his becoming a member of the same society, standing on the same footing of right and privilege with his master.

That the African negro is an inferior variety of the human race, is, I think, now generally admitted, and his distinguishing characteristics are such as peculiarly mark him out for the situation which he occupies among us. And these are no less marked in their original country, than as we have daily occasion to observe them. The most remarkable is their indifference to personal liberty. In this they have followed their instincts since we have any knowledge of their continent, by enslaving each other; but contrary to the experience of every race, the possession of slaves has no material effect in raising the character, and promoting the civilization of the master. Another trait is the want of domestic affections, and insensibility to the ties of kindred. In the travels of the Landers, after speaking of a single exception, in the person of a woman who betrayed some transient emotion in passing by the country from which she had been torn as a slave, the authors add: "that Africans, generally speaking, betray the most perfect indifference on losing their liberty, and being deprived of their relatives, while love of country is equally a stranger to their breasts, as social tenderness or domestic affection." "Marriage is celebrated by the nations as unconcernedly as possible; a man thinks as little of taking a wife, as of cutting an ear of corn—affection is altogether out of the question." They are, however, very submissive to authority, and seem to entertain great reverence for chiefs, priests, and masters. No greater indignity can be offered an individual, than to throw opprobrium on his parents. On this point of their character I think I have remarked, that, contrary to the instinct of nature in other races, they entertain less regard for children than for parents, to whose authority they have been accustomed to submit. Their character is thus summed up by the travellers quoted: "The few opportunities we have had of studying their characters, induce us to believe that they are a simple, honest, inoffensive, but weak, timid, and cowardly race. They seem to have no social tenderness, very few of those amiable private virtues which could win our affections, and none of those public qualities that claim respect or command admiration. The love of country is not strong enough in their bosoms to incite them to defend it against a despicable foe; and of the active energy, noble sentiments, and contempt of danger which distinguishes the North American tribes and other savages, no traces are to be found among this slothful people. Regardless of the past, as reckless of the future, the present alone influences their actions. In this respect, they approach nearer to the nature of the brute creation, than perhaps any other people on the face of the globe." Let me ask if this people do not furnish the very material out of which slaves ought to be made, and whether it be not an improving of their condition to make them the slaves of civilized masters? There is a variety in the character of the tribes. Some are brutally and savagely ferocious and bloody, whom it would be mercy to enslave. From the travellers' account, it seems not unlikely that the negro race is tending to extermination, being daily encroached on and overrun by the superior Arab race. It may be, that when they shall have been lost from their native seats, they may be found numerous, and in no unhappy condition, on the continent to which they have been transplanted.

The opinion which connects form and features with character and intellectual power, is one so deeply impressed on the human mind, that perhaps there is scarcely any man who does not almost daily act upon it, and in some measure verify its truth. Yet in spite of this intimation of nature, and though the anatomist and physiologist may tell them that the races differ in every bone and muscle, and in the proportion of brain and nerves, yet there are some who, with a most bigoted and fanatical determination to free themselves from what they have prejudged to be prejudice, will still maintain that this physiognomy, evidently tending to that of the brute, when compared to that of the Caucasian race, may be enlightened by as much thought, and animated by as lofty sentiment. We who have the best opportunity of judging, are pronounced to be incompetent to do so, and to be blinded by our interest and prejudices—often by those who have no opportunity at all—and we are to be taught to distrust or disbelieve that which we daily observe, and familiarly know, on such authority. Our prejudices are spoken of. But the truth is, that, until very lately, since circumstances have compelled us to think for ourselves, we took our opinions on this subject, as on every other, ready formed from the country of our origin. And so deeply rooted were they, that we adhered to them, as most men will do to deeply rooted opinions, even against the evidence of our own observation, and our own senses. If the inferiority exists, it is attributed to the apathy and degradation produced by Slavery. Though of the hundreds of thousand scattered over other countries, where the laws impose no disability upon them, none has given evidence of an approach to even mediocrity of intellectual excellence; this, too, is attributed to the slavery of a portion of their race. They are regarded as a servile caste, and degraded by opinion, and thus every generous effort is repressed. Yet though this should be the general effect, this very estimation is calculated to produce the contrary effect in particular instances. It is observed by Bacon, with respect to deformed persons and eunuchs, that though in general there is something of perversity in the character, the disadvantage often leads to extraordinary displays of virtue and excellence. " Whoever hath any thing fixed in his person that doth induce contempt, hath also a perpetual spur in himself, to rescue and deliver himself from scorn." So it would be with them, if they were capable of European aspirations—genius, if they possessed it, would be doubly fired with noble rage to rescue itself from this scorn. Of course, I do not mean to say that there may not be found among them some of superior capacity to many white persons; but that great intellectual powers are, perhaps, never found among them, and that in general their capacity is very limited, and their feelings animal and coarse—fitting them peculiarly to discharge the lower, and merely mechanical offices of society.

And why should it not be so ? We have among domestic animals infinite varieties, distinguished by various degrees of sagacity, courage, strength, swiftness, and other qualities. And it may be observed, that this is no objection to their being derived from a common origin, which we suppose them to have had. Yet these accidental qualities, as they may be termed, however acquired in the first instance, we know that they transmit unimpaired to their posterity for an indefinite succession of generations. It is most important that these varieties should be preserved, and that each should be applied to the purposes for which it is best adapted. No philo-zoost, I believe, has suggested it as desirable that these varieties should be melted down into one equal, undistinguished race of curs or road horses.

Slavery, as it is said in an eloquent article published in a Southern periodical work,* to which I am indebted for other ideas, " has done more to elevate a degraded race in the scale of humanity ; to tame the savage ; to civilize the barbarous; to soften the ferocious; to enlighten the ignorant, and to spread the blessings of Christianity among the heathen, than all the missionaries that philanthropy and religion have ever sent forth." Yet unquestionable as this is, and though human ingenuity and thought may be tasked in vain to devise any other means by which these blessings could have been conferred, yet a sort of sensibility which would be only mawkish and contemptible, if it were not mischievous, affects still to weep over the wrongs of "injured Africa." Can there be a doubt of the immense benefit which has been conferred on the race, by transplanting them from their native, dark, and barbarous regions, to the American continent and islands ! There, three-fourths of the race are in a state of the most deplorable personal Slavery. And those who are not, are in a scarcely less deplorable condition of political Slavery, to barbarous chiefs—who value neither life nor any other human right, or enthralled by priests to the most abject and atrocious superstitions. Take the following testimony of one of the few disinterested observers, who has had an opportunity of ob-

* Southern Literary Messenger, for January, 1835. *Note to Blackstone's Commentaries.*

serving them in both situations.* "The wild savage is the child of passion, unaided by one ray of religion or morality to direct his course, in consequence of which his existence is stained with every crime that can debase human nature to a level with the brute creation. Who can say that the slaves in our colonies are such? Are they not, by comparison with their still savage brethren, enlightened beings? Is not the West Indian negro, therefore, greatly indebted to his master for making him what he is—for having raised him from the state of debasement in which he was born, and placed him in a scale of civilized society? How can he repay him? He is possessed of nothing—the only return in his power is his servitude. The man who has seen the wild African, roaming in his native woods, and the well fed, happy looking negro of the West Indies, may, perhaps, be able to judge of their comparative happiness; the former, I strongly suspect, would be glad to change his state of boasted freedom, starvation, and disease, to become the slave of sinners, and the commiseration of saints." It was a useful and beneficent work, approaching the heroic, to tame the wild horse, and subdue him to the use of man; how much more to tame the nobler animal that is capable of reason, and subdue him to usefulness?

We believe that the tendency of Slavery is to elevate the character of the master. No doubt the character—especially of youth—has sometimes received a taint and premature knowledge of vice, from the contact and association with ignorant and servile beings of gross manners and morals. Yet still we believe that the entire tendency is to inspire disgust and aversion towards their peculiar vices. It was not without a knowledge of nature, that the Spartans exhibited the vices of slaves by way of negative example to their children. We

* Journal of an officer employed in the expedition, under the command of Capt. Owen, on the Western Coast of Africa, 1822.

flatter ourselves that the view of this degradation, mitigated as it is, has the effect of making probity more strict, the pride of character more high, the sense of honor more strong, than is commonly found where this institution does not exist. Whatever may the prevailing faults or vices of the masters of slaves, they have not commonly been understood to be those of dishonesty, cowardice, meanness, or falsehood. And so most unquestionably it ought to be. Our institutions would indeed be intolerable in the sight of God and man, if, condemning one portion of society to hopeless ignorance and comparative degradation, they should make no atonement by elevating the other class by higher virtues, and more liberal attainments—if, besides degraded slaves, there should be ignorant, ignoble, and degraded freemen. There is a broad and well marked line, beyond which no slavish vice should be regarded with the least toleration or allowance. One class is cut off from all interest in the State—that abstraction so potent to the feelings of a generous nature. The other must make compensation by increased assiduity and devotion to its honor and welfare. The love of wealth—so laudable when kept within proper limits, so base and mischievous when it exceeds them—so infectious in its example—an infection to which I fear we have been too much exposed—should be pursued by no arts in any degree equivocal, or at any risk of injustice to others. So surely as there is a just and wise governor of the universe, who punishes the sins of nations and communities, as well of individuals, so surely shall we suffer punishment, if we are indifferent to that moral and intellectual cultivation of which the means are furnished to us, and to which we are called and incited by our situation.

I would to heaven I could express, as I feel, the conviction how necessary this cultivation is, not only to our prosperity and consideration, but to our safety and very existence. We, the slaveholding States, are in a hopeless minority in our own confederated Republic—to say nothing of the great confederacy of civilized States. It is admitted, I believe, not only by slaveholders, but by others, that we have sent to our common councils more than our due share of talent, high character and eloquence. Yet in spite of all these most strenuously exerted, measures have been sometimes adopted which we believed to be dangerous and injurious to us, and threatening to be fatal. What would be our situation, if, instead of these, we were only represented by ignorant and grovelling men, incapable of raising their views beyond a job or petty office, and incapable of commanding bearing or consideration? May I be permitted to advert—by no means invidiously—to the late contest carried on by South-Carolina against Federal authority, and so happily terminated by the moderation which prevailed in our public counsels. I have often reflected, what one circumstance, more than any other, contributed to the successful issue of a contest, apparently so hopeless, in which one weak and divided State was arrayed against the whole force of the Confederacy—unsustained, and uncountenanced, even by those who had a common interest with her. It seemed to me to be, that we had for leaders an unusual number of men of great intellectual power, co-operating cordially and in good faith, and commanding respect and confidence at home and abroad, by elevated and honorable character. It was from these that we—the followers at home—caught hope and confidence in the gloomiest aspect of our affairs. These, by their eloquence and the largeness of their views, at least shook the faith of the dominant majority in the wisdom and justice of their measures—or the practicability of carrying them into successful effect; and by their bearing and well known character, satisfied them that South-Carolina would do all that she had pledged herself to do. Without these, how different might have been the result? And who shall say what at this day would have been the aspect of the now flourishing fields and cities of South-Carolina? Or rather, without these, it is probable the contest would never have been begun; but that, without even the animation of a struggle, we should have sunk silently into a hopeless and degrading subjection. While I have memory—in the extremity of age—in sickness —under all the reverses and calamities of life—I shall have one source of pride and consolation—that of having been associated—according to my humbler position—with the noble spirits who stood prepared to devote themselves for Liberty— the Constitution—the Union. May such character and such talent never be wanting to South-Carolina.

I am sure that it is unnecessary to say to an assembly like this, that the conduct of the master to his slave should be distinguished by the utmost humanity. That we should indeed regard them as wards and dependants on our kindness, for whose well-being in every way we are deeply responsible. This is no less the dictate of wisdom and just policy, than of right feeling. It is wise with respect to the services to be expected from them. I have never heard of an owner whose conduct in their management was distinguished by undue severity, whose slaves were not in a great degree worthless to him. A cheerful and kindly demeanor, with the expression of interest in themselves and their affairs, is, perhaps, calculated to have a better effect on them, than what might be esteemed more substantial favors and indulgences. Throughout nature, attachment is the reward of attachment. It is wise, too, in relation to the civilized world around us, to avoid giving occasion to the odium which is so industriously excited against ourselves and our institutions. For this reason, public opinion should, if possible, bear even more strongly and indignantly than it does at present, on masters who practise any wanton cruelty on their slaves. The miscreant who is guilty of this, not only violates the law of God and of humanity, but as far as in him lies, by bringing odium upon, endangers the institutions of his country, and the safety of his countrymen. He casts a shade upon the character of every individual of his fellow-citizens, and does every one of them a personal injury. So of him who indulges in any odious excess of intemperate or licentious passion. It is detached instances of this sort, of which the existence is, perhaps, hardly known among ourselves, that, collected with pertinacious and malevolent industry, affords the most formidable weapons to the mischievous zealots, who array them as being characteristic of our general manners and state of society.

I would by no means be understood to intimate, that a vigorous, as well as just government, should not be exercised over slaves. This is part of our duty towards them, no less obligatory than any other duty, and no less necessary towards their well-being than to ours. I believe that at least as much injury has been done and suffering inflicted by weak and injudicious indulgence, as by inordinate severity. He whose business is to labor, should be made to labor, and that with due diligence, and should be vigorously restrained from excess or vice. This is no less necessary to his happiness than to his usefulness. The master who neglects this, not only makes his slaves unprofitable to himself, but discontented and wretched—a nuisance to his neighbors and to society.

I have said that the tendency of our institution is to elevate the female character, as well as that of the other sex, and for similar reasons. In other states of society, there is no well defined limit to separate virtue and vice. There are degrees of vice, from the most flagrant and odious, to that which scarcely incurs the censure of society. Many individuals occupy an unequivocal position; and as society becomes accustomed to this, there will be a less peremptory requirement of purity in female manners and conduct; and often the whole of the society will be in a tainted and uncertain condition with respect to female virtue. Here, there is that certain and marked line, above which there is no toleration or allowance for any approach to license of manners or conduct, and she who falls below it, will fall far below even the slave. How many will incur this penalty?

And permit me to say, that this elevation of the female character is no less important and essential to us, than the moral and intellectual cultivation of the other sex. It would indeed be intolerable, if, when one class of the society is necessarily degraded in this respect, no compensation were made by the superior elevation and purity of the other. Not only essential purity of conduct, but the utmost purity of manners, and I will add, though it may incur the formidable charge of affectation or prudery,—a greater severity of decorum than is required elsewhere, is necessary among us. Always should be strenuously resisted the attempts which have been sometimes made to introduce among us the freedom of foreign European, and especially of continental manners. This freedom, the remotest in the world from that which sometimes springs from simplicity of manners, is calculated and commonly intended to confound the outward distinctions of virtue and vice. It is to prepare the way for licentiousness—to produce this effect—that if those who are clothed with the outward color and garb of vice, may be well received by society, those who are actually guilty may hope to be so too. It may be said, that there is often perfect purity where there is very great freedom of manners. And, I have no doubt, this may be true in particular instances, but it is never true of any soci-

ety in which this is the general state of manners. What guards can there be to purity, when every thing that *may possibly* be done innocently, is habitually practised; when there can be no impropriety which is not vice. And what must be the depth of the depravity when there is a departure from that which they admit as principle. Besides, things which may perhaps be practised innocently where they are familiar, produce a moral dilaceration in the course of their being introduced where they are new. Let us say, we will not have the manners of South-Carolina changed.

I have before said that free labor is cheaper than the labor of slaves, and so far as it is so the condition of the free laborer is worse. But I think President Dew has sufficiently shown that this is only true of Northern countries. It is matter of familiar remark that the tendency of warm climates is to relax the human constitution and indispose to labor. The earth yields abundantly—in some regions almost spontaneously—under the influence of the sun, and the means of supporting life are obtained with but slight exertion; and men will use no greater exertion than is necessary to the purpose. This very luxuriance of vegetation, where no other cause concurs, renders the air less salubrious, and even when positive malady does not exist, the health is habitually impaired. Indolence renders the constitution more liable to these effects of the atmosphere, and these again aggravate the indolence. Nothing but the coercion of Slavery can overcome the repugnance to labor under these circumstances, and by subduing the soil, improve and render wholesome the climate.

It is worthy of remark, that there does not now exist on the face of the earth, a people in a tropical climate, or one approaching to it, where Slavery does not exist, that is in a state of high civilization, or exhibits the energies which mark the progress towards it. Mexico and the South American Republics,* starting on their new career of independence, and having gone through a farce of abolishing slavery, are rapidly degenerating, even from semi-barbarism. The only portion of the South American continent which seems to be making any favorable progress, in spite of a weak and arbitrary civil government, is Brazil, in which slavery has been retained. Cuba, of the same race with the continental republics, is daily and rapidly advancing in industry and civilization; and this is owing exclusively to her slaves. St. Domingo is struck out of the map of civilized existence, and the British West Indies will shortly be so. On the other continent, Spain and Portugal are degenerate, and their rapid progress is downward. Their southern coast is infested by dis-

* The author of England and America thus speaks of the Colombian Republic:
"During some years, this colony has been an independent state; but the people dispersed over this vast and fertile plain, have almost ceased to cultivate the good land at their disposal; they subsist principally, many of them entirely, on the flesh of wild cattle; they have lost most of the arts of civilized life; not a few of them are in a state of deplorable misery; and if they should continue. as it seems probable they will, to retrograde as at present, the beautiful pampas of Buenos Ayres will soon be fit for another experiment in colonization. Slaves, black or yellow, would have cultivated those plains, would have kept together, would have been made to assist each other; would, by keeping together and assisting each other, have raised a surplus produce exchangeable in distant markets; would have kept their masters together for the sake of markets; would, by combination of labor, have preserved among their masters the arts and habits of civilized life." Yet this writer, the whole practical effect of whose work, whatever he may have thought or intended, is to show the absolute necessity, and immense benefits of Slavery, finds it necessary to add, I suppose in deference to the general sentiment of his countrymen, "that Slavery might have done all this, seems not more plain, than that so much good would have been bought too dear, if its price had been Slavery." Well may we say that the word makes men mad .

ease, arising from causes which industry might readily overcome, but that industry they will never exert. Greece is still barbarous, and scantily peopled. The work of an English physician, distinguished by strong sense and power of observation,* gives a most affecting picture of the condition of Italy,—especially south of the Appenines. With the decay of industry, the climate has degenerated towards the condition from which it was first rescued by the labor of slaves. There is poison in every man's veins, affecting the very springs of life, dulling or extinguishing, with the energies of the body, all energy of mind, and often exhibiting itself in the most appalling forms of disease. From year to year the pestilential atmosphere creeps forward, narrowing the circles within which it is possible to sustain human life. With disease and misery, industry still more rapidly decays, and if the process goes on, it seems that Italy too will soon be ready for another experiment in colonization.

Yet once it was not so, when Italy was possessed by the masters of slaves; when Rome contained her millions, and Italy was a garden; when their iron energies of body corresponded with the energies of mind which made them conquerors in every climate and on every soil; rolled the tide of conquest, not as in later times, from the South to the North; extended their laws and their civilization, and created them lords of the earth.

> "What conflux issuing forth or entering in;
> Prætors, pro-consuls to their provinces,
> Hasting, or on return in robes of state.
> Lictors and rods, the ensigns of their power,
> Legions and cohorts, turms of horse and wings:
> Or embassies from regions far remote,
> In various habits, on the Appian road,

* Johnson on Change of Air.

> Or on th' Emilian ; some from farthest South,
> Syene, and where the shadow both way falls,
> Meroe, Nilotic isle, and more to West,
> The realms of Bocchus to the Blackmoor sea;
> From th' Asian kings, and Parthian among these;
> From India and the golden Chersonese,
> And utmost India's isle, Taprobona,
> Dusk faces, with white silken turbans wreathed;
> From Gallia, Gades, and the British West;
> Germans, and Scythians, and Sarmatians, North
> Beyond Danubius to the Tauric Pool!
> All nations now to Rome obedience pay."

Such was, and such is, the picture of Italy. Greece presents a contrast not less striking. What is the cause of the great change? Many causes, no doubt, have occurred; but though

> "War, famine, pestilence, and flood and fire,
> Have dealt upon the seven-hilled city's pride,"

I will venture to say that nothing has dealt upon it more heavily than the loss of domestic slavery. Is not this evident? If they had slaves, with an energetic civil government, would the deadly miasma be permitted to overspread the Campagna, and invade Rome herself? Would not the soil be cultivated, and the wastes reclaimed? A late traveller* mentions a canal, cut for miles through rock and mountain, for the purpose of carrying off the waters of the lake of Celano, on which thirty thousand Roman slaves were employed for eleven years, and which remains almost perfect to the present day. This, the government of Naples was ten years in repairing with an hundred workmen. The imperishable works of Rome which remain to the present day were, for the most part, executed by slaves. How different would be the condition of Naples,

* Eight days in the Abruzzi.—*Blackwood's Magazine, November,* 1835.

if for her wretched lazzaroni were substituted negro slaves, employed in rendering productive the plains whose fertility now serves only to infect the air!

To us, on whom this institution is fastened, and who could not shake it off, even if we desired to do so, the great republics of antiquity offer instruction of inestimable value. They teach us that slavery is compatible with the freedom, stability, and long duration of civil government, with denseness of population, great power, and the highest civilization. And in what respect does this modern Europe, which claims to give opinions to the world, so far excel them—notwithstanding the immense advantages of the Christian religion and the discovery of the art of printing? They are not more free, nor have performed more glorious actions, nor displayed more exalted virtue. In the higher departments of intellect—in all that relates to taste and imagination—they will hardly venture to claim equality. Where they have gone beyond them in the results of mechanical philosophy, or discoveries which contribute to the wants and enjoyments of physical life, they have done so by the help of means with which they were furnished by the Grecian mind—the mother of civilization—and only pursued a little further the tract which that had always pointed out. In the development of intellectual power, they will hardly bear comparison. Those noble republics in the pride of their strength and greatness, may have anticipated for themselves—as some of their poets did for them,—an everlasting duration and predominance. But they could not have anticipated, that when they had fallen under barbarous arms, that when arts and civilization were lost, and the whole earth in darkness—the first light should break from their tombs—that in a renewed world, unconnected with them by ties of locality, language or descent, they should still be held the models of all that is profound in science, or elegant in literature, or all that is great in character, or elevated in imagination. And perhaps when England herself, who now leads the war with which we are on all sides threatened, shall have fulfilled her mission, and like the other glorious things of the earth, shall have passed away; when she shall have diffused her noble race and noble language, her laws, her literature, and her civilization, over all quarters of the earth, and shall perhaps be overrun by some Northern horde—sunk into an ignoble and anarchical democracy,* or subdued to the dominion of some Cæsar,—demagogue and despot,—then, in Southern regions, there may be found many republics, triumphing in Grecian arts and civilization, and worthy of British descent and Roman institutions.

If, after a time, when the mind and almost the memory of the republic were lost, Romans degenerated, they furnish conclusive evidence that this was owing not to their domestic, but to their political Slavery. The same thing is observed over all the Eastern monarchies; and so it must be, wherever property is insecure, and it is dangerous for a man to raise himself to such eminence by intellectual or moral excellence, as would give him influence over his society. So it is in Egypt; and the other regions bordering the Mediterranean, which once comprehended the civilization of the world, where Carthage, Tyre, and Phœnicia flourished. In short, the uncontradicted experience of the world is, that in the Southern States where good government and predial and domestic Slavery are found, there are prosperity and greatness; where either of these conditions is wanting, degeneracy and barbarism. The former, however, is equally essential in all climates and under all institutions. And can we suppose it to be the

---

* I do not use the word democracy in the Athenian sense, but to describe the government in which the slave and his master have an equal voice in public affairs.

design of the Creator, that these regions, constituting half of the earth's surface, and the more fertile half, and more capable of sustaining life, should be abandoned forever to depopulation and barbarism? Certain it is that they will never be reclaimed by the labor of freemen. In our own country, look at the lower valley of the Mississippi, which is capable of being made a far greater Egypt. In our own State, there are extensive tracts of the most fertile soil, which are capable of being made to swarm with life. These are at present pestilential swamps, and valueless, because there is abundance of other fertile soil in more favorable situations, which demand all and more than all the labor which our country can supply. Are these regions of fertility to be abandoned at once and forever to the alligator and tortoise—with here and there perhaps a miserable, shivering, crouching *free* black savage? Does not the finger of heaven itself seem to point to a race of men—not to be enslaved by us, but already enslaved, and who will be in every way benefitted by the change of masters—to whom such climate is not uncongenial, who, though disposed to indolence, are yet patient and capable of labor, on whose whole features, mind and character, nature has indelibly written—slave;—and indicate that we should avail ourselves of these in fulfilling the first great command to subdue and replenish the earth.

It is true that this labor will be dearer than that of Northern countries, where, under the name of freedom, they obtain cheaper and perhaps better slaves. Yet it is the best we can have, and this too has its compensation. We see it compensated at present by the superior value of our agricultural products. And this superior value they must probably always have. The Southern climate admits of a greater variety of productions. Whatever is produced in Northern climates, the same thing, or something equivalent, may be produced in the Southern. But the Northern have no equivalent for the products of Southern climates. The consequence will be, that the products of Southern regions will be demanded all over the civilized world. The agricultural products of Northern regions are chiefly for their own consumption. They must therefore apply themselves to the manufacturing of articles of luxury, elegance, convenience, or necessity,—which requires cheap labor—for the purpose of exchanging them with their Southern neighbors. Thus nature herself indicates that agriculture should be the predominating employment in Southern countries, and manufactures in Northern. Commerce is necessary to both—but less indispensable to the Southern, which produce within themselves a greater variety of things desirable to life. They will therefore have somewhat less of the commercial spirit. We must avail ourselves of such labor as we can command. The slave must labor, and is inured to it; while the necessity of energy in his government, of watchfulness, and of preparation and power to suppress insurrection, added to the moral force derived from the habit of command, may help to prevent the degeneracy of the master.

The task of keeping down insurrection is commonly supposed by those who are strangers to our institutions, to be a very formidable one. Even among ourselves, accustomed as we have been to take our opinions on this as on every other subject, ready formed from those whom we regarded as instructors, in the teeth of our own observation and experience, fears have been entertained which are absolutely ludicrous. We have been supposed to be nightly reposing over a mine, which may at any instant explode to our destruction. The first thought of a foreigner sojourning in one of our cities, who is awakened by any nightly alarm, is of servile insurrection and massacre. Yet if any thing is certain in human affairs, it is certain and from the most obvious considerations, that we are more secure in this respect than any civilized and fully peopled society upon the face of the earth. In every such society, there is a much larger proportion than with us, of persons who have more to gain than to lose by the overthrow of government, and the embroiling of social order. It is in such a state of things that those who were before at the bottom of society, rise to the surface. From causes already considered, they are peculiarly apt to consider their sufferings the result of injustice and misgovernment, and to be rancorous and embittered accordingly. They have every excitement, therefore, of resentful passion, and every temptation which the hope of increased opulence, or power or consideration can hold out, to urge them to innovation and revolt. Supposing the same disposition to exist in equal degree among our slaves, what are their comparative means or prospect of gratifying it? The poor of other countries are called free. They have, at least, no one interested to exercise a daily and nightly superintendence and control over their conduct and actions. Emissaries of their class may traverse, unchecked, every portion of the country, for the purpose of organizing insurrection. From their greater intelligence, they have greater means of communicating with each other. They may procure and secrete arms. It is not alone the ignorant, or those who are commonly called the poor, that will be tempted to revolution. There will be many disappointed men, and men of desperate fortune—men perhaps of talent and daring—to combine them and direct their energies. Even those in the higher ranks of society who contemplate no such result, will contribute to it, by declaiming on their hardships and rights.

With us, it is almost physically impossible that there should be any very extensive combination among the slaves. It is absolutely impossible that they should procure and conceal efficient arms. Their emissaries traversing the country, would carry their commissions on their foreheads. If we suppose among them an individual of sufficient talent and energy to qualify him for a revolutionary leader, he could not be so extensively known as to command the confidence, which would be necessary to enable him to combine and direct them. Of the class of freemen, there would be no individual so poor or degraded (with the exception perhaps of here and there a reckless and desperate outlaw and felon) who would not have much to lose by the success of such an attempt; every one, therefore, would be vigilant and active to detect and suppress it. Of all impossible things, one of the most impossible would be a successful insurrection of our slaves, originating with themselves.

Attempts at insurrection have indeed been made—excited, as we believe, by the agitation of the abolitionists and declaimers on Slavery; but these have been in every instance promptly suppressed. We fear not to compare the riots, disorder, revolt and bloodshed, which have been committed in our own, with those of any other civilized communities, during the same lapse of time. And let it observed under what extraordinary circumstances our peace has been preserved. For the last half century, one half of our population has been admonished in terms the most calculated to madden and excite, that they are the victims of the most grinding and cruel injustice and oppression. We know that these exhortations continually reach them, through a thousand channels which we cannot detect, as if carried by the birds of the air— and what human being, especially when unfavorably distinguished by outward circumstances, is not ready to give credit when he is told that he is the victim of injustice and oppression? In effect, if not in terms, they have been continually exhorted to insurrection. The master has been painted as a criminal, tyrant and robber, justly obnoxious to the vengeance of God and man, and they have been assured of the countenance and sympathy, if not of the active assistance, of all the rest of the world. We ourselves have in some measure pleaded guilty to the impeachment. It is not long since a great majority of our free population, servile to the opinions of those whose opinions they had been accustomed to follow, would have admitted Slavery to be a great evil, unjust and indefensible in principle, and only to be vindicated by the stern necessity which was imposed upon us. Thus stimulated by every motive and passion which ordinarily actuate human beings—not as to a criminal enterprise, but as to something generous and heroic—what has been the result? A few imbecile and uncombined plots—in every instance detected before they broke out into action, and which perhaps if undetected would never have broken into action. One or two sudden, unpremeditated attempts, frantic in their character, if not prompted by actual insanity, and these instantly crushed. As it is, we are not less assured of safety, order, and internal peace, than any other people; and but for the pertinacious and fanatical agitations of the subject, would be much more so.

This experience of security, however, should admonish us of the folly and wickedness of those who have sometimes taken upon themselves to supersede the regular course of law, and by rash and violent acts to punish supposed disturbers of the peace of society. This can admit of no justification or palliation whatever. Burke, I think, somewhere remarked something to this effect,—that when society is in the last stage of depravity—when all parties are alike corrupt, and alike wicked and unjustifiable in their measures and objects, a good man may content himself with standing neuter, a sad and disheartened spectator of the conflict between the rival vices. But are we in this wretched condition? It is fearful to see with what avidity the worst and most dangerous characters of society seize on the occasion of obtaining the countenance of better men, for the purpose of throwing off the restraints of law. It is always these who are most zealous and forward in constituting themselves the protectors of the public peace. To such men—men without reputation, or principle, or stake in society—disorder is the natural element. In that, desperate fortunes and the want of all moral principle and moral feeling constitute power. They are eager to avenge themselves upon society. Anarchy is not so much the absence of government, as the government of the worst—not aristocracy, but kakistocracy—a state of things, which to the honor of our nature, has seldom obtained amongst men, and which perhaps was only fully exemplified during the worst times of the French revolution, when that horrid hell burnt with its most lurid flame. In such a state of things, to be accused is to be condemned—to protect the innocent is to be guilty; and what perhaps is the worst effect, even men of better nature, to whom their own deeds are abhorrent, are goaded by terror to be forward and emulous in deeds of guilt and violence. The scenes of lawless violence which have been acted in some portions of our country, rare and restricted as they have been, have done more to tarnish its reputation than a thousand libels. They have done more to discredit, and if anything could, to endanger, not only our domestic, but our republican institutions, than the abolitionists themselves. Men can never be permanently and effectually disgraced but by themselves, and rarely endangered but by their own injudicious conduct, giving advantage to the enemy. Better, far better, would it be to encounter the dangers with which we are supposed to be threatened, than to employ such means for averting them. But the truth is, that in relation to this matter, so far as respects actual insurrection, when alarm is once excited, danger is absolutely at an end. Society can then employ legitimate and more effectual measures for its own protection. The very commission of such deeds is proof that they are unnecessary. Let those who attempt them, then, or make any demonstration towards them, understand that they will meet only the discountenance and abhorrence of all good men, and the just punishment of the laws they have dared to outrage.

It has commonly been supposed, that this institution will prove a source of weakness in relation to military defence against a foreign enemy. I will venture to say that in a slaveholding community, a larger military force may be maintained permanently in the field, than in any State where there are not slaves. It is plain that almost the whole of the able bodied free male population, making half of the entire able bodied male population, may be maintained in the field, and this without taking in any material degree from the labor and resources of the country. In general, the labor of our country is performed by slaves. In other countries, it is their laborers that form the material of their armies. What proportion of these can be taken away without fatally crippling their industry and resources? In the war of the revolution, though the strength of our State was wasted and paralyzed by the unfortunate divisions which existed among ourselves, yet it may be said with general truth, that every citizen was in the field, and acquired much of the qualities of the soldier.

It is true that this advantage will be attended with its compensating evils and disadvantages; to which we must learn to submit, if we are determined on the maintenance of our institutions. We are, as yet, hardly at all aware how little the maxims and practices of modern civilized governments will apply to us. Standing armies, as they are elsewhere constituted, we cannot have; for we have not, and for generations cannot have, the materials out of which they are to be formed. If we should be involved in serious wars, I have no doubt but that some sort of conscription, requiring the service of all citizens for a considerable term, will be necessary. Like the people of Athens, it will be necessary that every citizen should be a soldier, and qualified to discharge efficiently the duties of a soldier. It may seem a melancholy consideration, that an army so made up should be opposed to the disciplined mercenaries of foreign nations. But we must learn to know our true situation. But may we not hope, that made up of superior materials, of men having home and country to defend; inspired by higher pride of character, of greater intelligence, and trained by an effective, though honorable discipline, such an army will be more than a match for mercenaries. The efficiency of an army is determined by the qualities of its officers, and may we not expect to have a greater proportion of men better qualified for officers, and possessing the true spirit of military command. And let it be recollected that if there were otherwise reason to apprehend danger from insurrection, there will be the greatest security when there is the largest force on foot within the country. Then it is that any such attempt would be most instantly and effectually crushed.

And, perhaps, a wise foresight should induce our State to provide, that it should have within itself such military knowledge and skill as may be sufficient to organize, discipline and command armies, by establishing a military academy or school of discipline. The school of the militia will not do for this. From the general opinion of our weakness, if our country should at any time come into hostile collision, we shall be selected for the point of attack; making us, according to Mr. Adams's anticipation, the Flanders of the United States. Come from what quarter it may, the storm will fall upon us. It is known that lately, when there was apprehension of hostility with France, the scheme was instantly devised of invading the Southern States and organizing insurrection. In a popular English periodical work, I have seen the plan suggested by an officer of high rank and reputation in the British army, of invading the Southern States at various points and operating by the same means. He is said to be a gallant officer, and certainly had no conception that he was devising atrocious crime, as alien to the true spirit of civilized warfare, as the poisoning of streams and fountains. But the folly of such schemes is no less evident than their wickedness. Apart from the consideration of that which experience has most fully proved to be true—that in general their attachment and fidelity to their masters is not to be shaken, and that from sympathy with the feelings of those by whom they are surrounded, and from whom they derive their impressions, they contract no less terror and aversion towards an invading enemy; it is manifest that this recourse would be an hundred fold more available to us than to such an enemy. They are already in our possession, and we might at will arm and organize them in any number that we might think proper. The Helots were a regular constituent part of the Spartan armies. Thoroughly acquainted with their characters, and accustomed to command them, we might use any strictness of discipline which would be necessary to render them effective, and from their habits of subordination already formed, this would be a task of less difficulty. Though morally most timid, they are by no means wanting in physical strength of nerve. They are excitable by praise; and directed by those in whom they have confidence, would rush fearlessly and unquestioning upon any sort of danger. With white officers and accompanied by a strong white cavalry, there are no troops in the world from whom there would be so little reason to apprehend insubordination or mutiny.

This, I admit, might be a dangerous resource, and one not to be resorted to but in great extremity. But I am supposing the case of our being driven to extremity. It might be dangerous to disband such an army, and reduce them with the habits of soldiers, to their former condition of laborers. It might be found necessary, when once embodied, to keep them so, and subject to military discipline—a permanent standing army. This in time of peace would be expensive, if not dangerous. Or if at any time we should be engaged in hostilities with our neighbors, and it were thought advisable to send such an army abroad to conquer settlements for themselves, the invaded regions might have occasion to think that the scourge of God was again let loose to afflict the earth.

President Dew has very fully shown how utterly vain are the fears of those, who, though there may be no danger for the present, yet apprehend great danger for the future, when the number of slaves shall be greatly increased. He has shown that the larger and more condensed society becomes, the easier it will be to maintain subordination, supposing the relative number of the different classes to remain the same— or even if there should be a very disproportionate increase of the enslaved class. Of all vain things, the vainest and that in which man most shows his impotence and folly, is the taking upon himself to provide for a very distant future—at all events by any material sacrifice of the present. Though experience has shown that revolutions and political movements—unless when they have been conducted with the most guarded caution and moderation—have generally terminated in results just the opposite of what was expected from them, the angry ape will still play his fantastic tricks, and put in motion machinery, the action of which he no more comprehends or foresees than he comprehends the mysteries of infinity. The insect that is borne upon the current will fancy that he directs its course. Besides the fear of insurrection and servile war, there is also alarm lest, when their numbers shall be greatly increased, their labor will become utterly unprofitable, so that it will be equally difficult for the master to retain and support them, or to get rid of them. But at what age of the world is this likely to happen? At present, it may be said that almost the whole of the Southern portion of this continent is to be subdued to cultivation; and in the order of providence, this is the task allotted to them. For this purpose, more labor will be required for generations to come than they will be able to supply. When that task is accomplished, there will be many objects to which their labor may be directed.

At present they are employed in accumulating individual wealth, and this in one way, to wit, as agricultural laborers—and this is, perhaps, the most useful purpose to which their labor can be applied. The effect of Slavery has not been to counteract the tendency to dispersion, which seems epidemical among our countrymen, invited by the unbounded extent of fertile and unexhausted soil, though it counteracts many of the evils of dispersion. All the customary trades, professions and employments, except the agricultural, require a condensed population for their profitable exercise. The agriculturist who can command no labor but that of his own hands, or that of his family, must remain comparatively poor and rude. He who acquires wealth by the labor of slaves, has the means of improvement for himself and his children. He may have a more extended intercourse, and consequently means of information and refinement, and may seek education for his children where it may be found. I say, what is obviously true, that he has the *means* of obtaining those advantages; but I say nothing to palliate or excuse the conduct of him who, having such means, neglects to avail himself of them.

I believe it to be true, that in consequence of our dispersion, though individual wealth is acquired, the face of the country is less adorned and improved by useful and ornamental public works, than in other societies of more condensed population, where there is less wealth. But this is an effect of that which constitutes perhaps our most conspicuous advantage. Where population is condensed, they must have the evils of condensed population, and among these is the difficulty of finding profitable employment for capital. He who has accumulated even an inconsiderable sum, is often puzzled to know what use to make of it. Ingenuity is therefore tasked to cast about for every enterprise which may afford a chance of profitable investment. Works useful and ornamental to the country, are thus undertaken and accomplished, and though the proprietors may fail of profit, the community no less receives the benefit. Among us, there is no such difficulty. A safe and profitable method of investment is offered to every one who has capital to dispose of, which is further recommended to his feelings by the sense of independence and the comparative leisure which the employment affords to the proprietor engaged in it. It is for this reason that few of our citizens engage in the pursuits of commerce. Though these may be more profitable, they are also more hazardous and more laborious.

When the demand for agricultural labor shall be fully supplied, then of course the labor of slaves will be directed to other employments and enterprises. Already it begins to be found, that in some instances it may be used as profitably in works of public improvement. As it becomes cheaper and cheaper, it will be applied to more various purposes and combined in larger masses. It may be commanded and combined with more facility than any other sort of labor; and the laborer, kept in stricter subordination, will be less dangerous to the security of society than in any other country, which is crowded and overstocked with a class of what are called free laborers. Let it be remembered that all the great and enduring monuments of human art and industry—the wonders of Egypt—the everlasting works of Rome—were created by the labor of slaves. There will come a stage in our progress when we shall have facilities for executing works as great as any of these—more useful than the pyramids—not less magnificent than the sea of Moeris. What the end of all is to be; what mutations lie hid in the womb of the distant future; to what convulsions our societies may be exposed—whether the master, finding it impossible to live with his slaves, may not be compelled to abandon the country to them—of all this it were presumptuous and vain to speculate.

I have hitherto, as I proposed, considered it as a naked, abstract question of the comparative good and evil of the institution of slavery. Very far different indeed is the practical question presented to us, when it is proposed to get rid of an institution which has interwoven itself with every fibre of the body politic; which has formed the habits of our society, and is consecrated by the usage of generations. If this be not a vicious prescription, which the laws of God forbid to ripen into right, it has a just claim to be respected by all tribunals of man. If the negroes were now free, and it were proposed to enslave them, then it would be incumbent on those who proposed the measure to show clearly that their liberty was incompatible with the public security. When it is proposed to innovate on the established state of things, the burden is on those who propose the innovation, to show that advantage will be gained from it. There is no reform, however necessary, wholesome or moderate, which will not be accompanied with some degree of inconvenience, risk or suffering. Those who acquiesce in the state of things which they found existing, can hardly be thought criminal. But most deeply criminal are they who give rise to the enormous evil with which great revolutions in society are always attended, without the fullest assurance of the greater good to be ultimately obtained. But if it can be made to appear, even probably, that no good will be obtained, but that the results will be evil and calamitous as the process, what can justify such innovations? No human being can be so mischievous—if acting consciously, none can be so wicked as those who, finding evil in existing institutions, rush blindly upon change, unforeseeing and reckless of consequences, and leaving it to chance or fate to determine whether the end shall be improvement, or greater and more intolerable evil. Certainly the instincts of nature prompt to resist intolerable oppression. For this resistance no rule can be prescribed, but it must be left to the instincts of nature. To justify it, however, the insurrectionists should at least have a reasonable probability of success, and be assured that their condition will be improved by success. But most extraordinary is it, when those who complain and clamor are not those who are supposed to feel the oppression, but persons at a distance from them, and who can hardly at all appreciate the good or the evil of their situation. It is the unalterable condition of humanity, that men must achieve civil liberty for themselves. The assistance of allies has sometimes enabled nations to repel the attacks of foreign power, never to conquer liberty as against their own internal government.

In one thing I concur with the abolitionists; that if emancipation is to be brought about, it is better that it should be immediate and total. But let us suppose it to be brought about in any manner, and then enquire what would be the effects.

The first and most obvious effect, would be to put an end to the cultivation of our great Southern staple. And this would be equally the result, if we suppose the emancipated negroes to be in no way distinguished from the free laborers of other countries, and that their labor would be equally effective. In that case, they would soon cease to be laborers for hire, but would scatter themselves over our unbounded territory, to become independent land owners themselves. The cultivation of the soil on an extensive scale, can only be carried on where there are slaves, or in countries superabounding with free labor. No such operations are carried on in any portions of our own country where there are not slaves. Such are carried on in England, where there is an overflowing population and intense competition for employment. And our institutions seem suited to the exigencies of our respective situations. There, a much greater number of laborers is required at one season of the year than at another, and the farmer may enlarge or diminish the quantity of labor he employs, as circumstances may require. Here, about the same quantity of labor is required at every season, and the planter suffers no inconvenience from retaining his laborers throughout the year Imagine an extensive rice or cotton plantation cultivated by free laborers, who might perhaps *strike* for an increase of wages, at a season when the neglect of a few days would insure the destruction of the whole crop. Even if it were possible to procure laborers at all, what planter would venture to carry on his operations under such circumstances? I need hardly say that these staples cannot be produced to any extent where the proprietor of the soil cultivates it with his own hands. He can do little more than produce the necessary food for himself and his family.

And what would be the effect of putting an end to the cultivation of these staples, and thus annihilating, at a blow, two-thirds or three-fourths of our foreign commerce? Can any sane mind contemplate such a result without terror? I speak not of the utter poverty and misery to which we ourselves would be reduced, and the desolation which would overspread our own portion of the country. Our Slavery has not only given existence to millions of slaves within our own territories, it has given the means of subsistence, and therefore existence, to millions of freemen in our confederates States; enabling them to send forth their swarms to overspread the plains and forests of the West, and appear as the harbingers of civilization. The products of the industry of those States are in general similar to those of the civilized world, and are little demanded in their markets. By exchanging them for ours, which are every where sought for, the people of these States are enabled to acquire all the products of art and industry, all that contributes to convenience or luxury, or gratifies the taste or the intellect, which the rest of the world can supply. Not only on our own continent, but on the other, it has given existence to hundreds of thousands, and the means of comfortable subsistence to millions. A distinguished citizen of our own State, than whom none can be better qualified to form an opinion, has lately stated that our great staple, cotton, has contributed more than any thing else of later times to the progress of civilization. By enabling the poor to obtain cheap and becoming clothing, it has inspired a taste for comfort, the first stimulus to civilization. Does not *self-defence*, then, demand of us steadily to resist the abrogation of that which is productive of so much good? It is more than self-defence. It it to defend millions of human beings, who are far removed from us, from the intensest suffering, if not from being struck out of existence. It is the defence of human civilization.

But this is but a small part of the evil which would be occasioned. After President Dew, it is unnecessary to say a single word on the practicability of colonizing our slaves. The two races, so widely separated from each other by the impress of nature, must remain together in the same country. Whether it be accounted the result of prejudice or reason, it is certain that the two races will not be blended together so as to form a homogenous population. To one who knows anything of the nature of man and human society, it would be unnecessary to argue that this state of things cannot continue; but that one race must be driven out by the other, or exterminated, or again enslaved. I have argued on the supposition that the emancipated negroes would be as efficient as other free laborers. But whatever theorists, who know nothing of the matter, may think proper to assume, we well know that this would not be so. We know that nothing but the coercion of Slavery can overcome their propensity to indolence, and that not one in ten would be an efficient laborer. Even if this disposition were not grounded in their nature, it would be a result of their position. I have somewhere seen it observed, that to be degraded by opinion, is a thousand fold worse, so far as the feelings of the individuals are concerned, than to be degraded by the laws. *They* would be thus degraded, and this feeling is incompatible with habits of order and industry. Half our population would at once be paupers. Let an inhabitant of New-York or Philadelphia conceive of the situation of their respective States, if one-half of their population consisted of free negroes. The tie which now connects them, being broken, the different races would be estranged from each other, and hostility would grow up between them. Having the command of their own time and actions, they could more effectually combine insurrection, and provide the means of rendering it formidable. Released from the vigilant superintendence which now restrains them, they would infallibly be led from petty to greater crimes, until all life and property would be rendered insecure. Aggression would beget retaliation, until open war—and that a war of extermination

—were established. From the still remaining superiority of the white race, it is probable that they would be the victors, and if they did not exterminate, they must again reduce the others to Slavery—when they could be no longer fit to be either slaves or freemen. It is not only in self-defence, in defence of our country and of all that is dear to us, but in defence of the slaves themselves, that we refuse to emancipate them.

If we suppose them to have political privileges, and to be admitted to the elective franchise, still worse results may be expected. It is hardly necessary to add anything to what has been said by Mr. Paulding on this subject, who has treated it fully. It is already known, that if there be a class unfavorably distinguished by any peculiarity from the rest of society, this distinction forms a tie which binds them to act in concert, and they exercise more than their due share of political power and influence—and still more, as they are of inferior character and looser moral principle. Such a class form the very material for demagogues to work with. Other parties court them, and concede to them. So it would be with the free blacks in the case supposed. They would be used by unprincipled politicians, of irregular ambition, for the advancement of their schemes, until they should give them political power and importance beyond even their own intentions. They would be courted by excited parties in their contests with each other. At some time, they may perhaps attain political ascendancy, and this is more probable, as we may suppose that there will have been a great emigration of whites from the country. Imagine the government of such legislators. Imagine then the sort of laws that will be passed, to confound the invidious distinction which has been so long assumed over them, and, if possible, to obliterate the very memory of it. These will be resisted. The blacks will be tempted to avenge themselves by oppression and proscription of the white race, for their long superiority. Thus matters will go on, until universal anarchy, or kakistocracy, the government of the worst, is fully established. I am persuaded that if the spirit of evil should devise to send abroad upon the earth all possible misery, discord, horror, and atrocity, he could contrive no scheme so effectual as the emancipation of negro slaves within our country.

The most feasible scheme of emancipation, and that which I verily believe would involve the least danger and sacrifice, would be that the *entire* white population should emigrate, and abandon the country to their slaves. Here would be triumph to philanthropy. This wide and fertile region would be again restored to ancient barbarism—to the worst of all barbarism—barbarism corrupted and depraved by intercourse with civilization. And this is the consummation to be wished, upon a *speculation*, that in some distant future age, they may become so enlightened and improved, as to be capable of sustaining a position among the civilized races of the earth. But I believe moralists allow men to defend their homes and their country, even at the expense of the lives and liberties of others.

Will any philanthropist say that the evils, of which I have spoken, would be brought about only by the obduracy, prejudices, and overweening self-estimation of the whites in refusing to blend the races by marriage, and so create an homogenous population? But what, if it be not prejudice, but truth, and nature, and right reason, and just moral feeling? As I have before said, throughout the whole of nature, like attracts like, and that which is unlike repels. What is it that makes so unspeakably loathsome, crimes not to be named, and hardly alluded to? Even among the nations of Europe, so nearly homogenous, there are some peculiarities of form and feature, mind and character, which may be generally distinguished by those accustomed to observe them. Though the exceptions are numerous, I will venture to say that not in one instance in a hundred, is the man of sound and unsophisticated tastes and propensities so likely to be attracted by the female of a foreign stock, as by one of his own, who is more nearly conformed to himself. Shakspeare spoke the language of nature, when he made the senate and people of Venice attribute to the effect of witchcraft, Desdemona's passion for Othello—though, as Coleridge has said, we are to conceive of him not as a negro, but as a high bred Moorish chief.

If the negro race, as I have contended, be inferior to our own in mind and character, marked by inferiority of form and features, then ours would suffer deterioration from such intermixture. What would be thought of the moral conduct of the parent who should voluntarily transmit disease, or fatuity, or deformity to his offspring? If man be the most perfect work of the Creator, and the civilized European man the most perfect variety of the human race, is he not criminal who would desecrate and deface God's fairest work; estranging it further from the image of himself, and conforming it more nearly to that of the brute? I have heard it said, as if it afforded an argument, that the African is as well satisfied of the superiority of his own complexion, form, and features, as we can be of ours. If this were true, as it is not, would any one be so recreant to his own civilization, as to say that his opinion ought to weigh against ours—that there is no universal standard of truth, and grace, and beauty—that the Hottentot Venus may perchance possess as great perfection of form as the Medicean? It is true, the licentious passions of men overcome the natural repugnance, and find transient gratification in intercourse with females of the other race. But this is a very different thing from making her the associate of life, the companion of the bosom and the hearth. Him who would contemplate such an alliance for himself, or regard it with patience, when proposed for a son, or daughter, or sister, we should esteem a degraded wretch—with justice, certainly, if he were found among ourselves—and the estimate would not be very different if he were found in Europe. It is not only in defence of ourselves, of our country, and of our own generation, that we refuse to emancipate our slaves, but to defend our posterity and race from degeneracy and degradation.

Are we not justified then in regarding as criminals, the fanatical agitators whose efforts are intended to bring about the evils I have described? It is sometimes said that their zeal is generous and disinterested, and that their motives may be praised, though their conduct be condemned. But I have little faith in the good motives of those who pursue bad ends. It is not for us to scrutinize the hearts of men, and we can only judge of them by the tendency of their actions. There is much truth in what was said by Coleridge. "I have never known a trader in philanthropy who was not wrong in heart somehow or other. Individuals so distinguished, are usually unhappy in their family relations—men not benevolent or beneficent to individuals, but almost hostile to them, yet lavishing money and labor and time on the race—the abstract notion." The prurient love of notoriety actuates some. There is much luxury in sentiment, especially if it can be indulged at the expense of others, and if there be added some share of envy or malignity, the temptation to indulgence is almost irresistible. But certainly they may be justly regarded as criminal, who obstinately shut their eyes and close their ears to all instruction with respect to the true nature of their actions.

It must be manifest to every man of sane mind that it is impossible for them to achieve ultimate success; even if every individual in our country, out of the limits of the slaveholding

States, were united in their purposes. They cannot have even the miserable triumph of St. Domingo—of advancing through scenes of atrocity, blood and massacre, to the restoration of barbarism. They may agitate and perplex the world for a time. They may excite to desperate attempts and particular acts of cruelty and horror, but these will always be suppressed or avenged at the expense of the objects of their truculent philanthropy. But short of this, they can hardly be aware of the extent of the mischief they perpetrate. As I have said, their opinions, by means to us inscrutible, do very generally reach our slave population. What human being, if unfavorably distinguished by outward circumstances, is not ready to believe when he is told that he is the victim of injustice? Is it not cruelty to make men restless and dissatisfied in their condition, when no effort of theirs can alter it? The greatest injury is done to their characters, as well as to their happiness. Even if no such feelings or designs should be entertained or conceived by the slave, they will be attributed to him by the master, and all his conduct scanned with a severe and jealous scrutiny. Thus distrust and aversion are established, where, but for mischievous interference, there would be confidence and good will, and a sterner control is exercised over the slave who thus becomes the victim of his cruel advocates.

An effect is sometimes produced on the minds of slaveholders, by the publications of the self-styled philanthropists, and their judgments staggered and consciences alarmed. It is natural that the oppressed should hate the oppressor. It is still more natural that the oppressor should hate his victim. Convince the master that he is doing injustice to his slave, and he at once begins to regard him with distrust and malignity. It is a part of the constitution of the human mind, that when circumstances of necessity or temptation induce men to continue in the practice of what they believe to be wrong, they become desperate and reckless of the degree of wrong. I have formerly heard of a master who accounted for his practising much severity upon his slaves, and exacting from them an unusual degree of labor, by saying that the thing (Slavery) was altogether wrong, and therefore it was well to make the greatest possible advantage out of it. This agitation occasions some slaveholders to hang more loosely on their country. Regarding the institution as of questionable character, condemned by the general opinion of the world, and one which must shortly come to an end, they hold themselves in readiness to make their escape from the evil which they anticipate. Some sell their slaves to new masters (always a misfortune to the slave) and remove themselves to other societies, of manners and habits uncongenial to their own. And though we may suppose that it is only the weak and the timid who are liable to be thus affected, still it is no less an injury and public misfortune. Society is kept in an unquiet and restless state, and every sort of improvement is retarded.

Some projectors suggest the education of slaves, with a view to prepare them for freedom—as if there were any method of a man's being educated to freedom, but by himself. The truth is, however, that supposing that they are shortly to be emancipated, and that they have the capacities of any other race, they are undergoing the very best education which it is possible to give. They are in the course of being taught habits of regular and patient industry, and this is the first lesson which is required. I suppose that their most zealous advocates would not desire that they should be placed in the high places of society immediately upon their emancipation, but that they should begin their course of freedom as laborers, and raise themselves afterwards as their capacities and characters might enable them. But how little would what are commonly called the rudiments of education, add to their qualifications as laborers? But for the agitation which exists, however, their education would be carried further than this. There is a constant tendency in our society to extend the sphere of their employments, and consequently to give them the information which is necessary to the discharge of those employments. And this, for the most obvious reason, it promotes the master's interest. How much would it add to the value of a slave, that he should be capable of being employed as a clerk, or be able to make calculations as a mechanic? In consequence, however, of the fanatical spirit which has been excited, it has been thought necessary to repress this tendency by legislation, and to prevent their acquiring the knowledge of which they might make a dangerous use. If this spirit were put down, and we restored to the consciousness of security, this would be no longer necessary, and the process of which I have spoken would be accelerated. Whenever indications of superior capacity appeared in a slave, it would be cultivated; gradual improvement would take place, until they might be engaged in as various employments as they were among the ancients—perhaps even liberal ones. Thus, if in the adorable providence of God, at a time and in a manner which we can neither foresee nor conjecture, they are to be rendered capable of freedom and to enjoy it, they would be prepared for it in the best and most effectual, because in the most natural and gradual manner. But fanaticism hurries to its effect at once. I have heard it said, God does good, but it is by imperceptible degrees; the devil is permitted to do evil, and he does it in a hurry. The beneficent processes of nature are not apparent to the senses. You cannot see the plant grow, or the flower expand. The volcano, the earthquake, and the hurricane, do their work of desolation in a moment. Such would be the desolation, if the schemes of fanatics were permitted to have effect. They do all that in them lies to thwart the beneficent purposes of providence. The whole tendency of their efforts is to aggravate present suffering, and to cut off the chance of future improvement, and in all their bearings and results, have produced, and are likely to produce, nothing but " pure, unmixed, dephlegmated, defecated evil."

If Wilberforce or Clarkson were living, and it were enquired of them " can you be sure that you have promoted the happiness of a single human being?" I imagine that, if they considered conscientiously, they would find it difficult to answer in the affirmative. If it were asked " can you be sure that you have not been the cause of suffering, misery and death to thousands,"—when we recollect that they probably stimulated the exertions of the *amis des noirs* in France, and that through the efforts of these the horrors of St. Domingo were perpetrated—I think they must hesitate long to return a decided negative. It might seem cruel, if we could, to convince a man who has devoted his life to what he esteemed a good and generous purpose, that he has been doing only evil—that he has been worshipping a horrid fiend, in the place of the true God. But fanaticism is in no danger of being convinced. It is one of the mysteries of our nature, and of the divine government, how utterly disproportioned to each other are the powers of doing evil and of doing good. The poorest and most abject instrument, that is utterly imbecile for any purpose of good, seems sometimes endowed with almost the powers of omnipotence for mischief. A mole may inundate a province—a spark from a forge may conflagrate a city—a whisper may separate friends—a rumor may convulse an empire—but when we would do benefit to our race or country, the purest and most chastened motives, the most patient thought and labor, with the humblest self-distrust, are hardly sufficient to assure us that the results may not disappoint our expectations, and that we may not do evil instead of good. But are we therefore to refrain from efforts to benefit our race and country? By no means: but these motives, this labor and self distrust are the only conditions upon which we are permitted to hope for success. Very different indeed is the course of those whose precipitate and ignorant zeal would overturn the fundamental institutions of society, uproar its peace and endanger its security, in pursuit of a distant and shadowy good, of which they themselves have formed no definite conception—whose atrocious philosophy would sacrifice a generation—and more than one generation—for any hypothesis.

HAMMOND'S LETTERS ON SLAVERY.

SILVER BLUFF, (So. CA.,) JANUARY 28, 1845.

SIR: I received, a short time ago, a letter from the Rev Willoughby M. Dickinson, dated at your residence, "Playford Hall, near Ipswich, 26th November, 1844," in which was enclosed a copy of your Circular Letter, addressed to professing Christians in our Northern States, having no concern with Slavery, and to others there. I presume that Mr. Dickinson's letter was written with your knowledge, and the document enclosed with your consent and approbation. I therefore feel that there is no impropriety in my addressing my reply directly to yourself, especially as there is nothing in Mr. Dickinson's communication requiring serious notice. Having abundant leisure, it will be a recreation to devote a portion of it to an examination and free discussion of the question of Slavery as it exists in our Southern States: and since you have thrown down the gauntlet to me, I do not hesitate to take it up.

Familiar as you have been with the discussions of this subject in all its aspects, and under all the excitements it has occasioned for sixty years past, I may not be able to present much that will be new to you. Nor ought I to indulge the hope of materially affecting the opinions you have so long cherished, and so zealously promulgated. Still, time and experience have developed facts, constantly furnishing fresh tests to opinions formed sixty years since, and continually placing this great question in points of view, which could scarcely occur to the most consummate intellect even a quarter of a century ago: and which may not have occurred yet to those whose previous convictions, prejudices, and habits of thought, have thoroughly and permanently biased them to one fixed way of looking at the matter: while there are peculiarities in the operation of every social system, and special local as well as moral causes materially affecting it, which no one, placed at the distance you are from us, can fully comprehend or properly appreciate. Besides, it may be possibly, a novelty to you to encounter one who conscientiously believes the domestic Slavery of these States to be not only an inexorable necessity for the present, but a moral and humane institution, productive of the greatest political and social advantages, and who is disposed, as I am, to defend it on these grounds.

I do not propose, however, to defend the African slave trade. That is no longer a question. Doubtless great evils arise from it as it has been, and is now conducted: unnecessary wars and cruel kidnapping in Africa: the most shocking barbarities in the middle passage: and perhaps a less humane system of Slavery in countries continually supplied with fresh laborers at a cheap rate. The evils of it, however, it may be fairly presumed, are greatly exaggerated. And if I might judge of the truth of transactions stated as occurring in this trade, by that of those reported as transpiring among us, I should not hesitate to say, that a large proportion of the stories in circulation are unfounded, and most of the remainder highly colored.

On the passage of the Act of Parliament prohibiting this trade to British subjects rests, what you esteem, the glory of your life. It required twenty years of arduous agitation, and the intervening extraordinary political events, to convince your countrymen, and among the rest your pious king, of the expediency of the measure: and it is but just to say, that no one individual rendered more essential service to the cause than you did. In reflecting on the subject, you cannot but often ask yourself: What, after all, has been accomplished; how much human suffering has been averted; how many human beings have been rescued from transatlantic Slavery? And on the answers you can give these questions, must in a great measure, I presume, depend the happiness of your life. In framing them, how frequently must you be reminded of the remark of Mr. Grosvenor, in one of the early debates upon the subject, which I believe you have yourself recorded, "that he had twenty objections to the abolition of the slave trade: the first was, *that it was impossible*—the rest he need not give." Can you say to yourself, or to the world, that this *first* objection of Mr. Grosvenor has been yet confuted? It was estimated at the commencement of your agitation in 1787, that forty-five thousand Africans were annually transported to America and the West Indies. And the mortality of the middle passage, computed by some at five, is now admitted not to have exceeded nine per cent. Notwithstanding your Act of Parliament, the previous abolition by the United States, and that all the powers in the world have subsequently prohibited this trade—some of the greatest of them declaring it piracy, and covering the African seas with armed vessels to prevent it—Sir Thomas Fowel Buxton, a coadjutor of yours, declared in 1840, that the number of Africans now annually sold into slavery beyond the sea, amounts, at the very least, to one hundred and fifty thousand souls; while the mortality of the middle passage has increased, in consequence of the measures taken to suppress the trade, to twenty-five or thirty per cent. And of the one hundred and fifty thousand slaves who have been captured and liberated by British men-of-war, since the passage of your Act, Judge Jay, an American abolitionist, asserts that one hundred thousand, or two-thirds, have perished between their capture and liberation. Does it not really seem that Mr. Grosvenor was a prophet? That though nearly all the "impossibilities" of 1787 have vanished, and become as familiar *facts* as our household customs, under the magic influence of steam, cotton, and universal peace, yet this wonderful prophecy still stands, defying time and the energy and genius of mankind. Thousands of valuable lives, and fifty millions of pounds sterling, have been thrown away by your government in fruitless attempts to overturn it. I hope you have not lived too long for your own happiness, though you have been spared to see that in spite of all your toils and those of your fellow-laborers, and the accomplishment of all that human agency could do, the African slave trade has increased three-fold under your own eyes—more rapidly, perhaps, than any other ancient branch of commerce—and that your efforts to suppress it have effected *nothing more* than a three-fold increase of its horrors. There is a God who rules this world—all-powerful—far-seeing: He does not permit his creatures to foil his designs. It is he who, for his all-wise, though to us often inscrutable purposes, throws "impossibilities" in the way of our fondest hopes and most strenuous exertions. Can you doubt this?

Experience having settled the point, that this trade *cannot be abolished by the use of force,* and that blockading squadrons serve only to make it more profitable and more cruel, I am surprised that the attempt is persisted in, unless it serves as a cloak to other purposes. It would be far better than it now is, for the African, if the trade was free from all restrictions, and left to the mitigation and decay which time and competition would surely bring about. If kidnapping, both secretly and by war made for the purpose, could be by any means prevented in Africa, the next greatest blessing you could bestow upon that country would be to transport its actual slaves in comfortable vessels across the Atlantic. Though they might be perpetual bondsmen, still they would emerge from darkness into light—from barbarism into civilization—from idolatry to Christianity—in short from death to life.

But let us leave the African slave trade, which has so signally defeated the *philanthropy* of the world, and turn to American Slavery, to which you have now directed your attention, and against which a crusade has been preached as enthusiastic and ferocious as that of Peter the Hermit—destined, I believe, to be about as successful. And here let me say, there is a vast difference between the two, though you may not acknowledge it. The wisdom of ages has concurred in the justice and expediency of establishing rights by prescriptive use, however tortious in their origin they may have been. You would deem a man insane, whose keen sense of equity would lead him to denounce your right to the lands you hold, and which perhaps you inherited from a long line of ancestry, because your title was derived from a Saxon or Norman conqueror, and your lands were originally wrested by violence from the vanquished Britons. And so would the New-England abolitionist regard any one who would insist that he should restore his farm to the descendants of the slaughtered red men, to whom God had as clearly given it as he gave life and freedom to the kidnapped African. That time does not consecrate wrong, is a fallacy which all history exposes; and which the best and wisest men of all ages and professions of religious faith have practically denied. The means, therefore, whatever they may have been, by which the African race now in this country have been reduced to Slavery, cannot affect us, since they are our property, as your land is yours, by inheritance or purchase and prescriptive right.

You will say that man cannot hold *property in man*. The answer is, that he can and *actually does* hold property in his fellow all the world over, in a variety of forms, and *has always done so*. I will show presently his authority for doing it.

If you were to ask me whether I am an advocate of Slavery in the abstract, I should probably answer, that I am not, according to my understanding of the question. I do not like to deal in abstractions. It seldom leads to any useful ends. There are few universal truths. I do not now remember any single moral truth universally acknowledged. We have no assurance that it is given to our finite understanding to comprehend abstract moral truth. Apart from revelation and the inspired writings, what ideas should we have even of God, salvation and immortality? Let the heathen answer. Justice itself is impalpable as an abstraction, and abstract liberty the merest phantasy that ever amused the imagination. This world was made for man, and man for the world as it is. We ourselves, our relations with one another and with all matter, are real, not ideal. I might say that I am no more in favor of Slavery in the abstract, than I am of poverty, disease, deformity, idiocy, or any other inequality in the condition of the human family; that I love perfection, and think I should enjoy a millennium such as God has promised. But what would it amount to? A pledge that I would join you to set about eradicating those apparently inevitable evils of our nature, in equalizing the condition of all mankind, consummating the perfection of our race, and introducing the millennium! By no means. To effect these things, belongs exclusively to a higher power. And it would be well for us to leave the Almighty to perfect his own works and fulfil his own covenants. Especially, as the history of the past shows how entirely futile all human efforts have proved, when made for the purpose of aiding Him in carrying out even his revealed designs, and how invariably he has accomplished them by unconscious instruments, and in the face of human expectation. Nay more, that every attempt which has been made by fallible man to extort from the world obedience to his "abstract" notions of right and wrong, has been invariably attended with calamities dire, and extended just in proportion to the breadth and vigor of the movement. On Slavery in the abstract, then, it would not be amiss to have as little as possible to say. Let us contemplate it as it is. And thus contemplating it, the first question we have to ask ourselves is, whether it is contrary to the will of God, as revealed to us in his Holy Scriptures—the only certain means given us to ascertain his will. If it is, then Slavery is a sin. And I admit at once that every man is bound to set his face against it, and to emancipate his slaves, should he hold any.

Let us open these Holy Scriptures. In the twentieth chapter of Exodus, seventeenth verse, I find the following words: "Thou shalt not covet thy neighbor's house, thou shalt not covet thy neighbor's wife, nor his man-servant, nor his maid-servant, nor his ox, nor his ass, nor anything that is thy neighbor's"—which is the tenth of those commandments that declare the essential principles of the great moral law delivered to Moses by God himself. Now, discarding all technical and verbal quibbling as wholly unworthy to be used in interpreting the Word of God, what is the plain meaning, undoubted intent, and true spirit of this commandment? Does it not emphatically and explicitly forbid you to disturb your neighbor in the enjoyment of his property; and more especially of that which is here specifically mentioned as being lawfully, and by this commandment made sacredly his? Prominent in the catalogue stands his "man-servant and his maid-servant," who are thus distinctly *consecrated as his property*, and guaranteed to him for his exclusive benefit, in the most solemn manner. You attempt to avert the otherwise irresistible conclusion, that Slavery was thus ordained by God, by declaring that the word "slave" is not used here, and is not to be found in the Bible. And I have seen many learned dissertations on this point from abolition pens. It is well known that both the Hebrew and Greek words translated "servant" in the Scriptures, mean also, and most usually, "slave." The use of the one word, instead of the other, was a mere matter of taste with the translators of the Bible, as it has been with all the commentators and religious writers, the latter of whom have, I believe, for the most part, adopted the term "slave," or used both terms indiscriminately. If, then, these Hebrew and Greek words include the idea of both systems of servitude, the conditional and unconditional, they should, as the major includes the minor proposition, be always translated "slaves," unless the sense of the whole text forbids it. The real question, then is, what idea is intended to be conveyed by the words used in the commandment quoted ? And it is clear to my mind, that as no limitation is affixed to them, and the express intention was to secure to mankind the peaceful enjoyment of every species of property, that the terms "men-servants and maid-servants" include all classes of servants, and establish a lawful, exclusive, and indefeasible interest equally in the "Hebrew brother who shall go out in the seventh year," and "the yearly hired servant," and "those purchased from the heathen round about," who were to be "bondmen forever," *as the property of their fellow-man.*

You cannot deny that there were among the Hebrews "bondmen forever." You cannot deny that God especially authorized his chosen people to purchase "bondmen forever" from the heathen, as recorded in the twenty-fifth chapter of Leviticus, and that they are there designated by the very Hebrew word used in the tenth commandment. Nor can you deny that a "BONDMAN FOREVER" is a "SLAVE;" yet you endeavor to hang an argument of immortal consequence upon the wretched subterfuge, that the precise word "slave" is not to be found in the *translation* of the Bible. As if the translators were canonical expounders of the Holy Scriptures, and *their words*, not *God's meaning*, must be regarded as his revelation.

It is vain to look to Christ or any of his Apostles to justify such blasphemous perversions of the word of God. Although Slavery in its most revolting form was everywhere visible around them, no visionary notions of piety or philanthropy ever tempted them to gainsay the LAW, even to mitigate the cruel severity of the existing system. On the contrary, regarding Slavery as an *established*, as well as *inevitable condition of human society*, they never hinted at such a thing as its termination on earth, any more than that "the poor may cease out of the land," which God affirms to Moses shall never be: and they exhort "all servants under the yoke" to "count their masters as worthy of all honor:" "to obey them in all things according to the flesh; not with eye-service as men-pleasers, but in singleness of heart, fearing God;" "not only the good and gentle, but also the froward:" "for what glory is it if when ye are buffetted for your faults ye shall take it patiently? but if when ye do well and suffer for it ye take it patiently, this is acceptable of God." St. Paul actually apprehended a runaway slave, and sent him to his master! Instead of deriving from the Gospel any sanction for the work you have undertaken, it would be difficult to imagine sentiments and conduct more strikingly in contrast, than those of the Apostles and the abolitionists.

It is impossible, therefore, to suppose that Slavery is contrary to the will of God. It is equally absurd to say that American Slavery differs in form or principle from that of the chosen people. *We accept the Bible terms as the definition of our Slavery, and its precepts as the guide of our conduct.* We desire nothing more. Even the right to "buffet," which is esteemed so shocking, finds its express license in the gospel. 1 Peter ii. 20. Nay, what is more, God directs the Hebrews to "bore holes in the ears of their brothers" to *mark* them, when under certain circumstances they become *perpetual slaves.* Exodus xxi. 6.

I think, then, I may safely conclude, and I firmly believe, that American Slavery is not only not a sin, but especially commanded by God through Moses, and approved by Christ through his apostles. And here I might close its defence; for what God ordains, and Christ sanctifies, should surely command the respect and toleration of man. But I fear there has grown up in our time a transcendental religion, which is throwing even transcendental philosophy into the shade—a religion too pure and elevated for the Bible; which seeks to erect among men a higher standard of morals than the Almighty has revealed, or our Saviour preached; and which is probably destined to do more to impede the extension of God's kingdom on earth than all the infidels who have ever lived. Error is error. It is as dangerous to deviate to the right hand as the left. And when men, professing to be holy men, and who are by numbers so regarded, declare those things to be sinful which our Creator has expressly authorized and instituted, they do more to destroy his authority among mankind than the most wicked can effect, by proclaiming that to be innocent which he has forbidden. To this self-righteous and self-exalted class belong all the abolitionists whose writings I have read. With them it is no end of the argument to prove your propositions by the text of the Bible, interpreted according to its plain and palpable meaning, and as understood by all mankind for three thousand years before their time. They are more ingenious at construing and interpolating to accommodate it to their new-fangled and etherial code of morals, than ever were Voltaire and Hume in picking it to pieces, to free the world from what they considered a delusion. When the abolitionists proclaim "man-stealing" to be a sin, and show me that it is so written down by God, I admit them to be right, and shudder at the idea of such a crime. But when I show them that to hold "bondmen forever" is ordained by God, *they deny the Bible, and set up in its place a law of their own making.* I must then cease to reason with them on this branch of the question. Our religion differs as widely as our manners. The great judge in our day of final account must decide between us.

Turning from the consideration of slaveholding in its relations to man as an accountable being, let us examine it in its influence on his political and social state. Though, being foreigners to us, you are in no wise entitled to interfere with the civil institutions of this country, it has become quite common for your countrymen to decry Slavery as an enormous political evil to us, and even to declare that our Northern States ought to withdraw from the Confederacy rather than continue to be contaminated by it. The American abolitionists appear to concur fully in these sentiments, and a portion, at least, of them are incessantly threatening to dissolve the Union. Nor should I be at all surprised if they succeed. It would not be difficult, in my opinion, to conjecture which region, the North or South, would suffer most by such an event. For one, I should not object, by any means, to cast my lot in a confederacy of States whose citizens might all be slaveholders.

I endorse without reserve the much abused sentiment of Governer M'Duffie, that "Slavery is the corner-stone of our republican edifice;" while I repudiate, as ridiculously absurd, that much lauded but nowhere accredited dogma of Mr. Jefferson, that "all men are born equal." No society has ever yet existed, and I have already incidentally quoted the highest authority to show that none ever will exist, without a natural variety of classes. The most marked of these must, in a country like ours, be the rich and the poor, the educated and the ignorant. It will scarcely be disputed that the very poor have less leisure to prepare themselves for the proper discharge of public duties than the rich; and that the ignorant are wholly unfit for them at all. In all countries save ours, these two classes, or the poor rather, who are presumed to be necessarily ignorant, are by law expressly excluded from all participation in the management of public affairs. In a Republican Government this cannot be done. Universal suffrage, though not essential in theory, seems to be in fact a necessary appendage to a republican system. Where universal suffrage obtains, it is obvious that the government is in the hands of a numerical majority; and it is hardly necessary to say that in every part of the world more than half the people are ignorant and poor. Though no one can look upon poverty as a crime, and we do not here generally regard it as any objection to a man in his individual capacity, still it must be admitted that it is a wretched and insecure government which is administered by its most ignorant citizens, and those who have the least at stake under it. Though intelligence and wealth have great influence here, as everywhere, in keeping in check reckless and unenlightened numbers, yet it is evident to close observers, if not to all, that these are rapidly usurping all power in the non-slaveholding States, and threaten a fearful crisis in republican institutions there at no remote period. In the slaveholding States, however, nearly one-half of the whole population, and those the poorest and most ignorant, have no political influence whatever, because they are slaves. Of the other half, a large proportion are both educated and independent in their circumstances, while those who unfortunately are not so, being still elevated far above the mass, are higher toned and more deeply interested in preserving a stable and well ordered government, than the same class in any other country. Hence, Slavery is truly the "corner-stone" and foundation of every well-designed and durable "republican edifice."

With us every citizen is concerned in the maintenance of order, and in promoting honesty and industry among those of the lowest class who are our slaves; and our habitual vigilance renders standing armies, whether of soldiers or policemen, entirely unnecessary. Small guards in our cities, and occasional patrols in the country, ensure us a repose and security known no where else. You cannot be ignorant that, excepting the United States, there is no country in the world whose existing government would not be overturned in a month, but for its standing armies, maintained at an enormous and destructive cost to those whom they are destined to overawe—so rampant and combative is the spirit of discontent wherever nominal free labor prevails, with its ostensive privileges and its dismal servitude. Nor will it be long before the "*free States*" of this Union will be compelled to introduce the same expensive machinery, to preserve order among their "free and equal" citizens. Already has Philadelphia organized a permanent battalion for this purpose; New-York, Boston and Cincinnati will soon follow her example; and then the smaller towns and densely populated counties. The intervention of their militia to repress violations of the peace is becoming a daily affair. A strong government, after some of the old fashions—though probably with a new name—sustained by the force of armed mercenaries, is the ultimate destiny of the non-slave-holding section of this confederacy, and one which may not be very distant.

It is a great mistake to suppose, as is generally done abroad, that in case of war slavery would be a source of weakness. It did not weaken Rome, nor Athens, nor Sparta, though their slaves were comparatively far more numerous than ours, of the same color for the most part with themselves, and large numbers of them familiar with the use of arms. I have no apprehension that our slaves would seize such an opportunity to revolt. The present generation of them, born among us, would never think of such a thing at any time, unless instigated to it by others. Against such instigations we are always on our guard. In time of war we should be more watchful and better prepared to put down insurrections than at any other periods. Should any foreign nation be so lost to every sentiment of civilized humanity, as to attempt to erect among us the standard of revolt, or to invade us with black troops, for the base and barbarous purpose of stirring up servile war, their efforts would be signally rebuked. Our slaves could not be easily seduced, nor would any thing delight them more than to assist in stripping Cuffee of his regimentals to put him in the cotton-field, which would be the fate of most black invaders, without any very prolix form of "apprenticeship." If, as I am satisfied would be the case, our slaves remained peaceful on our plantations, and cultivated them in time of war under the superintendence of a limited number of our citizens, it is obvious that we could put forth more strength in such an emergency, at less sacrifice, than any other people of the same numbers. And thus we should in every point of view, "out of this nettle danger, pluck the flower safety."

How far Slavery may be an advantage or disadvantage to those not owning slaves, yet united with us in political association, is a question for their sole consideration. It is true that our representation in Congress is increased by it. But so are our taxes; and the non slave-holding States, being the majority, divide among themselves far the greater portion of the amount levied by the Federal Government. And I doubt not that, when it comes to a close calculation, they will not be slow in finding out that the balance of profit arising from the connection is vastly in their favor.

In a social point of view the abolitionists pronounce Slavery to be a monstrous evil. If it was so, it would be our own peculiar concern, and superfluous benevolence in them to lament over it. Seeing their bitter hostility to us, they might leave us to cope with our own calamities. But they make war upon us out of excess of charity, and attempt to purify by covering us with calumny. You have read and assisted to circulate a great deal about affrays, duels and murders, occurring here, and all attributed to the terrible demoralization of Slavery. Not a single event of this sort takes place among us, but it is caught up by the abolitionists, and paraded over the world, with endless comments, variations and exaggerations. You should not take what reaches you as a mere sample, and infer that there is a vast deal more you never hear. You hear all, and more than all, the truth.

It is true that the point of honor is recognized throughout the slave region, and that disputes of certain classes are frequently referred for adjustment, to the "trial by combat." It would not be appropriate for me to enter, in this letter, into a defence of the practice of duelling, nor to maintain at length, that it does not tarnish the character of a people to acknowledge a standard of honor. Whatever evils may arise from it, however, they cannot be attributed to Slavery, since the same custom prevails both in France and England. Few of your Prime Ministers, of the last half-century even, have escaped the contagion, I believe. The affrays, of which so much is said, and in which rifles, bowie-knives and pistols are so prominent, occur mostly in the frontier States of the South-West. They are naturally incidental to the condition of society, as it exists in many sections of these recently settled countries, and will as naturally cease in due time. Adventurers from the older States, and from Europe, as desperate in character as they are in fortune, congregate in these wild regions, jostling one another and often forcing the peaceable and honest into rencontres in self-defence. Slavery has nothing to do with these things. Stability and peace are the first desires of every slave-holder, and the true tendency of the system. It could not possibly exist amid the eternal anarchy and civil broils of the ancient Spanish dominions in America. And for this very reason, domestic Slavery has ceased there. So far from encouraging strife, such scenes of riot and bloodshed, as have within the last few years disgraced our Northern cities, and as you have lately witnessed in Birmingham and Bristol and Wales, not only never have occurred, but I will venture to say, never will occur in our slave-holding States. The only thing that can create a mob (as you might call it) here, is the appearance of an abolitionist, whom the people assemble to chastise. And this is no more of a mob, than a rally of shepherds to chase a wolf out of their pastures would be one.

But we are swindlers and repudiators! Pennsylvania is not a slave State. A majority of the States which have failed to meet their obligations punctually are non-slave-holding; and two-thirds of the debt said to be repudiated is owed by these States. Many of the States of this Union are heavily encumbered with debt—none so hopelessly as England. Pennsylvania owes $22 for each inhabitant—England $222, counting her paupers in. Nor has there been any repudiation definite and final, of a lawful debt, that I am aware of. A few States have failed to pay some instalments of interest. The extraordinary financial difficulties which occurred a few years ago will account for it. Time will set all things right again. Every dollar of both principal and interest, owed by any State, North or South, will be ultimately paid, *unless the abolition of Slavery overwhelms us all in one common ruin.* But have no other nations failed to pay? When were the French Assignats redeemed? How much interest did your National Bank pay on its immense circulation, from 1797 to 1821, during which period that circulation was inconvertible, and for the time *repudiated?* How much of your national debt has been incurred for money borrowed to meet the interest on it, thus avoiding delinquency in detail, by insuring inevitable bankruptcy and repudiation in the end? And what sort of operation was that by which your present Ministry recently expunged a handsome amount of that debt, by substituting, through a process just not compulsory, one species of security for another? I am well aware that the faults of others do not excuse our own, but when failings are charged to Slavery, which are shown to occur to equal extent where it does not exist, surely Slavery must be acquitted of the accusation.

It is roundly asserted, that we are not so well educated nor so religious here as elsewhere. I will not go into tedious statistical statements on these subjects. Nor have I, to tell the truth, much confidence in the details of what are commonly set forth as statistics. As to education, you will probably admit that slave-holders should have more leisure for mental culture than most people. And I believe it is charged against them, that they are peculiarly fond of power, and ambitious of honors. If this be so, as all the power and honors of this country are won mainly by intellectual superiority, it might be fairly presumed, that slave-holders would not be neglectful of education. In proof of the accuracy of this presumption, I point you to the facts, that our Presidential chair has been occupied for forty-four out of fifty-six years, by slaveholders; that another has been recently elected to fill it for four more, over an opponent who was a slave-holder also; and that in the Federal Offices and both Houses of Congress, considerably more than a due proportion of those acknowledged to stand in the first rank are from the South. In this arena, the intellects of the free and slave States meet in full and fair competition. Nature must have been unusually bountiful to us, or we have been at least reasonably assiduous in the cultivation of such gifts as she has bestowed—unless indeed you refer our superiority to moral qualities, which I am sure *you* will not. More wealthy we are not; nor would mere wealth avail in such rivalry.

The piety of the South is unobtrusive. We think it proves but little, though it is a confident thing for a man to claim that he stands higher in the estimation of his Creator, and is less a sinner than his neighbor. If vociferation is to carry the question of religion, the North, and probably the Scotch, have it. Our sects are few, harmonious, pretty much united among themselves, and pursue their avocations in humble peace. In fact, our professors of religion seem to think— whether correctly or not—that it is their duty "to do good in secret," and to carry their holy comforts to the heart of each individual, without reference to class *or color*, for his special enjoyment, and not with a view to exhibit their zeal before the world. So far as numbers are concerned, I believe our clergymen, when called on to make a showing, have never had occasion to blush, if comparisons were drawn between the free and slave States. And although our presses do not teem with controversial pamphlets, nor our pulpits shake with excommunicating thunders, the daily walk of our religious communicants furnishes, apparently, as little food for gossip as is to be found in most other regions. It may be regarded as a mark of our want of excitability—though that is a quality accredited to us in an eminent degree—that few of the remarkable religious *Isms* of the present day have taken root among us. We have been so irreverent as to laugh at Mormonism and Millerism, which have created such commotions farther North; and modern prophets have no honor in our country. Shakers, Rappists, Dunkers, Socialists, Fourrierists and the like, keep themselves afar off. Even Puseyism has not yet moved us. You may attribute this to our domestic Slavery if you choose. I believe you would do so justly. There is no material here for such characters to operate upon.

But your grand charge is, that licentiousness in intercourse between the sexes, is a prominent trial of our social system, and that it necessarily arises from Slavery. This is a favorite theme with the abolitionists, male and female. Folios have been written on it. It is a common observation, that there is no subject on which ladies of eminent virtue so much delight to dwell, and on which in especial learned old maids, like Miss Martineau, linger with such an insatiable relish. They expose it in the slave States with the most minute observance and endless iteration. Miss Martineau, with peculiar gusto, relates a series of scandalous stories, which would have made Boccacio jealous of her pen, but which are so ridiculously false as to leave no doubt, that some wicked wag, knowing she would write a book, has furnished her materials—a game too often played on tourists in this country. The constant recurrence of the female abolitionists to this topic, and their bitterness in regard to it, cannot fail to suggest to even the most charitable mind, that

"Such rage without betrays the fires within."

Nor are their immaculate coadjutors of the other sex, though perhaps less specific in their charges, less violent in their denunciations. But recently in your Island, a clergyman has, at a public meeting, stigmatized the whole slave region as a "brothel." Do these people thus cast stones, being "without sin?" Or do they only

> "Compound for sins they are inclined to
> By damning those they have no mind to."

Alas that David and Solomon should be allowed to repose in peace—that Leo should be almost canonized, and Luther more than sainted—that in our own day courtezans should be formally licensed in Paris, and tenements in London rented for years to women of the town for the benefit of the Church, with the knowledge of the Bishop—and the poor slave States of America alone pounced upon, and offered up as a holocaust on the altar of immaculateness, to atone for the abuse of natural instinct by all mankind; and if not actually consumed, at least exposed, anathematized and held up to scorn, by those who

> "Write,
> Or with a rival's or an eunuch's spite."

But I do not intend to admit that this charge is just or true. Without meaning to profess uncommon modesty, I will say that I wish the topic could be avoided. I am of opinion, and I doubt not every right-minded man will concur, that the public exposure and discussion of this vice, even to rebuke, invariably does more harm than good; and that if it cannot be checked by instilling pure and virtuous sentiments, it is far worse than useless to attempt to do it, by exhibiting its deformities. I may not, however, pass it over; nor ought I to feel any delicacy in examining a question, to which the slave-holder is invited and challenged by clergymen and virgins. So far from allowing, then, that licentiousness pervades this region, I broadly assert, and I refer to the records of our courts, to the public press, and to the knowledge of all who have ever lived here, that among our white population there are fewer cases of divorce, separation, crim. con., seduction, rape and bastardy, than among any other five millions of people on the civilized earth. And this fact I believe will be conceded by the abolitionists of this country themselves. I am almost willing to refer it to them and submit to their decision on it. I would not hesitate to do so, if I thought them capable of an impartial judgment on any matter where Slavery is in question. But it is said, that the licentiousness consists in the constant intercourse between white males and colored females. One of your heavy charges against us has been, that we regard and treat these people as brutes; you now charge us with habitually taking them to our bosoms. I will not comment on the inconsistency of these accusations. I will not deny that some intercourse of the sort does take place. Its character and extent, however, are grossly and atrociously exaggerated. No authority, divine or human, has yet been found sufficient to arrest all such irregularities among men. But it is a known fact, that they are perpetrated here, for the most part, in the cities. Very few mulattoes are reared on our plantations. In the cities, a large proportion of the inhabitants do not own slaves. A still larger proportion are natives of the North, or foreigners. They should share, and justly, too, an equal part in this sin with the slave-holders. Facts cannot be ascertained, or I doubt not, it would appear that they are the chief offenders. If the truth be otherwise, then persons from abroad have stronger prejudices against the African race than we have. Be this as it may, it is well known, that this intercourse is regarded in our society as highly disreputable. If carried on habitually, it seriously affects a man's standing, so far as it is known; and he who takes a colored mistress—with rare and extraordinary exceptions—loses caste at once. You will say that *one* exception should damn our whole country. How much less criminal is it to take a white mistress? In your eyes it should be at least an equal offence. Yet look around you at home, from the cottage to the throne, and count how many mistresses are kept in unblushing notoriety, without loss of caste. Such cases are nearly unknown here, and down even to the lowest walks of life, it is almost invariably fatal to a man's position and prospects to keep a mistress openly, whether white or black. What Miss Martineau relates of a young man's purchasing a colored concubine from a lady, and avowing his designs, is too absurd even for contradiction. No person would dare to allude to such a subject, in such a manner, to any decent female in this country.

After all, however, the number of the mixed breed, in proportion to that of the black, is infinitely small, and out of the towns next to nothing. And when it is considered that the African race has been among us for two hundred years, and that those of the mixed breed continually intermarry—often rearing large families—it is a decided proof of our continence, that so few comparatively are to be found. Our misfortunes are two-fold. From the prolific propagation of these mongrels among themselves, we are liable to be charged by tourists with delinquencies where none have been committed, while, where one has been, it cannot be concealed. Color marks indelibly the offence, and reveals it to every eye. Conceive that, even in your virtuous and polished country, if every bastard, through all the circles of your social system, was thus branded by nature and known to all, what shocking developments might there not be! How little indignation might your saints have to spare for the licentiousness of the slave region. But I have done with this disgusting topic. And I think I may justly conclude, after all the scandalous charges which tea-table gossip, and long-gowned hypocrisy have brought against the slave-holders, that a people whose men are proverbially brave, intellectual and hospitable, and whose women are unaffectedly chaste, devoted to domestic life, and happy in it, can neither be degraded nor demoralized, whatever their institutions may be. My decided opinion is, that our system of Slavery contributes largely to the development and culture of these high and noble qualities.

In an economical point of view—which I will not omit—Slavery presents some difficulties. As a general rule, I agree it must be admitted, that free labor is cheaper than slave labor. It is a fallacy to suppose that ours is *unpaid labor*. The slave himself must be paid for, and thus his labor is all purchased at once, and for no trifling sum. His price was, in the first place, paid mostly to your countrymen, and assisted in building up some of those colossal English fortunes, since illustrated by patents of nobility, and splendid piles of architecture, stained and cemented, if you like the expression, with the blood of kidnapped innocents; but loaded with no heavier curses than abolition and its begotten fanaticisms have brought upon your land—some of them fulfilled, some yet to be. But besides the first cost of the slave, he must be fed and clothed, well fed and well clothed, if not for humanity's sake, that he may do good work, retain health and life, and rear a family to supply his place. When old or sick, he is a clear expense, and so is the helpless portion of his family. No poor law provides for him when unable to work, or brings up his children for our service when we need them. These are all heavy charges on slave labor. Hence, in all countries where the denseness of the population has reduced it to a matter of perfect certainty, that labor can be obtained, whenever wanted, and the laborer be forced, by sheer necessity, to hire for the smallest pittance that will keep soul and body together, and rags upon his back while in actual employment—dependent at all other times on alms or poor rates—in all such countries it is found cheaper to pay this pittance, than to clothe, feed, nurse, support through childhood, and pension in old age, a race of slaves. Indeed, the advantage is so great as speedily to compensate for the loss of the value of the slave. And I have no hesitation in saying, that if I could cultivate my lands on these terms, I would, without a word, resign my slaves, provided they could be properly disposed of. But the question is, whether free or slave labor is cheapest to us in this country, at this time, situated as we are. And it is decided at once by the fact that we cannot avail ourselves of any other than slave labor. We neither have, nor can we procure, other labor to any extent, or on anything like the terms mentioned. We must, therefore, content ourselves with our dear labor, under the consoling reflection that what is lost to us, is gained to humanity; and that, inasmuch as our slave costs us more than your free man costs you, by so much is he better off. You will promptly say, emancipate your slaves, and then you will have free labor on suitable terms. That might be if there were five hundred where there now is one, and the continent, from the Atlantic to the Pacific, was as densely populated as your Island. But until that comes to pass, no labor can be procured in America on the terms you have it.

While I thus freely admit that to the individual proprietor slave labor is dearer than free, I do not mean to admit as equally clear that it is dearer to the community and to the State. Though it is certain that the slave is a far greater consumer than your laborer, the year round, yet your pauper system is costly and wasteful. Supported by your community at large, it is not administered by your hired agents with that interested care and economy—not to speak of humanity—which mark the management of ours, by each proprietor, for his own non-effectives; and is both more expensive to those who pay, and less beneficial to those who receive its bounties.

Besides this, Slavery is rapidly filling up our country with a hardy and healthy race, peculiarly adapted to our climate and productions, and conferring signal political and social advantages on us as a people, to which I have already referred.

I have yet to reply to the main ground on which you and your coadjutors rely for the overthrow of our system of Slavery. Failing in all your attempts to prove that it is sinful in its nature, immoral in its effects, a political evil, and profitless to those who maintain it, you appeal to the sympathies of mankind, and attempt to arouse the world against us by the most shocking charges of tyranny and cruelty. You begin by a vehement denunciation of "the irresponsible power of one man over his fellow men." The question of the responsibility of power is a vast one. It is the great political question of modern times. Whole nations divide off upon it and establish different fundamental systems of government. That "responsibility," which to one set of millions seems amply sufficient to check the government, to the support of which they devote their lives and fortunes, appears to another set of millions a mere mockery of restraint. And accordingly as the opinions of these millions differ, they honor each other with the epithets of "serfs" or "anarchists." It is ridiculous to introduce such an idea as this into the discussion of a mere domestic institution; but since you have introduced it, I deny that the power of the slave-holder in America is "irresponsible." He is responsible to God. He is responsible to the world—a responsibility which abolitionists do not intend to allow him to evade—and in acknowledgment of which, I write you this letter. He is responsible to the community in which he lives, and to the laws under which he enjoys his civil rights. Those laws do not permit him to kill, to maim, or to punish beyond certain limits, or to overtask, or to refuse to feed and clothe his slave. In short, they forbid him to be tyrannical or cruel. If any of these laws have grown obsolete, it is because they are so seldom violated, that they are forgotten. You have disinterred one of them, from a compilation by some Judge Stroud of Philadelphia, to stigmatize its inadequate penalties for killing, maiming, &c. Your object appears to be—you can have no other—to produce the impression, that it must be often violated on account of its insufficiency. You say as much, and that it marks our estimate of the slave. You forget to state that this law was enacted by *Englishmen*, and only indicates *their* opinion of the reparation due for these offences. Ours is proved by the fact, though perhaps unknown to Judge Stroud or yourself, that we have essentially altered this law; and the murder of a slave has for many years been punishable with death in this State. And so it is, I believe, in most or all the slave States. You seem well aware, however, that laws have been recently passed in all these States, making it penal to teach slaves to read. Do you know what occasioned their passage, and renders their stringent enforcement necessary? I can tell you. It was the abolition agitation. If the slave is not allowed to read his bible, the sin rests upon the abolitionists; for they stand prepared to furnish him with a key to it, which would make it, not a book of hope, and love, and peace, but of despair, hatred and blood; which would convert the reader, not into a christian, but a demon. To preserve him from such a horrid destiny, it is a sacred duty which we owe to our slaves, not less than to ourselves, to interpose the most decisive means. If the Catholics deem it wrong to trust the bible to the hands of ignorance, shall we be excommunicated because we will not give it, and with it the corrupt and fatal commentaries of the abolitionists, to our slaves? Allow our slaves to read your writings, stimulating them to cut our throats! Can you believe us to be such unspeakable fools?

I do not know that I can subscribe in full to the sentiment so often quoted by the abolitionists, and by Mr. Dickinson in his letter to me: "*Homo sum humani nihil a me alienum puto*," as translated and practically illustrated by them. Such a doctrine would give wide authority to every one for the most dangerous intermeddling with the affairs of others. It will do in poetry—perhaps in some sorts of philosophy—but the attempt to make it a household maxim, and introduce it into the daily walks of life, has caused many a "homo" a broken crown; and probably will continue to do it. Still, though a slaveholder, I freely acknowledge my obligations as a man; and that I am bound to treat humanely the fellow-creatures whom God has entrusted to my charge. I feel, therefore, somewhat sensitive under the accusation of cruelty, and disposed to defend myself and fellow-slaveholders against it. It is certainly the interest of all, and I am convinced that it is also the desire of every one of us, to treat our slaves with proper kindness. It is necessary to our deriving the greatest amount of profit from them. Of this we are all satisfied. And you snatch from us the only consolation we Americans could derive from the opprobrious imputation of being wholly devoted to making money, which your disinterested and gold-despising countrymen delight to cast upon us, when you nevertheless declare that we are ready to sacrifice it for the pleasure of being inhuman. You remember that Mr. Pitt could not get over the idea that self-interest would ensure kind treatment to slaves, until you told him your woful stories of the middle passage. Mr. Pitt was right in the first instance, and erred, under your tuition, in not perceiving the difference between a temporary and permanent ownership of them. Slaveholders are no more perfect than other men. They have passions. Some of them, as you may suppose, do not at all times restrain them. Neither do husbands, parents and friends. And in each of these relations, as serious suffering as frequently arises from uncontrolled passions, as ever does in that of master and slave, and with as little chance of indemnity. Yet you would not on that account break them up. I have no hesitation in saying that our slaveholders are kind masters, as men usually are kind husbands, parents and friends—as a general rule, kinder. A bad master—he who overworks his slaves, provides ill for them, or treats them with undue severity—loses the esteem and respect of his fellow-citizens to as great an extent as he would for the violation of any of his social and most of his moral obligations. What the most perfect plan of management would be, is a problem hard to solve. From the commencement of Slavery in this country, this subject has occupied the minds of all slaveholders, as much as the improvement of the general condition of mankind has those of the most ardent philanthropists; and the greatest progressive amelioration of the system has been effected. You yourself acknowledge that in the early part of your career you were exceedingly anxious for the *immediate* abolition of the slave trade, lest those engaged in it should so mitigate its evils as to destroy the force of your arguments and facts. The improvement you then *dreaded* has gone on steadily here, and would doubtless have taken place in the slave trade, but for the measures adopted to suppress it.

Of late years we have been not only annoyed, but greatly embarrassed in this matter, by the abolitionists. We have been compelled to curtail some privileges; we have been debarred from granting new ones. In the face of discussions which aim at loosening all ties between master and slave, we have in some measure to abandon our efforts to attach them to us, and control them through their affections and pride. We have to rely more and more on the power of fear. We must, in all our intercourse with them, assert and maintain strict mastery, and impress it on them that they are slaves. This is painful to us, and certainly no present advantage to them. But it is the direct consequence of the abolition agitation. We are determined to continue masters, and to do so we have to draw the rein tighter and tighter day by day to be assured that we hold them in complete check. How far this process will go on, depends wholly and solely on the abolitionists. When they desist, we can relax. We may not before. I do not mean by all this to say that we are in a state of actual alarm and fear of our slaves; but under existing circumstances we should be ineffably stupid not to increase our vigilance and strengthen our hands. You see some of the fruits of your labors. I speak freely and candidly—not as a colonist, who, though a slaveholder, has a master; but as a free white man, holding, under God, and resolved to hold, my fate in my own hands; and I assure you that my sentiments, and feelings, and determinations, are those of every slaveholder in this country.

The research and ingenuity of the abolitionists, aided by the invention of runaway slaves—in which faculty, so far as improvising falsehood goes, the African race is without a rival —have succeeded in shocking the world with a small number of pretended instances of our barbarity. The only wonder is, that considering the extent of our country, the variety of our population, its fluctuating character, and the publicity of all our transactions, the number of cases is so small. It speaks well for us. Yet of these, many are false, all highly colored, some occurring half a century, most of them many years ago; and no doubt a large proportion of them perpetrated by foreigners. With a few rare exceptions, the emigrant Scotch and English are the worst masters among us, and next to them our Northern fellow-citizens. Slaveholders born and bred here are always more humane to slaves, and those who have grown up to a large inheritance of them, the most so of any—showing clearly that the effect of the system is to foster kindly feelings. I do not mean so much to impute innate inhumanity to foreigners, as to show that they come here with false notions of the treatment usual and necessary for slaves, and that newly acquired power here, as everywhere else, is apt to be abused. I cannot enter into a detailed examination of the cases stated by the abolitionists. It would be disgusting, and of little avail. I know nothing of them. I have seen nothing like them, though born and bred here, and have rarely heard of anything at all to be compared to them. Permit me to say that I think most of *your* facts must have been drawn from the West Indies, where undoubtedly slaves were treated much more harshly than with us. This was owing to a variety of causes, which might, if necessary, be stated. One was, that they had at first to deal more extensively with barbarians fresh from the wilds of Africa; another, and a leading one, the absenteeism of proprietors. Agents are always more unfeeling than owners, whether placed over West Indian or American slaves, or Irish tenantry. We feel this evil greatly even here. You describe the use of *thumb screws*, as one mode of punishment among us. I doubt if a thumb screw can be found in America. I never saw or heard of one in this country. Stocks are rarely used by private individuals, and confinement still more seldom, though both are common punishments for whites, all the world over. I think they should be more frequently resorted to with slaves, as substitutes for flogging, which I consider the most injurious and least efficacious mode of punishing them for serious offences. It is not degrading, and unless excessive, occasions little pain. You may be a little astonished, after all the flourishes that have been made about "cart whips," &c., when I say flogging is not the most degrading punishment in the world. It may be so to a white man in most countries, but how is it to the white boy? That necessary coadjutor of the schoolmaster, the "birch," is never thought to have rendered infamous the unfortunate victim of pedagogue ire; nor did Solomon in his wisdom dream that he was counselling parents to debase their offspring, when he exhorted them not to spoil the child by sparing the rod. Pardon me for recurring to the now exploded ethics of the Bible. Custom, which, you will perhaps agree, makes most things in this world good or evil, has removed all infamy from the punishment of the lash to the slave. Your blood boils at the recital of stripes inflicted on a man; and you think you should be frenzied to see your own child flogged. Yet see how completely this is ideal, arising from the fashions of society. You doubtless submitted to the rod yourself, in other years, when the smart was perhaps as severe as it would be now; and you have never been guilty of the folly of revenging yourself on the Preceptor, who, in the plenitude of his "irresponsible power," thought proper to chastise your son. So it is with the negro, and the negro father.

As to chains and irons, they are rarely used; never, I believe, except in cases of running away. You will admit that if we pretend to own slaves, they must not be permitted to abscond whenever they see fit; and that if nothing else will prevent it, these means must be resorted to. See the inhumanity necessarily arising from Slavery, you will exclaim. Are such restraints imposed on no other class of people, giving no more offence? Look to your army and navy. If your seamen, impressed from their peaceful occupations, and your soldiers, recruited at the gin-shops—both of them as much kidnapped as the most unsuspecting victim of the slave trade, and doomed to a far more wretched fate—if these men manifest a propensity to desert, the heaviest manacles are their mildest punishment. It is most commonly death, after summary trial. But armies and navies, you say, are indispensable, and must be kept up at every sacrifice. I answer, that they are no more indispensable than Slavery is to us—and to *you* ; for you have enough of it in your country, though the form and name differ from ours.

Depend upon it that many things, and in regard to our slaves, most things which appear revolting at a distance, and to slight reflection, would, on a nearer view and impartial comparison with the customs and conduct of the rest of mankind, strike you in a very different light. Remember that on our estates we dispense with the whole machinery of public police and public courts of justice. Thus we try, decide, and execute the sentences, in thousands' of cases, which in other countries would go into the courts. Hence, most of the acts of our alleged cruelty, which have any foundation in truth. Whether our patriarchal mode of administering justice is less humane than the Assizes, can only be determined by careful enquiry and comparison. But this is never done by the abolitionists. All our punishments are the outrages of "irresponsible power." If a man steals a pig in England, he is transported—torn from wife, children, parents, and sent to the antipodes, infamous, and an outcast forever, though probably he took from the superabundance of his neighbor to save the lives of his famishing little ones. If one of our well fed negroes, merely for the sake of fresh meat, steals a pig, he gets perhaps forty stripes. If one of your cottagers breaks into another's house, he is hung for burglary. If a slave does the same here, a few lashes, or it may be, a few hours in the stocks, settles the matter. Are our courts or yours the most humane? If Slavery were not in question, you would doubtless say ours is mistaken lenity. Perhaps it often is ; and slaves too lightly dealt with sometimes grow daring. Occasionally, though rarely, and almost always in consequence of excessive indulgence, an individual rebels. This is the highest crime he can commit. It is treason. It strikes at the root of our whole system. His life is justly forfeited, though it is never intentionally taken, unless after trial in our public courts. Sometimes, however, in capturing, or in self-defence, he is unfortunately killed. A legal investigation always follows. But, terminate as it may, the abolitionists raise a hue and cry, and another "shocking case" is held up to the indignation of the world by tender-hearted male and female philanthropists, who would have thought all right had the master's throat been cut, and would have triumphed in it.

I cannot go into a detailed comparison between the penalties inflicted on a slave in our patriarchal courts, and those of the Courts of Sessions, to which freemen are sentenced in all civilized nations; but I know well that if there is any fault in our criminal code, it is that of excessive mildness.

Perhaps a few general facts will best illustrate the treatment this race receives at our hands. It is acknowledged that it increases at least as rapidly as the white. I believe it is an established law, that population thrives in proportion to its comforts. But when it is considered that these people are not recruited by immigration from abroad, as the whites are, and that they are usually settled on our richest and least healthy lands, the fact of their equal comparative increase and greater longevity, outweighs a thousand abolition falsehoods, in favor of the leniency and providence of our management of them. It is also admitted that there are incomparably fewer cases of insanity and suicide among them than among the whites. The fact is, that among the slaves of the African race these things are almost wholly unknown. However frequent suicide may have been among those brought from Africa, I can say that in my time I cannot remember to have known or heard of a single instance of deliberate self-destruction, and but of one of suicide at all. As to insanity, I have seen but one permanent case of it, and that twenty years ago. It cannot be doubted that among three millions of people there must be some insane and some suicides; but I will venture to say that more cases of both occur annually among every hundred thousand of the population of Great Britain, than among all our slaves. Can it be possible, then, that they exist in that state of abject misery, goaded by constant injuries, outraged in their affections, and worn down with hardships, which the abolitionists depict, and so many ignorant and thoughtless persons religiously believe?

With regard to the separation of husbands and wives, parents and children, nothing can be more untrue than the inferences drawn from what is so constantly harped on by abolitionists. Some painful instances perhaps may occur. Very few that can be prevented. It is, and it always has been, an object of prime consideration with our slaveholders, to keep families together. Negroes are themselves both perverse and comparatively indifferent about this matter. It is a singular trait, that they almost invariably prefer forming connexions with slaves belonging to other masters, and at some distance. It is, therefore, impossible to prevent separations sometimes, by the removal of one owner, his death, or failure, and dispersion of his property. In all such cases, however, every reasonable effort is made to keep the parties together, if they desire it. And the negroes forming these connexions, knowing the chances of their premature dissolution, rarely complain more than we all do of the inevitable strokes of fate. Sometimes it happens that a negro prefers to give up his family rather than separate from his master. I have known such instances. As to wilfully selling off a husband, or wife, or child, I believe it is rarely, very rarely done, except when some offence has been committed demanding "transportation." At sales of estates, and even at Sheriff's sales, they are always, if possible, sold in families. On the whole, notwithstanding the migratory character of our population, I believe there are more families among our slaves, who have lived and died together without losing a single member from their circle, except by the process of nature, and in the enjoyment of constant, uninterrupted communion, than have flourished in the same space of time, and among the same number of civilized people in modern times. And to sum up all, if pleasure is correctly defined to be the absence of pain—which, so far as the great body of mankind is concerned, is undoubtedly its true definition—I believe our slaves are the happiest three millions of human beings on whom the sun shines. Into their Eden is coming Satan in the guise of an abolitionist.

As regards their religious condition, it is well known that a majority of the communicants of the Methodist and Baptist churches of the South are colored. Almost everywhere they have precisely the same opportunities of attending worship that the whites have, and, besides special occasions for themselves exclusively, which they prefer. In many places not so accessible to clergymen in ordinary, missionaries are sent, and mainly supported by their masters, for the particular benefit of the slaves. There are none I imagine who may not, if they like, hear the gospel preached at least once a month—most of them twice a month, and very many every week. In our thinly settled country the whites fare no better. But in addition to this, on plantations of any size, the slaves who have joined the church are formed into a class, at the head of which is placed one of their number, acting as deacon or leader, who is also sometimes a licensed preacher. This class assembles for religious exercises weekly, semi-weekly, or oftener, if the members choose. In some parts, also, Sunday schools for blacks are established, and Bible classes are orally instructed by discreet and pious persons. Now where will you find a laboring population possessed of greater religious advantages than these? Not in London, I am sure, where it is known that your churches, chapels, and religious meeting-houses, of all sorts, cannot contain one-half of the inhabitants.

I have admitted, without hesitation, what it would be untrue and profitless to deny, that slaveholders are responsible to the world for the humane treatment of the fellow-beings whom God has placed in their hands. I think it would be only fair for you to admit, what is equally undeniable, that every man in independent circumstances, all the world over, and every government, is to the same extent responsible to the whole human family, for the condition of the poor and laboring classes in their own country, and around them, wherever they may be placed, to whom God has denied the advantages he has given themselves. If so, it would naturally seem the duty of true humanity and rational philanthropy to devote their time and labor, their thoughts, writings and charity, first to the objects placed as it were under their own immediate charge. And it must be regarded as a clear evasion and skilful neglect of this cardinal duty, to pass from those whose destitute situation they can plainly see, minutely examine and efficiently relieve, to enquire after the condition of others in no way entrusted to their care, to exaggerate evils of which they cannot be cognizant, to expend all their sympathies and exhaust all their energies on these remote objects of their unnatural, not to say dangerous, benevolence; and finally, to calumniate, denounce, and endeavor to excite the indignation of the world against their unoffending fellow-creatures for not hastening, under their dictation, to redress wrongs which are stoutly and truthfully denied, while they themselves go but little farther in alleviating those chargeable on them than openly and unblushingly to acknowledge them. There may be indeed a sort of merit in doing so much as to make such an acknowledgment, but it must be very modest if it expects appreciation.

Now I affirm, that in Great Britain the poor and laboring classes of your own race and color, not only your fellow-beings, but your *fellow-citizens*, are more miserable and degraded, morally and physically, than our slaves; to be elevated to the actual condition of whom, would be to these, *your fellow-citizens*, a most glorious act of *emancipation*. And I also affirm, that the poor and laboring classes of our older free States would not be in a much more enviable condition, but for our Slavery. One of their own Senators has declared in the United States Senate, "that the repeal of the Tariff would reduce New-England to a howling wilderness." And the American Tariff is neither more nor less than a system by which the slave States are plundered for the benefit of those States which do not tolerate Slavery.

To prove what I say of Great Britain to be true, I make the following extracts from the Reports of Commissioners appointed by Parliament, and published by order of the House of Commons. I can make but few and short ones. But similar quotations might be made to any extent, and I defy you to deny that these specimens exhibit the real condition of your operatives in every branch of your industry. There is of course a variety in their sufferings. But the same incredible amount of toil, frightful destitution, and utter want of morals, characterize the lot of every class of them.

Collieries.—" I wish to call the attention of the Board to the pits about Brampton. The seams are so thin that several of them have only two feet headway to all the working. They are worked altogether by boys from eight to twelve years of age, on all-fours, with a dog belt and chain. The passages being neither ironed nor wooded, and often an inch or two thick with mud. In Mr. Barnes' pit these poor boys have to drag the barrows with one hundred weight of coal or slack sixty times a day sixty yards, and the empty barrows back, without once straightening their backs, unless they choose to stand under the shaft, and run the risk of having their heads broken by a falling coal."—*Report on Mines*, 1842, p. 71. "In Shropshire the seams are no more than eighteen or twenty inches."—*Ibid*, p. 67. "At the Booth pit," says Mr. Scriven, "I walked, rode, and crept eighteen hundred yards to one of the nearest faces."—*Ibid*. "Chokedamp, firedamp, wild fire, sulphur and water, at all times menace instant death to the laborers in these mines." "Robert North, aged 16: Went into the pit at seven years of age, to fill up skips. I drew about twelve months. When I drew by the girdle and chain my skin was broken, and the blood ran down. I durst not say anything. If we said anything, the butty, and the reeve, who works under him, would take a stick and beat us."—*Ibid*. "The usual punishment for theft is to place the culprit's head between the legs of one of the biggest boys, and each boy in the pit—sometimes there are twenty—inflicts twelve lashes on the back and rump with a cat."—*Ibid*. "Instances occur in which children are taken into these mines to work as early as four years of age, sometimes at five, not unfrequently at six and seven, while from eight to nine is the ordinary age at which these employments commence."—*Ibid*. "The wages paid at these mines is from two dollars fifty cents to seven dollars fifty cents per month for laborers, according to age and ability, and out of this they must support themselves. They work twelve hours a day."—*Ibid*.

In Calico Printing.—"It is by no means uncommon in all the districts for children five or six years old to be kept at work fourteen to sixteen hours consecutively."—*Report on Children*, 1842, p. 59.

I could furnish extracts similar to these in regard to every branch of your manufactures, but I will not multiply them. Everybody knows that your operatives habitually labor from twelve to sixteen hours, men, women, and children, and the men occasionally twenty hours per day. In lace-making, says the last quoted report, children sometimes commence work at two years of age.

Destitution.—It is stated by your Commissioners that forty thousand persons in Liverpool, and fifteen thousand in Manchester, live in cellars; while twenty-two thousand in England pass the night in barns, tents, or the open air. "There have been found such occurrences as seven, eight, and ten persons in one cottage, I cannot say for one day, but for whole days, without a morsel of food. They have remained on their beds of straw for two successive days, under the impression that in a recumbent posture the pangs of hunger were less felt."—*Lord Brougham's Speech*, 11*th July*, 1842. A volume of frightful scenes might be quoted to corroborate the inferences to be necessarily drawn from the facts here stated. I will not add more, but pass on to the important enquiry as to

Morals and Education.—"Elizabeth Barrett, aged 14: I always work without stockings, shoes, or trowsers. I wear nothing but a shift. I have to go up to the headings with the men. *They are all naked there.* I am got used to that."—*Report on Mines.* "As to illicit sexual intercourse it seems to prevail universally, and from an early period of life." "The evidence might have been doubled, which attest the early commencement of sexual and promiscuous intercourse among boys and girls." "A lower condition of morals, in the fullest sense of the term, could not, I think, be found. I do not mean by this that there are many more prominent vices among them, but that moral feelings and sentiments do not exist. *They have no morals.*" "Their appearance, manners, and moral natures—so far as the word *moral* can be applied to them—are in accordance with their half-civilized condition."—*Report on Children.* "More than half a dozen instances occurred in Manchester, where a man, his wife, and his wife's grown-up sister, habitually occupied the same bed."—*Report on Sanitary Condition.* "Robert Crucilow, aged 16 : I don't know anything of Moses—never heard of France. I don't know what America is. Never heard of Scotland or Ireland. Can't tell how many weeks there are in a year. There are twelve pence in a shilling, and twenty shillings in a pound. There are eight pints in a gallon of ale."—*Report on Mines.* "Ann Eggly, aged 18 : I walk about and get fresh air on Sundays. I never go to church or chapel. I never heard of Christ at all."—*Ibid.* Others : "The Lord sent Adam and Eve on earth to save sinners." "I don't know who made the world; I never heard about God." "I don't know Jesus Christ—I never saw him—but I have seen Foster who prays about him." "Employer : You have expressed surprise at Thomas Mitchel's not hearing of God. I judge there are few colliers here about that have."—*Ibid.* I will quote no more. It is shocking beyond endurance to turn over your records, in which the condition of your laboring classes is but too faithfully depicted. Could our slaves but see it, they would join us in lynching the abolitionists, which, by the by, they would not now be loth to do. We never think of imposing on them such labor, either in amount or kind. We never put them to *any work*, under ten, more generally at twelve years of age, and then the very lightest. Destitution is absolutely unknown—never did a slave starve in America; while in moral sentiments and feelings, in religious information, and even in general intelligence, they are infinitely the superiors of your operatives. When you look around you, how dare you talk to us before the world of Slavery? For the condition of your wretched laborers, you, and every Briton who is not one of them, are responsible before God and man. If you are really humane, philanthropic, and charitable, here are objects for you. Relieve them. Emancipate them. Raise them from the condition of brutes, to the level of human beings—of American slaves, at least. Do not for an instant suppose that the *name* of being freemen is the slightest comfort to them, situated as they are, or that the bombastic boast that "whoever touches British soil stands redeemed, regenerated, and disenthralled," can meet with anything but the ridicule and contempt of mankind, while that soil swarms, both on and under its surface, with the most abject and degraded wretches that ever bowed beneath the oppressor's yoke.

I have said that Slavery is an established and inevitable condition to human society. I do not speak of the *name*, but the *fact*. The Marquis of Normanby has lately declared your operatives to be "*in effect slaves.*" Can it be denied? Probably, for such philanthropists as your abolitionists care nothing for facts. They deal in terms and fictions. It is the *word* "slavery" which shocks their tender sensibilities; and their imaginations associate it with "hydras and chimeras dire." The thing itself, in its most hideous reality, passes daily under their view unheeded—a familiar face, touching no chord of shame, sympathy or indignation. Yet so brutalizing is your iron bondage that the English operative is a bye-word through the world. When favoring fortune enables him to escape his prison house, both in Europe and America he is shunned. With all the skill which fourteen hours of daily labor from the tenderest age has ground into him, his discontent, which habit has made second nature, and his depraved propensities, running riot when freed from his wonted fetters, prevent his employment whenever it is not a matter of necessity. If we derived no other benefit from African Slavery in the Southern States than that it deterred your *freedmen* from coming hither, I should regard it as an inestimable blessing.

And how unaccountable is that philanthropy, which closes its eyes upon such a state of things as you have at home, and turns its blurred vision to our affairs beyond the Atlantic, meddling with matters which no way concern them—presiding, as you have lately done, at meetings to denounce the "iniquity of our laws" and "the atrocity of our practices," and to sympathize with infamous wretches imprisoned here for violating decrees promulgated both by God and man? Is this doing the work of "your Father which is in heaven," or is it seeking only "that you may have glory of man?" Do you remember the denunciation of our Saviour, "Woe unto you, Scribes and Pharisees; hypocrites! for ye make clean the outside of the cup and platter, but within they are full of extortion and excess."

But after all, supposing that every thing you say of Slavery be true, and its abolition a matter of the last necessity, how do you expect to effect emancipation, and what do you calculate will be the result of its accomplishment? As to the means to be used, the abolitionists, I believe, affect to differ, a large proportion of them pretending that their sole purpose is to apply "moral suasion" to the slaveholders themselves. As a matter of curiosity, I should like to know what their idea of this "moral suasion" is. Their discourses—yours is no exception—are all tirades, the exordium, argument and peroration, turning on the epithets "tyrants," "thieves," "murderers," addressed to us. They revile us as "atrocious monsters," "violators of the laws of nature, God and man," our homes the abode of every iniquity, our land a "brothel." We retort, that they are "incendiaries" and "assassins." Delightful argument! Sweet, potent "moral suasion!" What slave has it freed—what proselyte can it ever make? But if your course was wholly different—if you distilled nectar from your lips, and discoursed sweetest music, could you reasonably indulge the hope of accomplishing your object by such means? Nay, supposing that we were all convinced, and thought of Slavery precisely as you do, at what era of "moral suasion" do you imagine you could prevail on us to give up a thousand millions of dollars in the value of our slaves, and a thousand millions of dollars more in the depreciation of our lands, in consequence of the want of laborers to cultivate them? Consider: were ever any people, civilized or savage, persuaded by any argument, human or divine, to surrender voluntarily two thousand millions of dollars? Would you think of asking five millions of Englishmen to contribute, either at once or gradually, four hundred and fifty millions of pounds sterling to the cause of philanthropy, even if the purpose to be accomplished was not of doubtful goodness? If you are prepared to undertake such a scheme, try it at home. Collect your fund—return us the money for our slaves, and do with them as you like. Be all the glory yours, fairly and honestly won. But you see the absurdity of such an idea. Away, then, with your pretended "moral suasion." You know it is mere nonsense. The abolitionists have no faith in it themselves. Those who expect to accomplish any thing count on means altogether different. They aim, first, to alarm us: that failing, to compel us by force to emancipate our slaves, at our own risk and cost. To these purposes they obviously direct all their energies. Our Northern liberty men endeavored to disseminate their destructive doctrine among our slaves, and excite them to insurrection. But we have put an end to that, and stricken terror into them. They dare not show their faces here. Then they declared they would dissolve the Union. Let them do it. The North would repent it far more than the South. We are not alarmed at the idea. We are well content to give up the Union sooner than sacrifice two thousand millions of dollars, and with them all the rights we prize. You may take it for granted that it is impossible to persuade or alarm us into emancipation, or to making the first step towards it. Nothing, then, is left to try, but sheer force. If the abolitionists are prepared to expend their own treasure and shed their own blood as freely as they ask us to do ours, let them come. We do not court the conflict; but we will not and we cannot shrink from it. If they are not ready to go so far; if, as I expect, their philanthropy recoils from it; if they are looking only for *cheap* glory, let them turn their thoughts elsewhere, and leave us in peace. Be the sin, the danger and the evils of Slavery all our own. We compel, we ask none to share them with us.

I am well aware that a notable scheme has been set on foot to achieve abolition by making what is by courtesy called "free" labor so much cheaper than slave labor as to force the abandonment of the latter. Though we are beginning to *manufacture with slaves*, I do not think you will attempt to pinch your operatives closer in Great Britain. You cannot curtail the rags with which they vainly attempt to cover their nakedness, nor reduce the porridge wh'ch barely, and not always, keeps those who have employment from perishing of famine. When you can do this, we will consider whether our slaves may not dispense with a pound or two of bacon per week, or a few garments annually. Your aim, however, is to cheapen labor in the tropics. The idea of doing this by exporting your "bold yeomanry" is, I presume, given up. Cromwell tried it when he *sold* the captured followers of Charles into *West Indian Slavery*, where they speedily found graves. Nor have your recent experiments on British and even Dutch constitutions succeeded better. Have you still faith in carrying thither your Coolies from Hindostan? Doubtless that once wild robber race, whose highest eulogium was that they did not murder merely for the love of blood, have been tamed down, and are perhaps "keen for immigration," for since your civilization has reached it, plunder has grown scarce in Guzerat. But what is the result of the experiment thus far? Have the Coolies, ceasing to handle arms, learned to handle spades, and proved hardy and profitable laborers? On the contrary, broken in spirit and stricken with disease at home, the wretched victims whom you have hitherto kidnapped for a bounty, confined in depots, put under hatches and carried across the ocean—forced into "voluntary immigration," have done little but lie down and die on the *pseudo* soil of freedom. At the end of five years two thirds, in some colonies a larger proportion, are no more! Humane and pious contrivance! To alleviate the fancied sufferings of the accursed posterity of Ham, you sacrifice by a cruel death two-thirds of the children of the blessed Shem—and demand the applause of Christians—the blessing of heaven! If this "experiment" is to go on, in God's name try your hand upon the Thugs. That other species of "immigration" to which you are resorting I will consider presently.

But what do you calculate will be the result of emancipation, by whatever means accomplished? You will probably point me, by way of answer, to the West Indies—doubtless to Antigua, the great boast of abolition. Admitting that it has succeeded there—which I will do for the sake of the argument—do you know the reason of it? The true and only causes of whatever success has attended it in Antigua are, that the population was before crowded, and all or nearly all the arable land in cultivation. The emancipated negroes could not, many of them, get away if they desired; and knew not where to go, in case they did. They had, practically, no alternative but to remain on the spot; and remaining, they must work on the terms of the proprietors, or perish—the strong arm of the mother country forbidding all hope of seizing the land for themselves. The proprietors, well knowing that they could thus command labor for the merest necessities of life, which was much cheaper than maintaining the non-effective as well as effective slaves in a style which decency and interest, if not humanity, required, willingly accepted half their value, and at once realized far more than the interest on the other half in the diminution of their expenses, and the reduced comforts of the *freemen*. One of your most illustrious judges, who was also a profound and philosophical historian, has said " that villeinage was not abolished, but went into decay in England." This was the process. This has been the process wherever (the name of) villeinage or slavery has been successfully abandoned. Slavery, in fact, " went into decay" in Antigua. I have admitted that, under similar circumstances, it might profitably cease here—that is, profitably to the individual proprietors. Give me half the value of my slaves, and compel them to remain and labor on my plantation, at ten to eleven cents a day, as they do in Antigua, supporting themselves and families, and you shall have them to-morrow, and if you like dub them " free." Not to stickle, I would surrender them without price. No—I recall my words: My humanity revolts at the idea. I am attached to my slaves, and would not have act or part in reducing them to such a condition. I deny, however, that Antigua, as a community, is, or ever will be, as *prosperous* under present circumstances, as she was before abolition, though fully ripe for it. The fact is well known. The reason is that the African, if not a distinct, is an inferior race, and never will effect, as it never has effected, as much in any other condition as in that of Slavery.

I know of no *slaveholder* who has visited the West Indies since Slavery was abolished, and published *his* views of it. All our facts and opinions come through the friends of the experiment, or at least those not opposed to it. Taking these, even without allowance, to be true as stated, I do not see where the abolitionists find cause for exultation. The tables of exports, which are the best evidences of the condition of a people, exhibit a woful falling off—excused, it is true, by unprecedented droughts and hurricanes, to which their free labor seems unaccountably more subject than slave labor used to be. I will not go into detail. It is well known that a large proportion of British legislation and expenditure, and that proportion still constantly increasing, is most anxiously devoted to repairing the monstrous error of emancipation. You are actually galvanizing your expiring colonies. The truth, deduced from all the facts, was thus pithily stated by the London Quarterly Review, as long ago as 1840: "None of the benefits anticipated by mistaken good intentions have been realized, while every evil wished for by knaves and foreseen by the wise has been painfully verified. The wild rashness of fanaticism has made the emancipation of the slaves equivalent to the loss of one-half of the West Indies, and yet put back the chance of negro civilization." (*Art. Ld. Dudley's Letters.*) Such are the *real fruits* of your never-to-be-too-much-glorified abolition, and the valuable dividend of your twenty millions of pounds sterling invested therein.

If any farther proof was wanted of the utter and well-known, though not yet openly avowed, failure of West Indian emancipation, it would be furnished by the startling fact, that THE AFRICAN SLAVE TRADE HAS BEEN ACTUALLY REVIVED

UNDER THE AUSPICES AND PROTECTION OF THE BRITISH GOVERNMENT. Under the specious guise of "immigration," they are replenishing those Islands with slaves from the coast of Africa. Your colony of Sierra Leone, founded on that coast to prevent the slave trade, and peopled, by the bye, in the first instance, by negroes stolen from these States during the Revolutionary War, is the depot to which captives taken from slavers by your armed vessels are transported. I might say returned, since nearly half the Africans carried across the Atlantic are understood to be embarked in this vicinity. The wretched survivors, who are there set at liberty, are immediately seduced to "immigrate" to the West Indies. The business is systematically carried on by black "delegates," sent expressly from the West Indies, where, on arrival, the "immigrants" are *sold into Slavery* for twenty-one years, under conditions ridiculously trivial and wickedly void, since few or none will ever be able to derive any advantage from them. The whole prime of life thus passed in bondage, it is contemplated, and doubtless it will be carried into effect, to turn them out in their old age to shift for themselves, and to supply their places with fresh and vigorous "immigrants." Was ever a system of Slavery so barbarous devised before? Can you think of comparing it with ours? Even your own religious missionaries at Sierra Leone denounce it " as worse than the slave state in Africa." And your black delegates, fearful of the influence of these missionaries, as well as on account of the inadequate supply of captives, are now preparing to procure the able-bodied and comparatively industrious Kroomen of the interior, by *purchasing from their head-men* the privilege of inveigling them to the West India market! So ends the magnificent farce—perhaps I should say tragedy, of West India abolition! I will not harrow your feelings by asking you to review the labors of your life and tell me what you and your brother enthusiasts have accomplished for "injured Africa," but while agreeing with Lord Stowell, that "villeinage decayed," and admitting that Slavery might do so also, I think I am fully justified by passed and passing events in saying, as Mr. Grosvenor said of the slave trade, that its *abolition* is "impossible."

You are greatly mistaken, however, if you think that the consequences of emancipation here would be similar and no more injurious than those which followed from it in your little sea-girt West India Islands, where nearly all were blacks. The system of Slavery is not in "decay" with us. It flourishes in full and growing vigor. Our country is boundless in extent. Dotted here and there with villages and fields, it is, for the most part, covered with immense forests and swamps of almost unknown size. In such a country, with a people so restless as ours, communicating of course some of that spirit to their domestics, can you conceive that any thing short of the power of the master over the slave, could confine the African race, notoriously idle and improvident, to labor on our plantations? Break this bond, but for a day, and these plantations will be solitudes. The negro loves change, novelty and sensual excitements of all kinds, *when awake*. "Reason and order," of which Mr. Wilberforce said "liberty was the child," do not characterize him. Released from his present obligations, his first impulse would be to go somewhere. And here no natural boundaries would restrain him. At first they would all seek the towns, and rapidly accumulate in squalid groups upon their outskirts. Driven thence by the "armed police," which would immediately spring into existence, they would scatter in all directions. Some bodies of them might wander towards the "free" States, or to the Western wilderness, marking their tracks by their depredations and their corpses. Many would roam wild in our "big woods." Many more would seek the recesses of our swamps for secure covert. Few, very few of them, could be prevailed on to do a stroke of work, none to labor continuously, while a head of cattle, sheep or swine could be found in our ranges, or an ear of corn nodded in our abandoned fields. These exhausted, our folds and poultry yards, barns and store-houses, would become their prey. Finally, our scattered dwellings would be plundered, perhaps fired, and the inmates murdered. How long do you suppose that we could bear these things? How long would it be before we should sleep with rifles at our bedsides, and never move without one in our hands? This work once begun, let the story of our British ancestors and the aborigines of this country tell the sequel. Far more rapid, however, would be the catastrophe. "Ere many moons went by," the African race would be exterminated, or reduced again to Slavery, their ranks recruited, after your example, by fresh "emigrants" from their fatherland.

Is timely preparation and gradual emancipation suggested to avert these horrible consequences? I thought your experience in the West Indies had, at least, done so much as to explode that idea. If it failed there, much more would it fail here, where the two races, approximating to equality in numbers, are daily and hourly in the closest contact. Give room for but a single spark of real jealousy to be kindled between them, and the explosion would be instantaneous and universal. It is the most fatal of all fallacies, to suppose that these two races can exist together, after any length of time, or any process of preparation, on terms at all approaching to equality. Of this, both of them are finally and fixedly convinced. They differ essentially, in all the leading traits which characterize the varieties of the human species, and color draws an indelible and insuperable line of separation between them. Every scheme founded upon the idea that they can remain together on the same soil, beyond the briefest period, in any other relation than precisely that which now subsists between them, is not only preposterous, but fraught with deepest danger. If there was no alternative but to try the "experiment" here, reason and humanity dictate that the sufferings of "gradualism" should be saved, and the catastrophe of "immediate abolition" enacted as rapidly as possible. Are you impatient for the performance to commence? Do you long to gloat over the scenes I have suggested, but could not hold the pen to portray? In your long life many such have passed under your review. You know that *they* are not "*impossible.*" Can they be to your taste? Do you believe that in laboring to bring them about, the abolitionists are doing the will of God? No! God is not there. It is the work of Satan. The arch-fiend, under specious guises, has found his way into their souls, and with false appeals to philanthropy, and foul insinuations to ambition, instigates them to rush headlong to the accomplishment of his diabolical designs.

We live in a wonderful age. The events of the last three quarters of a century appear to have revolutionized the human mind. Enterprise and ambition are only limited in their purposes by the horizon of the imagination. It is the transcendental era. In philosophy, religion, government, science, arts, commerce, nothing that has been is to be allowed to be. Conservatism, in any form, is scoffed at. The slightest taint of it is fatal. Where will all this end? If you can tolerate one ancient maxim, let it be that the best criterion of the future is the past. That, if anything, will give a clue. And, looking back only through your time, what was the earliest feat of this same transcendentalism? The rays of the new moral Drummond Light were first concentrated to a focus at

Paris, to illuminate the universe. In a twinkling it consumed the political, religious and social systems of France. It could not be extinguished there until literally drowned in blood. And then, from its ashes arose that supernatural man, who, for twenty years, kept affrighted Europe in convulsions. Since that time, its scattered beams, refracted by broader surfaces, have, nevertheless, continued to scathe wherever they have fallen. What political structure, what religious creed, but has felt the galvanic shock, and even now trembles to its foundations? Mankind, still horror-stricken by the catastrophe of France, have shrunk from rash experiments upon social systems. But they have been practising in the East, around the Mediterranean, and through the West India Islands. And growing confident, a portion of them seem desperately bent on kindling the all-devouring flame in the bosom of our land. Let it once again blaze up to heaven, and another cycle of blood and devastation will dawn upon the world. For our own sake, and for the sake of those infatuated men who are madly driving on the conflagration; for the sake of human nature, we are called on to strain every nerve to arrest it. And be assured our efforts will be bounded only with our being. Nor do I doubt that five millions of people, brave, intelligent, united, and prepared to hazard every thing, will, in such a cause, with the blessing of God, sustain themselves. At all events, come what may, it is ours to meet it.

We are well aware of the light estimation in which the abolitionists, and those who are taught by them, profess to hold us. We have seen the attempt of a portion of the Free Church of Scotland to reject our alms, on the ground that we are "slave-drivers," after sending missionaries to solicit them. And we have seen Mr. O'Connell, the "irresponsible master" of millions of ragged serfs, from whom, poverty stricken as they are, he contrives to wring a splendid privy purse, throw back with contumely, the "tribute" of his own countrymen from this land of "miscreants." These people may exhaust their slang, and make black-guards of themselves, but they cannot defile us. And as for the suggestion to exclude slaveholders from your London clubs, we scout it. Many of us, indeed, do go to London, and we have seen your breed of gawky lords, both there and here, but it never entered into our conceptions to look on them as better than ourselves. The American slaveholders, collectively or individually, ask no favors of any man or race who tread the earth. In none of the attributes of men, mental or physical, do they acknowledge or fear superiority elsewhere. They stand in the broadest light of the knowledge, civilization and improvement of the age, as much favored of heaven as any of the sons of Adam. Exacting nothing undue, they yield nothing but justice and courtesy, even to royal blood. They cannot be flattered, duped, nor bullied out of their rights or their propriety. They smile with contempt at scurrility and vaporing beyond the seas, and they turn their backs upon it where it is "irresponsible;" but insolence that ventures to look them in the face, will never fail to be chastised.

I think I may trust you will not regard this letter as intrusive. I should never have entertained an idea of writing it, had you not opened the correspondence. If you think anything in it harsh, review your own—which I regret that I lost soon after it was received—and you will probably find that you have taken your revenge before hand. If you have not, transfer an equitable share of what you deem severe, to the account of the abolitionists at large. They have accumulated against the slaveholders a balance of invective, which, with all our efforts, we shall not be able to liquidate much short of the era in which your national debt will be paid. At all events,

I have no desire to offend you personally, and, with the best wishes for your continued health, I have the honor to be,
Your obedient servant,
J. H. HAMMOND.

Thos. Clarkson, Esq.

Silver Bluff, S. C., March 24, 1845.

Sir—In my letter to you of the 28th January—which I trust you have received ere this—I mentioned that I had lost your circular letter soon after it had come to hand. It was, I am glad to say, only mislaid, and has within a few days been recovered. A second perusal of it induces me to resume my pen. Unwilling to trust my recollections from a single reading, I did not, in my last communication, attempt to follow the course of your argument, and meet directly the points made and the terms used. I thought it better to take a general view of the subject, which could not fail to traverse your most material charges. I am well aware, however, that for fear of being tedious, I omitted many interesting topics altogether, and abstained from a complete discussion of some of those introduced. I do not propose now to *exhaust* the subject; which it would require volumes to do; but without waiting to learn—which I may never do—your opinion of what I have already said, I sit down to supply some of the deficiencies of my letter of January, and, with your circular before me, to reply to such parts of it as have not been fully answered.

It is, I perceive, addressed, among others, to "such as have never visited the Southern States" of this confederacy, and professes to enlighten their ignorance of the actual "condition of the poor slave in their own country." I cannot help thinking you would have displayed prudence in confining the circulation of your letter altogether to such persons. You might then have indulged with impunity in giving, as you have done, a picture of Slavery, drawn from your own excited imagination, or from those impure fountains, the Martineaus, Marryatts, Trollopes and Dickenses, who have profited by catering, at our expense, to the jealous sensibilities and debauched tastes of your countrymen. Admitting that you are familiar with the history of Slavery, and the past discussions of it, as I did, I now think rather broadly, in my former letter, what can *you know* of the true *condition* of the "poor slave" here? I am not aware that you have ever visited this country, or even the West Indies. Can you suppose, that because you have devoted your life to the investigation of the subject—commencing it under the influence of an enthusiasm, so melancholy at first, and so volcanic afterwards, as to be nothing short of hallucination—pursuing it as men of *one idea* do everything, with the single purpose of establishing your own view of it—gathering your information from discharged seamen, disappointed speculators, factious politicians, visionary reformers and scurrilous tourists—opening your ears to every species of complaint, exaggeration and falsehood, that interested ingenuity could invent, and never for a moment questioning the truth of anything that could make for your cause—can you suppose that all this has qualified you, living the while in England, to form or approximate towards the formation of a correct opinion of the condition of slaves among us? I know the power of self-delusion. I have not the least doubt, that you think yourself the very best informed man alive on this subject, and that many think so likewise. So far as facts go, even after deducting from your list a great deal that is not fact, I will not deny that, probably, your collection is the most extensive in existence. But as to the *truth* in regard to Slavery, there is not an adult in this region but knows more of it than you do. *Truth* and *fact* are, you are aware, by no means synonymous terms. Ninety-nine facts may constitute a falsehood: the hundredth, added or alone, gives the truth. With all your knowledge of facts, I undertake to say that you are entirely and grossly ignorant of the real condition of our slaves. And from all that I can see, you are equally ignorant of the essential principles of human association revealed in history, both sacred and profane, on which Slavery rests, and which will perpetuate it forever in some form or other. However you may declaim against it; however powerfully you may array atrocious incidents; whatever appeals you may make to the heated imaginations and tender sensibilities of mankind, believe me, your total blindness to the *whole truth*, which alone constitutes *the truth*, incapacitates you from ever making an impression on the sober reason and sound common sense of the world. You may seduce thousands—you can convince no one. Whenever and wherever you or the advocates of your cause can arouse the passions of the weak-minded and the ignorant, and bringing to bear with them the interests of the vicious and unprincipled, overwhelm common sense and reason—as God sometimes permits to be done—you may triumph. Such a triumph we have witnessed in Great Britain. But I trust it is far distant here; nor can it, from its nature, be extensive or enduring. Other classes of reformers, animated by the same spirit as the abolitionists, attack the institution of marriage, and even the established relations of parent and child. And they collect instances of barbarous cruelty and shocking degradation, which rival, if they do not throw into the shade, your Slavery statistics. But the rights of marriage and parental authority rests upon truths as obvious as they are unchangeable—coming home to every human being,—self-impressed forever on the individual mind, and cannot be shaken until the whole man is corrupted, nor subverted until civilized society becomes a putrid mass. Domestic Slavery is not so universally understood, nor can it make such a direct appeal to individuals or society beyond its pale. Here, prejudice and passion have room to sport at the expense of others. They may be excited and urged to dangerous action, remote from the victims they mark out. They may, as they have done, effect great mischief, but they cannot be made to maintain, in the long run, dominion over reason and common sense, nor ultimately put down what God has ordained.

You deny, however, that Slavery is sanctioned by God, and your chief argument is, that when he gave to Adam dominion over the fruits of the earth and the animal creation, he stopped there. "He never gave him any further right over his fellow-men." You restrict the descendants of Adam to a very short list of rights and powers, duties and responsibilities, if you limit them solely to those conferred and enjoined in the first chapter of Genesis. It is very obvious that in this narrative of the Creation, Moses did not have it in view to record any part of the law intended for the government of man in his social or political state. Eve was not yet created; the expulsion had not yet taken place; Cain was unborn; and no allusion whatever is made to the manifold decrees of God to which these events gave rise. The only serious answer this argument deserves, is to say, what is so manifestly true, that God's not expressly giving to Adam "any right over his fellow-men" by no means excluded him from conferring that right on his descendants; which he in fact did. We know that Abraham, the chosen one of God, exercised it and held property in his fellow-man, even anterior to the period when property in land was acknowledged. We might infer that God had authorized it. But we are not reduced to inference or conjecture. At the hazard of fatiguing you by repetition, I will again refer you to the ordinances of the Scriptures. Innumerable instances might be quoted where God has given and commanded men to assume dominion over their fellow-men. But one will suffice. In the twenty-fifth chapter of Leviticus, you will find *domestic Slavery—precisely such as is maintained at this day in these States—ordained and established by God, in language which I defy you to pervert so as to leave a doubt on any honest mind that this institution was founded by him, and decreed to be perpetual.* I quote the words:

Leviticus xxv. 44–46 : " Both thy bondmen and thy bondmaids which thou shalt have, shall be of the heathen [Africans] that are round about you : of *them ye shall buy bondmen and bondmaids.*

" Moreover, of the children of the strangers that do sojourn among you, of them shall ye buy, *and of their families that are with you which they begat in your land* [descendants of Africans?] and they shall be your possession.

" *And ye shall take them as an inheritance for your children after you, to inherit them for a possession.* THEY SHALL BE YOUR BONDMEN FOREVER."

What human legislature could make a decree more full and explicit than this? What court of law or chancery could defeat a title to a slave couched in terms so clear and complete as these? And this is the *law of God*, whom you pretend to worship, while you denounce and traduce us for respecting it.

It seems scarcely credible, but the fact is so, that you deny this law so plainly written, and in the face of it have the hardihood to declare that " though Slavery is not *specifically*, yet it is *virtually, forbidden* in the Scriptures, because all the crimes which necessarily arise out of Slavery, and which can arise from no other source, are reprobated there and threatened with divine vengeance." Such an unworthy subterfuge is scarcely entitled to consideration. But its gross absurdity may be exposed in few words. I do not know what crimes you particularly allude to as arising from Slavery. But you will perhaps admit—not because they are denounced in the decalogue, which the abolitionists respect only so far as they choose, but because it is the *immediate interest* of most men to admit—that disobedience to parents, adultery, and stealing, are crimes. Yet these crimes " necessarily arise from " the relations of parent and child, marriage, and the possession of private property; at least they " can arise from no other sources." Then, according to your argument, it is " virtually forbidden" to marry, to beget children, and to hold private property! Nay, it is forbidden to live, since murder can only be perpetrated on living subjects. You add that " in the same way the gladiatorial shows of old, and other barbarous customs, were not specifically forbidden in the New Testament, and yet Christianity was the sole means of their suppression." This is very true. But these shows and barbarous customs thus suppressed were not *authorized by God*. They were not ordained and commanded by God for the benefit of his chosen people and mankind, as the purchase and holding of bondmen and bondmaids were. Had they been they would never have been " suppressed by Christianity " any more than Slavery can be by your party. Although Christ came " not to destroy but fulfil the law," he nevertheless did formally abrogate some of the ordinances promulgated by Moses, and all such as were at war with his mission of " peace and good will on earth." He " specifically " annuls, for instance, one " barbarous custom " sanctioned by those ordinances, where he says, "ye have heard that it hath been said, an eye for an eye, and a tooth for a tooth; but I say unto you that ye resist not evil, but whosoever shall smite thee on the right cheek, turn to him the other also." Now, in the time of Christ, it was usual for masters to put their slaves to death on the slightest provocation. They even killed and cut them up to feed their fishes. He was undoubtedly aware of these things, as well as of the law and commandment I have quoted. He could only have been restrained from denouncing them, as he did the "*lex talionis*," because he knew that in despite of these barbarities the institution of Slavery was at the bottom a sound and wholesome, as well as lawful one. Certain it is, that in his wisdom and purity he did not see proper to interfere with it. In your wisdom, however, you make the sacrilegious attempt to overthrow it.

You quote the denunciation of Tyre and Sidon, and say that "the chief reason given by the prophet Joel for their destruction, was, that they were notorious beyond all others for carrying on the slave trade." I am afraid you think we have no Bibles in the Slave States, or that we are unable to read them. I cannot otherwise account for your making this reference, unless indeed your own reading is confined to an expurgated edition, prepared for the use of abolitionists, in which everything relating to Slavery that militates against their view of it is left out. The prophet Joel denounces the Tyrians and Sidonians, because "the children also of Judah and the children of Jerusalem have ye sold unto the Grecians." And what is the divine vengeance for this "notorious slave trading?" Hear it. "And I will sell your sons and daughters into the hands of the children of Judah, and they shall sell them to the Sabeans, to a people far off; for the Lord hath spoken it." Do you call this a condemnation of slave trading? The prophet makes God himself a participator in the crime, if that be one. "The Lord hath spoken it," he says, that the Tyrians and Sidonians shall be *sold into slavery* to strangers. Their real offence was, in enslaving the chosen people; and their sentence was a repetition of the old command, to makes slaves of the heathen round about.

I have dwelt upon your scriptural argument, because you profess to believe the Bible; because a large proportion of the abolitionists profess to do the same, and to act under its sanction; because your circular is addressed in part to "professing Christians;" and because it is from that class mainly that you expect to seduce converts to your anti-christian, I may say, infidel doctrines. It would be wholly unnecessary to answer you, to any one who reads the Scriptures for himself, and construes them according to any other formula than that which the abolitionists are wickedly endeavoring to impose upon the world. The scriptural sanction of Slavery is in fact so palpable, and so strong, that both wings of your party are beginning to acknowledge it. The more sensible and moderate admit, as the organ of the Free Church of Scotland, the North British Review, has lately done, that they "*are precluded by the statements and conduct of the Apostles from regarding mere slaveholding as essentially sinful,*" while the desperate and reckless, who are bent on keeping up the agitation at every hazard, declare, as has been done in the Anti-Slavery Record, "If our inquiry turns out in favor of Slavery, IT IS THE BIBLE THAT MUST FALL, AND NOT THE RIGHTS OF HUMAN NATURE." You cannot, I am satisfied, much longer maintain before the world the Christian platform from which to wage war upon our institutions. Driven from it, you must abandon the contest, or, repudiating REVELATION, rush into the horrors of NATURAL RELIGION.

You next complain that our slaves are kept in bondage by the "law of force." In what country or condition of mankind do you see human affairs regulated merely by the law of love? Unless I am greatly mistaken, you will, if you look over the world, find nearly all certain and permanent rights, civil, social, and I may even add religious, resting on and ultimately secured by the "law of force." The power of majorities—of aristocracies—of kings—nay of priests, for the most part, and of property, resolves itself at last into "force," and could not otherwise be long maintained. Thus, in every turn of your argument against our system of Slavery, you advance, whether conscious of it or not, radical and revolutionary doctrines calculated to change the whole face of the world, to overthrow all government, disorganize society, and reduce man to a state of nature—red with blood, and shrouded once more in barbaric ignorance. But you greatly err, if you suppose, because we rely on force in the last resort to maintain our supremacy over our slaves, that ours is a stern and unfeeling domination, at all to be compared in hard-hearted severity to that exercised, not over the mere laborer only, but by the higher over each lower order, wherever the British sway is acknowledged. You say, that if those you address were "to spend one day in the South, they would return home with impressions against Slavery never to be erased." But the fact is universally the reverse. I have known numerous instances, and I never knew a single one, where there was no other cause of offence, and no object to promote by falsehood, that individuals from the non-slaveholding States did not, after residing among us long enough to understand the subject, "return home" *to defend our Slavery.* It is matter of regret that you have never tried the experiment yourself. I do not doubt you would have been converted, for I give you credit for an honest though perverted mind. You would have seen how weak and futile is all abstract reasoning about this matter, and that, as a building may not be less elegant in its proportions, or tasteful in its ornaments, or virtuous in its uses, for being based upon granite, so a system of human government, though founded on force, may develope and cultivate the tenderest and purest sentiments of the human heart. And our patriarchal scheme of domestic servitude is indeed well calculated to awaken the higher and finer feelings of our nature. It is not wanting in its enthusiasm and its poetry. The relations of the most beloved and honored chief, and the most faithful and admiring subjects, which, from the time of Homer, have been the theme of song, are frigid and unfelt compared with those existing between the master and his slaves—who served his father, and rocked his cradle, or have been born in his household, and look forward to serve his children—who have been through life the props of his fortune, and the objects of his care—who have partaken of his griefs, and looked to him for comfort in their own—whose sickness he has so frequently watched over and relieved—whose holidays he has so often made joyous by his bounties and his presence; for whose welfare, when absent, his anxious solicitude never ceases, and whose hearty and affectionate greetings never fail to welcome him home. In this cold, calculating, ambitious world of ours, there are few ties more heartfelt, or of more benignant influence, than those which mutually bind the master and the slave, under our ancient system, handed down from the father of Israel. The unholy purpose of the abolitionists, is to destroy by defiling it; to infuse into it the gall and bitterness which rankle in their own envenomed bosoms; to poison the minds of the master and the servant; turn love to hatred, array "*force*" *against force*, and hurl all

"With hideous ruin and combustion, down
To bottomless perdition."

You think it a great "crime" that we do not pay our slaves

14*

"wages," and on this account pronounce us "robbers." In my former letter, I showed that the labor of our slaves was not without great cost to us, and that in fact they themselves receive more in return for it than your hirelings do for theirs. For what purpose do men labor, but to support themselves and their families in what comfort they are able? The efforts of mere physical labor seldom suffice to provide more than a livelihood. And it is a well known and shocking fact, that while few operatives in Great Britain succeed in securing a comfortable living, the greater part drag out a miserable existence, and sink at last under absolute want. Of what avail is it that you go through the form of paying them a pittance of what you call "wages," when you do not, in return for their services, allow them what alone they ask—and have a just right to demand—enough to feed, clothe and lodge them, in health and sickness, with reasonable comfort. Though we do not give "wages" *in money*, we do this for *our slaves*, and they are therefore better rewarded than *yours*. It is the prevailing vice and error of the age, and one from which the abolitionists, with all their saintly pretensions, are far from being free, to bring everything to the standard of money. You make gold and silver the great test of happiness. The American slave must be wretched indeed, because he is not compensated for his services *in cash*. It is altogether praiseworthy to pay the laborer a shilling a day, and let him starve on it. To supply all his wants abundantly, and at all times, yet withhold from him *money*, is among "the most reprobated crimes." The fact cannot be denied, that the mere laborer is now, and always has been, everywhere that barbarism has ceased, enslaved. Among the innovations of modern times, following "the decay of villeinage," has been the creation of a new system of Slavery. The primitive and patriarchal, which may also be called the sacred and natural system, in which the laborer is under the personal control of a fellow-being endowed with the sentiments and sympathies of humanity, exists among us. It has been almost everywhere else superseded by the modern *artificial money power system*, in which man—his thews and sinews, his hopes and affections, his very being, are all subjected to the dominion of *capital*—a monster without a heart—cold, stern, arithmetical—sticking to the bond—taking ever " the pound of flesh,"—working up human life with engines, and retailing it out by weight and measure. His name of old was "Mammon, the least erected spirit that fell from heaven." And it is to extend his empire that you and your deluded coadjutors dedicate your lives. You are stirring up mankind to overthrow our heaven-ordained system of servitude, surrounded by innumerable checks, designed and planted deep in the human heart by God and nature, to substitute the absolute rule of this "spirit reprobate," whose proper place was hell.

You charge us with looking on our slaves "as chattels or brutes," and enter into a somewhat elaborate argument to prove that they have "human forms," "talk," and even "think." Now the fact is, that however you may indulge in this strain for effect, it is the abolitionists, and not the slave-holders, who, practically, and in the most important point of view, regard our slaves as "chattels or brutes." In your calculations of the consequences of emancipation, you pass over entirely those which must prove most serious, and which arise from the fact of their being *persons*. You appear to think that we might abstain from the use of them as readily as if they were machines to be laid aside, or cattle that might be turned out to find pasturage for themselves. I have heretofore glanced at some of the results that would follow from breaking the bonds of so many *human beings*, now peacefully and happily linked into our social system. The tragic horrors, the decay and ruin that would for years, perhaps for ages, brood over our land, if it could be accomplished, I will not attempt to portray. But do you fancy the blight would, in such an event, come to us alone? The diminution of the sugar crop of the West Indies affected Great Britain only, and there chiefly the poor. It was a matter of no moment to capital, that labor should have one comfort less. Yet it has forced a reduction of the British duty on sugar. Who can estimate the consequences that must follow the annihilation of the cotton crop of the slaveholding States? I do not undervalue the importance of other articles of commerce, but no calamity could befall the world at all comparable to the sudden loss of two millions of bales of cotton annually. From the deserts of Africa to the Siberian wilds—from Greenland to the Chinese wall,—there is not a spot of earth but would feel the sensation. The factories of Europe would fall with a concussion that would shake down castles, palaces, and even thrones; while the "purse-proud, elbowing insolence" of our Northern monopolist would soon disappear forever under the smooth speech of the pedlar, scourging our frontiers for a livelihood, or the bluff vulgarity of the South Sea whaler, following the harpoon amid storms and shoals. Doubtless the abolitionists think we could grow cotton without slaves, or that at worst the reduction of the crop would be moderate and temporary. Such gross delusions show how profoundly ignorant they are of our condition here.

You declare that "the character of the people of the South has long been that of *hardened infidels*, who fear not God, and have no regard for religion." I will not repeat what I said in my former letter on this point. I only notice it to ask you how you could possibly reconcile it to your profession of a Christian spirit, to make such a malicious charge—to defile your soul with such a calumny against an unoffending people?

> "You are old;
> Nature in you stands on the very verge
> Of her confine. You should be ruled and led
> By some discretion."

May God forgive you.

Akin to this, is the wanton and furious assault made on us by Mr. Macaulay, in his late speech on the sugar duties, in the House of Commons, which has just reached me. His denunciations are wholly without measure, and, among other things, he asserts "that Slavery in the United States wears its worst form; that, boasting of our civilization and freedom, and frequenting Christian churches, we breed up slaves, nay, beget children for slaves, and sell them at so much a-head." Mr. Macaulay is a reviewer, and he knows that he is "nothing if not critical." The practice of his trade has given him the command of all the slashing and vituperative phrases of our language, and the turn of his mind leads him to the habitual use of them. He is an author, and as no copy-right law secures for him from this country a consideration for his writings, he is not only independent of us, but naturally hates everything American. He is the representative of Edinburgh; it is his cue to decry our Slavery, and in doing so he may safely indulge the malignity of his temper, his indignation against us, and his capacity for railing. He has suffered once, for being in advance of his time in favor of abolition, and he does not intend that it shall be forgotten, or his claim passed over, to any crumb which may now be thrown to the vociferators in the cause. If he does not know that the statements he has made respecting the slaveholders of this country are vile and atrocious falsehoods, it is because he does not think it worth his while to be sure he speaks the truth, so that he speaks to his own purpose.

> "Hic niger est, hunc tu, Romane caveto."

Such exhibitions as he has made, may draw the applause of a British House of Commons, but among the sound and high-minded thinkers of the world they can only excite contempt and disgust.

But you are not content with depriving us of all religious feelings. You assert that our Slavery has also "demoralized the Northern States," and charge upon it not only every common violation of good order there, but the "Mormon murders," the "Philadelphia riots," and all "the exterminating wars against the Indians." I wonder that you did not increase the list by adding that it had caused the recent inundation of the Mississippi, and the hurricane in the West Indies—perhaps the insurrection of Rebecca, and the war in Scinde. You refer to the law prohibiting the transmission of abolition publications through the mail, as proof of general corruption! You could not do so, however, without noticing the late detected espionage over the British post office by a minister of state. It is true, as you say, it "occasioned a general outburst of national feeling"—from the opposition; and a "Parliamentary enquiry was instituted"—that is, moved, but treated quite cavalierly. At all events, though the fact was admitted, Sir James Graham yet retains the Home Department. For one, I do not undertake to condemn him. Such things are not against the laws and usages of your country. I do not know fully what reasons of state may have influenced him and justified his conduct. But I do know that there is a vast difference in point of "national morality" between the discretionary power residing in your government to open any letter in the public post office, and a well-defined and limited law to prevent the circulation of certain specified incendiary writings by means of the United States mail.

Having now referred to everything like argument on the

subject of Slavery, that is worthy of notice in your letter, permit me to remark on its tone and style, and very extraordinary bearing upon other institutions of this country. You commence by addressing certain classes of our people, as belonging to "a nation whose character is *now so low* in the estimation of the civilized world;" and throughout you maintain this tone. Did the Americans who were "under your roof last summer" inform you that such language would be gratifying to their fellow-citizens "having no practical concern with slaveholding?" Or do the infamous libels on America, which you read in our abolition papers, induce you to believe that all that class of people are, like the abolitionists themselves, totally destitute of patriotism or pride of country? Let me tell you that you are grossly deceived. And although your stock-brokers and other speculators, who have been bitten in American ventures, may have raised a stunning "cry" against us in England, there is a vast body of people here besides slaveholders, who justly

"Deem their own land of every land the pride,
Beloved by heaven o'er all the world beside,"

and who *know* that at this moment we rank among the first powers of the world—a position which we not only claim, but are always ready and able to maintain.

The style you assume in addressing your Northern friends, is in perfect keeping with your apparent estimation of them. Though I should be the last, perhaps, to criticise mere style, I could not but be struck with the extremely simple manner of your letter. You seem to have thought you were writing a tract for benighted heathen, and telling wonders never before suggested to their imagination, and so far above their untutored comprehension as to require to be related in the primitive language of "the child's own book." This is sufficiently amusing; and would be more so, but for the coarse and bitter epithets you continually apply to the poor slaveholders—epithets which appear to be stereotyped for the use of abolitionists, and which form a large and material part of all their arguments.

But, perhaps, the most extraordinary part of your letter is your bold denunciation of "*the shameful compromises*" of our constitution, and your earnest recommendation to those you address to overthrow or revolutionize it. In so many words you say to them, "*you must either separate yourselves from all political connection with the South, and make your own laws; or if you do not choose such a separation, you must break up the political ascendancy which the Southern have had for so long a time over the Northern States.*" The italics in this, as in all other quotations, are your own. It is well for those who circulate your letter here, that the constitution you denounce requires an overt act to constitute treason. It may be tolerated for an American by birth, to use on his own soil the freedom of speaking and writing which is guaranteed him, and abuse our constitution, our Union, and our people. But that a foreigner should use such seditious language, in a circular letter addressed to a portion of the American people, is a presumption well calculated to excite the indignation of all. The party known in this country as the abolition party has long since avowed the sentiments you express, and adopted the policy you enjoin. At the recent presidential election, they gave over 62,000 votes for their own candidate, and held the balance of power in two of the largest States—wanting but little of doing it in several others. In the last four years their vote has quadrupled. Should the infatuation continue, and their vote increase in the same ratio for the next four years, it will be as large as the vote of the *actual slaveholders* of the Union. Such a prospect is, doubtless, extremely gratifying to you. It gives hope of a contest on such terms as may insure the downfall of Slavery or our constitution. The South venerates the constitution, and is prepared to stand by it forever, *such as it came from the hands of our fathers;* to risk every thing to defend and maintain it *in its integrity*. But the South is under no such delusion as to believe that it derives any *peculiar* protection from the Union. On the contrary, it is well known we incur *peculiar danger*, and that we bear far more than our proportion of the burdens. The apprehension is also fast fading away that any of the dreadful consequences commonly predicted will necessarily result from a separation of the States. And *come what may*, we are firmly resolved that OUR SYSTEM OF DOMESTIC SLAVERY SHALL STAND. The fate of the Union, then—but, thank God, not of republican government—rests mainly in the hands of the people to whom your letter is addressed—the "professing Christians of the Northern States having no concern with slaveholding," and whom with incendiary zeal you are endeavoring to stir up to strife—without which fanaticism can neither live, move, nor have any being.

We have often been taunted for our sensitiveness in regard to the discussion of Slavery. Do not suppose it is because we have any doubts of our rights, or scruples about asserting them. There was a time when such doubts and scruples were entertained. Our ancestors opposed the introduction of slaves into this country, and a feeling adverse to it was handed down from them. The enthusiastic love of liberty fostered by our revolution strengthened this feeling. And before the commencement of the abolition agitation here, it was the common sentiment that it was desirable to get rid of Slavery. Many thought it our duty to do so. When that agitation arose, we were driven to a close examination of the subject in all its bearings, and the result has been an *universal conviction* that in holding slaves we violate no law of God,—inflict no injustice on any of his creatures—while the terrible consequences of emancipation to all parties and the world at large, clearly revealed to us, make us shudder at the bare thought of it. The slaveholders are, therefore, indebted to the abolitionists for perfect ease of conscience, and the satisfaction of a settled and unanimous determination in reference to this matter. And could their agitation cease now, I believe, after all, the good would preponderate over the evil of it in this country. On the contrary, however, it is urged on with frantic violence, and the abolitionists, reasoning in the abstract, as if it were a mere moral or metaphysical speculation, or a minor question in politics, profess to be surprised at our exasperation. In their ignorance and recklessness, they seem to be unable to comprehend our feelings or position. The subversion of our rights, the destruction of our property, the disturbance of our peace and the peace of the world, are matters which do not appear to arrest their consideration. When revolutionary France proclaimed "hatred to kings and unity to the republic," and inscribed on her banners "France risen against tyrants," she professed to be only worshipping "abstract rights." And if there can be such things, perhaps she was. Yet all Europe *rose* to put her sublime theories down. They declared her an enemy to the common peace; that her doctrines alone violated the "law of neighborhood," and, as Mr. Burke said, justly entitled them to anticipate the "damnum nondum factum" of the civil law. Danton, Barrere, and the rest were apparently astonished that umbrage should be taken. The parallel between them and the abolitionists holds good in all respects.

The rise and progress of this fanaticism is one of the phenomena of the age in which we live. I do not intend to repeat what I have already said, or to trace its career more minutely at present. But the legislation of Great Britain will make it historical, and doubtless you must feel some curiosity to know how it will figure on the page of the annalist. I think I can tell you. Though I have accorded and do accord to you and your party, great influence in bringing about the parliamentary action of your country, you must not expect to go down to posterity as the only cause of it. Though *you* trace the progenitors of abolition from 1516, through a long stream with divers branches, down to the period of its triumph in your country, it has not escaped contemporaries, and will not escape posterity, that England, without much effort, sustained the storm of its scoffs and threats, until the moment arrived when she thought her colonies fully supplied with Africans; and declared against the slave trade, only when she deemed it unnecessary to her, and when her colonies, full of slaves, would have great advantages over others not so well provided. Nor did she agree to West India emancipation, until, discovering the error of her previous calculation, it became an object to have slaves free throughout the Western world, and, on the ruins of the sugar and cotton growers of America and the Islands, to build up her great slave empire in the East; while her indefatigable exertions, still continued, to engraft the right of search upon the law of nations, on the plea of putting an end to the forever increasing slave trade, are well understood to have chiefly in view the complete establishment of her supremacy at sea.* Nor must you flatter yourself that your party will derive historic dignity from the

* On these points, let me recommend you to consult a very able Essay on the Slave Trade and Right of Search, by M. Jollivet, recently published; and as you say, since writing your Circular Letter, that you " burn to try your hand on another little Essay, if a subject could be found," I propose to you to " try " to answer this question, put by M. Jollivet to England : " *Pourquoi sa philanthropie n'a pas deigne, jusqu' a present, doubler le cap de Bonne-Esperance ?*"

names of the illustrious British statesmen who have acted with it. Their country's ends were theirs. They have stooped to use you, as the most illustrious men will sometimes use the vilest instruments, to accomplish their own purposes. A few philanthropic common places and rhetorical flourishes, "in the abstract," have secured them your "sweet voices," and your influence over the tribe of mawkish sentimentalists. Wilberforce may have been yours, but what was he besides, but a wealthy county member? You must, therefore, expect to stand on your own merits alone before posterity, or rather that portion of it that may be curious to trace the history of the delusions which, from time to time, pass over the surface of human affairs, and who may trouble themselves to look through the ramifications of transcendentalism, in this era of extravagances. And how do you expect to appear in their eyes? As Christians, piously endeavoring to enforce the will of God, and carry out the principles of Christianity? Certainly not, since you deny or pervert the Scriptures in the doctrines you advance; and in your conduct, furnish a glaring contrast to the examples of Christ and the Apostles. As philanthropists, devoting yourselves to the cause of humanity, relieving the needy, comforting the afflicted, creating peace and gladness and plenty round about you? Certainly not, since you turn from the needy, the afflicted; from strife, sorrow and starvation which surround you; close your eyes and hands upon them; shut out from your thoughts and feelings the human misery which is real, tangible, and within your reach, to indulge your morbid imagination in conjuring up woes and wants among a strange people in distant lands, and offering them succor in the shape of costless denunciations of their best friends, or by scattering among them "firebrands, arrows and death." Such folly and madness, such wild mockery and base imposture, can never win for you, in the sober judgment of future times, the name of philanthropists. Will you even be regarded as worthy citizens? Scarcely, when the purposes you have in view, can only be achieved by revolutionizing governments and overturning social systems, and when you do not hesitate, zealously and earnestly, to recommend such measures. Be assured, then, that posterity will not regard the abolitionists as Christians, philanthopists, or virtuous citizens. It will, I have no doubt, look upon the mass of the party as silly enthusiasts, led away by designing characters, as is the case with all parties that break from the great, acknowledged ties which bind civilized man in fellowship. The leaders themselves will be regarded as *mere ambitious men;* not taking rank with those whose ambition is "eagle-winged and sky-aspiring," but belonging to that mean and selfish class, who are instigated by "rival-hating envy," and whose base thirst is for *notoriety;* who cloak their designs under vile and impious hypocrisies, and, unable to shine in higher spheres, devote themselves to fanaticism, as a trade. And it will be perceived that, even in that, they shunned the highest walk. Religious fanaticism was an old established vocation, in which something brilliant was required to attract attention. They could not be George Foxes, nor Joanna Southcotes, nor even Joe Smiths. But the dullest pretender could discourse a jumble of pious bigotry, natural rights, and drivelling philanthropy. And, addressing himself to aged folly and youthful vanity, to ancient women, to ill-gotten wealth, to the reckless of all classes, who love excitement and change, offer each the cheapest and the safest glory in the market. Hence, their numbers; and, from number and clamor, what impression they have made on the world.

Such, I am persuaded, is the light in which the abolitionists will be viewed by the posterity their history may reach. Unless, indeed—which God forbid—circumstances should so favor as to enable them to produce a convulsion which may elevate them higher on the "bad eminence" where they have placed themselves.

    I have the honor to be
      Your obedient servant,
          J. H. HAMMOND.
THOMAS CLARKSON, Esq.

NOTE.—The foregoing Letters were not originally intended for publication. In preparing them for the press, they have been revised. The alterations and corrections made, however, have been mostly verbal. Had the writer felt at liberty to condense the two letters into one, and bring up the history of abolition to the period of publication, he might have presented a more concise and perfect argument, and illustrated his views more forcibly, by reference to facts recently developed. For example, since writing the first, the letter of Mr. Clarkson, as President of the British Anti-Slavery Society, to Sir Robert Peel, denouncing the whole scheme of "Immigration," has reached him; and after he had forwarded the last, he saw it stated, that Mr. Clarkson had, as late as the first part of April, addressed the Earl of Aberdeen, and declared, that all efforts to suppress the African slave trade had fully failed. It may be confidently expected, that it will be ere long announced from the same quarter, that the "experiment" of West India emancipation has also proved a complete abortion.

Should the terms which have been applied to the abolitionists appear to any as unduly severe, let it remembered, that the direct aim of these people is to destroy us by the most shocking of all processes; and that, having a large portion of the civilized world for their audience, they daily and systematically heap upon us the vilest calumnies and most unmitigated abuse. Clergymen lay aside their bibles, and females unsex themselves, to carry on this horrid warfare against slave holders.

THE MORALS OF SLAVERY.*

INTRODUCTION.

THE original of the essay which follows was originally published in the pages of the *Southern Literary Messenger*, sometime in the year 1837. At that period the subject had not so greatly engaged the attention of the Southern people, as in more recent years; the progress of the anti-Slavery sentiment, in the Northern States and other regions, not having shown itself so active, pressing and insolent as it has since become. The very favorable opinion with which the article was, at the time, received, and the demand for copies, prompted its republication, in the form of a separate pamphlet, which appeared in 1838. This pamphlet was dedicated to the *Honorable, the Delegates from South Carolina, in the Congress of the United States*, in the following language:
"GENTLEMEN :

"If I did not regard you as representatives, not less of the interests of the slave of Carolina, than of the rights of his owner, I should not trouble you with this inscription, nor the press with the publication of this little essay. Originally put forth in one of our Southern periodi-

---

* Being a brief review of the writings of Miss Martineau, and other persons, on the subject of Negro Slavery, as it now exists in the United States. By W. GILMORE SIMMS, Esq., of South Carolina.

cals, it has been so far honored by the approbation of its readers, as to make it desirable, in the estimation of many, that it should have a more extended circulation. This it should not have, if I could bring myself for an instant to believe, that I was moved to its preparation by any motive but a sincere desire for the truth; or, if I could doubt that it contains principles which no sophistry can subvert, and no misapplied ingenuity, whether of sheer cunning or of self-blinding philanthropy, could keep from the ultimate reception of mankind. The argument, indeed, is chiefly drawn from what would seem to be the inevitable sense of mankind upon the subject of which it treats, as that sense is illustrated and shown by the practices and the necessities of men throughout the world, and through all its successive ages, from its known beginning. I will not seek, therefore, to fortify my views by the accumulation of authorities which he who runs may read. In my humble notion, the whole world of human experience is tributary to their maintenance; and I would as soon doubt that it is truth which I profess, as question the final triumph of those opinions upon which the practice of all nations has invariably settled down. I speak now, only, as I deem it desirable that we should facilitate the advent of truth, and not because I have any doubts of her final coming. We should labor in her assistance, not so much because she may need our service, as because our feeble race stands so grievously in need of hers. This we can best do, not by persuasive and specious doctrines, and fine flexible sayings, but simply by a firm adherence to what we know, and to what we think we have already gained. As yet, we have, confessedly, but partial glimmerings of her divine presence,—her fixed and all sufficing light!—we must treasure up these gleams and glimpses, few and feeble though they be, until, to our more familiar eyes, star by star, she unfolds her perfect form, and, with the loveliness and the light of heaven, irradiates the dim cloud that now hangs between her and the earth. That we shall pray long and vainly for this ideal of the moral world—that we shall look for it, with but little hope, whether in your day or in mine,—is not a matter of difficult prediction while there are so many, and so bold, prophets that proclaim themselves adversely throughout the land. But, that the continued and cheering presence of this blessed hope in the hearts of the few, will at length achieve what they so earnestly seek and sometimes die to realize, may be predicted with not less confidence. Let us, at least, labor that we may verify our own desires, and find renewed impulse to our labors, as we behold the industry of those who toil against us, and those things, which we conceive to be justified by their perfect consonance with the divine law. We may neither of us do much in this holy cause, but, if we gather, each, but a single shell from the great ocean of truth—to employ the fancy of one whose constant thought was the best philanthropy—we shall at least diminish the toils of those who shall follow in our footsteps along the shores of the same solitary and unknown regions."

There is nothing in the tone or sentiment of the preceding that the author would change, and the interval which has elapsed since the publication of the essay and the present time, has confirmed him in most of his convictions, while enabling him greatly to enlarge the sphere of his observations, and to add to the number of his facts.

It is thought by the present publishers, that the views here expressed, may still serve a useful purpose, in connection with those of óthers, in the defence of a domestic institution, which we hold to be not simply within the sanctions of justice and propriety, but as constituting one of the most essential agencies, under the divine plan, for promoting the general progress of civilization, and for elevating, to a condition of humanity, a people otherwise barbarous, easily depraved, and needing the help of a superior condition—a power from without—to rescue them from a hopelessly savage state. In consenting to this republication, I am not unaware of the disadvantages under which it must labor, in comparison with other essays subsequently written. When I wrote, but little had been said in defence of African Slavery in America. Prescription was against it everywhere. All our maxims, our declamation, the pet phrases, equally of philanthropy and of demagogueism, were designed to render it odious and criminal; and, in the defence usually offered, on the part of those who maintained it, it was generally admitted that a wrong had been done, and that a social evil did exist, which expediency alone denied that we should seek to repair, or put away from us. The author was among the very few who took other and higher grounds. He denied that any wrong had been done to the African, in making him labor in America. He denied that any evil, but rather a great good and blessing, accrued from his appropriate but subordinate employment in the States of the South. He contended, that the institution of Slavery, *per se*, was not in violation of the divine law; that it had existed, in all ages, and from the earliest periods, under the immediate sanction of Heaven; and that most nations, while it endured among them, were in the enjoyment of the highest human prosperity. But the argument of the essay need not be anticipated here. Enough that, under certain slavish habits of thinking, many of these opinions were regarded as heresies, even in the South. It was not easy, even with the interests of the community to support the truth, to eradicate that falsehood from their minds, which had been the growth of prescription and the habit of thought, of phrase and formula, for a hundred years—errors of opinion, when habitual, being entirely hostile to all independent and honest thinking. But the progress of fifteen years, since the first publication of this essay, has effected a corresponding progress to independence in the opinion and sentiment of our people. Forced, by external and hostile pressure, to re-examine the argument, the grounds upon which their title rests to the labor of their slaves, they have found themselves fortified by higher authority than they had originally claimed in mere expediency. It is one of the happy results of evil always, according to the benign decree of providence, that it must ultimately work out the fruits of good, in despite of its malicious contriver; and it should be a subject of great gratification to the people of the South, that abolition, with all its annoyances and offences against our peace and safety, has resulted in our moral reässurance,—in the establishing, to our own perfect conviction, our right to the labor of our slaves, and in relieving us from all that doubt, that morbid feeling of weakness in respect to the moral of our claim, which was undoubtedly felt so long as we forebore the proper consideration of the argument. Twenty years ago, few persons in the South undertook to justify Negro Slavery, except on the score of necessity. Now, very few persons in the same region, question their perfect right to the labor of their slaves,—and more,—their moral obligation to keep them still subject, as slaves, and to compel their labor, so long as they remain the inferior beings which we find them now, and which they seem to have been from the beginning. This is a great good, the fruit wholly of the hostile pressure. It has forced us to examine into the sources of the truth; to reject the specious formula, which originally deluded us, and still deludes so many; and to feel the strength of our argument, by which we are justified to our own consciences, and to know our justification, as slave-holders, to be complete, according to all proper morals, and in accordance equally with sacred and profane experience.

I have but to add that, in the revision of the review which follows, I have not confined myself to a consideration of the case, according to the condition of the country when it was written, the lights then possessed and the opinions entertained. I have not scrupled to make such additions, alterations and amendments, as my own longer experience, as well as that of our people, and the subsequent thought given to the subject, shall have suggested as proper and useful to the discussion. In the plan of my paper, I have made no changes. It has seemed to me proper that I should still address myself to Miss Martineau, as fairly representing that tribe whose restless eagerness, morbid self-esteem, and complacent philanthropy—never so well satisfied as when, preaching reform, it designs revolution—are at the bottom of all the dangers which threaten the existing civilization and safety of mankind. In showing up her mistakes of fact and opinion, I do but indicate those which are common to her sect; and, what is desultory in the manner of the essay, may be forgiven, in consideration of the freedom which it affords; by which the gravity of the discussion is relieved, and the occasional employment of what is personal and anecdotical, is made the better to illustrate the case.

CHARLESTON, July 1, 1852.

THE MORALS OF SLAVERY.

In the course of my wanderings, last summer, in some of the Northern States, a friend, who had possessed himself of the volumes of Miss Martineau, descriptive of her Western Travel, drew my attention to those portions of her work which related especially to South-Carolina. He was anxious that, as a native of that State, who had resided in it all his life, and who might, accordingly, be assumed to know the condition and character of its society, I should say in what degree the good lady had erred in the statement of her facts. Her inferences in respect to them, we were both agreed, might be reserved for after consideration. Her report, I need not say, had been by no means a grateful one. She had seen many things which she understood unfavorably. She had reported many other *unseen* things, equally unfavorable, on the authority of others; and her conjectures, and doubts, and suspicions, were of a sort sufficiently to show, that the indulgent entertainment which she had found in Carolina, had not tended very materially to raise her estimate of a people, whom, it was evident, she was prepared to study only through the medium of her prejudices. My friend, who was a northern man, agreed that Miss Martineau was a very favorable sample of the more intelligent among the abolitionists; that she had embodied pretty generally their authorities and arguments, and that her alleged facts, and the inferences drawn from them, were such as constituted the materials of warfare commonly employed by the fraternity. To expose her errors and to answer her charges, was sufficiently to answer all; and as he was really curious, and, I believe, in good faith solicitous of the truth, I was not unwilling to undertake the task which he pointed out, and to go over with him, page by page, the two thick duodecimos of the philanthropic lady. Pencil in hand, we noted all her points, not only in respect to Carolina, but all the States, so far as the subjects were familiar to either of us; and the result was the expression, on his part, of a wish, that I should take up the matter in some of our periodicals, and answer to her, as I had done to him, the charges which she had made against my particular province. It was only a natural opinion that, to expose her blunders in regard to one of the States, we should reasonably compel a proper caution, on the part of the reader, in the adoption of her authority in respect to any; and it might be that the sectional labors of one citizen would thus persuade others, in other regions which the lady traveller had disparaged, to undertake the patriotic labor of following her footsteps, and correcting her blunders, as fast as she committed them. It was agreed, between us, that the first essential was to disprove the facts of the abolitionists. They had relied upon these alleged facts in the first instance, to create an antipathy to the slaveholder. To paint the horrors of Slavery, so as to revolt the sensibilities of humanity, was the first great means by which to show that the institution was unnatural and irreligious, and its tendencies necessarily inhuman. The rest was easy. Our first business, accordingly, was with the facts; to dispose of these, was to clear the way to an inquiry into the institution of Slavery, *per se*, as a moral question. No matter how seemingly insignificant was the fact asserted, it thus became important to the discussion; and the insignificance of the details was not a sufficient reason for shoving them aside from consideration. The common mind rarely reasons independently of practical considerations ; and its prejudices, by which the most wholesome laws are overthrown, are morally founded in matters of fact, which, intrinsically, have, perhaps, no sort of bearing upon the morals of the subject. To assert, as we do in argument, that there is no course so illogical as that which reasons from the abuse against the use, is scarcely sufficient for our purpose when dealing with the ignorant. It must be our care, also, to show the gross exaggeration, if not utter mis-statement, in the matter of the abuse;—show that the morals of the philanthropist do not deny that he should lie *ad libitum*, even when he proposes nothing less than a holy warfare in the cause of truth ; and that if Slavery in the States of the South is to be overthrown, it must be by argument drawn from intrinsic considerations of the institution itself, and not from the alleged inhumanity of the slave-holder.

I was not unwilling to comply with the request of my friend—not unwilling to assist the stranger to our country in arriving at a knowledge—which appears so equally difficult and necessary —of a region of the world, which our foreign brethren are so well pleased to insist upon as barbarous. But here, at the very threshold of the subject, my pride revolted at the task. Why should we account to these people ? What are they that they should subject us to the question ? We are their equals ; sprung from the same stocks, in possession of the same authorities, learning at the same schools, taught from the same books, by the same great masters of thought and language, and in the full assertion of an equal civilization and freedom. Speaking once with Miss C. Sedgwick,—a lady whom, in spite of her abolition prejudices, I greatly esteem,—in respect to the gradual progress of the negro under our care and tuition, to the exercise of a higher moral and intellect than he had ever exhibited, as a freeman in his own or in any country, she asked "But what security do you give us that you will continue to advance him?" The natural reply was immediate. "Give *you* security? You mistake. We offer you none. We are your equals. We owe you no accountability. Our responsibility is to God and our own consciencies alone." The same natural pride would prompt us to answer the scorner with scorn, and the assailant with defiance. What we offer is voluntary. What we put on record, is not in our defence, but in the assertion of the truth, and that we may furnish the due authorities to history. The very approach to the subject, on the part of the stranger, is an implied impertinence. It goes on the assumption of our inferiority, as well as our error. The Southern people form a nation, and, as such, it derogates from their dignity that they should be called to answer at the tribunals of any other nation. When that call shall be definitely or imperatively made, they will answer with their weapons, and in no other language than that of war to the knife.

As individuals, the annoyance of such an approach is more acutely felt, since it outrages their personal self-esteem. The Southron asks with indignation, why it is that he and his people should be supposed guilty of brutalities and cruelties to the negro race, which are inconsistent with the civilization of that race to which he belongs? What do you see in us, our manners, tastes, opinions or habits, to lead you to think us less humane and intelligent than yourselves; less considerate of the claims, less solicitous of the sympathies of the inferior? And he may well ask these questions, with astonishment, since, what he sees, elsewhere, is by no means calculated to prompt his doubts of an inferior humanity in his own bosom. Yet the daily narrative and clamor of the abolitionists teaches this very doubt, which it is their policy to inculcate. In conflict with this assumption of our assailants, it is usual to ascribe to the people of the South a somewhat superior refinement. Their grace of manner, courteous bearing, gentleness of deportment, studious forbearance and unobtrusiveness—their social characteristics, in general—all assumed to spring from the peculiar institution of Negro Slavery, as affording superior time, as well as leisure, to the controlling race—are usually admitted without question. The testimony of the intelligent European is commonly to this effect. That these traits should be held consistent with brutal practice, savage passions, and a reckless tyranny over inferiors, is naturally a great difficulty in the way of those whose habit it is to recognize good manners as, in some degree, a warranty for good morals. In regard to the former, the Southron, who is something of a traveller, has rarely occasion to feel mortified at the comparison with the people among whom he travels; and his wonder is even greater than his mortification, when he finds himself charged with crimes against humanity, such as are in strange conflict with his social attainments and position. To these charges it is not his custom to offer any reply; his scorn of the imputation usually rendering him unconscious of the assailant, whom he regards rather as a slanderer than an adversary.

What is true of the relations of the Southern people with the Northern, is, in a great degree, true of the general relations of both people with the British; and the inordinate self-esteem of the latter, coupled with quite an adequate share of ignorance, makes it almost impossible to teach them, through any processes, except those of war, to accord the simplest justice to their cis-Atlantic descendants. In ordinary cases— viewing the proposition abstractly—and a colony, it will be taken for granted, must resemble, in all substantial particulars, the country from which it goes forth. In its habits and pursuits, its tastes and objects, its general modes of thinking, and the common carriage of society, its people will exhibit, with very trifling modifications, the race from which they sprang. This, which is true as a rule, is yet not without its exceptions; and it is the pleasure of the people of Great Britain to regard those of America as falling very far short of those superior standards, of mind and society, which they have set up as their own. Their travellers, accordingly, when they come among us, and write about us, do so with the air of persons surveying the savages of some newly found country—some Polynesia or Australasia—that fifth portion of the world for which they are only now providing fine names and probably foul destinies. Their very first approaches among us are made with an air of superiority; either of an insolence which contemns, or of a patronage which is scarcely less offensive; and they speak with certain assumptions forever in their mouths, by which we are required to waive altogether the advantages of ancestry—forego any claims that might result to us from the possession of an origin, a language and a literature, in common with themselves,—and content ourselves with that place, on the lower form, from which it is scarcely possible, or to be permitted, that we shall at any time emerge into honorable consideration. Our intercourse, *in limine*, begins with a distinct assertion of our inferiority and degeneracy; and the pert noble, or the unsexed spinster, never rising to a consideration of what has been done by our branch of the family, almost single-handed, will impudently set themselves up as the social and political teachers of a people, which, from its own ranks, has produced, in modern and recent times, many of the master spirits of the world. One of the consequences of this practice, is, to exclude all such persons from the society of those who could best enlighten them in American facts, and give them the most just notions of American morals and manners. Persons having a becoming sense of their own claims, and those of their country, never permit these boors to enter their habitations. They fall, accordingly, into the hands of those only who seek notoriety;—of those who, conscious of inferior position at home, are eager to seize upon the titled or the notorious foreigner—any one, indeed, who can, by any possibility, lift them into local consideration. These persons conciliate the visitor by such concessions as, did they represent the nation, would wholly degrade it; and, not the least of the evils accruing from their *toadyism* is, that they suffer, without denial, the assumptions of the stranger at the expense of their country. This is the fruit equally of their desire to flatter the guest, and of their incapacity to engage in the argument. The enlightened Englishman will find little difficulty in recognizing the better society of the United States in those who make him the fewest possible approaches;—those who let him see, at the outset, that their desire of society, however eager, is not to be gratified at the sacrifice of their proper self-esteem. The reserve of this class, towards the foreigner, is in due degree with the eagerness with which the merely *pretentious* press torwads him. What he hears and learns from the latter, in respect to parties, sections, or the country at large, must always be taken with a due caution, which never, at any time, overlooks the doubtful moral of that authority which begins with the surrender of the individual *amour propre*.

The misfortune of Miss Martineau was in falling very frequently into such hands as these, when she came to this country; a circumstance which, in addition to the farther fact that her abolition sympathies conducted her naturally into the embraces of those who were hostile to the South, served sufficiently to fill her mind with false facts, as it had already been sufficiently stored with false philosophy. That she saw many intelligent and worthy people, besides, we do not deny;

but she saw them, and sought them, only that she might exercise her favorite passion for polemics. She sought them for the purposes of encounter; and frequently chuckled, in fancied triumphs, over statesmen and philosophers, who preferred temporary submission to her tongue, rather than encounter the toil of appealing to a mind which, on certain subjects, was, to the full, as inaccessible as her ears.

When Miss Martineau, after acknowledging the peculiar disability under which she labors, in being deaf, proceeds to hunt up and to dilate upon some of the advantages of such an infirmity; and, with an ingenuity which deserves credit, (and in New-England might have found it, had she withheld her remarks upon that region,) dilates upon the winning power which her trumpet exercises in a tête-a-tête—we, at once, discover the sort of person with whom we have to deal. Had she written volumes with the design of illustrating the peculiar properties of her own mind, she could have said nothing which better conveys the idea of the adroit casuist, ready and able to make the best case out of the worst;—to raise subtle hypotheses,—to suggest means of fight and defence in the worst cases,—to plan sorties and escapes; and, whatever might be the fate of the conflict, if she did not " change sides," at least "still continue to dispute." The passage of her preface, in which this singular stretch of self deception (if we may so style it) occurs, is truly an amusing one. Her accuracy of information, she insists, is not diminished in consequence of her deafness; for her trumpet is one of " singular fidelity," and she " gains more in a tête-a-tête, than is given to people who hear general conversation." This is one of those passages, with which the volume abounds, which most admirably illustrate the perfect assurance of the author. What person beside herself would undertake to argue for the advantages of being deaf? To prove that the ears are but surplusage, is certainly to suggest to the deity a process of improvement, by which the curtailment of a sense will help the endowments of a philosopher. Here, she assumes cognizance of a subject, and decides a preference, which she is physically incapable of considering; and, without thought—for the reflection of a single instant would have saved her from the absurdity—proceeds to determine upon a point obviously beyond her capacity. Satisfied, herself, with the "charm of her trumpet," and fully persuaded, as she seems to be, of the truth of what she has said, she is yet dubious that there will be some unwisely skeptical whom it is yet necessary to convince; and the reason which she gives for the truth that is in her, may amuse many whom it will certainly fail to satisfy.

"*Its charm* (the charm of chatting through a trumpet with a deaf damsel of a 'certain age!') consists in the new feeling which it imparts, of ease and privacy!"

It does not seem to strike her for an instant that, among a people, like the Americans, who are singularly susceptible of the ridiculous, there would be nothing half so awkward as to be subjected to this charming tête-a-tête. Yet such was the case. We know many intelligent persons who declined to make the lady's acquaintance while in this country, simply on account of her trumpet, and the awkwardness of such a chat in company, who, otherwise, would have been very well pleased to know her, and who might have afforded her some very useful information. This latter opinion, she, perhaps, will not so readily believe; since she tells us, in brief, that, during her travels of nearly two years among the Americans, seldom more than two weeks in any one place, and thus dividing her time among fifteen or eighteen millions of persons, she made the acquaintance of nearly all of the distinguished people, and believes that she "heard every argument that can possibly be adduced in vindication or palliation of Slavery!" In a note, only a few pages apart from this precious sample of assurance, she gives a little anecdote which will answer all the purposes of a commentary upon it. She says:

"A fact regarding Mr. Gallatin, shows what the obscurity of country life in the United States may be. His estate was originally in Virginia. By a new division it was thrown into the back part of Pennsylvania. He ceased to be heard of for some years. . . . . During this time an advertisement appeared in a newspaper, asking for tidings of 'one Albert Gallatin,' and adding, that if he were still living, he might, on making a certain application, hear of something to his advantage."

So much for the story, which may be true or not. It is highly probable. And yet, it will be remembered—that the hardihood of our traveller may be the better understood—that Mr. Albert Gallatin has the reputation of being one of our most celebrated economists—a statesman highly distinguished for his acumen and frequently employed;—an ethnologist of no mean reputation. It was left for Miss Martineau, in spite of the "obscur'ty of country life in the United States,"—which is peculiarly the nation of great distances,—to find out all the distinguished men, and to hear all the arguments that were worth hearing. The "charm" of her trumpet, however, being taken into consideration, some of the difficulties of the achievement were, no doubt, readily overcome.

A little proem taken from a paper in the Edinburgh Review, furnishes the text for a portion of her preface. This text dilates, though summarily, upon the folly and impertinence of any traveller assuming, by a brief race through a neighboring country, to generalize, for the people thereof, from his own partial and hasty observations. Miss Martineau, with an air of no little humility at first, acknowledges the force of this paragraph; and is almost resolved, as she felt the reasonableness of its suggestions, to say nothing "in print on the condition of society in the United States." But she does not keep in this mind long. Indeed, how could she, in utter disregard of the leading habit of her life? To quote the paragraph, was only to serve its suggestions, as she does so many conversational ninepins which she sets up, here and there, throughout her two volumes, simply to show how well she can bowl them down. This is her obvious purpose in making the quotation; and she concludes not to mind its arguments, but to print and generalize, for good or for evil; contenting herself with saying, most illogically, in defence of her resolve, that " men will never arrive at a knowledge of each other, if those who have the power of foreign observation refuse to relate what they think they have learned; or even to lay before others the materials from which they themselves hesitate to construct a theory, or draw large conclusions."

No wonder error should breed so fast, and attain a growth so vigorous, when this sort of morals is to be inculcated. " I am not sure," says our author, " that what I tell you is the truth, but never mind, it looks sufficiently like the truth for all common purposes, and with my dressing; and better that than nothing. If we scruple to say what we conjecture, we should perhaps know but little of each other, and an ingenious conjecture is certainly a good substitute for an unknown fact. Be thankful, with Sancho, and look not the gift horse too narrowly in the mouth."

This is the *gist* of the argument. It does not occur to the good lady that the task of unlearning the error is perhaps one of the greatest difficulties in the way of the progress to the truth. But allowing all the credit claimed for her reasoning, it could only apply to a region of which there is no means to acquire better information. In regard to the United States, of which the people of Great Britain have it in their power to know so much; to which their travellers crowd daily; of which they publish accounts daily; with which their intercourse, of the most imposing and valuable kind, is constant, absorbing, and hourly increasing, the suggestion is a mere absurdity. The good lady knew of this intimate relation quite as well as any body else; but she had a policy in forestalling the opinions and inferences of others. It belonged to her philosophy that she should furnish the guide points and the clues to the traveller; that she should shape his facts and construct his philosophies; and this, not because she desired the perversion of the truth, but that she was sworn to the progress of a theory which served all the purposes of a perfect truth to her.

The same preface affords us another marvellous statement, in regard to the condition of Miss Martineau's mind, when she proposed to visit the United States. To those who know the lady, whether from her writings or from personal intercourse, the following passage will seem as perfect an absurdity as any of the many in her volumes. She tells us that she "went with a mind, *she* believes, as nearly as possible unprejudiced about America; with a strong disposition to admire democratic institutions; but an entire ignorance how far the people of the United States lived up to or fell below, their own theory. *She* had read whatever she could lay hold of that had been written about them; but was unable to satisfy herself that, after all, she understood anything whatever of their condition. As to knowledge of them, her mind was nearly a blank; as to opinion of their state, she did not carry the germ of one."

If this be the truth, Miss Martineau was capable of far more forbearance, on the subject of the United States, than is her usual habit on most other subjects. She was a democrat in England, writing incessantly on topics, and in regard to institutions and objects, which necessarily involved a close consideration of a region which, to her class, conveyed in some degree an ideal realm of security and happiness,—perfect freedom and proper philanthropy. She tells us that she had read all that she could lay hands on in relation to America, yet had learned nothing. Is it possible that such was the case; that the people of Great Britain, down to this the day of her writing, had left themselves so utterly uninformed as to a people with whom their original relations were so intimate; with whom they had fought two bloody wars; with whom they carried on the most profitable commercial intercourse? *Credat Judæas!* Miss Martineau, at least, could never have left herself thus ignorant, whatever had been the indifference of her people upon this subject. She is one of those coarse, eager, bold, disputatious persons, strong of will, restless in search, keen and persevering, who are never satisfied with themselves, until they have acquired some leading notions upon every topic to which their minds may be addressed. She will store her memory with facts, or such as she deems so, drawn from no matter what quarter, and she will brood upon these facts until she shapes and resolves them all into tributary groups for the maintenance of whatsoever view of the case may have obtained predominance in her mind. She has formed a habit of speculating as she goes,—a very good habit, if her mind were not always subject to a bias,—and with this habit she has formed another, a far less valuable one, of declaiming her philosophies aloud, as fast as they accumulate in her thought. Nothing escapes her tongue, however much avoids her ear. No subject is felt too great, none proves too little, for her scrutiny. She shrinks from neither extreme. The shallows and the deeps, alike, form her elements, though she shows herself ludicrously striving to dive in the one, and to wade upright in the other. To those who, not caring either to wade or dive in such waters, will content themselves with simply glancing at the ambitious heads of her chapters, her sections, and her subdivisions, the surprise will be unqualified at her universality. The distich occurs naturally as you read—

"Still the wonder *grows*,
That one small head can carry all she *knows*."

While other travellers, rating themselves modestly, are satisfied usually to relate only what they see and hear, and only now and then to dilate upon some single topic, with which they assume to be particularly acquainted; our author, with a surprising capacity, and a boldness rather remarkable than attractive, theorizes upon all. "Politics," "the apparatus of government," "the morals of politics," "public and private economy," "agriculture," "internal improvements," "manufactures," "commerce," "morals of economy," "civilization," "honor," "woman," "children," "sufferers," "utterance," "religion,"—"its science, its spirit, and its administration"—these are the heads under which come up a thousand specifications and subdivisions, upon all of which she is equally copious, bold and dogmatical. How far she may have been ignorant of the United States before she came to this country, and how utterly opinionless she was thereon,—though reading every book she could lay hold of, which treated of the subject,—I will not pretend to determine. Certain it is, she has been anything but slow in forming opinions since her visit. Her *knowledge* of the subject is another matter; and, after all her journeys and essays, I am prepared to give her credit for as little real information, in regard to America, as at the moment of her disembarcation upon our shores. But the want of knowledge in her case implies no want of speech. Her readiness to discuss the theme of which she hears for the first time, reminds us of the happy declaration, a few years ago, by a member of Congress, whose confession, like that of

Miss Martineau, should have prepared us for any other course. "Mr. Speaker," he said *naively*, "I know nothing of the subject under discussion, but I intend to go on argufying it, until I l'arn all the necessary knowledge," &c.

Miss Martineau argues, no doubt, with the same hope, though it is clear that her progress is not exactly in the direction of the desired result. I do not doubt her real ignorance of the subject of America, for the simple reason that all the facts in the world will not avail to make a simple truth, in the case of one who perverts them to the maintenance of a prejudice. As to the passiveness of her mind, in the formation of opinions touching this country, prior to her visit, we may be permitted to doubt a little. She deceived herself, I am very sure, as most English travellers do, on the subject of this dispassionateness. The Halls', Hamilton's, Trollope's, *et id omne genus*, all allege the same grateful impartiality; nay, the greater number of them insist, with Miss Martineau, upon their absolutely democratic tendencies; as if any well educated Englishman could be a democrat, in the vulgar sense of the term, and at the same time an honest man. But the word democrat, with the modern Englishman—I am not now speaking of the Chartists—has really no signification more profound than was implied in the old word Dissenter. Their notion of it implied no revolution—no absolute change, perhaps,—nothing more than a modification of existing conditions,—with a more indulgent recognition on the part of those in power, of the great merits of many, who sat in the king's porch, upon anxious benches—waiters upon providence, in better phrase. But American democracy was an argument in the mouths of these good people, since it is sometimes necessary to appeal to the apprehensions, as well as the wisdom, of men in power. For this reason, American democracy had to be studied, and, if possible, understood. A similar necessity existed in France, and that gave us De Tocqueville. Miss Martineau, possibly, had some design of doing for England, in this respect, what the former had done for France. She might well fancy that there was some special call upon her to do this work. As a democrat after the English fashion—nay, something more,—as a perfect leveller, for the time, in England, the government and institutions of the United States (Slavery always excepted) might well loom up before her imagination in beautiful contrast with those of her own government. Our theories more completely harmonized with her own,—nay, most probably helped to originate them. She could not, accordingly, by any possibility, have escaped the formation of a large body of opinions in relation to our people, society, and institutions; and that she had formed such opinions, and very decisive ones, too, in respect to them, is everywhere apparent in these volumes. It is, indeed, from opinions thus previously formed, upon imperfect data, or facts vitiated by her anomalous theories, that most of her errors have arisen. Her notions of democracy, for example, lead her constantly to overlook the fact, that, whatever may be our abstractions or her own, we have a limited and restraining charter—a constitutional compact—which overrules and overrides, or should do so, every enactment of Congress and the laws. This fact is continually conflicting, in its operations, with the cherished idea in her head. Of course, whenever this happens, we fall short of our theories—our plan is defective—the charter is anomalous—the people are corrupt. The ideal of the good lady furnishes the only correct standard.

On the subject of Slavery in America, her detestation is avowed as having been entertained long before she entered the slave States. It was entertained long before she left England; and very naturally so. The subject, from the labors of Clarkson and others, had been the philanthropic hobby of the

British government and people for many years past. The wisest among their statesmen doubted of the wisdom of this; and the number of doubters among their wise men, increases daily, as the results of the emancipation experiment declare themselves. But, for a considerable period, it was the favorite subject of British declamation; that which cant most delighted to indulge in, and to which national vanity was most pleased to listen. The insane and cruel act which set free the slaves of the British West Indies, to the ruin of that region as well as themselves, was one of those tremendous acts of legislation, by which pride and vanity rear themselves monuments; but, too frequently, at the expense of their country. Abolition, naturally, under the sanction of such an act, became the national cry, the popular watch-word, the subject upon which every well-fed British subject felt himself entitled to expatiate. The habit was prescriptive. There was no opinion in the matter. It was the result of no thought, no examination of the subject. It was simply the embodiment of a self-glorifying phrase, uttered and uttered falsely long before, which proclaimed that the chains fell from the limbs of the slave the moment that he touched the soil of Britain; and this, while Britain was planting African Slavery in America, and subjecting the free-born chiefs and people of the East to war, havoc, spoliation, and the most cruel bondage. Verily, the only monument which truth and the future will rear to the atrocious hypocrisy of such an act of grace as the emancipation of the West India negroes, must be that "whited sepulchre," which, in Scripture language, is made to illustrate that shameless looking up, and challenging the praise of heaven, while doing the work of hell!

It belonged to the generally levelling tendencies of Miss Martineau's character that she should be hostile to the institution of Negro Slavery without regard to its facts. She shared the prejudices of her times and country, and, though a strong-minded woman in many respects, it suited too well with her usual modes of thinking, to set aside the national prejudices, and, looking behind the mere name of odium, which attached to the institution, to inquire into its substantial working and results, by which, alone, the moral uses and propriety of any institution could be determined. Had it not been for this name of odium, and that Slavery had been assimilated with those features of government policy which it was her cue to obliterate, we shou'd have seen her, as we have in latter days seen Carlyle, boldly looking through all the mists and mystifications of the subject, and probing it with an independent analysis, with which neither prescription, nor prejudices, nor selfish policy, could be permitted to interfere. Her self-relying nature would have sufficed for this, had she not determined against Slavery, before acquiring any just knowledge of that condition which has received this name. On this topic, at least, her sentiments were decided long before she left Europe. When she reached New-England, the brotherly love of that region served to heighten this detestation, which thenceforward became so cordial, that all things and thoughts, whatever she saw or heard, only gave it added aliment. It was fed, we are not sorry to add, in most cases, at the previous sacrifice of truth. I do not mean to say that Miss Martineau wilfully related falsehoods, or willingly adopted them. Far from it. I must do her the justice to say that I regard her volumes, as written throughout in good faith, and with a mind of the most perfect integrity; so far as integrity may be predicated of a mind in a condition only of partial sanity. But on the one subject she is a monomaniac, with all the wonderful ingenuity, to pervert the truth, and shape the fanciful to her purposes, which marks the nature of the monomaniac. Biassed and bigoted to the last degree on the subject of Slavery, she could neither believe the truth, when it spoke in behalf of the slaveholder, nor question the falsehood, however gross, when it fell from the lips of the abolitionist. The morbid quality in her mind effectually impaired her ordinary capacity, strong in most other respects, to observe and judge with vigilance and sagacity. Thus, for example, in proof not less of this bias, than of its demoralizing influence upon her mind, we are told that the abolitionists sent no incendiary tracts among the slaves, and that they use no direct means towards promoting their objects in the slave States. "It is wholly untrue that they insinuate their publications into the South." Such is her bold assertion; yet, "Mr. Madison made the charge, so did Mr. Clay, so did every slaveholder and merchant with whom I conversed. I chose afterwards to hear the other side of the whole question; and I found, to my amazement, that this charge was wholly groundless." Here the lady undertakes to decide a question of veracity, with singular composure, in favor of her friends, and at the expense of the first names of the country. Would Miss Martineau have done this, and that too in the assertion of a negative, if she were in full possession of her wits? But, so far from the denial being valid, " of the other side," the matter is one of public notoriety throughout the country; leading, in some cases, to demonstrations, which were beyond question the gutting of post-offices, filled with incendiary documents, and public bonfires of their contents in the streets of large cities.

"Nor did it occur to me," she writes, "that, as slaves cannot read," &c.

This is one of her assertions, her facts, which is as notoriously false as her previous statement. Thousands of negro slaves do read, as any body may see who has ever visited the cities of the South; but, the slaveholders allege—though the abolitionists may deny—that, lest the slave should labor under this disability, and for the better conveying the lesson to the thousands that do read, gross *cuts* are employed in these abolition newspapers, and are even stamped upon manufactured cottons, of the kind usually furnished for negro consumption, and insinuated, here and there, at decent intervals, among the bales designed for the Southern market. Such bales were laid bare to public examination, in the city of Charleston, but a few years before the visit of Miss Martineau. She might have obtained ample evidence from New-England authority, on this point, had she desired it, when in that city.

"Slavery," says our author, "*of a very mild kind*, has been abolished in the northern parts of the Union." What knowledge had Miss Martineau, except from interested parties, by which to enable her to pronounce so authoritatively upon the character of the institution at the North? Slavery, properly speaking, never was abolished at all, in any of the States where it originally obtained. It simply died out, when it ceased to be profitable. In some of the States, no formal enactment was necessary; and we believe it is only within five years that Massachusetts placed any such decree among her statutes; if, indeed, she has yet done so. The New-England States were never, to any great extent, slave-holding; their virtues were chiefly exercised in slave-selling. To New-England and Old England, the South almost wholly owes her slaves. They stole the African from his native land, and bartered him away, without a care what became of him afterwards; their philanthropy by no means disquieted at the reflection that he might fall into the hands of those who might brutally entreat him—a people, not like themselves, proverbially God-fearing and men-loving. They kept but few of their captives among themselves, and those only who were least saleable. It was not profitable to use negro labor in the cold and sterile regions of New-England; nor did any act of abolition, when it did occur, help many of the slaves of that country. The great bulk of their negroes were sold to the South long before it could go into operation. Few were suffered to remain to taste its benefits (?) except the infirm, and here and there an old servant of some wealthy family, who could very well afford to give him that liberty which the dependent rarely sought to assert. This is the true history of Slavery in New-England. We may add—what may be new to our British philanthropists—that it was from the Southern colonies that the prayer was first heard to arise, to the British Parliament, to arrest the further traffic in, and importation of, slaves; a prayer to which the mother country turned a deaf ear always. New-England continued to steal and sell the property which she did not care to keep, and for which she now refuses all warranty. She would still continue to do so, if she could. Her ships still continue the trade at the perils of piracy. The South gave up one of its best securities against New-England morals when it assented to the abolition of the slave trade. But, to proceed with our author.

It is one part of the policy of the abolitionists to urge the continual insecurity which attends the condition of the slaveholder; to show that he sleeps upon the pillow of fear, and that his own convictions forever prompt the dread of vengeance at the hands of his serviles. There is an argument to be deduced from this apprehension, if it could be shown to exist, since any human institution, thus guarded by terror, would seem to be in conflict with the design and decree of Providence. The condition would seem an unnatural one, and the moral which might be drawn from it would appear to be fatal to its propriety. Such, at least, is the assumption; and it is one which we should by no means deny, if the danger arose from the natural movements of the servile mind, and were not instigated from without. But, without engaging in the discussion of this principle, it is enough that we join issue with our enemies upon the fact. Miss Martineau contributes, in a small way, to this portion of the subject, by retailing a number of petty anecdotes;—some ludicrous enough, and others merely foolish and vicious without being ludicrous, to show the feeling of insecurity of the whites of the South, and their dread of the negro population. I quote a single paragraph, by way of sample, from the collection of the lady, and will proceed to analyze it, in order to show the absurdity of the statement. In doing this, it will be seen how singularly obtuse the mind may become, even in the case of one so generally acute as Miss Martineau, when it is inveterate in the pursuit of a given object, and held in bondage to a controlling prejudice.

"At Charleston, when a fire breaks out, the gentlemen all go home on the ringing of the alarm bell; the ladies rise and dress themselves and their children. It may be the signal of insurrection; and the fire burns on, for any help the citizens give, till a battalion of soldiers marches down to put it out."

Now, I take it, that, in any city in the world, slave or free, the gentleman who happens to be absent from his family when the fire-bell rings, will be apt to hurry home to see that all is safe, and to quiet the alarm of his wife and children—particularly, indeed, in a large city, where it is not so easy, at all times, to determine in what quarter the fire rages. It may be in your precincts, or in mine, but while neither of us know, we had better both depart and see. There is nothing at all remarkable in such a proceeding, let it occur among men in any city. Were they not to do so, it would argue a singular degree of indifference to the fate of objects and interests, which, in every community, are considered sufficiently precious. There is surely nothing remarkable in the fact, nor is it peculiar to Charleston, or to any other city in which slaves are held. But, in a city that is largely built of wood—which in comparatively recent times was almost wholly built of wood, and that of the most inflammable kind—the resinous pine—where a fire extends with amazing rapidity, and where the ravages of fire have been alike frequent and terrible,—it becomes especially necessary that the gentlemen should not only make all haste in getting home, but that the lady should be equally prompt in getting her children and other jewels ready for rapid flight. All this would seem natural enough, and these necessities would seem sufficiently justified on other grounds than those of Slavery. "But," says Miss Martineau, blindly as well as deafly blundering into speech, which a single moment of reflection would have made her quietly avoid—"The fire burns on for any help the citizens give, till a battalion of soldiers marches down to put it out." This is grave fooling enough. *Who are the soldiers in Charleston, but the citizens*, and how can *soldiers extinguish a fire?* By guns and bayonets? These two simple questions, had the lady allowed herself sufficient time for inquiry, would have saved her from the emission of such an absurdity. We have none but a citizen soldiery in Charleston, unless you regard the hundred and fifty cadets at the military academy as so many regulars, and count the score or two employées at the United States arsenal, as sufficient guarantees against the negroes in time of fire; but, it so happens, that neither of these bodies leave their separate stations, at such a period, or seek, in any way, the scene of conflagration. But it is easy to account for the lady's error. She had got hold of the tail, rather than the head of the fact, and was resolute to twist it to the required direction, in obedience to her fixed bias. There is just truth enough in her story for the purposes of falsehood; but even this slender capital was too imperfectly understood by our author, to be used with effect. She was too eager to launch her shaft at the slaveholders, to observe that she aimed at them the notched, and not the barbed, extremity. Let us explain. There is an arrangemnt in Charleston, by which a certain portion of the city militia—amounting probably to two hundred men,—is required to appear on parade whenever the alarm of fire is given. This body acts simply as a military police, and is really auxiliary in its duties to the ordinary city police and watch. It did originate, we believe, at the period of the anticipated negro insurrection in Charleston, in 1822; an affair which, we are disposed to think, stands quite alone in the domestic history of that place, and the scheme of which originated in an imported mulatto. But the original cause for the creation of this military police is no longer recognized as the necessity for its continuance. It has other uses. It preserves public order, which is always liable to disturbance on occasions of fire, and protects the property which has been rescued from the flames. So little is the popular apprehension of the slaves, that, of fifteen or twenty fire engines owned by the city, a large number of these is entirely worked by negroes. Those who have seen their excitement on occasions of public duty, have heard the Babel-like uproar of their conflicting tongues, their shouts, cries, clamor, and peculiar eloquence, would be very apt to suppose that they had never been taught the first lesson in subordination.* Certainly no one would suppose that they

* These facts were true when this pamphlet was originally written. There may be some alteration in the present arrangement, with which the writer is less familiar; at that date, the fire system in Charleston was supposed to be particularly complete. The city had so frequently and fearfully suffered, that improvement in the system, and refinement upon it, was inevitable. The citizen soldiery, we

entertained any lurking jealousies or suspicions of their masters, or stood on such doubtful terms with them as might, by possibility, require sharp application from the bayonets of the guard on duty. A sudden shower from the engines would be more calculated to arouse their terror, and would be the most obvious resort of the firemen, in the event of their subordinates showing themselves lazy or unruly—the former exhibition being by far the most likely of the two.

But, even did there exist among the people of Charleston and the South generally, an apprehension of mutiny and revolt among their serviles, to what would it amount? What would it prove? What argument would Miss Martineau and the abolitionist brethren draw from the fact? That the slave is a discontent. That the superior authority anticipates trouble and prepares for strife! Suppose we grant it, and in what then does our condition as a community, and our relations with our slaves, differ from that of any European people? Why are there standing armies in all the states of Europe? Why do grim sentries environ the highways, the posts, stations, railway trains, public walks? Why do the citadels

need not say, do nothing towards extinguishing the fire, as the dear old lady states. That is left to well-drilled companies—hose, and axe and engine. The city watch consists of about 100 men. Thus, to a population of 44,000, is moderate enough; and, during a fire, would be of small value in preserving order. The fire guard, in brief, is an auxiliary police. The detachment is relieved every three months. Their duty, as stated in the text, is chiefly to receive and protect the rescued goods, and to preserve order; since fires are most commonly the work of incendiaries, who avail themselves of the public alarm to plunder. Nor is this the only respect in which the fire police in Charleston is superior There is a salaried officer,—an engineer—who, with certain assistants, is required to appear at every fire, properly provided with powder made up into certain forms, and with the necessary *chevaux-de frise*, for blowing up houses—not negroes!—in order to the more summary arresting of the conflagration by making a vacuum.

look down with grinning muzzles upon the streets of the peaceful city? Why is the simple traveller, the single man, compelled to carry his passport, and get it *viséd* at every stage in his journey—nay, why is he denied to journey in certain of the states of Europe at all? Why are the walks of the great city garrisoned with spies to report the sayings and doings of the populace? Why does England growl at the bare mention of Ireland, and present her bayonets, if she but stirs, in her stagnating sleep? And why does France burden herself with the support of half a million of armed men? Why does Russia the same? Why is Austria only a great camp? Why does New-York call out its militia to support the sheriff and collect the rents of the Patroon—and unavailingly? But why multiply the questions which can have but one answer? It is because authority every where dreads the revolt of the impatient, toiling, vexed, weary and ignorant inferiority—because, slavish and superstitious, anxious to luxuriate in forbidden pleasures; loathing the decreed toils which are wholesome; envious of the wealth which they have not patience to wait for, or virtue to forbear to crave,—they would have the day's pay without doing the day's work, and long to vote themselves ease and affluence out of the possessions of the wealthier classes. That the people of the Southern States should adopt some precautions—some regulations, by which to make their repose secure—is only what is done in Europe, at greater expense,—in more imposing array,—with greater ostentation of men and weapons. It is absolutely absurd to speak of such police regulations as prevail in Carolina, as of any significance at all, when we consider the precautions of the same sort which distinguish every state in Europe; but, when we add, that the civil and military police of South-Carolina, and of any of the Southern States, bears no such proportion to the total of the population as occurs in the states and cities of the North, we may quietly suffer this count in Miss Martineau's indictment to remain without more waste of words in answer. The police of Charleston is nothing to that of New-York, making a due relative estimate of the two populations; yet, in the former, such a thing as a riot is never heard of. There, no portion of the population, the blackest and the poorest, is so degraded as to need to be shot down by scores for the maintenance of order and the security of society.

In the chapter devoted to "Revenue and Expenditure," we are told, in an extraneous sentence, which is closed with a note of exclamation, that in "South-Carolina there is a tax on free people of color!" Had it not been that Miss Martineau was too well satisfied with the surface of the fact, she would have inquired farther; in the New-England States she certainly would have done so; but it was quite enough to show that in Carolina a special poll tax was levied upon the unhappy free negro. Let us complete the fact, and probably do away with the mystery and injustice, by stating that the same free person of color enjoys an exemption from militia, from patrol, jury, guard and other duties, and is required to perform no military service in time of war. For such exemption the white mechanic and laborer—indeed, most white men—would be very well pleased to pay ten times the amount paid by the free negro as a capitation tax. But, says the abolitionist, these duties are privileges, and the exemption of the free negro, however grateful to his love of ease, is still in the nature of a forfeiture. Precisely; but it is such a forfeiture as is conceived proper to his natural disabilities. Our women are similarly exempt. The system with us, whether it regards the free negroes or the slave, goes on the assumption that he belongs to an inferior race, to whom such trusts, where the rights of the superior race are concerned, would be improperly confided. I shall have something further to say on this topic in another place.

In the remarks of our author upon the policy and institutions of Carolina, to which I chiefly confine myself, there are numerous other points, like the preceding, involving error, either of fact or inference, which might be exposed with little difficulty, were it worth my while to pursue such small game. But, merely to multiply instances, when a few can be made to illustrate the whole, would trespass, without profitable result, upon the time of the reader. All these blunders of our author are to be ascribed to the one cause—her bias on the subject of Slavery. This bias has been of a character so tyrannical, as to derange her intellect, and utterly to baffle her reasoning faculties, the moment she recurs to it. She can make no correct observations, or exercise any proper judgment, in any matter with which this subject is coupled, however remotely or incidentally. To those who think for themselves, and examine honestly,—her errors, in the greater number of cases, as in those we have instanced. carry their refutation on the face of them. They were unavoidable in a progress such as hers, and could not but occur to a person who, like herself, pursued her travels, and made her observations, with regard simply to a support of her theories. What one wills to see is readily seen; what one resolves to believe, for that he will find sufficient proofs; and that which already constitutes a controlling faith in the mind, will never lack for a cloud of witnesses. Miss Martineau can summon any number. The vague apprehensions of women, filled with fears and suspicions in due degree with their ignorance, are already gravely written in her chronicles. Her informants are frequently Northern women, who have married and removed to the South. If not readily admitted into society, they revenge themselves upon it by their slanders. Such persons are always anxious to get away from a region where they can make no figure; and their lives are wasted in envious repinings, in complainings and vaporings, and in a studied misconstruction of the circumstances in which they live. What Miss Martineau hears of the fears of the Southern people, are from such witnesses; and they serve her in stead on all occasions. It needs, for all such persons, but the slenderest support of fact, to justify the most monstrous revelations. These charges against the South, drawn from such sources, are of the most hotch-potch character, and, of whatever sort, they are fastened, as a matter of course, upon Slavery. Of the rapes, hangings, burnings, murders, which have happened upon the Southern border for fifty years, Miss Martineau makes a grateful collection, and licks her lips over them with the air of one about to gratify a very avid appetite. She records many of which the people of the South never heard. She enters into no such statistics at the North,— but sets out, seemingly, with the assumption that they are to be looked for only in the precincts of the slaveholder. She does not seem to have asked about the offences against good morals in New-York and Philadelphia, or the quality and color of the offenders in those cities. If she hears that a slave poisons an owner in Carolina, though this event may occur once in a hundred years, she crows over it lustily. The very instance which she records was given to her as a remarkable one, yet she wilfully assumes it to be a common occurrence, in spite of its notorious isolation. But the crimes of the free negroes at the North, with whose condition alone, the comparison should be made of the Southern slave, entirely escape her attention. Crimes and atrocities which occur in all communities, and which simply indicate the bad passions and vicious heart of the criminal, are assumed to be peculiar to the state of Slavery; while, the truth is, the South is confessedly the region of all the United States, where the criminal never prospers. Compare its criminal reports with those that reach us daily from the North. How many women are cruelly murdered in the Northern cities—sometimes by priests, sometimes by professors; by merchants and merchants' clerks. What a volume of depravity was unfolded in the trial of Robinson; and there was the case of Avery, and the case of Colt, and the case of Webster—a series of the most bloody, base, cowardly murders, ar d all for money, or to get rid of an importunate creditor. So deliberately done, too, the crime—beguiling the creditor to the shambles, butchering him and cutting him up, and pickling him, and packing him away, in boxes, coal holes, privies; decomposing him with lime, and acids and vitriol. And the criminals all among " our best citizens!" Of course, the offender mostly escapes, if he be not poor. If he be poor, he goes to the gallows or the state prison. The finding of the jury, declaring that the supposed murderer is not guilty, does not do away with the fact that the poor victim, man or woman, is murdered—nor does it diminish the aggravation that they are almost invariably murdered with impunity. The newspapers frequently record forgeries by priests, by priests' sons, and by the founders of splendid cities; and while they wonder passingly that such good people should turn out so bad, their chief regrets are, the loss of such enterprising citizens to the fine cities for which they did so much. Alleged rapes, by negroes upon white girls, are frequently stated by Northern journalists. We refer to Mr. Tappan for such particulars as resulted from the examination of the Commissioners of the Magdalen Asylum into the morals of New-York; and we regret that Miss Martineau had not looked more closely into the negro quarters, and into the various police trials of negro offenders in the different cities of the free States. Had she done this, she would have spared us the entire chapter on the morals of Slavery. Indeed, had she as narrowly examined the brothels, and the stews, and the alleys, and sinks of London—with as keen a nostril as she has thrust into the Southern country, she would have paused before taking ship for the New World; and, as a good Christian, would have addressed herself to the augean duty of cleansing out her own stables. It is a modern British statistician who tells us that, in London alone, there are five thousand persons who will cut your throat for a shilling. But why linger upon that royal lazar-house of suffering, infamy and crime, which England offers, in all her recesses, to the hopeless inspection of the philosopher. We have only to read the narratives of her own statesmen, descriptive of the sable horrors of the collieries, to feel that rebuke from Britain is the saddest and stupidest of all impertinences. It is to take a harder test, for trying the South, that we invite the comparison with the free States of our own country. Our crimes in the South are not only fewer, but very different in character from theirs. With us, such a thing as the murder of a woman is never heard of, or so rarely as to make the event a marvel. Our men engage in deadly combat with one another—proud, passionate men, filled with mortified ambition, and goaded by public indignity. But secret murders are infrequent. Throat-cutting to escape a debt or dun, is not among our chronicles; you never hear, among us, of infernal machines sent into a family, in the guise of innocent mahogany cases, to explode when opened, and blow a fearful household into eternity. But why pursue the contrast? It is one that every day's intelligence only serves to heighten.

The antipathy of Miss Martineau to the slaveholder, sometimes results in an amusing exposure of her absurd injustice. Take a sample or two. At page 44, vol. i, she says:

"In the Senate, the people's right of petition is invaded. Last session, it was ordained that all petitions and memorials relating to a particular subject—Slavery in the District of Columbia—should be laid on the table, unread, and never recurred to. Of course the people will not long submit to this!"

Mark how her tone changes, in a case exactly parallel—when it is *my* bull which has gored *your* ox! At page 70, of the same volume, we find a similar proceeding of Congress dismissed with a complacency quite remarkable, when compared with the evident indignation of the preceding paragraph. She is now speaking of Carolina nullification, and the violent opposition of the State Rights portion of the country to the protective policy of the Eastern States.

"Congress," says she, "went on legislating about the tariff without regard to this opposition; and the *protests of certain States*, against their proceedings, *were quietly laid on the table as impertinences!*"

The hatred of the white towards the colored population is a subject of her notice, and she tells an anecdote, of which she has probably heard only a portion of the particulars.

"Lafayette," says she, "on his last visit to the United States, expressed his astonishment at the increase of the prejudice against color. He remembered, he said, how the black soldiers used to mess with the whites in the revolutionary war."

Had Miss Martineau asked the particulars of this change, which she should have done, she would have found that it was a change altogether confined to those regions where Slavery had been done away with! The black soldiers were employed, as such, at a time when their brethren (and themselves also, probably) were *slaves*, and were modestly satisfied with their condition of inferiority. By emancipation, and the pettings of philanthropy, the coarse and uneducated negro became lifted into a condition to which his intellect did not entitle him, and to which his manners were unequal;—he became presumptuous accordingly, and consequently offensive;—and the whites, who could have tolerated him in his proper and inferior condition, were naturally outraged by the impudence of the creature when lifted out of place. There is no doubt that he is an object of dislike and hatred in the Northern cities, and with good reason. He is a rival without being an equal; a competitor without like responsibilities with those to whom he opposes himself. He is presumptuous in due degree with his sense of irresponsibility. His habits of idleness increase his presumption, while lessening his moral, wretchedly feeble from the first. The complaint of the white population of the North is always to this effect. The blacks do not labor on the same terms with the whites. In fact, they will not labor at all if they can escape it. They will do jobs, do light *chores*, brush boots, go on errands, sweep, tinker, and thieve,—the latter upon the same petty scale which marks all their performances. They skulk all manly and honorable toils, such as the white prefers, boldly undertakes, and vigorously performs. The black still seeks the position of the menial, and is despised accordingly; in that position he is easily rendered impudent, for his conceit is intolerable when at large, like that of a monkey; when impudent he grows offensive, and hence hateful. He must be always despicable in any community which leaves him at liberty, and where he shrinks from grappling with the higher toils and purposes which alone can dignify the possession of freedom.

The case is far otherwise where Negro Slavery exists. In the South, the negro is not an object of dislike or hatred. There, he never offends by obtrusiveness; he occupies his true position, and, while he fills it modestly, he is regarded with favor, nay, respect and love, and is treated with kindness and affection. And this would be the result, North as well as South, if he did not contend for an equality of position with a people to whom he is morally and physically inferior. When he does this, he provokes hatred inevitably, and must live in a condition of perpetual insecurity. If his moral were not so glaringly inferior to his assumptions, and those made for him, at the North, he would be torn to pieces by the laboring classes among the whites. As it is, he frequently incurs this danger. I need not surely refer to the frequent drubbings which he receives, even in his wigwam, in the negro quarters of the great cities. It is to him no castle. He is sometimes torn out of it, neck and heels, by the mob, and his den demolished about his ears. But, when these things take place, our benevolent abolitionists ascribe the outrage to the influence of the slaveholders. Listen to Miss Martineau, at one moment, and she will persuade you that these slaveholders absolutely rule the Northern cities; that their influence is sovereign for evil every where; and is mortally vexed at certain friendly relations between Boston and Charleston, of which cities she deals in terms not less insulting to their communities than complimentary to the minds by which they are supposed to be governed. But, a moment after, she forgets the prodigious influence over the North for which she has given credit to the South, and then tells us, that the latter seeks for disunion *because she is without influence.* She then treats us to a stock of anecdotes, showing the envy and hatred of the latter towards the North, because of this deficiency. Envy of the North by the South! The boot is on the other leg, perhaps. So far from envy, the error of the South is in the indulgence of quite too complacent an estimate of its own resources. The South is frequently made indignant at the assumptions of the North, resenting frequent injustice and wrong which, in other countries, would be called rank robbery! But envy—never! That is not the Southern vice or weakness, though it may have many vices for which to answer.

I could multiply extracts, page on page, to show the heated, the malignant prejudices which darken the eyes, and baffle the faculties of our author;—but of what use? A few specimens may serve. She looks at all things in our country as through a blackened glass. The eyes of her mind are jaundiced—they are not healthy—they never will be healthy, until she substitutes Christianity for that shrewd sort of philosophy which is so grateful to human vanity, and which so betrays the heart. Her eyes need the helping hand of that benign occulist, Truth; and truth will only be able to touch them successfully, when she has first had them well washed by that gentle handmaid, whom moralists call Humility. As yet, neither of them can do any thing for her case. Could she enjoy the restoration of one faculty, by the forfeit of another;—could she recover her hearing by the surrender of her speech;—there might be hope of her. Now, she is too talkative to listen, too deaf to hear, too confident of herself to learn, even should Truth, in visible embodiment, descend divinely to become her teacher! But let us proceed with our instances.

"When to all this is added that tremendous curse, the possession of irresponsible power over slaves," &c.

There is no such irresponsibility in America. Ordinarily, and in most cases, the interests of the owner are sufficient protection for the slave. It is his policy to prolong his life, to preserve his health, to promote his strength, and to give him contentment. These objects imply adequate food and clothing, indulgent nurture, moderate tasks, and, as much, if not more leisure, than is allotted usually to the laboring classes in any country. The laws protect him also—as a being of inferior *caste*, it is true—but they do protect him, in correspondence with what is the obvious policy of the master. He is as effectually secured against wrong and murder as the white man, and his securities are as unfrequently outraged. The murder of the negro, slave or free, is punished with death. Wanton injuries against him are redressed by the courts, as in the case of the white man, and the courts will entertain an action for damages for an assault even upon his character. That there will be instances in which he suffers wrong, blows, brutalities and loss of life, are undeniable; but these risks are not peculiar to the slave. It will be time enough to ascribe these offences against humanity, to the institution of Slavery, when it is shown that free states and communities enjoy exemption from them. We insist, and challenge investigation, that the crimes of all descriptions, brutality, murder and violence, occur less frequently in the slave than in the free States, and that, even as they occur in the slave States, the negro is less frequently the sufferer than the white man.

"A planter," says Miss Martineau, "stated to a sugar refiner in New-York, that it was found the best economy to work off the stock of negroes once in seven years."

Miss Martineau's credulity, on the subject of slave atrocities, is sufficiently English. Such an assertion should not be made but upon the most unquestionable authority. It would, I fancy, be a subject of some difficulty to point out the Louisiana planter who finds it the best economy to wear out his machinery as rapidly as possible. It would be equally difficult, I apprehend, to bring forth the sugar refiner to support the indictment. As an honest man,—as a man of any sort—he should have denounced by name the heartless wretch by whom the speech was made. But this is of a piece with the usual fictions of the abolitionists, which most commonly defeat their malice by their absurdities. It is possible that such a speech *was* made; but supposing it true, it proves nothing. To show that there is an individual monster in the slave States, argues nothing against their morals. It must be shown that his case is not the exception, but the ordinary history. There is a work of fiction, recently published by Mrs. Stowe, which is just now the rage with the abolitionists; the great error of which, throughout, consists in the accumulation of all the instances that can be found of cruelty or crime among the slaveholders. Admit all her statements to be true, and they prove nothing. Her facts may be susceptible of proof, while her inferences are wholly false. Take an example from this very work of fiction, (Uncle Tom's Cabin,) which illustrates this error of reasoning among our enemies. She shows us a planter of Louisiana, as one of the most heartless, bloody, brutal, gross, loathsome and ignorant wretches under the sun. She gives us the most shocking details of his inhumanities; but, in doing so, *she herself isolates him.* She shows that *he resides in a remote, and scarcely inaccessible swamp region, where his conduct comes under no human cognizance.* How is society answerable for his offences? How does he represent the condition and character of the slaveholder? The very isolation of his position and of the case, is conclusive against its application. When to this we add, that the equal necessities of truth and fiction seem to have compelled her, though a Yankee, to admit that this brutal specimen is a Yankee also, we may reasonably, without shaking our skirts, refer his responsibilities back to his native parish.

We have been apt, in the South, to think and to assert, that there are few people so very well satisfied with their condition as the negroes,—so happy of mood, so jocund, and so generally healthy and cheerful. Such has been the general admission of the traveller. But Miss Martineau, seeing through her own eyes, gives very different testimony. She never saw " in any brute, an expression of countenance so low, so lost, as in the most degraded classes of negroes. There is some life and intelligence in the countenance of every animal; even in that of the silly sheep; nothing so dead as the vacant, unheeding look of the depressed slave is to be seen."

The *depressed* slave, we suppose, will look depressed, just as the white man in a state of depression. There is no combating the statement as it is made; but it is so put as to convey the idea that such is the usual appearance of the slave, and as the natural result of his condition. Unless this be meant, the passage is simply absurd and gratuitous; nobody need be told that men who suffer will be apt to look like sufferers. It is the testimony of travellers generally—British mostly—and Miss Martineau among them—that the American countenance generally (that of the whites) is that of a people care-worn and prematurely old. This is ascribed by the same charitable persons to the greedy avarice of the people, the degrading, intense and unintermitted worship of the " eternal dollar." The exceptions which they have made, when this sarcasm was to be established, were all in favor of the slave. Even in the pages of our author, we might find a dozen passages which go to this effect, and thus conflict with that which we have quoted; and, but that it appeared to serve the purposes of Miss Martineau's single object and argument, to show the brutalizing processes of slavery upon its subjects, we think it very probable that she would have seen very differently. The prevailing desire of the mind but too commonly imparts its own color to the eyes, and when it fails to do so, the perversely hostile soon discovers some ingenious method by which to evade the argument which is suggested by the senses. Thus, when Dr. Lardner was in this country, and on a visit to Carolina, he found himself forced to wonder at the exceeding comfort, and great cheerfulness and contentment of the negro. He freely admitted that nowhere were the laboring classes better, if so well treated, as our slaves. Their sprightliness particularly commanded his notice, their buoyancy and happy *abandon*. So far, his eyes beheld things through a different medium from Miss Martineau; but the Doctor was philosophically perverse; and more ingenious, in the adoption and use of the fact, than the lady in rejection of it. His regret and complaint were that the silly negroes were so cheerful, so content, so happy, so well fed, clothed, and generally entreated. Why? do you suppose? "*Because, it permanently reconciled them to their condition!*" We ask, with surprise— Well! if so, is not this *primâ facie* evidence that the condition is the very best for them? "Not so!" the Doctor substantially replies, "for the sufficient reason that *it conflicts with certain ideas in my mind on that subject!*" This is the difficulty with all these people. The Doctor was a better observer than philosopher. He blundered in this case, as he did in his relations with Mrs. Heavyside. The Doctor's eyes showed him, truly, that the lady was fair to look upon; it was his moral philosophy that failed him, not his senses, when he broke the commandments, and lusted after his neighbor's wife.

In further illustration of the tendency of our minds to control our capacities for observation, and the just use of our senses, I give another instance, in the case of another traveller in the South. Mr. Charles Hoffman, of New-York, a gentleman of good family, and the author of several works of merit, recently (1836) put forth a couple of volumes of travels in the South and West. On his arrival in Virginia, he is startled with a spectacle, such as he has never before witnessed, and which painfully reminds him that he is in a slave

State. What is that spectacle? A stout, able-bodied white man is beheld, sitting, or lying at ease, in his piazza, while an old negro is at work, hoe in hand, in the contiguous fields! Is it not curious that Mr. Hoffman should never have seen this spectacle a thousand times a day in the streets of New-York;—should not have beheld the wealthy nabob at his palace windows, along Broadway, or Fifth Avenue, reclining in state, under crimson or azure curtains, canopied like a prince, while the aged laborer plies his weary toil, without cessation, in the streets below;—driving the iron ram down upon the unmalleable stone, paving the highways, or, in midsummer, piling bricks, bearing the hod to the house-top, sawing wood and lifting luggage, performing toils a thousand times more heavy than any task which is put upon the shoulders of the Southern slave? The one condition proves the existence of slavery no more than the other; and there is no sort of reason why the spectacle should give pain in one more than in the other instance. They both simply declare for the universal inequalities of fortune in all parts of the world. But it was the contrast of color which smote the eyes, and drew the attention, of our traveller to the fact in Virginia, which he had never witnessed in New-York. In New-York, the negro is seldom caught doing hard work of any sort, and he wins that sympathy in the South, from the Northern traveller, which the latter does not seem to have accorded to the sufferings of the working class at home.

"There is an obligation by law to keep an overseer, to obviate insurrection."

This is said of Alabama. It may be true or not. It is possible that there is a similar regulation in Carolina. If so, it is pretty nearly obsolete. There is scarcely any need of such a law; and certainly none, in reference to the event which is assigned as the reason for its enactment. It would seem sufficiently to justify the practice of keeping an overseer, on estates where the owner is not present, that the profit of the plantation would dwindle to nothing without one. In Carolina and Alabama, as in New-England, the interests of the proprietor would sufficiently suggest the necessity of such an employée. I know, indeed, of no part of the world, in which, if the subordinates be numerous, the overseer can safely be dispensed with. He is employed, if not necessary, in every factory of the free States. According to Miss Martineau, the purpose of the overseer is to prevent that which, as a white man, it would be equally his policy to resist and prevent, though not employed as an overseer. He is in the same ship with his employer, and the storm which would sink the one, would not be likely to spare the other. But what would the efforts of one overseer, a single man, in charge frequently of an hundred slaves, avail against their outbreak? The suggesiton is an absurdity. He is empolyed with regard to other objects; to regulate, to direct, the labor of the negroes; to see that they work; that they make a crop; to keep them from roving about the country, robbing hog-pens and hen-roosts, and doing those things which occur to the negro, as, perhaps, the only advantages that could possibly result to him from his freedom. As for insurrection, nobody who knows any thing of the country, or its people, has any apprehensions on the subject. Men retire to their beds at night, on plantations surrounded with slaves, without locking a door or bolting a window.

"For any responsible service," says Miss Martineau, "slaves are quite unfit."

This is not true. But, assuming it to be true, she infers that it is because they are slaves that they are thus irresponsible. What is the fitness of the free negro at the North—what his responsibility? In the South, we have ample evidence of their *fitness*, whenever they are faithful. The Virginia and Carolina negro is not only superior to the African savages, from whom they sprung, but, when they have had the advantages of training among the whites, they prove themselves very far superior to the free redmen of the country. The latter defer to them in most seasons of difficulty. They make them frequently their own and the "sense-keepers" of the nation. The negro slave, Abraham, was the master mind among the Seminoles. He guided the councils of "Micanopy" and others; and had the policy of the United States been a little more subtle, they might have prevented the last war with the Seminoles, by proper *douceurs* to Abraham. In respect to this subject of the negro intellect in the slave condition, Miss Martineau's book is full of contradictions. In one place, we are told that the slaves show themselves susceptible of education in numberless respects; in another, they are denied the capacity to cut out their own garments. In the assertion of either case, the good lady makes it prove the curse and crime of slavery. If the negro is shown to have improved, she insists that it is an improvement in spite, and not in consequence, of his subjection; and that his progress in a free condition would have been far greater;—if he fails, and shows himself incapable, it is only because he is degraded by his bonds into fatuity. In the South, nobody denies their susceptibility to training; none who do not readily acknowledge and assert their improvement. There are certain arts in which they may excel—certain employments for which they are specially fitted. Some of the best dress makers and tailors in the South are slaves. The mulatto has a genius for barbering and hair-dressing. The black makes a first rate butcher, and as a fish and melon vender is incomparable. His eloquence in crying his wares, however rude, is very efficient. In the cities of the South, the barbers, many of the butchers, and several of the tavern keepers, are slaves or free negroes, quite respected, shrewd, intelligent, and usually prosperous in all these occupations.

Miss Martineau not unfrequently takes the position of the slaveholder, and argues his case for him, simply to show the weakness of his cause. The defence is usually pitiful enough. To show our own inequality to the argument, she records all our angry speeches; and the disputant whom, on another subject, she would scorn to notice, is honored with a heedful ear, and a chronicled remembrance, when he utters himself, in a heat, and savagely, on a topic which is at all times apt to provoke us. " We have our slaves and mean to keep them," was never spoken by any Southern gentleman, by way of *argument* on the subject of Slavery ; but in defiance ; shortly, to answer an insolent party seeking to exercise a power in the councils of the Federal Government, in relation to a subject over which the Southron denies that government shall exercise any jurisdiction ; or in answer, perhaps, to some impudent foreigner, stupidly pressing upon a mood which his own provocations have rendered irritable to the last degree.

Speaking of the Southampton insurrection, Miss Martineau says—" It happened *before* the abolition movement began ; for it is remarkable that no insurrections have taken place since the friends of the slave have been busy *afar off ;*" " whereas rebellions broke out as often as once a month before ; there have been none since." Of this frequency of rebellion we hear for the first time. In regard to the rest of this matter, we shall say but few words. Our author confounds cause with effect. She should have said that the Southampton insurrection broke out before the secret workings of the abolitionists had been generally detected or suspected. The insurrections ceased the moment that the loving labors of the abolitionists were discovered, and when they were constrained to be "busy *only* afar off." The fact, as well as the phrase, is a very significant one. The moment that the South roused itself, grew angry, drove the abolitionists off, and burned their pamphlets and tracts, the insurrections, "which had broke out as often as once a month before," entirely ceased! There have been none since. The good lady needs glass eyes!

The failure of Christian preaching among the slaves, in making them any better, is next insisted on as the result of slavery; as if slavery, which requires submission and obedience on the part of the inferior, was not really an auxiliary to the Christian preliminary of humility. But any one who should report an improved condition of religion at the North, in the *free States*, black or white, would greatly peril his honest conscience.

"The testimony of slaveholders was explicit as to no moral improvement having taken place in consequence of the introduction of religion. There was less singing and dancing; but as much lying, drinking and stealing as ever."

The question might here be asked, who are the authorities for the statement? It is too general and sweeping to be true. In regard to some regions, the report is false; and in others it is, perhaps, only true, in consequence of the peculiar quality of the so-called religion which wast aught. But the vices named are not confined to the slaves; and the budget of horrors, brutalities and miscellaneous crimes, which the book of Miss M. unfolds, as of occurrence among the free people of the country, should have taught her to hesitate ere she ascribed the short-comings of the negro to slavery. The very abolition of singing and dancing, as the result of the religion, must sufficiently show the sort of religion which was busy; and should certainly have produced some doubt, in the mind of one so subtle on most subjects as the writer, whether the religion itself which, at the outset, subverted the innocent and natural recreations of a simple people, was not likely to produce even greater evils than it professed to cure. The philosophical mind has long since been anxiously watchful of the fearful progress of a gloomy bigotry throughout the land. Miss Martineau should not have treated it so blindly—suffering her own infirmity to obscure to her view a subject of the greatest popular importance. She should have remembered, while ascribing to slavery the defeat and failure of the professors of religion to make any impression upon the slaves, what she has herself said of their progress among the red men, who are freed from all the restraints which she deems so pernicious to the black. The gloomy and ascetic doctrines of our teachers have resulted only in the greater depravation of the savage: while the French Catholics, who taught an easier faith, and indulgent laws of exercise and recreation, have been eminently successful in improving them. "Near Little Traverse, in the north-west part of Michigan," says Miss Martineau, "there is an Indian village, full of orderly and industrious inhabitants, employed chiefly in agriculture. The English and Americans have never succeeded with the aborigines so well as the French; *and it may be doubted whether the clergy have been a much greater blessing than the traders.*"

There is one passage in Miss Martineau's book which calls for the serious attention of the philosopher. We quote the passage entire. She is describing the State asylum for lunatics, in Columbia, South-Carolina. "I observed that no people of color were visible in any part of the establishment. I inquired whether negroes were as subject to insanity as whites. Probably; but no means were known to have been taken to ascertain the fact. From the violence of their passions, there could be no doubt that insanity must exist among them.

Were such insane negroes ever seen? No one present had ever seen any. Where were they, then? It was some time before I could get a clear answer to this: *but my friend, the physician, said, at length, that he had no doubt they were kept in outhouses, chained to logs, to prevent their doing mischief.*"

It is singular, indeed, that we should find so very few insane persons among the blacks. The absence of all care for the morrow, for the future, for their own support in age, and the support of their children, together with the restraints of labor, tending to the subjection of those intense passions of which Miss Martineau speaks, and which are not in consequence so active, I am inclined to think, in the negro, as in the white man, must greatly abridge the tendency to insanity; and it may be that the generally inferior activity of their minds, is one cause of their freedom from this dreadful malady. Certain it is, that we have few or no madmen among the negroes. The idea that they are chained in out-houses to logs, is idle enough; since, in that condition, they would require the constant attention of one or more able slaves, which a master would not be willing to afford; and would be, in other respects, a monstrous annoyance. Were insanity at all common among them, "it would be," in Miss Martineau's own language, " the interest of masters to provide for their useless or mischievous negroes;"—and this—were there sufficient occasion—would have been the case. But, in truth, there is little or no madness in South-Carolina, whether among black or white.* The lunatic asylum is not a popular

* Since these passages were penned, the United States census confirms our facts, and thus justifies our inferences. The reader need not be reminded of the official statement of Mr. Calhoun, when Secretary of State, under Tyler, comparing the relative insanity of the North and South, and the blind rage which followed the exposure among the abolitionists.

institution in the State, as it is known to be unprofitable, and was believed to be unnecessary. The patients are usually very few—not enough to support the establishment—and these, in half the number of instances, are drawn from other States. The few cases of madness known in the State, prior to the establishment of the present asylum, were kept in a small building, devoted to the purpose, in Charleston, connected with the Poor establishment of that city. Among the inmates there were one or two negroes, both women—I do not think that there were more. The number was greater during the revolution, when the building appropriated to their confinement stood in the same neighborhood with the fabric more recently put to their use, and both within a short distance of the place of arms, or arsenal, which, when Charleston fell into the possession of the British, was assigned as the depôt for the reception of the weapons of the defenders. A melancholy fate attended the maniacs, in consequence of this propinquity. The American prisoners, ordered to deposit their arms in the arsenal, under the feelings of mortified pride and shame, which, naturally enough, followed the surrender of their city, threw the weapons and ammunition confusedly together, into the hall designed for them, without any heed to the danger of such carelessness. The consequences were dreadful. The building was blown up, the guard of British soldiers, fifty in number, destroyed, and the contiguous houses, the poor-house and mad-house, destroyed also, with the greater number of their unhappy inmates.

But, to return to our author. Miss Martineau does not let this opportunity slip, of conveying an imputation of inhumanity at the expense of the slaveholders.

"No member of society is charged with the duty of investigating cases of disease and suffering among slaves, who cannot make their own state known. They are wholly at the mercy of their owners."

We had almost called these wilful misstatements. The grand juries of the country are bound to take cognizance of all such matters, and do so whenever occasion requires. The slaves, themselves, will always contrive to make their sufferings known, and have few scruples in complaining, whether they have cause or not. A brutal master is sometimes punished, and always known; and his offences against law and humanity, in the treatment of his slaves, are quite as often the subject of public inquiry and prosecution, as in any other cases over which juries possess jurisdiction. But it is not often that he offends by their ill-treatment. His interest in the life and health of his slave obviates the necessity of any particular supervision of the subject by the public authorities. No better security has ever yet been devised by man, for the safety of man, and the proper observance of humane laws by the citizen, than that which the Southern slaveholder offers, in the continual presence of his leading interests. It would be fortunate for the country if the securities of the abolitionist to society were half so good. As for the chaining of the negro lunatic in outhouses, the notion is ridiculous. A case of temporary necessity like this may have occurred, but nothing more. A madman, chained in an outhouse, would be a sufficient source of disquiet to all the country round; and the neighborhood would soon rise, *en masse*, and compel his removal to a place of safe-keeping.

There is one painful chapter in these two volumes, under the head of "Morals of Slavery." It is painful, because it is full of truth. It is devoted to the abuses, among slaveholders, of the institution of slavery; and it gives a collection of statements which are, no doubt, in too many cases, founded upon fact, of the illicit and foul conduct of some among us, who make their slaves the victims and the instruments, alike, of the most licentious passions. Regarding our slaves as a dependent and inferior people, we are their natural and only guardians; and to treat them brutally, whether by wanton physical injuries, by a neglect, or perversion of their morals, is not more impolitic than it is dishonorable. We do not quarrel with Miss Martineau for this chapter. The truth—though it is not all truth—is quite enough to sustain her and it; and we trust that its utterance may have that beneficial effect upon the relations of master and slave in our country, which the truth is, at all times, most likely to have every where. Still, we are not satisfied with the spirit with which Miss M. records the grossness which fills this chapter. She has exhibited a zest in searching into the secrets of our prison-house, in the slave States, which she does not seem to have shown in any other quarter. The female prostitution of the South is studiously looked after, as if it were the peculiar result of slavery. She makes no corresponding inquiry into the *prostitution of the North*. She picks up no tales of vice in that quarter—no rapes—no murders—no robberies—no poisoning—no stabbing. She has addressed her whole mind to the search after these things in the *slave States;* and, with a strange singleness of vision, she has entirely forborne the haunts of the negro at the North, and the degraded classes in the free States. She says nothing whatsoever about them. Had she demanded of Mr. Tappan a copy of the report of the Commissioners of the Magdalen Asylum, of New-York, of which he was the President, and one of the founders, she would have been told by that publication, that, in the city of New-York alone, not including blacks, there are ten thousand professional prostitutes. We do not answer for the truth of this assertion; but as Miss M. has bestowed, elsewhere, a most lavish eulogy upon the veracity and general good character of the abolitionists, and as Mr. Tappan has been heretofore regarded as the very Coryphœus of that fraternity, she will be able to determine for herself the degree of confidence which she should yield to this statement. The fact is, that, in the Southern States, the prostitutes of the communities are usually slaves, unless when imported from the free States. The negro and the colored woman, in the South, supply the place which, at the North, is usually filled with factory and serving girls. The evil is one for which good morals can offer no apology in any region; but this may be said of it in the South, that it affects, there, a race which has not yet been lifted into sensibilities, the possession of which necessarily brings, with indulgence in the vice, the consciousness of degradation. It does not debase the civilized, as is the case with prostitution at the North. It scarcely, in any way, affects the mind of the negro, and does not materially affect his social *status*. The case is far otherwise with white prostitution. The only way to judge of the vice, in connection with slavery, is to compare its practice in both regions, North and South. Prostitution seems to be an incident of humanity, in its fallen state. Napoleon, finding it ineradicable from the community, legislated for it, and thus ameliorated some of its evils. If the practice were not great in, and common to, all communities, savage and civilized, bond and free, it might be permitted to dwell upon its aspects, as they show themselves especially in the slave States; but not as the matter stands with all. We may, and do, acknowledge our guilt in the South, but not as slaveholders; and, looking at all the regions of the earth, we may add, "those, only, who are least guilty, may be permitted to cast the stone!"

We are perfectly safe in saying that two-thirds of these volumes are devoted to the slavery question, and in the States of the South. Now, the lady gives us a body of assumed facts; now, her declamations upon them; and, anon, a subtle topic of metaphysics, by way of novel speculation. Setting forth evidently with the resolve to uproot and utterly destroy an institution which she has previously resolved to be evil, she sees no aspect of it which is not so. The kindness of the master to the slave is likened to the kindness which he has for his dog; the affection of the slave, and his respect for one whom he looks up to as greatly superior, is ascribed to the fear of punishment, or the utter fatuity of his intellect. Every anecdote of cruelty which she hears is religiously written down, and honestly believed; and even the jealous apprehensions of a jaundiced wife, who fears that her husband is no better than he should be, are chronicled with a sad solemnity—which is amusing enough—as the fruit of slavery. The outrages of the borderers—the frontier law of "regulation," or "lynching," which is common to new countries, all over the world—are ascribed to slavery. Miss M., along with too many others, seems to think that none but well-bred, quiet, peaceable men, should tame the wilderness. All her stories of great crimes, of burning, and hanging, and stabbing, which she has raked up with such exquisite care, are stories of the borders. They belong to that period in the history of society, when civilization sends forth her pioneer to tame the wilderness. Your well-bred city gentleman is no pioneer—he belongs to a better condition of things, and to after times. It is the bold, reckless adventurer, the dissolute outcast, the exile from crime, or from necessities of one sort or another, who goes forth to contend with the wild beasts, the stubborn forests, and the savage tribes who prowl among them. These people, naturally enough, become as wild, almost, as those whom they conquer; but they have their uses. They are the lower limbs of civilization, and the links which connect the wilderness with the city. They prepare the way for civilization, if uncivilized themselves; and, however much we may deplore the crimes which they sometimes commit, we must content ourselves with the knowledge that these crimes seem to be unavoidable, under the circumstances, and will continue to be committed, by the same class of men, whenever, in a new country, the presence of such adventurers becomes necessary. This is said simply, by way of statement. It is only a record of the fact, which I do not seek to excuse, let it happen South or North. I look upon all violence and all injustice as brutal, whether it be the burning of the convent, the assault upon the trembling nuns, and their subsequent denial of justice, the frequent murders of women in places professing to be civilized, and where they are pleased to declaim very much about the outrages upon the borders, or the cruel "lynchings," at the South, of the sturdy incendiary. These atrocities, in the settled communities of our country, may, most generally, be ascribed to the constant appeals which are made to what is called " public opinion ;" an appeal to a something—a power beyond the law—which is expected to take the form of an equitable jurisdiction, and remedy its supposed deficiencies. This I take to be one of the great causes of so much mobbing, and burning, and rioting, and lynching, in recent times, among us. "Public opinion," so called, is very apt to become public action; and the mob, whom an editor invokes to ridicule the militia law, will not hesitate long to tar and feather the colonel, who is something of a martinet, and desires to sustain it. But it is not public opinion which is thus invoked; it is popular passion, and a vain insolence, which are cherished and brought into activity by such appeals, and which then become a tyranny, being out of its place. Public opinion is of very slow, very temperate, and very judicious formation. It is the aggregate of small truths, and the experience of successive days and years, which, heaped together, form a general principle, which is of final conviction in every bosom. It only requires to receive a name, in order to become a law; and a law which is precipitately imposed upon a people, in advance of the formation of this sort of public opinion, will soon be openly abolished, or become obsolete, in the progress of events. For my own part, I am satisfied with the existing laws, until the gradual and naturally formed convictions of the community, and the progress of experience, shall call for their improvement. I have no respect for those who set themselves up for makers of public opinion; and as for the "hell-broth" so compounded, I know not any draught which would not be more wholesome than that which makes the body politic a body plethoric, and leaves no remedy to the physician but the cautery and the knife. The evils of this sort, thus originating, are, by the way, far less frequent in the slave than in the free States, which really do not appear to possess a single principle of permanence and stability.

A goodly portion of the two volumes of Miss Martineau is compiled from the conversations and opinions of Americans, who are nameless, followed by her examination of them. She sets up these argumentative nine-pins with the utmost gravity, and bowls them down with great rapidity and wonderful adroitness. Many of her arguments are carried on with women; and as there are very few women so "cunning of fence," on her own ground, as this professional disputant, it is easy to see, not only that she obtains an easy victory, but that she derives no increase of knowledge from the controversy. Her own estimate of the mental pretensions of the American women should have saved her from a misplaced confidence either in their evidence or judgment. Indeed, she only confides in their opinions when it answers her purpose to

20*

do so. She describes them as little above fatuity. The three chapters devoted to this subject, under the general head of "Woman," present a singular and contradictory compound of truth and error, which nothing but a rabid desire for publication could have suffered her to put forth. The minds of the American women, according to her estimate, with few exceptions, are little else than a blank. They have little or no practical philosophy—no thought;—and they confound learning with wisdom. Wherever she heard of a woman having a local celebrity, she was sure to find her a mere linguist; and she winds up her generally contemptuous estimate of the sex, by ascribing drunkenness to the more enlightened among them—a vice, perhaps, more utterly foreign to the American woman, than to the woman of any other country on the face of the globe. "It is no secret, on the spot, that the habit of intemperance is not unfrequent among women of station and education, in the most enlightened parts of the country. I witnessed some instances, and heard of more. It does not seem to me to be regarded with all the dismay which such a symptom ought to excite." The wonder is, with such an estimate of the sex, she should have drawn most of her authorities from them. This she does, commonly, on the subject of slavery. Her dialogues are mostly had with women; and those which she reports are certainly silly enough, in most cases, to support her estimate. Fortunately, since the days of Lady Blessington's protracted conversations with Lord Byron, men are not satisfied with reports of this description, unless they have proof that the stenographer has been by, all the while, and busy.

Another source of authority, with Miss Martineau, are the public men of our country—the members of Congress, of both parties, and those, seemingly, among the most violent. It does appear to me that she could not have erred more strikingly than in this particular: since the furious partizan, whether in England or America, is usually the last person in the world from whom the unprejudiced and ungarbled truth can be derived. That she should not have given the most implicit confidence to their statements, is the legitimate conclusion from her own report of them. She tells us that they strove to make a partizan of her—sought to secure her favorable opinions—and, on all occasions, exhibited much more earnestness in making proselytes *to the party*, than they would have done in securing them to the cause of truth. It is true, she is, here and there, annoyed with something in their conduct that seems to startle her with the semblance of an inconsistency; but she does not, even then, doubt the good faith of the speaker—when it serves her turn, or supports her favorite idea. She suspects the judgment first—aye, always—with a self-confidence in her own, which is thoroughly English—the weakness—anything but the prejudice and the interest of party. The politicians of Carolina give heed, and bow ready assent to all her anti-slavery propositions; and when she believes that she has them all snugly within the hem of her garment, she is thunderstruck to hear them vote aloud in approbation of Governor McDuffie's thoroughgoing, yet only half-elaborated, opinions in favor of slavery. To this day, she does not suspect that a polite Southern gentleman, in a ball-room, would infinitely prefer bowing assent to all her propositions, than gravely undertake to refute them, through the medium of her "charming" trumpet.

"It was necessary to purchase Florida, because it was a retreat for runaways."

This was one reason, perhaps; but Miss M. seems to have been imperfectly acquainted with the history of Florida. It may be well to inform her, that the best reason for the purchase of that country, is kindred to that which prompts the United States and Great Britain to maintain so jealous a watch upon the Island of Cuba, in order to keep it from falling into the possession of any great maritime power. From the first, Florida, under the Spaniards, had been the scourge of the Southern States. As Colonies and States, they were subjected to the continual incursions of the savages, under Spanish influence; and the wars of the borders, between the two people, were among the most sanguinary of those that ever took place in America. St. Augustine was emphatically styled, by the early English settlers in the South, as the "Sallee of America." In later days, a more urgent necessity arose for the acquisition of this territory, as it furnished a foothold, during the war of 1812, to our affectionate mother, England, to plant her standard upon it, and summon her red brethren to pile up the scalps of her banished children beneath it. Had Miss Martineau read the history, she might have found stronger reasons for the acquisition of this territory by the United States, than the recovery of its fugitive slaves; though that would be reason quite enough, in our estimation, to justify the purchase. But, he who knows any thing of the American people, needs not to hunt up a necessity, of any kind, for their acquisition of territory, or any reason better than the greed and strength of appetite. It is quite enough that the land is in the neighborhood, and accessible, to be lusted after; and the lust does not often scruple at the process by which it gratifies itself.

Miss Martineau deals in unmeasured invective, in respect to the annexation of Texas, an event then only in anticipation. She has her nice little story, of abolition manufacture, touching this region also, which is quite different from that told by the Texans themselves. But I need not linger upon this topic.

THE MORALS OF SLAVERY. 237

Of the causes of the war with the Seminoles, she gives us the following history:

"According to the laws of the slave States, the children of the slaves follow the fortunes of the *mother*. It will be seen, at a glance, what consequences follow upon this; how it operates as a premium upon licentiousness among white men; how it prevents any but mock-marriages among slaves; and, also, what effect it must have upon any Indians with whom slave women have taken refuge. The late Seminole war arose out of this law. The escaped slaves had intermarried with the Indians. The masters claimed the children. The Seminole fathers would not deliver them up. Force was used, to tear the children from their parents' arms, and the Indians began their desperate, but very natural war, of extermination."

Such is the story of Miss Martineau. Without doubt, it came from the mint of the abolitionists—the people of such veracity. This version is entirely new in the South. It is a budget of errors, one growing out of the other. The laws of Florida do not prevail over the Indians. The children of slaves only follow the condition of the mother, where the laws prevail. If a runaway woman is recovered from the Indian territory, her child will, of course, follow her condition, under the laws of the State whence she escapes; and there may have been an instance where the child of an Indian father is thus recovered, with the slave mother, and carried back into bondage; but I am disposed to doubt even this. The occurrence is rare, if it ever does or did take place. The Seminoles own slaves, which are either brought from the Island of Cuba, or have been stolen from the whites, at remote periods. They are only transferred from one kind of slavery to another, since they are held by the Indians without any restraints of law whatsoever, and are liable to all their caprices, of sudden rage, drunkenness, gloomy ferocity, and a malice which seems natural to them. Under these influences, the slave is frequently murdered, and the murderer goes unpunished. It is only such philanthropists as modern abolition provides, who esteem it better for the negro to be the slave to the savage than to the civilized man. The Indians do not often have intercourse with their slaves. They are a cold and sterile people, as is the case with most of the wandering tribes. Fecundity is one of the fruits of a settled and stationary population. The marriages among the negro slaves of the whites are much more formal, and quite as rigidly observed, as among the Indians, who are polygamists or anything. They are creatures of impulse, having nothing but the mood of the moment for their laws. The rule, that the child shall follow the condition of the mother, is not a stimulant to licentiousness among the whites, and we almost wonder to find Miss Martineau meditating such a matter. She certainly knows but little of human passion, if she supposes that, in matters of this nature, the mercenary desire of gain will prompt the white man to such excesses, other provocatives being wanting. So far from this being the motive, it may be stated here with perfect safety, that the greater number of the Southern mulattoes have been made free, in consequence of their relationship to their owners. In fact, mulatto slaves are not liked. They are a feebler race than the negro, and less fitted for the labors of the field. Of late years, some arbitrary laws have been passed in Carolina, which forbid the citizens to free their slaves. I do not approve of these laws myself; but they have their advocates among the majority, and reasons of State policy are given in their behalf, which are imposing enough, if not altogether sound. I am persuaded that it would be a wholesome policy to revoke these laws. It would, in the first place, prevent their frequent evasion. A more important consideration is, that it would give to the owner a power now denied, of doing full justice to the claims of the faithful and the intellectual, without compelling him to banish them from their native homes, while bestowing upon them their own mastery. The war in Florida arose from other and more natural causes, which the philosophical mind of Miss Martineau would have soon enough ferreted out, if the demon of abolition had not possessed her brain, and too entirely darkened her vision. The hunting grounds of the red men were too much circumscribed, by the gradual gathering of the whites around them, to permit them to procure sustenance after their ordinary habits. The game had become scarce, and, as they had not yet been taught the first lesson of christianity, as it is the first decree of God—namely, the necessity of labor—they were half the time in a state of starvation. Their contact with the civilized must always result—as such contact has everywhere resulted—either in their subjection as inferiors, or their extermination. Their only safety will be found in their enslavement, or in their removal to a region where the hunting grounds are open and uncircumscribed. They must perish or remove, unless they conform to the established usages of the States in which they linger, and fall into the customs of the superior people. The government of the United States has aimed at their removal for many years; but this removal has been resisted in various quarters, and chiefly by the instrumentality of those universal philanthropists, who are now known as abolitionists. They were strenuous in opposing it, and did not confine their opposition to the councils of our own nation. They preached resistance to the Indians themselves, and encouraged them to stay where they were, and starve. Their eloquence, in these exhortations, overlooked the absolute *necessities* of the Indian; and was chiefly devoted to the imaginary privations consequent upon his removal.

They dwelt pathetically upon the loss of his home, and his banishment from his forefathers' graves; and, in dilating upon privations such as these, they entirely forgot all the more serious evils arising from the state of sufferance in which he dwelt, in an abridged territory, and under a government whose regulations, his necessities, and his ignorance alike, drove him momently to violate. He must either beg, steal or starve. In seeking to avoid the latter, the commission of crime is frequent. The red men become embroiled with the whites, whom they despoil of their hogs and cattle, and whatever else they can lay their hands on; they refuse obedience to the authorities they offend; they fly from the officers of justice, and seek for shelter in their wild recesses, their swamps and everglades. They are pursued, and, from their refractoriness, are treated, naturally enough, as outlaws, by their pursuers. The numbers, on both sides, accumulate; and blood is shed, and can only cease to be shed in the utter extermination of the inferior class. To avoid this dreadful necessity, the government has been laboring to remove them to other homes, and a wider extent of country, where they may follow, without let or hindrance, the customs which they like. And this removal is but a small and partial evil, in comparison with the many evils which must follow upon their stay. Our homes depend, for their comfort, not so much upon the associations of our childhood, as upon their fitness for our mental and moral condition. Men—civilized men—whose sensibilities upon such matters are duly educated, and made fine and susceptible by the institutions of society, daily dispose of their dwellings, and depart into strange lands; and while we doubt not that all men must feel a sense of regret at parting from the homes of infancy and youth, we should be paying but a sorry tribute to their manliness, and proper nature, in regarding this as a sore and overwhelming evil. The Indian, too, of all people in the world, is the last to feel much, if any regret, at such a necessity. It is no great sacrifice for him. From the moment that his eyes opened upon the light, he has been a wanderer. He has never known a fixed abode, until the appearance and settlement of the whites formed a point of attraction, to which, with all the consciousness of his inferiority, he tacitly inclined. His fathers before him were wanderers, and, according to their histories, their whole lives have been passed in bearing their stakes from the wilderness to the seaside, and from the seaside to the wilderness again. The habitations of the Indians prove all this.* During the space of three hundred years—the time of our acquaintance with them—they have made no improvements; they have built no house of sufficient comfort or importance to be occupied by two successive generations. Their habitations have been such, only, as they could readily remove, or leave, without loss, to the use of some succeeding occupant. Their towns—if the collections of filthy wigwams in which they fester and breed vermin may be called towns—are few, far between, and the men seldom in them. Their women have ever been their drudges, in the most degrading slavery—brutes denied in-

---

* The account which the aborigines gave of themselves to the first discoverers, represented them to be the invaders of a people far superior to themselves in civilization, which their greater numbers and savage ferocity destroyed. This was the boast of the Indian to the white man. The antique remains of works, fortifications, temples, and other fabrics, which are dispersed all over the country, confirm this intelligence, without regarding the obvious fact that these were remains utterly beyond the ability of the Indians to erect. This history, we may add, is the history of the world, as we read it everywhere. The moment that civilization pauses in her conquests, she is overrun by the savage. She cannot rest in her conquests. She must conquer, not only to improve the savage, but to save herself. Let her pause, with an inferior tribe beside her, not acknowledging her sway, and she is overthrown.

dulgence, and slaves to the most vicious caprices of their masters, without restraint or redress, unless it comes in the sudden vengeance of some irritable relative. Such a people have no idea of home. That is their best home which gives them elbow room, and full forests in which to hunt. The Florida war sprung entirely from want of such freedom, and we may add, that most of our Indian wars have arisen from the same single cause. The philanthropists who would keep them in a region in which they have no resources of life, are those only to whom such wars are to be ascribed. Still, we do not deny the wanton injustice, and the occasional cruelty, of the base white borderer. It would be wonderful, indeed, if such people did forbear the commission of injustice. Their labors are not of such a sort as would lead us to hope for their forbearance; and the necessities of the savage give them but too frequent provocation for the exercise of their unrestrained and brutal propensities. The true evil is in the condition of things which keeps the two races in contact, yet not in connection. The inferior people must fly from the presence, or perish before the march of approaching civilization.

I come now to a point upon which the abolitionists, and the Northern people universally, are more profoundly ignorant than upon almost any other subject. This is the assumed greater dependence of the South, than any other section, upon the confederacy. Miss Martineau, in this matter, is the unreluctant mouth-piece of their crudities. Of course, the weakness of the South, in these relations, is due to slavery.

"In case of war," says the good lady, "they might be only too happy if their slaves did run away, instead of rising up against them at home."

The wish is very much the father of the thought.* Per-

* I stept, not long since, into one of the book shops of Broadway, and, in a new magazine lying upon the counter, read a letter from a

haps there is nothing in the world that the people of the South less apprehend, than this, of the insurrection of their negroes. The attempts of this people at this object have been singularly infrequent, and perhaps never would be dreamed of, were their bad passions not appealed to by the abolitionists or their emissaries. They are not a warlike people; are, indeed, rather a timid race; have no concert, no system, and are too well content with their condition, to the great grief of such philosophers as Dr. Lardner, to desire any change. And this has been the case from the beginning. I must remind these reformers of a history which will scarcely add strength to their convictions. The slave population in Carolina was quite equal to its white population in 1776. That conflict was one which obviously held forth the best opportunities for an outbreak, had the slaves desired it. The British authorities were not unfriendly to any proceedings, on their part, which would have distressed their owners. They did encourage them to take up arms, and undertook to form separate bands of negro troops, to uniform them in their scarlet, and furnish them with arms; yet succeeded in persuading only a single regiment to their ranks. The entire mass of the slave population adhered, with unshaken fidelity, to their masters—numbers followed or accompanied them to the field, and fought at their sides, while the greater body faithfully pursued their labors on the plantations—never deserting them in trial, danger or privation, and exhibiting, amidst every re-

visitor in Charleston, who stated that, such was the apprehension entertained of slave insurrections, that all the houses are enclosed with brick or stone walls! There are not half a dozen such walls in the city. The enclosures are mostly of wood, and such as a strong man would hew down with an axe in half a dozen strokes. But the absurdbecomes most intelligible, when it is remembered that the slaves of each household are lodgers *within* each enclosure.

verse of fortune, that respect, that propriety of moral, which did not presume in adversity, and took no license from the disorder of the times; and this decorum and fidelity were shown at a time when, to the presence of an overwhelming foreign enemy, was added the greater curse of a reckless and unsparing civil war, before their eyes, and among their own masters. Perhaps the whole world cannot exhibit a history more remarkable, or more worthy of grateful remembrance, than the conduct of the serviles of the South, during the war of the revolution. The few who were incorporated in the ranks of the British were of little service, behaved with no courage, and were soon dispersed or cut to pieces. Where they survived, they probably shared the fate of thousands more, whom the enemy found it much easier to convert into slaves, in the West Indies, than soldiers in the Carolinas. This history ought surely to suffice, to settle any doubts, or hopes, of our philanthropic brethren, in regard to our securities on this head. Of the remaining causes of Southern insecurity from foreign war, it is perhaps quite enough to state that the people of the South are born to the use of arms, and are fearless in the employment of them. They have never received any help from the North, at any period of their fortunes, either before or since the formation of the confederacy. They have, on the contrary, frequently sent their troops to the succor of the Northern States. In the recent war with Mexico, of the volunteers in the conquest of that country, under Taylor and Scott, their contribution, in proportion to that of the North, was as two to one. The people of the Southern States are emphatically a military people. The very fact that the tillage of the earth is confided mostly to an inferior race, affords them leisure for war, for constant exercise with weapons, and on horseback. The point, however, need not be pursued. Enough, that the people of the South are conscious of their strength, and entertain no sort of doubt of their capacity to maintain themselves equally against the danger from within and the foe without.

I have now gone through most of the points, in these volumes, which, directly or indirectly, affect the moral and the fact, in the case of South-Carolina. I have confined myself mostly to the one State, as better prepared to speak as a witness on the subject, and satisfied that the argument, in the case of one, will apply more or less thoroughly to that of all the slave States. It would have been quite easy to expose many other errors in these books, relating to the whole country. the result of Miss Martineau's self-conceit, her monomania, and her habit of generalizing from imperfect and inferior sources of fact; but this sort of labor is not very grateful, and the game would be scarce worth the candle. I must leave the task to other pens, more able and ready, in the regions which she has wronged by her report I commend it to them. A book like that of this lady, who *appears* to think, and certainly labors to do so, after a fashion of her own, is the proper sort of work for dissection. She arrays before us all our alleged offences, and thus makes it easy to turn at once to page and chapter, when we would make up the issue with her. I had marked sundry little anecdotes which she gives us, which, true in themselves, are yet false, in consequence of her employment of them for the illustration of the truth in general. But, as they involve no principles likely to affect the question, and are so commonly in conflict with other matters which the same pages develope, we may leave it to the reader to detect and contrast the examples for himself. They will do no harm, even if they escape all objection. Indeed, the book itself can do no harm. On the contrary, I am half disposed to think it may be of some benefit, if it brings us only to the knowledge of some of our errors. Like the spiteful octavo of Mrs. Trollope, it tells us an occasional home truth, North and South, which we may ponder, and upon which we may improve. And yet there may be some unkindness, in requiring the reader to toil through this weary wilderness of chaff, in the hope of such small wheat as it promises.

Miss Martineau is a monstrous proser. She has a terrible power of words, and is tyrannical as she is powerful, in the use of them. We have no doubt she is herself free from stain or reproach; but her tongue is wretchedly incontinent. She is probably one of those persons who never believe that they have been talking all the while. She declaims constantly, and is forever searching after exceptions. She scruples at no game, fears no opponent, and, whether the meat be washed or unwashed, hawk or heron, it is all the same to her. She discusses the rights of man, and—heaven save the mark!—the rights of women too, with her chambermaid, when she cannot corner a senator. Smart exceedingly, well practised in the minor economies of society, and having at her tongue's end all the standards of value in the grain, cotton, beef and butter markets, she does not scruple to apply them to the more mysterious involutions of the mind and society. It is but too evident that, with all her cleverness, she lacks that more advantageous wisdom which begins with humility. She is too dogmatical ever to be wise. She comes to teach, not to learn. She gets nothing from her hearer, for she does not hear him. If she listens, it is simply because she is confident that her answer is ready. That she has never listened, while in America, is evident from these volumes; though I doubt not that a great many words have gone through her trumpet. Miss Martineau came to America with two or three texts in her memory, which she assumed to be the only right standards by which our people were to be tried and their institutions judged. These texts are so many broad and bold assumptions, that have obtained currency, rather in consequence of the audacity by which they have been urged, and perhaps by some latent vitality, the result of partial truth within them, than because of their complete and triumphant endurance of the tests of experience and severe analysis. With her, as with most European philosophers of her order, they are assumptions only—specious or imposing—which have been taken on trust; according, perhaps, with the particular temperament of the individual. To a woman of the bold, free, masculine nature of Miss Martineau, impatient of the restraints of her sex, and compelled to seek her distinction in fields which women are rarely permitted to penetrate, democracy is one of the most attractive of social philosophies, as conservatism must be necessarily the most offensive. With her, the doctrine of majorities is the voice of God. She has a fast faith in the proverb. The will of the majority, she insists, will be right—right, always, *in the end*—a faith which we should not care to dispute, since we can readily conceive of a people, after having boxed the compass in experiments, and bruised its shins, or broken its limbs, over a thousand errors, arriving, at last, at the goal which it had never conjectured, and had not the capacity to seek or to foresee. Let "*the end*" be sufficiently remote, and we hardly question but that, in God's mercy, all his scattered flocks will find their way into the saving fold. But need this be a matter of chance, and need there be any such long delay about it? May not the thousand sorrows, trials, hurts and bruises of the race be lessened, and the road to right be shortened, under other auspices? Are not the delay and the suffering the strict consequence of following such blind guides as our own capricious passions, headlong will, fierce impulse, and impudent presumption—following *the multitude*, in short, to do evil; and has not God appointed safer guides, specially gifted beings, whom we were wiser to seek and follow, and who would conduct us to the great object of our pilgrimage, at no such peril, and with no such delay as now attends the progress? I confess that, though not unwilling to suppose *the majority may be right in the end*, I am half disposed to *prefer a minority that is right in the beginning*. But that would not suit Miss Martineau, who prefers to work out her own problems, at any cost, so that she can do the work for herself. She takes this doctrine of majorities lovingly in hand, and, applying it to sundry cases in her own mind—to which it is not customary to apply it in America—she is alarmed at the annoying inconsistency which follows. Hence her wild chapter about the "Rights of Women," her groans and invectives because of their exclusion from the offices of state, the right of suffrage, the exercise of political authority. In all this, the error of the declaimer consists in the very first movement of the mind. "The "Rights of *Women*" may all be conceded to the sex, yet the rights of *men* withheld from them. Here is all the difficulty. The knot of the subject lies in this little respect; and the untying of it, by no A'exandrine process—we had almost said Cæsarian—may enable us still to insist upon our American understanding of the doctrine of majorities, yet leave the tender sex without any legitimate cause of complaint. Certainly, if mere numbers are to be considered the proper sources of power in a state, the inference follows that women must have a share in the administration of affairs. The fact that they are *not*, in a country which yet professes to be ruled by a majority, should have prompted Miss Martineau to a closer inquiry into the source of the peculiar rights of the majority. It is important to know what was the peculiar sense, on this subject, of the founders of our laws, customs, and constitution. We are in possession of a good many very subtle and ingenious expositions of the secret principle by which the larger claims to rule the smaller body. But I doubt the whole of them, and am not sure that the whole moral of it is not an agreeable political fiction, by which to save trouble, avoid difficulty, escape danger, and have leisure for more personal matters; just as the elevation of a pretty young woman to the throne of England, following the *prescribed* order of events, prevents a constant recurrence of struggles, ending in bloody wars, with regard to the disputed succession. There must be, for the general safety, some rule on these subjects, of general recognition, and this of the majority is most in accordance with the genius, as it is the preference, of the people. There may be found a substantial reason for it at bottom, which may be suggestive to Miss Martineau why women are not to be taken into the account. The truth is, the doctrine of majorities simply determines the presence of physical power, displayed by simple arithmetic, by which we obviate any necessity for the application of the brute force, when we assert our rights, and seek their exercise by swaying over the rights of others. The majority tells us where the brute force lies, and we submit to it, with what philosophy we can, in all cases where the authority which governs, entails upon us no such evils as would follow from our physical struggle to shake it off. Whenever the wrongs and injustice of the majority pass beyond the ordinary bounds of patience, it is resisted, and the *ultima ratio* is resorted to by the minority, either in hope or desperation. There is no abstract charm, in mere numbers, to compel the submission of those who are wronged, or who think themselves so. But when it is known that votes represent men—able-bodied and armed men—the case is different. We at once see the enemy with which we have to contend, and the superior capacities which he possesses of coercion. The doctrine of majorities is, in truth, no new doctrine. It is as old as the hills. The only difference between times past and times present, consists, simply, in the superior facilities which, in modern times, we enjoy, of determining where the power lies, without any resort to blows. It is more easy, now-a-days, to compute the strength of the opposition, than it was in the distant periods when war was almost invariably the result of ignorance on both hands; and never was the doctrine more clearly illustrated than in the wars of Napoleon Bonaparte, whose many successes were the sheer result of his attention to this fact. His mode of concentrating his force at a given point, in advance of his enemy, was the true secret of his wonderful victories. Like all dexterous politicians, his aim was to be always in a majority. Minorities would never submit to the frequent injustice of majorities, but that they well know that the court of dernier resort is one just as little likely to give them redress, as the power which robs them of their rights by a mere resort to the numeration table.

It is only one of many of the subjects of disquiet which Miss Martineau finds, when she compares the *working* of our system with its prescribed standards. The governing principles of our political condition, and the laws and practice under them, she finds in frequent conflict; and *her* trouble is that of the European generally. One of her points of difficulty is in the famous passage in the declaration of American independence, which announces that "all men are created equal." The declaration has been one of long dispute, with all sorts of philosophers, and the decision upon the vexed question is not likely to be made in our day. Our excellent forefathers, when they pronounced this truth to be self-evident, were not in the best mood to become philosophers, however well calculated to approve themselves the best of patriots. They were much excited, nay, rather angry, in the days of the "declaration," and hence it is that what they alleged to

THE MORALS OF SLAVERY.

be self evident *then*, is, at this time, when we are comparatively cool, a source of very great doubt and disputation. But, the truth is, the phrase was simply a finely sounding one, significant of that sentimental French philosophy, then so current, which was destined to bear such sanguinary fruits in after periods. Jefferson inclined to that school of philosophers, so long as its sentimentality constituted its chief characteristic, and before the paradisaical fancies of which it was so prolific had been literally swallowed up in a sea of human blood. How could Rousseau, or Jefferson, determine how men were created—in what degrees—in what equality? The only record which we have, shows us, under the ordinary interpretation of the churchmen, that there was never but a single man *created* by the hands of God; the rest were born, under laws such as prevail uniformly through the animal world—in different climates, different realms, under different conditions, victims to poverty, to exposure, to want, to disease, or pets of vanity, and pride, and opulence—all differing, everywhere, in health, strength, size, circumstance—under no uniformity of culture, training, education;—as *unequal* a scattered family—color, race, tribe, feature—as if it had been the studious purpose of the Deity that there should be as great a variety in the human family, as among the brute and vegetable nations. And I have no doubt that such really was his plan, conforming to all the analogies in nature. But the statement of the case, as made in the "declaration of independence," is, in its very nature, wholly indeterminable. Nobody, now-a-days, is born naked. Indeed, man was hardly ever, at any period, in what we describe as a state of nature. The artifices of a social condition were woven about him from the earliest periods, and the essential inequalities of such conditions, in differing societies, must always have had the effect of establishing corresponding inequalities among the individuals composing tribes and families, even if it had not been the benevolent purpose of God that such inequalities should constitute an essential feature of his plan of creation. But, be sure that our good fathers, in the revolution, never contemplated so wide a survey of the subject, when they insisted upon the perfect equality of the sons of men. They made the assertion in a more limited sense, evidently thinking not so much of the *accouchement* of Eve, as of the *delivery* of the American people. Their assertion meant no more than this: "You, George the Third, whom we think a tyrant, have presumed to call us, John Hancock, Samuel Adams, Thomas Jefferson, etc., traitors and rebels. Now, look you, George, we owe you no allegiance. We are as good men as you, any day. We are your equals. God created, or made, us so. Stand up and compare with us, if you dare. Compare with us your best men—your Norths, and Butes, and Germaines—and let us see where your superiority lies. Physically, we are fully your match; morally and intellectually, your superiors. And so will our people compare with yours, and with the whole world. God has endowed them, equally with your people, with the capacity to govern and control themselves." And this was the amount of it, and such was the argument, as against a rival people. Within their own tribes, they no doubt held the farther doctrine, that all men were equal in the sight of God—that is, that he was incapable of partialities. He had made them equally his care—he had decreed their equal accountability; and, by proper analogy, the authors of the declaration might well declare, in behalf of the equal recognition, by the laws and government, of the claims of the citizen, *each in his place;* each, while he obeyed the laws and complied with his public duties, having an equal right with his neighbor to the protection of society, in his life and liberty, his pursuits and his possessions. We are not to subject such a performance as the declaration of independence to a too critical scrutiny, in respect to its generalizations. These are put briefly, and the circumstances of the revolutionary movement were such as required that they should be put *strongly*. It was necessary that they should be pronounced with emphasis, since the revolution was an event which, while it fixed the attention of the civilized world, required that it should also compel its popular sympathies. It was, perhaps, something of policy that dictated the employment of phrases which should particularly commend it to the French philosophers of that day; and I have no question but that many of the statesmen who signed the paper were thus made the endorsers of sundry sentiments which they never swallowed at all. The Adamses, of Massachusetts, could not well have bolted the doctrine of universal equality; while it is very certain that the aristocrats of Carolina, in that day, must, if they did swallow it, have done so with monstrous wry faces. But the doubtful matter did not then provoke a question, since nobody gave it, then, any construction more authoritative than that which I have here assigned it.

How should they, indeed, unless blinder than the beasts that perish, with staring proofs to the contrary surrounding them, even while they deliberated and wrote? That God has not created men alike, or equal, whether morally or physically, is not less notorious, than it is in perfect harmony with all his other creations. The most striking development, every where, in and about the beautiful world which we inhabit, is in striking proof of his purpose to crown it with as much diversity as life. Nothing, indeed, can be more remarkable, or more delightful, to the mind and eye, surveying the works of the Creator, than the endless varieties, and the boundless inequalities, of his creations. Not only is no void unfilled, but no void is filled in the same manner. Size, form, color, order, power, in all living objects, are graduated endowments, which enable one to fly, while another creeps; one to dilate in grandeur, while another trembles in insignificance; one to loom out, like some bright creature of the elements, while another nestles, with sombre garment, in a corresponding shadow. Whether we survey the globe which we inhabit, the sky which canopies, the seas which surround us, or the systems which give us light and loveliness, we are perpetually called upon to admire that infinite variety of the Creator, which nothing seems to stale. The stars are lovely in their inequalities; the hills, the trees, the rivers and the seas; and it is from their very inequalities that their harmonies arise. Were it otherwise, the eye would be pained by the monotony of the prospect everywhere. As it is, we love to look abroad upon nature, and it is with a pleasure no less sensible than that of the savage, that we learn "how to name the bigger light, and how the less." They have their names, only as they are unlike and unequal. It is because these shine *in their places*, however inferior to other orbs, that they are lovely. They are all unequal, but each keeps its place; and the beauty which they possess and yield us, results entirely from their doing so. A greater philosopher than Thomas Jefferson—and we may add, after a long interval, Jeremy Bentham and Miss Martineau—has given us a noble passage, devoted to this subject, which is no less philosophical than poetical—indeed, it is the true poet, alone, who is the perfect and universal philosopher. Let us hear William Shakspeare. I quote from "Troilus and Cressida." The speech is made by Ulysses, at the close of the seventh year of the siege of Troy, when the Greeks, emulous of each other, each striving for sway, defeat their own objects, and begin to despair of success in the continued disappointments of the war. After a prefatory passage, he says:

> "*Degree being vizarded*,
> The *unworthiest* shows as fairly in the mask.
> The heavens themselves, the planets, and this centre,
> Observe degree, priority and place,
> Insisture, course, proportion, season, form,
> Office and custom, in all line of order:
> And therefore is the glorious planet, Sol,
> In noble eminence enthroned and sphered
> Amidst the other, whose med'cinable eye
> Corrects the ill aspects of planets evil,
> And posts, like the commandment of a king,
> Sans check, to good and bad: *But when the planets,*
> *In evil mixture, to d'sorder wander,*
> *What plagues, and what portents! What mutiny!*
> *What raging of the sea! shaking of earth!*
> *Commotion in the winds!—frights, changes, horrors,*
> *Divert and crack, rend and deracinate*
> *The unity and married calm of states**
> *Quite from their fixture!* Oh, when degree is shak'd,
> *Which is the ladder of all high designs,*
> *The enterprise is sick!* How could communities,
> Degrees in schools, and brotherhoods in cities,
> Peaceful commerce from dividable shores,
> The primogenitive and due of birth,
> Prerogative of age, crowns, sceptres, laurels,
> But by degree, stand in authentic place?
> *Take but degree away, untune that string,*
> *And hark! what discord follows! Each thing meets*
> *In mere oppugnancy:* The bounded waters
> Should lift their bosoms higher than the shores,
> And make a sop of all this solid globe;

* Were our federal union what it should be, how happily would this line serve as the motto of the confederacy.

Strength should be lord of imbecility,
And the rude son should strike his father dead;
Force should be right; or, rather, right and wrong
(Between whose endless jars justice resides)
Should lose their names, and so should justice too.
Then everything includes itself in power,
Power into will, will into appetite;
And appetite, an universal wolf,
So doubly seconded by will and power,
Must make, perforce, an universal prey,
And last, eat up himself. Great Agamemnon,
This chaos, when degree is suffocate,
Follows the choking."*

---

* Pope, too, not to speak of a hundred others, has like authority.

" Order is heaven's first law, and this confest,
Some are, and *must be*, greater than the rest."

The laws of society are not intended to disturb the natural degrees of humanity, but to reconcile them—to make them consistent with, and dependent upon, one another—not to make the butcher a judge, or the baker a president; but to protect them, according to their claims as butcher and baker. Let us illustrate these distinctions by some well known cases. In a claim for maintenance, the jury will inquire what have been the habits, what is the education, the tastes, sensibilities, etc., of the wife—in an action for damages, in slander, the words being the same, the jury will adjudge the amount of damages according to the profession, the moral and intellectual standing, of the slandered person; and this, too, without reflecting that it is wholly in defiance of this doctrine of universal equality. Yet the trial by jury is, perhaps, even beyond that of representation—nay, it is the most vital sort of representation—the most conspicuous showing of the equal rights principle. The jury, drawn from all classes, recognizes, as by an instinct, what is due to superior social position, and, just in degree as the character is eminent, which they have to redress, will make exemplary the damages. Here is the whole subject. If we thus guage the degree of wrong done to the individual, as an individual, and according to his special claims, it is because we have first recognized the individual superiority of his rights.

This noble passage is full of force and meaning. It does not too highly rate, to society, the importance of order—degree—or men, as well as things, in their right places. All harmonies, whether in the moral or physical worlds, arise wholly from the inequality of their tones and aspects; and all things, whether in art or nature, social or political systems, but for this inequality, would give forth only monotony or discord. That equality which the leveller insists upon would result in general confusion—the breaking down of every necessary barrier of distinction—the universal forfeiture of names to things. There could be no hope, there would be no ambition, where

"*Degree*, being vizarded,
The unworthiest shows us fairly"*

as the noblest. The motive to honorable performance would be lost; and that, too, without lessening, in any degree, the scramble, on all hands, for place and power. The very nature of man is in conflict with this law of universal equality. His perpetual, and proper effort, is to rise honorably above his fellows. It is thus, and thus only, that he asserts an individuality of character and endowment, which is the secret of all greatness, whether of possession or performance. It was never the intention of the fathers of the country to destroy this individuality, to deny its assertion, or to bring about that dead level condition in society, in which everything but stagnates. They may have been democrats; but in their notion of democracy, it was not levelling in its character. They rather found in it that harmony of relation in the moral world, in which all the agents and operatives, playing together, wrought out from their correspondence the best music of humanity—that music which builds the great city, and secures peace and prosperity to man, in the prosecution of his labors. The democracy which they asserted not only recognized, but insisted upon inequalities—its laws declaring, not the fitness of all men for any place, but that all should be secured in the quiet possession of their individual right of place—that there should be no usurpation—no assertion of power, in hostility to right—no arrogant assumption, upon artificial bases, of any natural right of one class of performers to the sway over another. Neither their acts nor their declarations, properly read and understood, asserted anything beyond the simple and reasonable law, that each man should enjoy the place to which he is justly entitled, by reason of his moral, his intellect, his strength, or his resource. Of the thing or position *proper to him*, that should he enjoy without molestation. Their understanding, and, as I read it, their definition of true liberty, is the enjoyment of that place in society to which our moral and intellect entitle us, and of the fruits of those efforts and enterprises, which we owe to our own performances. Here, I may offer a few brief definitions, the better to convey my notion of what was theirs.

He is in the enjoyment of freedom, whatever his condition, who is suffered to occupy his proper place.

He, only, is the slave, who is forced into a position in society which is below the claim of his intellect and moral.

He cannot but be a tyrant—a wrong-doer at least—who forces or makes his way into a position for which his moral is unfitted or unprepared, and for the duties of which his intellect is unprepared.

That such were the definitions of democracy, in the days of the declaration, is fairly inferrible from the fact, that they left the condition of their social world precisely as they found it. They might, indeed, have held, as an abstract notion, that, in a state of nature, men were born equal—equally helpless, of themselves, certainly, and equally dependant and incapable—but they certainly never held that they must of right continue equal; nor is this a fair conclusion, from what they say. The birthright of man may be alienated in a thousand ways, and it never was an unqualified one.

Of these inalienable rights of man,

"All men," says the declaration of independence, "are created equal; they are endowed by their Creator with certain inalienable rights; among these are life, liberty, and the pursuit of happiness," etc.

Now, is this true, in whole or in part? Is it true that life, liberty, and the pursuit of happiness, are inalienable, under the practice of our government, or any other? Do we not alienate them every day? Men are hung for rapes, for treason, for murder, for forgery, for burglary, and many other offences. We cast them into prisons, and deprive them of their liberty; we sue them in the courts, and take from them their property. On what pretence, if these rights of man be inalienable, do we deprive him of them? There is some mystery in all this, not to be explained by a resort to the ordinary mode of argumentation; and those who insist, as Miss Martineau does, upon the unlimited and the unqualified meaning of these natural laws—for natural rights are natural laws—will certainly be at a loss to reconcile a difficulty like this. In fact, these are only *conditional* possessions or endowments. We must look farther. There must be a qualified acceptation of these principles and phrases, or they are nothing. *The truth is, that our natural rights depend entirely upon the degree of obedience which we pay to the laws of our creation. All our rights, whether from nature or from society*—and these are the only two sources of right known to us—*result from the performance of our duties* Unless we perform our duties, we have no rights; or they are alienable, in consequence of our *lâchesse*. The man has no rights by nature, unless by a compliance with the laws of nature; as he would have no rights from society, unless by a compliance with its laws. Refusing to obey, he is *outlawed*, and society thus only recognizes, instinctively, the remorseless decree of nature. *These laws, in a state of nature, require from the man the application of his mental and physical energies, to the improvement of the passive world around him.* It was given to him for this single purpose. The Indian, who finds himself upon a hillock, has no more right to it, by nature, than the hog which burrows along its borders, until he proves his right by the exhibition of faculties superior to those which the hog possesses. He is no more a man than the hog, until he complies with the natural laws of his being. This he does, when he builds himself a cabin from the woods around him; when he bends the branches into a bower overhead, and covers the roof with leaves, and strews the floor with rushes, and thus protects himself against the elements; when he gathers fuel, and, by rubbing two dried sticks together, builds himself a fire, and warms himself against the cold; when he plants his maize and beans, and provides against future hunger. These prove his superiority to the brute, and maintain for him the proper rights which his superior powers have fairly established to be in him. He literally obeys the first decree of God to the expatriated man, and, by tilling the earth, obtains his bread in the sweat of his brow.* As he proceeds, Labor, which, alone, is but a blind Polyphemus at the best, receives a divine assistant from heaven, in the shape of Art. She gives life and animation to his toils, cheers him with her smiles and her songs, and,

---

* And this is one of the first elements of religion, as it is the prime element of human prosperity. Genesis is studied in vain, unless this be the conclusion of the student.

when his work is ended, with a plastic hand, smoothes down its roughnesses, and, from the rude block, commands the upspringing presence of Beauty. In the progress of time, Nature supplies him, from his own resources, with another ally, of whom he had no previous knowledge, in the shape of Science. This ally is many-winged and many-handed, and makes all the elements subservient to his purposes. He shows labor where to place his shoulder, and the mountain is heaved from its base. He tells where he shall strike, and the crag is cleft by his stroke. He hews down the high trees of the forest at his bidding, and guides his dwelling-place even upon the waters. These gifts prepare man properly for life. The crowning and last gift, which is spiritual religion, prepares him for death. But the inevitable law must be first obeyed, or he gains none of these blessings. He must first *labor*. This is the destiny from which he is forever seeking to escape.* It is only by a compliance with this, the first law of his creation, that he can hope to be secure in life, successful in his pursuits, benefitted by society, and made happy by religion. It is the key-stone of religion itself; and the missionary who seeks to teach the mysteries of christianity to the wandering savage, can never hope to be successful, so long as he neglects to inform him of the first duty consequent upon his creation.

* The desire to escape this destiny is one of the true causes of the present distress of our country. We are all toiling to avoid toil; and we cog, lie, swindle, speculate—do anything but delve and dig. We import our labor— the most useful and necessary arm of our population— from a foreign country; and a long train of evils must ensue in consequence, which the narrow mind will always be unwilling to trace back to this seemingly unimportant origin. It is a moral disgrace to a nation such as ours, not less than a political and social evil, when we are compelled to import from foreign lands our grain. our bread stuffs, and the forage for our cattle. Land was given us for cultivation; not for speculation.—*Note written in* 1837.

The result of labor, to the man, is property. The possession of property is the first cause which brings about any enlarged formation of society: numbers become necessary to defend wealth from the barbarians, who do not labor, and who have none. As society improves and increases—and it must inevitably do so, while it continues to comply with its natural and obvious laws—it extends its dominion, and controls the surrounding tribes, for its own safety. These succumb, are enslaved, and, as they improve in intellectual respects, are lifted, by regular degrees, into the bosom of that society which has first enslaved them.* The superior people, which conquers, also educates the inferior; and their reward, for this good service, is derived from the labor of the latter, which being, in all moral respects, the inferior people, can yield no other recompense. Unless the civilized and superior nation does this, it will inevitably fall a victim to the barbarous tribes which gather around it—forever poor, desperate and daring—having no possessions to lose, and, from their bestial improvidence, compelled, in all inclement seasons, to resort to war with their neighbors, to avoid starvation. It is no less the duty than the necessity, therefore, of civilization, to overcome these tribes—to force the tasks of life upon them—to compel their labor—to teach them the arts of economy and providence, and, with a guiding hand and unyielding sway, conduct them to the moral Pisgah, from whence they may behold the lovely and inviting Canaan of a higher and holier condition, spread out before them, and praying them to come. When civilization ceases to extend her con-

* This is a natural, and therefore an inevitable result. Without referring to the moral law to this effect, the Southern slaveholder finds it his interest to lift the more intelligent slave into stations of higher responsibility, and more honorable trust, than are commonly yielded to his fellows.

quests, she falls, like Rome, the victim to the savage. The war is as endless between her and her foe, as between any two diametrically opposite principles in the same moral circle ; and as her sway is the more gentle, and as she conquers only to improve, while the savage conquers only to destroy, it follows, inevitably, that hers is the only legitimate conquest, and every other is but tyranny.

Every primitive nation, of which we have any knowledge in the world's history, has been subjected to long periods of bondage. They have been all elevated and improved by its tasks and labors, and a positive sanction for the use of slavery, and a proof of its necessity, are fairly to be inferred from this inevitable consequence ; but, as if this were not enough for the purposes of authority, God himself, we are given to understand, actually, in two remarkable instances, placed a favorite people in foreign slavery, making them hewers of wood and drawers of water, in the land of the stranger ; as, from their refusal to comply with the laws of their creation, they had shown themselves unfitted even for the very comparative degree of social liberty allotted to men at those periods—requiring them thus, through that ordeal, which is improperly called slavery, but which is simply a process of preparation for an improving and improved condition, to work out their own moral deliverance. For, truly is it, that we shall not only gain our bread by the sweat of our brow, but thus subdue those barbarous appetites, and degrading brutal propensities, without the subjection of which, our minds could never have that due play and exercise, which can alone fit them for social dependance, and the friendly restraints of a guardian government. The nature of man is one of continual conflicts, and those chiefly with himself; and the proverb which inculcates the victory over himself as the most glorious of all victories, is one strictly and philosophically growing out of a just knowledge of his own attributes, and the difficulties which oppose their exercise.

Our general views, in modern times, on the subject of slaves and slavery, are distressingly narrow. Our forefathers were less precipitate, but more certain in their philosophy. They did not scruple to go forward, but they were first sure that they were right in doing so. We do not resemble them in this. We are too ready to follow multitudes to do evil. Having commenced our political career by a grand innovation upon the existing condition of things, we would still innovate; and, like any other good principle suffering abuse, the zeal which released us from a foreign yoke would also release us from our allegiance to higher influences than kings. We are losing our veneration fast. We are overthrowing all sacred and hallowing associations and authorities. Marriage is now a bond which we may rend at pleasure. The Sabbath is a wrong and a superstition. Such is the progress of opinion and doctrine among those very classes which show themselves hostile to Southern slavery. The cry is "On!" and we do not see the beginning of the end. Never was fanaticism more mad than on the subject of slavery; which was a very good thing enough when "England and the North" sold slaves, and the South bought them; and it is a good thing now, if we would only reason rightly, and find out what slavery is. We make no distinction between those restraints which impose labor upon the body—improving its health, bringing out its symmetry and strength, and fulfilling a destiny, which the analogies of all history, not less than the faith which we profess, teach us is the decree of the Universal Parent—and that bondage of the mind, and that denial of its exercise, which are always the aim of tyrannies, and which, as in the case of some of the *unlaboring* people of Europe, must result in the utter enervation, sluggishness, and shame of body and mind alike. Pity it is, that the lousy and lounging lazzaroni of Italy, cannot be made to labor in the fields, under the whip of a severe task-master! They would then be a much freer—certainly a much nobler animal—than we can possibly esteem them now;—and far better had it been for our native North American savage, could he have been reduced to servitude, and, by a labor imposed upon him, within his strength, and moderately accommodated to his habits, have been preserved from that painful and eating decay, which has left but a raw and naked skeleton of what was once a numerous and various people—a people, that needed nothing but an Egyptian bondage of four hundred years to have been saved for the future, and lifted into a greatness to which Grecian and Roman celebrity might have been a faint and failing music.*

This clamor about liberty and slavery, is, after all, unless we get some certain definitions to begin with, the most arrant nonsense. "License they mean when they cry liberty!"—and we may add, "license they mean when they cry slavery!" The extremes are near kindred, and in all these clamors they are sure to meet. The Russian boor is called a slave, and

* I will be referred to the experiment of this nature, made by the Spaniards in the Island of Cuba, in which the poor savages were utterly destroyed. But this is no parallel case to the proposition in the text. The reason why the Spaniards failed, and the Indians perished under the *repartimiento* system, arose from the fact, that the masters had only a *temporary* and not a *permanent* interest in their services. The Spanish governors were compelled to arrive at sudden wealth, or not at all; and they worked the savages to death in order to obtain it. Had the Indians been allotted to them, not according to geographical, but numerical divisions, such result would not have followed. They should have had a limited number of slaves, and in these they should have had a life interest. Their policy, then, must have been to economize that labor, of which, under the existing circumstances, they were inhumanly profligate. The fate of the Indians, under such rule, might have been predicted.

the German subject of Austria is called a slave, and the Italian is called a slave, and the negro in the Southern States is called a slave,—and yet, how unlike to one another is the condition of all these slaves! The right of ruling themselves, at pleasure, is that which is assumed to be the test of freedom. The native African has that right, and what is the rule of Africa? A sufficient commentary upon it will be found in the naked, unmarked outlines, hanging upon the walls of our houses, and dignified with the title of maps of Africa. Murder awaits the missionary and the traveller who penetrate the country; and civilization seems to be as far remote as ever from their attainment. And how should it be otherwise? And how should they improve, having never taken the first step in such a progress? They cannot improve until they learn to labor,—they will not learn to labor until they become stationary; and the wandering savage has seldom yet become stationary, unless by the coercion of a superior people.* But the right to govern themselves requires, first, a capacity for such government. The right can only result from a compliance with the laws of their creation; and the capacity requires long ages of preparation, of great trial, hardship, severe labor and perilous enterprise. The responsibilities and the duties of self-government, demand a wonderful and wide-spread knowledge and practice of morals,

* For the sake of the African world, it is to be regretted that, instead of abolishing the slave trade, the nations had not contented themselves with regulating it. Vessels should have been licensed for the trade, of particular burden and construction, and carrying limited numbers; by which means the disgusting and dreadful horrors which resulted from the compression of the unhappy captives, in great numbers, into fœtid and narrow dungeons, would have been avoided, with all of the evils consequent upon their change of condition; leaving them only to the thousand benefits, which make the American slave so superior an animal to the African freemen.

before such a capacity can arise; and it would be an awkward and difficult inquiry at this moment to discover any one of the leading nations of the globe where such a capacity exists. *I will not even believe it to exist in the United States, until I see the people willing to tax themselves directly for their own protection. I will not believe it, so long as they need to be deceived by indirect and circuitous taxation, into the expenditures which are necessary for their own good. They are not yet willing to look in the face the cost of their own liberties.* The practice of the English government denies the existence of any such capacity among its people;* and France!—what

* Great Britain has freed her slaves, yet denies equality to a large portion of her own people—yea, denies them equal liberties of conscience. But how has she freed the blacks? If they had an unqualified right of freedom, by what right has she limited their freedom, in making them apprentices for a term of years? Their rights, if absolute, demanded, on her part, an absolute release of them. While I write, I am reminded of a paragraph in the Table Talk of Coleridge. It is kindred to our notions, and we give it accordingly. He says · "You are always talking of the *rights* of the negroes. As a rhetorical mode of stimulating the people of England *here*, I do not object; but I utterly condemn your frantic practice of declaiming about their rights to the blacks themselves. They ought to be forcibly reminded of the state in which their brethren in Africa still are, and taught to be thankful for the providence which has placed them within the means of grace. *I know no right except such as flows from righteousness;* and as every Christian believes his righteousness to be imputed, so must his right be an imputed right too. *It must flow out of a duty,* and it is under that name that the process of humanization ought to begin and to be conducted throughout." In another paragraph, devoted more distinctly to the proceedings of the British parliament, Mr. Coleridge speaks thus: "Have you been able to discover any principle in this emancipation bill for the slaves, except a principle of fear of the abolition party struggling with a fear of causing some monstrous calamity to the empire at large? *Well! I will not prophesy; and God grant that this tremendous and unprecedented act of positive enactment may not do the harm to the cause of humanity and freedom which I cannot but fear!"*

have all her bloody days, through successive ages, effected for her liberties, but cries for more blood, an increasing discontent, and the fever and phrensy which continually defy and defeat her own laws, in the appetite which calls for fresher uproar? Perhaps, the very homogeneousness of a people is adverse to the most wholesome forms of liberty. It may make of a selfish people (which has succeeded by the aid of other nations in the attainment of a certain degree of moral enlargement) a *successful* people—in the merely worldly sense of the word—but it can never make them, morally, a great one.* For that most perfect form of liberty, which prompts us to love justice for its own sake, it requires strange admixtures of differing races—the combination and comparison of the knowledge which each has separately arrived at—the long trials and conflicts which precede their coming together; and their perfect union in the end, after that subjection on the part of the inferior class, which compels them to a knowledge of what is possessed by the superior. This was the history of the Saxon boors under the Norman conquest—a combination, which has resulted in the production of one of the most perfect specimens of physical organization and moral susceptibilities, which the world has ever known. And where this amalgamation cannot be effected—as in the case of the Israelites—who are too homogeneous for commixture or even communion with other people,—the slave, in the progress of

* The moment that a people boasts of its homogeneousness, we may begin to doubt its farther improvement, particularly if the community be a small one. The homogeneousness of the Jews is, probably, the true reason of their national inferiority. They are a people, without a nation. All insulated communities degenerate; until, in time, they cease even to have issue. The intermarriages of islanders, villagers, and other homogeneous people, should be forbidden by law; and so should the intermarriages among cousins. *Perhaps, it would be well, if our men in America always chose their wives from other States and sections than their own.*

events, acquires the knowledge of the master. When Moses could emulate the Egyptian priesthood, he was able to embody and to represent his people, and to lead them forth from bondage; for then they had acquired all the knowledge which was possessed by the Egyptian; and as they could derive nothing further from the instruction of their masters, the period had naturally arrived for their emancipation. Upon this susceptibility of acquisition, on the part of the slave, depends the whole secret of his release from bondage. It is his mental and moral inferiority which has enslaved, or subjected him to a superior. It is his rise, morally and intellectually, into the same form with his master, which alone can emancipate him.—(*See Appendix.*) It is possible that a time will come, when, taught by our schools, and made strong by our training, the negroes of the Southern States may arrive at freedom; then, at least, his condition may be such as would entitle him to go forth out of bondage. It may be, when that time comes, that, like Pharoah, we too shall prove unwilling to give up our bondmen. But that that time is very far remote, is sufficiently evident from the condition of the free negroes in the Northern States, and elsewhere—the British West Indies, for example. There, in both regions, without restraints of any kind, they rather decline to a worse brutality, with every increase of privilege. In the former region, after a fifty years' enjoyment of their own rule, they have yet founded no city to themselves, raised no community of their own; but are willing to remain the boot-cleaners and the bottle-washers of the whites, in a state of degrading inferiority, which they are too obtuse to feel; and are only made conscious of their degradation, by the occasional kicks and cuffs which they are made to endure, at the humor of the whites, and without any prospect of redress. They have not that moral courage—the true source of independence—which would prompt them, like the poor white pioneer, to sally forth into the wilderness, hew out their homes, and earn their rights by a compliance with their duties. They feel their inferiority to the whites, even when nominally freemen; and sink into the condition of serviles, in fact, if not in name, in compliance with their natural dependence, and unquestionable moral deficiencies. What they show themselves now, with every example around them stimulating them to freedom and ambition, taken in connection with what they have been shown to be from the earliest known periods of history, ought to be conclusive, with every person of common sense, not only that they have no capacity for an individual independent existence, but that they were always designed for a subordinate one. And why should we assume for the Deity, that he has set out with a design, in the creation and government of men, differing from those laws which he has prescribed in the case of all his other creatures. Why should there not be as many races of men, differing in degree, in strength, capacity, art, endowment, as we find them differing in shape, stature, color, organization? Why, indeed, should there not be differing organizations among men, which shall distinctly shadow forth the several duties, and the assigned stations, which they are to fulfil and occupy in life. This would seem to be a necessity, analogous to what is apparent every where in all the other works of God's creation. Nay, is it not absolutely consistent with all that we learn from history of the uses of men and nations? As we note their progress, we detect their mission; and, this done, they themselves disappear. The African seems to have his mission. He does *not* disappear, but he still remains a slave or a savage! I do not believe that he ever will be other than a slave, or that he was made to be otherwise; but that he is designed as an implement in the hands of civilization always. You may eradicate him from place, but not from life. If he ceases to exist in Virginia or Carolina, Georgia or Louisiana, it is only because he is doing the allotted tasks of his master in regions farther South. I look upon Negro Slavery as the destined agent for the civilization of all the states of Mexico, and all the American states beyond.

The circumstance which, more than any thing beside — apart from his original genius—prepared the Anglo-American for the comparative condition of freedom which he enjoys, was the desperate adventure, the trying necessity, and the thousand toils through which he had to go, in contending with the sterility of an unfriendly soil, and the continual and thwarting hostility of surrounding and savage men. The very sterility of New-England, by imposing upon all classes the necessity of labor, gave strength and energy to her sons, and stability to her institutions. Her severe austerity arose even more from her own toils and trials, than from her puritan ancestry; and, bating the bigotry and miserable exclusiveness which, among the vast majority of her people, can find no greatness and little worth beyond her own borders, she confessedly stands among the most successful, in worldly affairs, of any people on the face of the earth. The fertility of the soil in the South, by readily yielding to the hands of Labor, is, without any paradox, the true source of our enervation, and of the doubtful prosperity of our country—as a country merely. Individuals are successful and prosperous, but not the face of the country; and however much this may be the subject of regret on the one hand, like the trumpet of Miss Martineau, it is not without its advantages. It results, we may state, in individuality of character among its people; who never, in consequence, devolve upon societies, combinations, or their neighbors, their several duties of charity, hospitality and friendship; and who sufficiently esteem their own morals, their sense of honor and humanity, to think they can do justice to the claims of their dependants, without the interference or tuition of any gratuitous philanthropy.

The chapter which Miss Martineau devotes to the "Morals of Slavery," should rather be styled the morals of the community. The excesses to which she refers, and in some respects particularizes, are excesses not confined to the slave States, and which do not, in any State, result from slavery. We contend for the morality of slavery among us, as we assert that the institution has wrought, and still continues to work, the improvement of the negro himself; and we confidently challenge a comparison between the slave of Carolina, and the natives of the region from which his ancestors have been brought. No other comparison, with any other people, can properly be made. We challenge comparison between the negro slave in the streets of Charleston, and the negro freeman—so called—in the streets of New-York. Compare either of these with the native Indian, and, so far as the civilized arts, and the ideas of civilization are involved in the comparison, you will find that the negro who has been taught by the white man, is always deferred to, in matters of counsel, by his own Indian master. The negro slave of a Muscoghee warrior, to my knowledge, in frequent instances, is commonly his best counsellor; and the primitive savage follows the direction of him, who, having been forced to obey the laws of his creation, has become wiser, in consequence, than the creature who wilfully refuses.*

---

* "The Indian," says Miss Martineau, "looks with silent wonder upon the settler, who becomes visibly a capitalist in nine months, on the same spot where the red man has remained equally poor all his life." Elsewhere and everywhere she describes the negro slaves of the Indians as looking better than their masters. She attributes this to the milder form of their slavery to that of the whites; though

This subjection to the superior mind is the process through which every inferior nation has gone, and the price which the inferior people must always pay, for that knowledge of, and compliance with, their duties, which alone can bring them to the possession of their rights, and to the due attainment of their liberties—these liberties always growing in value and number with the improving tastes and capacities for their appreciation. Show me any people, which, complying with this inevitable condition, has not improved! Show me one, refusing to comply, which has not perished! Look at the history of man throughout the world, with the eye of a calm, unselfish, deliberate judgment, and say if this be not so. Regard the slave of Carolina, with a proper reference to the condition of the cannibal African from whom he has been rescued, and say if his bondage has not increased his value to himself, not less than to his master. We contend that it found him a cannibal, destined in his own country to eat his fellow, or to be eaten by him;—that it brought him to a land in which he suffers no risk of life or limb, other than that to which his owner is equally subjected;—that it in-

the obvious inference should have been the greater advantages of white slavery in so educating the inferior African, as to lift him into a mental condition vastly superior to that of the red man, who, in a state of nature, is decidedly more intellectual than the black in a like state. She says, speaking of the religious education of the Indian— " I fear that the common process has here been gone through, of taking from the savage the venerable and true which he possessed, and to force upon him something else which is neither venerable nor true." This is one of those vague phrases and seeming philosophies with which the book abounds. The fact is, that the only " venerable and true" which is necessary, for the improvement of the Indian, is the compulsion of labor, whose laws are surely sufficiently venerable, and as surely ought to be true, considering where we find them— the venerable and true which he never yet has been taught, and is not now very likely to acquire.

creases his fecundity infinitely beyond that of the people from whom he has been taken—that it increases his health and strength, improves his physical symmetry and animal organization—that it elevates his mind and morals—that it extends his term of life—that it gives him better and more certain food, better clothing, and more kind and valuable attendance when he is sick. These clearly establish the morality of the slave institutions in the South; and, though they may not prove them to be as perfect as they may be made, as clearly show their propriety and the necessity of preserving them. Indeed, the slaveholders of the South, having the moral and physical guardianship of an ignorant and irresponsible people under their control, are the great moral conservators, in one powerful interest, of the entire world. Assuming slavery to be a denial of justice to the negro, there is no sort of propriety in the application of the name of slave to the servile of the South. He is under no despotic power. There are laws which protect him, *in his place*, as inflexible as those which his proprietor is required to obey, *in his place*. *Providence has placed him in our hands, for his good, and has paid us from his labor for our guardianship.** The question with us is, simply, as to the manner in which we have fulfilled our trust. How have we employed the talents which were given us—how have we discharged the duties of our guardianship? What is the condition of the dependant? Have we been careful to graduate his labors to his capacities? Have we

---

* The slaveholder has no right to free his slave—unless he is perfectly assured of a mental and moral capacity in the slave, sufficiently strong and fixed, to enable him not only to maintain his elevation, but to improve it. Having done so, let him appear before God, if he dare, and account for the trust committed to his hands. The moral and mental worth of the slave, can, alone, give us the right to discharge him from his dependance.

bestowed upon him a fair proportion of the fruits of his industry? Have we sought to improve his mind in correspondence with his condition? Have we raised his condition to the level of his improved mind? Have we duly taught him his moral duties—his duties to God and man? And have we, in obedience to a scrutinizing conscience, been careful to punish only in compliance with his deserts, and never in brutali'y or wantonness? These are the grand questions for the tribunal of each slaveholder's conscience. He must answer them to his God. These are the only questions, and they apply equally to all his other relations in society. Let him carefully put them to himself, and shape his conduct, as a just man, in compliance with what he should consider a sacred duty, undertaken to God and man alike.

APPENDIX.

In farther illustration of some of the topics embodied in this, and other passages of this essay, I make an extract from a dialogue contained in the collection entitled "The Wigwam and the Cabin :"

"Savages are children in all but physical respects. To do anything with them, you must place them in that position of responsibility, and teach them that law, without the due recognition of which, any attempt to educate a child must be an absurdity—you must teach them obedience. They must be made to know, at the outset, that they know nothing, and they must implicitly defer to the superior. This lesson they will never learn, so long as they possess the power, at any moment, to withdraw from his control."

"Yet, even were this to be allowed, there must be a limit. There must come a time when you will be required to emancipate them. In what circumstances will you find that time? You cannot keep them under this coercion always; when will you set them free?"

"When they are fit for freedom."

"How is that to be determined? Who shall decide their fitness?"

"Themselves; as in the case of the children of Israel. The children of Israel went out from bondage as soon as their own intellectual advancement had been such as to enable them to produce from their own ranks a leader like Moses:—one whose genius was equal to that of the people by whom they had been educated, and sufficient for their own proper government thereafter."

"But has not an experiment of this sort already been tried in our country?"

"Nay, I think not—I know of none."

"Yes: an Indian boy was taken, in infancy, from his parents, carried to one of the Northern States, trained in all the learning and habits of a Northern college and society, associated only with whites, beheld no manners, and heard no morals, but those which are known to Christian communities. His progress was satisfactory—he learned rapidly—was considered something of a prodigy, and graduated with eclât. He was then left, with the same option which the rest enjoyed, to the choice of a profession. And what was his choice? Do you not remember the beautiful little poem of Freneau on this subject? He chose the buckskin leggins, the moccasins, bow and arrows, and the wide, wild forests, where his people dwelt."

"Freneau's poem tells the story somewhat differently. The facts upon which it is founded, however, are, I believe, very much as you tell them. But what an experiment it was! How very silly! They take a copper-colored boy from his people, and carry him, while yet an infant, to a remote region. Suppose, in order that the experiment may be fairly tried, that they withhold from him all knowledge of his origin. He is brought up precisely as the other lads around him. But what is the first discovery which he makes? That he is a copper-colored boy; that he is, alone, the only copper-colored boy; that, wherever he turns, he sees no likenesses of himself. This begets his wonder, then his curiosity, and finally his suspicion. He soon understands—for his suspicion sharpens every faculty of observation—that he is an object of experiment. Nay, the most cautious policy in the world could never entirely keep this from a keen-thoughted urchin. His fellow pupils teach him this. He sees that, to them, he is an object of curiosity and study. They regard him, and he soon regards himself, as a creature set apart, and separated, for some peculiar purposes, from all the rest. A stern and singular sense of individuality and isolation is thus forced upon him. He asks—Am I, indeed, alone?—Who am I?—What am I? These inquiries naturally occasion others. Does he read? Books give him the history of his race. Nay, his own story probably meets his eye, in the newspapers. He learns that he is descended from a nation dwelling among the secret sources of the Susquehannah. He pries in all corners for more information. The more secret his search, the more keenly does he pursue it. It becomes the great passion of his mind. He learns that his people are fierce warriors and famous hunters. He hears of their strifes with the white man—their successful strifes, when the nation could send forth its thousand bow-men, and the whites were few and feeble. Perhaps the young pale faces around him speak of his people, even now, as enemies; at least, as objects of suspicion, and possibly antipathy. All these things tend to elevate and idealize, in his mind, the history of his people. He cherishes a sympathy, even beyond the natural desires of the heart, for the perishing race from which he feels himself, 'like a limb, cast bleeding and torn.' The curiosity to see his ancestry—the people of his tribe and country—would be the most natural feeling of the white boy, under similar circumstances; shall we wonder that it is the predominant passion in the bosom of the Indian, whose very complexion forces him away from all connection with the rest! My idea of the experiment—if such a proceeding can be called an experiment—is soon spoken. As a statement of facts, I see nothing to provoke wonder. The result was the most natural thing in the world, and a man of ordinary powers of reflection might easily have predicted it, precisely as it happened. The only wonder is that there should be found, among persons of ordinary education and sagacity, men who should have undertaken such an experiment, and fancied that they were busy in a moral and philosophical problem."

"Why, how would you have the experiment tried?"

"As it was tried upon the Hebrews, upon the Saxons, upon every savage people who ever became civilized. It cannot be tried upon an individual; it must be tried upon a nation—at least upon a community, sustained by no succor from without—having no forests or foreign shores, upon which to turn their eyes for refuge—having no mode or hope of escape—under the full control of an already civilized people—and sufficiently numerous among themselves to find sympathy against those necessary rigors which at first will seem oppressive, but which will be the only hopeful process by which to enforce the work of improvement. They must find this sympathy from beholding others, like themselves in aspect, form, feature and condition, subject to the same unusual restraints. In this contemplation, they will be content to pursue their labors, under a rule which they cannot displace. But the natural law must be satisfied. There must be opportunities yielded for the indulgence of the legitimate passions. The young, of both sexes, among the subjected people, must commune and form ties, in obedience to the requisitions of nature and according to their national customs. What if the Indian student, on whom the 'experiment' was tried, had paid his addresses to a white maiden? What a revulsion of the moral and social sense would have followed his proposition, in the mind of the Saxon damsel; and, were she to consent, what a commotion in the community in which she lived! And this revulsion and commotion would be perfectly natural, and, accordingly, perfectly proper. God has made an obvious distinction between the races of men, setting them apart, and requiring them to be kept so, by subjecting them to the resistance and rebuke of one of the most jealous sentinels of sense which we possess—the eye. The prejudices of this sense require that the natural barriers should be maintained, and hence it becomes necessary that the race in subjection should be sufficiently numerous to enable it to carry out the great object of every distinct community, though, perchance, it may happen to be an inferior one. In process of time, the beneficial and blessing effects of labor would be felt and understood by the most ignorant and savage of the race. Perhaps not in one generation, or in two, but after the fifth and seventh, as it is written, 'of those who keep my commandments.' They would soon discover that, though compelled to toil, their toils neither enfeebled their strength nor impaired their happiness; that, on the contrary, they still resulted in their increasing strength, health and comfort; that their food, which before was precarious, depending on the caprices of the seasons, or the uncertainties of the chase, was now equally plentiful, wholesome and certain. They would also perceive that, instead of the sterility which is usually the destiny of all wandering tribes, and one of the processes by which they perish, the fecundity of their people was wonderfully increased. These discoveries—if time be allowed to make them—would tacitly reconcile them to that inferior position of their race, which is proper and inevitable, so long as their intellectual inferiority shall continue. And what would have been the effect upon our Indians—decidedly the noblest race of aborigines that the world has ever known—if, instead of buying their scalps, at prices varying from five to fifty shillings, each, we had conquered and subjected them? Will any one pretend to say that they would not have increased, with the restraints and enforced toils of our superior genius?—that they would not, by this time, have formed a highly valuable and noble integral in the formation of our national strength and character? Perhaps their civilization would have been comparatively easy. The Hebrews required four hundred years; the Britons and Saxons, possibly, half that time, after the Norman Conquest. Differing in color from their conquerors, though, I suspect, with a natural genius superior to that of the ancient Britons, at the time of the Roman invasion under Julius Cæsar, the struggle between the two races must have continued for some longer time; but the union would have been finally effected, and then, as in the case of the Englishman, we should have possessed a race, in their progeny, which, in moral and physical structure, might have challenged competition with the world."

"Ay, but the difficulty would have been in the conquest."

"True, that would have been the difficulty. The American colonists were few in number and feeble in resource. The nations from which they emerged put forth none of their strength, in sending them forth. Never were colonies so inadequately provided, so completely left to themselves; and hence the peculiar injustice and insolence of the subsequent exactions of the British, by which they required their colonies to support their schemes of aggrandizement and expenditure, by submitting to extreme taxation. Do you suppose, if the early colonists had been powerful, that they would have ever deigned to treat for lands with the roving hordes of savages whom they found on the continent? Never! Their purchases and treaties were not for lands, but tolerance. They bought permission to remain without molestation. The amount professedly paid for land was simply a tribute, paid to the superior strength of the Indian, precisely as we paid it to Algiers and the Mussulmens, until we grew strong enough to whip them into respect. If, instead of a few ships, and a few hundred men, timidly making their approaches along the shores of Manhattan, Penobscot and Ocracocke, some famous leader, like Æneas, had brought his entire people—suppose them to be the persecuted Irish—what a wondrous difference would have taken place. The Indians would have been subjected—would have sunk into their proper position of humility and dependence—and, by this time, might have united with their conquerors, producing, perhaps, along the great ridge of the Alleghany, the very noblest specimens of humanity, in mental and bodily stature, that the world has ever witnessed. The Indians were taught to be insolent, by the fears and feebleness of the whites. They were flattered by fine words, by rich presents, and abundance of deference, until the ignorant savage—but a single degree above the brute—who, until then, had never been sure of his porridge for more than a day ahead—took airs upon himself, and became one of the most conceited and arrogant lords in creation. The colonists grew wiser as they grew stronger; but the evil was already done, and we are reaping some of the bitter fruits, at this day, of seed unwisely sown in that. It may be that we shall yet see the experiment tried fairly."

"Ah, indeed—where?"

"In Mexico, by the Texans. Let the vain, capricious, ignorant and dastardly wretches, who now occupy and spoil the face and fortunes of the former country, persevere in pressing war upon those sturdy adventurers, and their doom is written. I *fear* it may be the sword; I *hope* it may be the milder fate of bondage and subjection. Such a fate would save, and raise them finally to a far higher condition than they have ever before enjoyed. Thirty thousand Texans, each with his horse and rifle, would soon make themselves masters of the city of Montezuma, and then may you see the experiment tried upon a scale sufficiently extensive to make it a fair one. But your Indian student, drawn from

'Susquehannah's farthest springs,'

and sent to Cambridge, would present you some such moral picture as that of the prisoner described by Sterne. His chief employment, day by day, would consist in notching upon his stick the undeviating record of his daily suffering. It would be, to him, an experiment almost as full of torture as that of the Scottish boot, the Spanish thumbscrew, or any of those happy devices of ancient days, for impressing pleasant principles upon the mind, by impressing unpleasant feelings upon the thews, joints and sinews. I wish that some one of our writers, familiar with mental analysis, would make this poem of Freneau the subject of a story. I think it would yield admirable material. To develope the thoughts and feelings of an Indian boy, taken from his people ere yet he has formed such a knowledge of them, or of others, as to have begun to discuss or compare their differences—follow him to a college such as that of Princeton or Cambridge—watch him within its walls—amid the crowd, but not of it—looking only within himself, while all others are looking into him, or trying to do so—surrounded by active, sharp-witted lads, of the Anglo-Norman race—undergoing an hourly repeated series of moral spasms, as he hears them wantonly or thoughtlessly dwell upon the wild and ignorant people from whom he is chosen—listening, though without seeming to listen, to their crude speculations upon the great problem, which is to be solved only by seeing how well he can endure his spasms, and what use he will make of his philosophy, if he survives it—then, when the toils of study and the tedious restraints and troubles of prayer and recitation are got over, to behold and describe the joy with which the happy wretch flings by his fetters, when he is dismissed from those walls which have witnessed his tortures, even supposing him to remain (which is very unlikely) until his course of study is pronounced to be complete! With what curious pleasure will he stop, in the shadow of the first deep forest, to tear from his limbs those garments which make him seem unlike his people! How quick will be the beating at his heart, as he endeavors to dispose about his shoulders the blanket robe, in the manner in which it is worn by the chief warrior of his tribe! With what keen effort—should he have had any previous knowledge of his kindred—will he seek to compel his memory to restore every, the slightest, custom or peculiarity which distinguished them, when his eyes were first withdrawn from the parental tribe; and how closely will he imitate their indomitable pride, and lofty, cold, superiority of look and gesture, as, at evening, he enters the native hamlet, and takes his seat, in silence, at the door of the council house, waiting, without a word, for the summons of the elders!"

"Quite a picture. I think with you, that, in good hands, such a subject would prove a very noble one."

"But the story would not finish here. Supposing all this to have taken place, just as we are told it did—supposing the boy to have graduated at college, and to have flung away the distinction—to have returned, as has been described, to his costume—to the homes and habits of his people;—it is not so clear that he will fling away all the lessons of wisdom, all the knowledge of facts, which he will have acquired from the tuition of the superior race. A natural instinct, which is above all lessons, must be complied with; but, this done, and when the first tumults of his blood have subsided, which led him to defeat the more immediate object of his social training, there will be a gradual resumption of the educational influence in his mind, and his intellectual habits will begin to exercise themselves anew. They will be provoked, necessarily, to this exercise, by what he beholds around him. He will begin to perceive, in its true aspects, the wretchedness of that hunter state, which, surveyed at a distance, appeared only the embodiment of stoical heroism and the most elevated pride. He will see and lament the squalid poverty of his people, which, his first lessons in civilization must have shown him, is due only to the mode of life and pursuits in which they are engaged. Their beastly intoxication will offend his tastes; their superstition and ignorance—the circumscribed limits of their capacity for judging of things and relations, beyond the life of the bird or beast of prey—will awaken in him a sense of shame, when he feels that they are his kindred. The insecurity of their liberties will awaken his fears, for he will instantly see that the great body of the people, in every aboriginal nation, are the veriest slaves in the world; and the degrading exhibitions which they make, in their filth and drunkenness, which reduce the man to a loathsomeness of aspect which is never reached by the vilest beast which he hunts or scourges, will be beheld by the Indian student in very lively contrast with all that has met his eyes during that novitiate among the white sages, the processes of which have been to him so humiliating and painful. His memory reverts to that period with feelings of reconciliation. The torture is over, and the remembrance of former pain, endured with manly fortitude, is comparatively a pleasure. A necessary reaction in his mind takes place; and, agreeably to the laws of nature, what will, and what should follow, but that he will seek to become the tutor and the reformer of his people? They, themselves, will tacitly raise him to this position; for the man of the forest will defer even to the negro who has been educated by the white man. He will try to teach them habits of greater method and industry; he will overthrow the altars of their false gods; he will seek to bind the wandering tribes together, under one head, and in one nation; he will prescribe uniform laws of government. He will succeed in some things; he will fail in others. He will offend the pride of the self-conceited and the mulish—the priesthood will be the first to declare against him—and he will be murdered, most probably, as was Romulus, and afterwards deified. If he escapes this fate, he will yet, most likely, perish from mortification under failure, or in consequence of those mental strifes which spring from that divided allegiance between the feelings belonging to his savage, and those which have had their origin in his Christian schools—those natural strifes between the acquisitions of civilization on the one hand, and those instinct tendencies of the blood which distinguish his connection with the inferior race. In this conflict, he will, at length, when the enthusiasm of his youthful zeal has become chilled by frequent and unexpected defeat, falter, and finally fail. But will there be nothing done for this people? Who can say? I believe that no seed falls, without profit, by the wayside. Even if the truth produces no immediate fruits, it forms a moral manure, which fertilizes the otherwise barren heart, in preparation for the more favorable season. The Indian student may fail, as his teachers did, in realizing the object for which he has striven; and this sort of failure is, by the way, one of the most ordinary of human allotment. The desires of man's heart, by an especial providence, that always wills him to act for the future, generally aim at something far beyond his own powers of performance. But the labor has not been taken in vain, in the progress of successive ages, which has achieved even a small part of its legitimate purposes. The Indian student has done for his people much more than the white man achieves, ordinarily, for his generation, if he has only secured to their use a single truth which they knew not before—if he has overthrown only one of their false gods—if he has smitten off the snaky head of only one of their superstitious prejudices. If he has added to their fields of corn a field of millet, he has induced one farther physical step towards moral improvement. Nay, if there be no other result, the very deference which they will have paid him, as the *elève* of the white man, will be a something gained, of no little importance, towards inducing their more ready, though still tardy, adoption of the laws and guidance of the superior race."

PROFESSOR DEW ON SLAVERY.*

In looking to the texture of the population of our country, there is nothing so well calculated to arrest the attention of the observer, as the existence of negro slavery throughout a large portion of the confederacy. A race of people, differing from us in color and in habits, and vastly inferior in the scale of civilization, have been increasing and spreading, "growing with our growth, and strengthening with our strength," until they have become intertwined and intertwisted with every fibre of society. Go through our Southern country, and every where you see the negro slave by the side of the white man; you find him alike in the mansion of the rich, the cabin of the poor, the workshop of the mechanic, and the field of the planter. Upon the contemplation of a population framed like this, a curious and interesting question readily suggests itself to the inquiring mind:—Can these two distinct races of people, now living together as master and servant, be ever separated? Can the black be sent back to his African home, or will the day ever arrive when he can be liberated from his thraldom, and mount upwards in the scale of civilization and rights, to an equality with the white? This is a question of

---

* Review of the debate in the Virginia Legislature, 1831-'32. By Thomas R. Dew, Professor of History, Metaphysics, and Political Law, William and Mary College, Virginia. Abolition of Slavery. 1. Debate in the Virginia Legislature of '31 '32, on the Abolition of Slavery. Richmond. 2. Letter of Appomattox to the People of Virginia, on the subject of the Abolition of Slavery. Richmond.

truly momentous character; it involves the whole framework of society, contemplates a separation of its elements, or a radical change in their relation, and requires, for its adequate investigation, the most complete and profound knowledge of the nature and sources of national wealth and political aggrandizement, an acquaintance with the elastic and powerful spring of population, and the causes which invigorate or paralyze its energies, together with a clear perception of the varying rights of man, amid all the changing circumstances by which he may be surrounded, and a profound knowledge of all the principles, passions, and susceptibilities which make up the moral nature of our species, and according as they are acted upon by adventitious circumstances, alter our condition, and produce all that wonderful variety of character which so strongly marks and characterizes the human family. Well, then, does it behoove even the wisest statesmen to approach this august subject with the utmost circumspection and diffidence; its wanton agitation even is pregnant with mischief; but rash and hasty action threatens, in our opinion, the whole Southern country with irremediable ruin. The evil of *yesterday's* growth may be extirpated *to-day*, and the vigor of society may heal the wound; but that which is the growth of *ages*, may require *ages* to remove. The Parliament of Great Britain, with all its philanthropic zeal, guided by the wisdom and eloquence of such statesmen as Chatham, Fox, Burke, Pitt, Canning and Brougham, has never yet seriously agitated this question, in regard to the West India possessions. Revolutionary France, actuated by the most intemperate and phrenetic zeal for liberty and equality, attempted to legislate the free people of color, in the Island of St. Domingo, into all the rights and privileges of the whites; and, but a season afterwards, convinced of her madness, she attempted to retrace her steps. But it was too late. The deed had been done.

The bloodiest and most shocking insurrection ever recorded in the annals of history had broken out, and the whole Island was involved in frightful carnage and anarchy, and France, in the end, has been stript " of the brightest jewel in her crown," the fairest and most valuable of all her colonial possessions. Since the revolution, France, Spain and Portugal, large owners of colonial possessions, have not only not abolished slavery in their colonies, but have not even abolished the slave trade in practice.

In our Southern slaveholding country, the question of emancipation has never been seriously discussed in any of our legislatures, until the whole subject, under the most exciting circumstances, was, during the last winter, brought up for discussion in the Virginia Legislature, and plans of partial or total abolition were earnestly pressed upon the attention of that body. It is well known that, during the last summer, in the county of Southampton, in Virginia, a few slaves, led on by Nat Turner, rose in the night, and murdered, in the most inhuman and shocking manner, between sixty and seventy of the unsuspecting whites of that county. The news, of course, was rapidly diffused, and, with it, consternation and dismay were spread throughout the State, destroying, for a time, all feeling of security and confidence; and, even when subsequent development had proved that the conspiracy had been originated by a fanatical negro preacher, (whose confessions prove, beyond a doubt, mental aberration,) and that this conspiracy embraced but few slaves, all of whom had paid the penalty of their crimes, still the excitement remained, still the repose of the commonwealth was disturbed, for the ghastly horrors of the Southampton tragedy could not immediately be banished from the mind—and *rumor*, too, with her thousand tongues, was busily engaged in spreading tales of disaffection, plots, insurrections, and even massacres, which frightened the timid, and harassed and mortified the whole of the slaveholding population. During this period of excitement, when reason was almost banished from the mind, and the imagination was suffered to conjure up the most appalling phantoms, and picture to itself a crisis, in the vista of futurity, when the overwhelming numbers of the blacks would rise superior to all restraint, and involve the fairest portion of our land in universal ruin and desolation, we are not to wonder that, even in the lower part of Virginia, many should have seriously inquired if this supposed monstrous evil could not be removed from our bosom? Some looked to the removal of the free people of color, by the efforts of the Colonization Society, as an antidote to all our ills. Some were disposed to strike at the root of the evil: to call on the General Government for aid, and, by the labors of *Hercules*, to extirpate the curse of slavery from the land. Others again, who could not bear that Virginia should stand towards the General Government (whose unconstitutional action she had ever been foremost to resist) in the attitude of a suppliant, looked forward to the legislative action of the State, as capable of achieving the desired result. In this state of excitement and unallayed apprehension, the Legislature met, and plans for abolition were proposed, and earnestly advocated in debate.

Upon the impropriety of this debate, we beg leave to make a few observations. Any scheme of abolition, proposed so soon after the Southampton tragedy, would necessarily appear to be the result of that most inhuman massacre. Suppose the negroes, then, to be really anxious for their emancipation, no matter on what terms, would not the extraordinary effect produced on the Legislature by the Southampton insurrection, in all probability, have a tendency to excite another? And we must recollect, from the nature of things, no plan of abolition could act suddenly on the whole mass of slave population in the State. Mr. Randolph's was not even to commence its operation till 1840. Waiting, then, one year or more, until the excitement could be allayed, and the empire of reason could once more have been established, would surely have been productive of no injurious consequences; and, in the mean time, a Legislature could have been selected, which would much better have represented the views and wishes of their constituents, on this vital question. Virginia could have ascertained the sentiments and wishes of other slaveholding States, whose concurrence, if not absolutely necessary, might be highly desirable, and should have been sought after and attended to, at least, as a matter of State courtesy. Added to this, the texture of the Legislature was not of that character calculated to ensure the confidence of the people, in a movement of this kind. If ever there was a question debated in a deliberative body, which called for the most exalted talent, the longest and most tried experience, the utmost circumspection and caution, a complete exemption from prejudice and undue excitement, where both are apt to prevail, an ardent and patriotic desire to advance the vital interests of the State, uncombined with mere desire for vain and ostentatious display, and with no view to party or geographical divisions, that question was the question of the *abolition* of *slavery*, in the Virginia Legislature. "*Grave* and *reverend* seniors," "the very fathers of the Republic," were indeed required, for the settlement of a question of such magnitude. It appears, however, that the Legislature was composed of an unusual number of young and inexperienced members, elected in the month of April, previous to the Southampton massacre, and at a time of profound tranquillity and repose, when, of course, the people were not disposed to call from their retirement their most distinguished and experienced citizens.

We are very ready to admit, that in point of ability and

eloquence, the debate transcended our expectations. One of the leading political papers in the State remarked, "We have never heard any debate so eloquent, so sustained, and in which so great a number of speakers had appeared, and commanded the attention of so numerous and intelligent an audience." . . . . . "Day after day, multitudes throng to the capital, and have been compensated by eloquence which would have illustrated Rome or Athens." But, however fine might have been the rhetorical display, however ably some isolated points may have been discussed, still we affirm, with confidence, that no enlarged, wise and practical plan of operations was proposed by the abolitionists. We will go farther, and assert that their arguments, in most cases, were of a wild and intemperate character, based upon false principles, and assumptions of the most vicious and alarming kind, subversive of the rights of property and the order and tranquillity of society, and portending to the whole slaveholding country—if they ever shall be followed out in practice—the most inevitable and ruinous consequences. Far be it, however, from us, to accuse the abolitionists in the Virginia Legislature of any settled or malevolent design to overturn or convulse the fabric of society. We have no doubt that they were acting conscientiously for the best; but it often happens that frail, imperfect man, in the too ardent and confident pursuit of imaginary good, runs upon his utter destruction.

We have not formed our opinion lightly upon this subject; we have given to the vital question of abolition the most mature and intense consideration which we are capable of bestowing, and we have come to the conclusion—a conclusion which seems to be sustained by facts and reasoning as irresistible as the demonstration of the mathematician—that every plan of emancipation and deportation which we can possibly conceive, is *totally* impracticable. We shall endeavor to prove that the attempt to execute these plans can only have a tendency to increase all the evils of which we complain, as resulting from slavery. If this be true, then the great question of abolition will necessarily be reduced to the question of emancipation, with a permission to remain, which, we think, can easily be shown to be utterly subversive of the interests, security and happiness of both the blacks and whites, and consequently, hostile to every principle of expediency, morality, and religion. We have heretofore doubted the propriety, even, of too frequently agitating, especially in a public manner, the question of abolition, in consequence of the injurious effects which might be produced on the slave population. But the Virginia Legislature, in its zeal for discussion, boldly set aside all prudential considerations of this kind, and openly and publicly debated the subject, before the world. The seal has now been broken—the example has been set from a high quarter; we shall, therefore, waive all considerations of a prudential character, which have hitherto restrained us, and boldly grapple with the abolitionists and this great question. We fear not the result, so far as truth, justice and expediency alone are concerned. But we must be permitted to say that we do most deeply dread the effects of misguided philanthropy, and the marked, and, we had like to have said, impertinent intrusion in this matter, of those who have no interest at stake, and who have not intimate and minute knowledge of the whole subject, so absolutely necessary to wise action.

Without further preliminary, then, we shall advance to the discussion of the question of abolition, noticing not only the plans proposed in the Virginia Legislature, but some others, likewise. And, as the subject of slavery has been considered in every point of view, and pronounced, in the *abstract*, at least, as entirely contrary to the law of nature, we propose taking, in the first place, a hasty view of the origin of slavery, and point out the influence which it has exerted on the progress of civilization, and to this purpose it will be necessary to look back to other ages—cast a glance at nations differing from us in civilization and manners, and see whether it is possible to mount to the source of slavery.

1. *Origin of Slavery, and its Effects on the Progress of Civilization.*

Upon an examination of the nature of man, we find him to be almost entirely the creature of circumstances—his habits and sentiments are, in a great measure, the growth of adventitious causes—hence the endless variety and condition of our species. We are almost ever disposed, however, to identify the course of nature with the progress of events in our own narrow contracted sphere; we look upon any deviation from the constant round in which *we* have been spinning out the thread of our existence, as a departure from nature's great system, and, from a known principle of our nature, our first impulse is to condemn. It is thus that the man born and matured in the lap of freedom, looks upon slavery as unnatural and horrible; and, if he be not instructed upon the subject, is sure to think that so unnatural a condition could never exist, but in few countries or ages, in violation of every law of justice or humanity; and he is almost disposed to implore the divine wrath, to shower down the consuming fire of heaven on the Sodoms and Gomorrahs of the world, where this unjust practice prevails.

But, when he examines into the past condition of mankind, he stands amazed at the fact which history develops to his view. "Almost every page of ancient history," says Wallace, in his Dissertation on the Numbers of Mankind, "demonstrates the great multitudes of slaves; which gives occasion to a melancholy reflection, that the world, when best peopled, was not a world of freemen, but of slaves."* "And in every age and country, until times comparatively recent," says Hallam, "personal servitude appears to have been the lot of a large, perhaps the greater portion of mankind."†

Slavery was established and sanctioned by divine authority, among even the elect of heaven, the favored children of Israel. Abraham, the founder of this interesting nation, and the chosen servant of the Lord, was the owner of *hundreds* of slaves. That magnificent shrine, the Temple of Solomon, was reared by the hands of slaves. Egypt's venerable and enduring piles were reared by similar hands. Slavery existed in Assyria and Babylon. The ten tribes of Israel were carried off in bondage to the former by Shalmanezar, and the two tribes of Judah were subsequently carried in triumph by Nebuchadnezzar, to beautify and adorn the latter. Ancient Phœnicia and Carthage had slaves. The Greeks and Trojans, at the siege of Troy, had slaves. Athens, and Sparta, and Thebes, indeed the whole Grecian and Roman worlds, had more slaves than freemen. And in those ages which succeeded the extinction of the Roman empire in the West, "*servi*, or slaves," says Dr. Robertson, "seem to have been the most numerous class."‡ Even in this day of civilization, and the regeneration of governments, slavery is far from being confined to our hemisphere alone. The serf and labor rents prevalent throughout the whole of Eastern Europe, and a portion of Western Asia, and the ryot rents throughout the extensive and over populated countries of the East, and over the dominions of the Porte in Europe, Asia and Africa, but too conclusively

* P. 93, Edinburgh edition.
† Middle Ages, vol. 1, p. 120, Philadelphia edition.
‡ See Robertson's Works, vol. 3, p. 186.

mark the existence of slavery over these boundless regions. And when we turn to the continent of Africa, we find slavery, in all its most horrid forms, existing throughout its whole extent, the slaves being at least three times more numerous than the freemen; so that, looking to the whole world, we may, even now, with confidence assert, that slaves, or those whose condition is infinitely worse, form by far the largest portion of the human race!

Well, then, may we here pause, and inquire a moment—for it is surely worthy of inquiry—how has slavery arisen and thus spread over our globe? We shall not pretend to enumerate accurately, and in detail, all the causes which have led to slavery; but we believe the principal may be summed up under the following heads: 1st. Laws of War; 2d. State of Property and Feebleness of Government; 3d. Bargain and Sale; and 4th. Crime.

1st. *Laws of War.*—There is no circumstance which more honorably and creditably characterizes modern warfare, than the humanity with which it is waged, and the mildness with which captives are treated. Civilized nations, with but few exceptions, now act in complete conformity with the wise rule laid down by Grotius, "that in war we have a right only to the use of those means which have a connection *morally necessary* with the end in view." Consequently, we have no just right, where this rule is adhered to by our adversary, to enslave or put to death enemies *non-combatant*, who may be in our possession: for this, in modern times, among civilized nations, is not *morally necessary* to the attainment of the end in view. On the contrary, if such a practice were commenced now, it would only increase the calamities of the belligerents, by converting their wars into wars of extermination, or rapine and plunder, terminated generally with infinitely less advantage, and more difficulty to each of the parties. But humane and advantageous as this mitigated practice appears, we are not to suppose it universal, or that it has obtained in all ages. On the contrary, it is the growth of modern civilization, and has been confined, in a great measure, to civilized Europe and its colonies.

Writers on the progress of society designate three stages in which man has been found to exist. First, the hunting or fishing state; second, the pastoral; third, agricultural. Man, in the hunting state, has ever been found to wage war in the most cruel and implacable manner, extermination being the object of the belligerent tribes. Never has there been a finer field presented to the philosopher, for a complete investigation of the character of any portion of our species, than the whole American hemisphere presented, for the complete investigation of the character of savages, in the hunting and fishing state.

Dr. Robertson has given us a most appalling description of the cruelties with which savage warfare was waged, throughout the whole continent of America, and the barbarous manner in which prisoners were everywhere put to death. He justly observes, that the bare description is enough to chill the heart with horror, wherever men have been accustomed, by milder institutions, to respect their species, and to melt into tenderness at the sight of human sufferings. The prisoners are tied naked to a stake, but so as to be at liberty to move round it. All who are present—men, women and children—rush upon them like furies. Every species of torture is applied, that the rancor of revenge can invent: some burn their limbs with red hot iron, some mangle their bodies with knives, others tear their flesh from their bones, pluck out their nails by the roots, and rend and twist their sinews. Nothing sets bounds to their rage but the dread of abridging the duration of their vengeance, by hastening the death of the sufferers; and such is their cruel ingenuity in tormenting, that, by avoiding industriously to hurt any vital part, they often prolong the scene of anguish for several days."*

Let us now inquire into the cause of such barbarous practices, and we shall find that they must be imputed principally to the passion of revenge. In the language of the same eloquent writer whom we have just quoted, "in small communities, every man is touched with the injury or affront offered to the body of which he is a member, as if it were a personal attack on his own honor and safety. War, which, between extensive kingdoms, is carried on with little animosity, is prosecuted by small tribes with all the rancor of a private quarrel. When polished nations have obtained the glory of victory, or have acquired an addition of territory, they may terminate a war with honor. But savages are not satisfied, until they extirpate the community which is the object of their hatred. They fight not to conquer, but destroy." "The desire of vengeance is the first, and almost the only principle, which a savage instils into the minds of his children. The desire of vengeance, which takes possession of the hearts of savages, resembles the instinctive rage of an animal, rather than the passion of a man."† Unfortunately, too, interest conspires with the desire of revenge, to render savage warfare horrible. The wants of the savage, it is true, are few and simple; but, limited as they are, according to their mode of life, it is extremely difficult to supply them. Hunting and fishing afford, at best, a very precarious subsistence. Throughout the extensive regions of America, population was found to be most sparsely settled; but, thin as it was, it was most wretchedly and scantily supplied with provisions. Under these circumstances, prisoners of war could

---

* See Robertson's America, Phil. ed., vol. 1, p. 197.
† Ibid., vol. 1, pp. 192, 193.

not be kept, for the feeding of them would be sure to produce a famine.* They would not be sent back to their tribe, for that would strengthen the enemy. They could not even make slaves of them, for their labor would have been worthless. Death, then, was, unfortunately, the punishment, which was prompted both by interest and revenge. And, accordingly, throughout the whole continent of America, we find, with but one or two exceptions, that this was the dreadful fate which awaited the prisoners of all classes, men, women and children. In fact, this has been the practice of war, wherever man was found in the first stages of society, living on the precarious subsistence of the chase. The savages of the Islands of Andaman, in the East, supposed by many to be lowest in the scale of civilization, of Van Diemen's Land, of New Holland, and of the Islands of the South Pacific,† are all alike—they all agree in the practice of exterminating enemies, by the most perfidious and cruel conduct, and, throughout many extensive regions, the horrid practice of feasting on the murdered prisoners prevailed.‡

* " If a few Spaniards settled in any district, such a small addition of supernumerary mouths soon exhausted their scanty store, and brought on famine."—Robertson, p. 182.

† Captain Cook says, of the natives in the neighborhood of Queen Charlotte's Sound, "If I had followed the advice of all our pretended friends, I might have extirpated the whole race, for the people of each hamlet or village, by turns, applied to me to destroy the other. . . . . It appears to me that the New Zealanders must live in perpetual apprehension of being destroyed by each other."

‡ " Among the Iroquois," says Dr. Robertson, " the phrase by which they express their resolution of making war against an enemy is, ' let us go and eat that nation.' If they solicit the aid of a neighboring tribe, they invite it to ' eat broth made of the flesh of their enemies.' " Among the Abnakis, according to the " Lettres Edif. et Curieuse," the chief, after dividing his warriors into parties, says to each, " to you is

What is there, let us ask, which is calculated to arrest this horrid practice, and to communicate an impulse towards civilization? Strange as it may sound in modern ears, it is the institution of property and the existence of slavery. Judging from the universality of the fact, we may assert that domestic slavery seems to be the only means of fixing the wanderer to the soil, moderating his savage temper, mitigating the horrors of war, and abolishing the practice of murdering the captives. In the pure hunting state, man has little idea of property, and consequently there is little room for distinction, except what arises from personal qualities. People in this state retain, therefore, a high sense of equality and independence. It is a singular fact, that the two extremes of society are most favorable to liberty and equality—the most savage, and the most refined and enlightened—the former, in consequence of the absence of the institution of property, and the latter from the diffusion of knowledge, and the consequent capability of self-government. The former is characterized by a wild, licentious independence, totally subversive of all order and tranquillity; and the latter by a well-ordered, well-established liberty, which, while it leaves to each the enjoyment of the fruits of his industry, secures him against the lawless violence and rapine of his neighbors. Throughout the whole American continent, this equality and savage independence seem to have prevailed, except in the comparatively great kingdoms of Mexico and Peru, where the right to property was established.

So soon as the private right to property is established,

---

given such a hamlet to eat, to you such a village," etc. Captain Cook, in his third voyage, says of the New Zealanders, " Perhaps the desire of making a good meal (on prisoners) is no small inducement " to go to war.

slavery commences; and with the institution of slavery, the cruelties of war begin to diminish. The chief finds it to his interest to make slaves of his captives, rather than put them to death. This system commences with the shepherd state, and is consummated in the agricultural. Slavery, therefore, seems to be the chief means of mitigating the horrors of war. Accordingly, wherever, among barbarous nations, they have so far advanced in civilization as to understand the use which may be made of captives, by converting them into slaves, there the cruelties of war are found to be lessened.

Throughout the whole continent of Africa, in consequence of the universal prevalence of slavery, war is not conducted with the same barbarous ferocity as by the American Indian. And hence it happens that some nations become most cruel to those whom they would most wish to favor. Thus, on the borders of Persia, some of the tribes of Tartars massacre all the true believers who fall into their hands, but preserve heretics and infidels, because their religion forbids them to make slaves of true believers, and allows them to use or sell all others, at their pleasure.*

In looking to the history of the world, we find that interest, and *interest* alone, has been enabled successfully to war against the fiercer passion of revenge. The only instance of mildness in war, among the savages of North America, results from the operation of interest. Sometimes, when the tribe has suffered great loss of numbers, and stands very much in need of recruits, the prisoner is saved, and adopted (says Robertson) as a member of the nation. Pastoral nations require but few slaves, and, consequently, they save but few prisoners for this purpose. Agricultural require more, and this state

* Tacitus tells us that civil wars are always the most cruel, because the prisoners are not made slaves.

is the most advantageous to slavery. Prisoners of war are generally spared by such nations, in consideration of the use which may be made of their labor.

It is curious, in this respect, to contemplate the varied success with which, under various circumstances, the principle of self-interest combats that of vengeance. The barbarians who overran the Roman Empire existed principally in the pastoral state. They brought along with them their wives and children, and consequently they required extensive regions for their support, and but few slaves. We find, accordingly, they waged a most cruel, exterminating war, not even sparing women and children. "Hence," says Dr. Robertson, in his preliminary volume to the History of Charles V., "if a man were called to fix upon a period in the history of the world, during which the condition of the human race was most calamitous and afflicted, he would, without hesitation, name that which elapsed from the death of Theodosius the Great, (A.D. 395.) to the reign of Alboinus in Lombardy." (A.D. 571.) At the last mentioned epoch, the barbarian inundations spent themselves, and, consequently, repose was given to the world.

Slavery was very common at the siege of Troy; but, in consequence of the very rude state of agriculture prevalent in those days, and the great reliance placed on the spontaneous productions of the earth, the same number of slaves was not required as in subsequent ages, when agriculture had made greater advances. Hence we find the laws of war of a very cruel character, the principle of revenge triumphing over every other. These are the evils, we are informed by Homer, that follow the capture of a town: "The men are killed, the city is burned to the ground, the women and children of all ranks are carried off for slaves." (Iliad, L. 9.) Again: "Wretch that I am," says the venerable Priam, "what evil does the great Jupiter bring on me in my old age? My sons slain, my daughters dragged into slavery, violence pervading even the chambers of my palace, and the very infants dashed against the ground, in horrid sport of war. I myself, slain in the vain office of defence, shall be the prey of my own dogs, perhaps, in the very palace gates!" (Iliad, L. 22.)

In after times, during the glorious days of the republics of both Greece and Rome, the wants of man had undergone an enlargement; agriculture had been pushed to a high state of improvement, population became more dense, and consequently a more abundant production, and more regular and constant application of labor, became necessary. At this period, slaves were in great demand, and, therefore, the prisoners of war were generally spared, in order that they might be made slaves. And this mildness did not arise so much from their civilization, as from the great demand for slaves. All the Roman generals, even the mild Julius, were sufficiently cruel to put to death, when they did not choose to make slaves of the captives. Hence, as cruel as were the Greeks and Romans in war, they were much milder than the surrounding barbarous nations. In like manner, the wars in Africa have been made, perhaps, more mild by the *slave trade* than they would otherwise have been. Instances are frequent, where the prisoner has been immediately put to death, because a purchaser could not be found. The report of the Lords, in 1789, speaks of a female captive in Africa, for whom an anker of brandy had been offered; but before the messenger arrived, her head had been cut off. Sir George Young saved the life of a beautiful boy, about five years old at Sierra Leone. The child was about to be thrown into the river by the person who had him to sell, because he was too young to be an object of trade; but Sir George offered a quarter cask of Madeira for him, which was accepted.* A

* See Edward's West Indies, vol. 2, book 4, chap. 4.

multitude of such instances might easily be cited, from commanders of vessels and travellers, who have ever visited Africa. And thus do we find, by a review of the history of the world, that slavery alone, which addresses itself to the principle of self-interest, is capable of overcoming that inordinate desire of vengeance which glows in the breast of the savage; and, therefore, we find the remark made by Voltaire, in his Phi. Dic., that "slavery is as ancient as war, and war as human nature," is not strictly correct: for many wars have been too cruel to admit of slavery.

Let us now close this head, by an inquiry into the justice of slavery, flowing from the laws of war. And here we may observe, in the first place, that the whole of the ancient world, and all nations of modern times verging on a state of barbarism, never for a moment doubted this right. All history proves that they looked upon slavery as a mild punishment, in comparison with what they had a right to inflict. And, so far from being conscience-stricken, when they inflicted the punishment of death or slavery, they seemed to glory in the severity of the punishment, and to be remorseful only when, from some cause, they had not inflicted the worst. "Why so tender-hearted," says Agamemnon to Menelaus, seeing him hesitate, while a Trojan of high rank, who had the misfortune to be disabled, by being thrown from his chariot, was begging for life, "are you and your horse so beholden to the Trojans? Let not one of them escape destruction from our hands—no, not the child within his mother's womb. Let all perish unmourned." And the poet even gives his sanction to this inhumanity of Agamemnon, who was never characterized as inhuman: "It was justly spoken, (says Homer,) and he turned his brother's mind." And the suppliant was murdered by the hand of the king of men. "When the unfortunate monarch of Troy came to beg the body of his heroic son, (Hector,) we find the conduct of Achilles marked by a superior spirit of generosity. Yet, in the very act of granting the pious request, he doubts if he is quite excusable to the soul of his departed friend, for remitting the extremity of vengeance which he had meditated, and restoring the corse to secure the rites of burial."* To ask them, whether men, with notions similar to these, had a right to kill or enslave the prisoners, would almost be like gravely inquiring into the right of tigers and lions to kill each other, and devour the weaker beasts of the forest. If we look to the republics of Greece and Rome, in the days of their glory and civilization, we shall find no one doubting the right to make slaves of those taken in war. "No legislator of antiquity," says Voltaire, "ever attempted to abrogate slavery; on the contrary, the people the most enthusiastic for liberty—the Athenians, the Lacedemonians, the Romans, and the Carthagenians—were those who enacted the most severe laws against their serfs. Society was so accustomed to this degradation of the species, that Epictetus, who was assuredly worth more than his master, never expresses any surprise at his being a slave."† Julius Cæsar has been reckoned one of the mildest and most clement military chieftains of antiquity, and yet there is very little doubt, that the principal object in the invasion of Britain, was to procure slaves for the Roman slave markets. When he left Britain, it became necessary to collect together a large fleet, for the purpose of transporting his captives across the channel. He sometimes ordered the captive chiefs to be executed, and he butchered the whole of Cato's Senate, when he became master of Utica. Paulus Emilius, acting under the special orders of the Roman Senate,

---

* See Mitford's Greece, vol. 1, chap. 2, sec. 4.
† See Philosophical Dictionary, title "Slaves."

laid all Epirus waste, and brought 150,000 captives in chains to Italy, all of whom were sold in the Roman slave markets. Augustus Cæsar was considered one of the mildest, most pacific, and most politic of the Roman Emperors; yet, when he rooted out the nation of the Salassii, who dwelt upon the Alps, he sold 36,000 persons into slavery. Cato was a large owner of slaves, most of whom he had purchased in the slave markets at the sale of prisoners of war.* Aristotle, the greatest philosopher of antiquity, and a man of as capacious mind as the world ever produced, was a warm advocate of slavery—maintaining that it was reasonable, necessary, and natural; and, accordingly, in his model of a republic, there were to be comparatively few freemen served by many slaves.†

If we turn from profane history to Holy Writ—that sacred fountain whence are derived those pure precepts, and holy laws and regulations by which the Christian world has ever been governed—we shall find that the children of Israel, under the guidance of Jehovah, massacred or enslaved their prisoners of war. So far from considering slavery a curse, they considered it a punishment much too mild, and regretted, from this cause alone, its infliction.

The children of Israel, when they marched upon the tribes of Canaan, were in a situation very similar to the northern invaders who overran the Roman Empire. They had their wives and children along with them, and wished to make Canaan their abode. Extermination, therefore, became necessary; and accordingly, we find that the Gibeonites alone, who practised upon the princes of Israel by a fraud, escaped the dreadful scene of carnage. They were enslaved, and so far from regretting their lot, they seem to have delighted in it; and the children of Israel, instead of mourning over the des-

* See Plutarch's Lives, Cato the Elder.
† Aristotle's Politics, book 1, chap. 4.

tiny of the enslaved Gibeonites, murmured that they were not massacred—"and all the congregation murmured against the princes." And the answer of the princes was, "we will even let them live, lest wrath be upon us, because of the oath which we swear unto them." "But let them be hewers of wood and drawers of water unto all the congregation, as the princes had promised them."*

But it is needless to multiply instances farther to illustrate the ideas of the ancient world in regard to their rights to kill or enslave at pleasure the unfortunate captive. Nor will we now cite the example of Africa, the great storehouse of slavery for the modern world, which so completely sustains our position in regard to the opinions of men on this subject, farther than to make an extract from a speech delivered in the British House of Commons, by Mr. Henniker, in 1789, in which the speaker asserts that a letter had been received by George III., from one of the most powerful of African potentates, the Emperor of Dahomey, which letter admirably exemplifies an African's notions about the right to kill or enslave prisoners of war. "He (Emperor of Dahomey) stated," said Mr. H., "that as he understood King George was the greatest of white kings, so he thought himself the greatest of black ones. He asserted that he could lead 500,000 men armed into the field, that being the pursuit to which all his subjects were bred, and the women only staying at home to plant and manure the earth. He had himself fought two hundred and nine battles, with great reputation and success, and had conquered the great king of Ardah. The king's head was to this day preserved with the flesh and hair; the heads of his generals were distinguished by being placed on each side of the doors of their Fetiches; with the heads of the inferior officers they paved the space before the doors; and the heads

* See 9th chapter of Joshua.

of the common soldiers formed a sort of fringe or outwork round the walls of the palace. Since this war, he had experienced the greatest good fortune, and he hoped in good time to be able to complete the out walls of all his great houses, to the number of seven, in the same manner."*

Mr. Norris, who visited this empire in 1772, actually testifies to the truth of this letter. He found the palace of the Emperor an immense assemblage of cane and mud tents, enclosed by a high wall. The skulls and jaw bones of enemies slain in battle, formed the favorite ornaments of the palaces and temples. The king's apartments were paved, and the walls and roof stuck over with these horrid trophies. And if a farther supply appeared at any time desirable, he announced to his general, that "his house wanted thatch," when a war for that purpose was immediately undertaken.† Who can for a moment be so absurd as to imagine that such a prince as this could doubt of his right to make slaves in war, when he *gloried* in being able to thatch his houses with the heads of his enemies? Who could doubt that any thing else than a strong sense of interest, would ever put an end to such barbarity and ferocity? Our limits will not allow us to be more minute, however interesting the subject.

And, therefore, we will now examine into the right, according to the law of nations—the strict *jus gentium*—and we shall find all the writers agree in the justice of slavery, under certain circumstances. Grotius says that, as the law of nature permits prisoners of war to be killed, so the same law has introduced the right of making them slaves, that the captors, in view to the benefit arising from the labor or sale of their prisoners, might be induced to spare them.‡ From

---

* See Haz'itz's British Eloquence, vol. 2.
† See Family Library, No. 16, p. 199.
‡ L 3, chap. 7, sec. 5. 4 Book 6, chap. 3.

the general practice of nations before the time of Puffendorf, he came to the conclusion that slavery has been established "by the free consent of the opposing parties."*

Rutherforth, in his Institutes, says, "since all the members of a nation, against which a just war is made, are bound to repair the damages that gave occasion to the war, or that are done in it, and likewise to make satisfaction for the expenses of carrying it on; the law of nations will allow those who are prisoners to be made slaves by the nation which takes them; that so their labor, or the price for which they are sold, may discharge these demands." But he most powerfully combats the more cruel doctrine laid down by Grotius, that the master has a right to take away the life of his slave. Bynkershoek contends for the higher right of putting prisoners of war to death: "We may, however, (enslave,) if we please," he adds, "and indeed we do sometimes still exercise that right upon those who enforce it against us. Therefore the Dutch are in the habit of selling to the Spaniards as slaves, the Algerines, Tunisians, and Tripolitans, whom they take prisoners in the Atlantic or Mediterranean. Nay, in the year 1661, the States General gave orders to their admiral to sell as slaves all the pirates that he should take. The same thing was done in 1664."† Vattel, the most humane of all the standard authors on national law, asks—"are prisoners of war to be made slaves?" To which he answers, "Yes; in cases which give a right to kill them, when they have rendered themselves personally guilty of some crime deserving death."‡ Even Locke, who has so ably explored all the faculties of the mind, and who so nobly stood forth against the monstrous and absurd doctrines of Sir Robert Filmer, and the

---

* Book, chap. 9, sec. 17.
† Treatise on the Law of War, Du Ponceau's Ed. p. 21.
‡ See Law of Nations, book 3, chap. 8, sec. 152.

passive submissionists of his day, admits the right to make slaves of prisoners whom we might justly have killed. Speaking of a prisoner who has forfeited his life, he says, " he to whom he has forfeited it may, when he has him in his power, delay to take it, and make use of him to his own service, and he does him no injury by it."* Blackstone, it would seem, denies the right to make prisoners of war slaves; for he says we had no right to enslave, unless we had the right to kill, and we had no right to kill, unless " in cases of absolute necessity, for self-defence; and it is plain this absolute necessity did not subsist, since the victor did not actually kill him, but made him prisoner."† Upon this we have to remark, 1st, that Judge Blackstone here speaks of slavery in its pure, unmitigated form, " whereby an unlimited power is given to the master over the life and fortune of the slave."‡ Slavery scarcely exists any where in this form, and if it did, it would be a continuance of a state of war, as Rousseau justly observes, between the captive and the captor. Again: Blackstone, in his argument upon this subject, seems to misunderstand the grounds upon which civilians place the justification of slavery, as arising from the laws of war. It is well known that most of the horrors of war spring from the principle of retaliation, and not, as Blackstone supposes, universally from " absolute necessity." If two civilized nations of modern times are at war, and one hangs up, without any justifiable cause, all of the enemy who fall into its possession, the other does not hesitate to inflict the same punishment upon an equal number of its prisoners. It is the " *lex talionis*," and not the absolute necessity, which gives rise to this.

The colonists of this country up to the revolution, during,

* On Civil Government, chap. 6.
† See Tucker's Blackstone, vol. 2, p. 423.
‡ Blackstone's Commentaries, in loco citato.

and even since that epoch, have put to death the Indian captives, whenever the Indians had been in the habit of massacreing indiscriminately. It was not so much absolute necessity as the law of retaliation, which justified this practice; and, the civilians urge that the greater right includes the lesser; and, consequently, the right to kill involves the more humane and more useful right of enslaving. In point of fact, it would seem that the Indians were often enslaved by the colonists.* Although we find no distinct mention made, by any of the historians, of the particular manner in which this slavery arose, yet it is not difficult to infer that it must have arisen from the laws of war, being a commutation of the punishment of death for slavery. Again: If the nation with which you are at war makes slaves of all your citizens falling into its possession, surely you have the right to retaliate and do so likewise. It is the "*lex talionis*," and not absolute necessity, which justifies you; and, if you should choose from policy to waive your right, your ability to do so would not, surely, prove that you had no right at all to enslave. Such a doctrine as this would prove that the rights of belligerents were in the inverse ratio of their strength— a doctrine which, pushed to the extreme, would always reduce the hostile parties to a precise equality—which is a perfect absurdity. If we were to suppose a civilized nation in the heart of Africa, surrounded by such princes as the King of Dahomey, there is no doubt that such a nation would be justifiable in killing or enslaving at its option, in time of war, and if it did neither, it would relinquish a *perfect right*.† We have now consi-

* See Tucker's Blackstone, vol 2, Appendix, note H.

† We shall hereafter see that our colony at Liberia may, at some future day, be placed in an extremely embarrassing condition from this very cause. It may not in future wars have strength sufficient to forego the exercise of the right of killing or enslaving, and if it

dered the most fruitful source of slavery—*laws of war*—and shall proceed more briefly to the consideration of the other three which we have mentioned, taking up—

2. *State of Property and Feebleness of Government.*—In tracing the manners and customs of a people who have emerged from a state of barbarism, and examining into the nature and character of their institutions, we find it of the first importance to look to the condition of property, in order that we may conduct our inquiries with judgment and knowledge. The character of the government, in spite of all its forms, depends more on the condition of property, than on any one circumstance beside. The relations which the different classes of society bear towards each other, the distinction into high and low, noble and plebeian, in fact, depend almost exclusively upon the state of property. It may be with truth affirmed, that the exclusive owners of the property ever have been, ever will, and perhaps ever ought to be, the virtual rulers of mankind. If, then, in any age or nation, there should be but one species of property, and that should be exclusively owned by a portion of citizens, that portion would become inevitably the masters of the residue. And if the government should be so feeble as to leave each one, in a great measure, to protect himself, this circumstance would have a tendency to throw the property into the hands of a few, who would rule with despotic sway over the many. And this was the condition of Europe during the middle ages, under what was termed the *feudal system*. There was, in fact, but one kind of property, and that consisted of land. Nearly all the useful arts had perished—commerce and manufactures could scarcely be said to exist at all, and a dark night

have the strength, it may not have the mildness and humanity. Revenge is sweet, and the murder of a brother or father, and the slavery of a mother or sister, will not easily be forgotten.

of universal ignorance enshrouded the human mind. The landholders of Europe, the feudal aristocrats, possessing all the property, necessarily and inevitably as fate itself, usurped all the power; and in consequence of the feebleness of government, and the resulting necessity that each one should do justice for himself, the laws of primogeniture and entails were resorted to as a device to prevent the weakening of families by too great a subdivision or alienation of property, and from the same cause, small *allodial* proprietors were obliged to give up their small estates to some powerful baron or large landholder, in consideration of protection, which he would be unable to procure in any other manner.* Moreover, the great landholders of those days had only one way of spending their estates, even when they were not barred by entails, and that was by employing a large number of retainers—for they could not then spend their estates as spendthrifts generally squander them, in luxuries and manufactures, in consequence of the rude state of the arts—all the necessities of man being supplied directly from the farms;† and the great author of the Wealth of Nations has most philosophically remarked, that few great estates have been spent from benevolence alone. And the people of those days could find no employment except on the land, and, consequently, were entirely dependant on the landlords, subject to their caprices and whims, paid according to their pleasure, and entirely

---

* Upon this subject, see Robertson's 1st vol. Hist. Charles V., Hallam's Middle Ages, Gilbert Stuart on the Progress of Society, and all the writers on feudal tenures.

† "There is not a vestige to be discovered, for several centuries, of any considerable manufactures. . . . . Rich men kept domestic artisans among their servants; even kings, in the ninth century, had their clothes made by the women upon their farms."—Hallam's Middle Ages, vol. 2, pp. 208, 361, Philad. edition.

under their control; in fine, they were *slaves complete*. Even the miserable cities of the feudal times were not independent, but were universally subjected to the barons or great landholders, whose powerful protection against the lawless rapine of the times, could only be purchased by an entire surrender of liberty.*

Thus the property of the feudal ages was almost exclusively of one kind. The feebleness of government, together with the laws of primogeniture and entails, threw that property into the hands of a few, and the difficulty of alienation, caused by the absence of all other species of property, had a tendency to prevent that change of possession which we so constantly witness in modern times. Never was there, then, perhaps, so confirmed and so permanent an aristocracy as that of the feudal ages; it naturally sprang from the condition of property and the obstacles to its alienation. The aristocracy alone embraced in those days the freemen of Europe; all the rest were slaves, call them by what name you please, and doomed by the unchanging laws of nature, to remain so, till commerce and manufactures had arisen, and with them had sprung into existence a new class of capitalists, the *tiers etat* of Europe, whose existence first called for new forms of government, and whose exertions either have or will revolutionize the whole of Europe. A revolution in the state of property is always a premonitory symptom of a revolution in government and in the state of society, and without the one you cannot meet with permanent success in the other. The slave of southern Europe could never have been emancipated, except through the agency of commerce and manufactures, and the consequent rapid rise of cities, accompanied with a more regular and better protected industry, producing a vast augmentation in the products which administer to our neces-

* Upon this subject, see both Hallam and Robertson.

sities and comforts, and increasing, in a proportionate degree, the sphere of our wants and desires. In the same way we shall show, before bringing this article to a close, that if the slaves of our southern country shall ever be liberated, and suffered to remain among us, with their present limited wants and longing desire for a state of idleness, they will fall, inevitable, by the nature of things, into a state of slavery, from which no government could rescue them, unless by a radical change of all their habits, and a most awful and fearful change in the whole system of property throughout the country. The state of property, then, may fairly be considered a very fruitful source of slavery. It was the most fruitful source during the feudal ages—it is the foundation of slavery throughout the north-eastern regions of Europe and the populous countries of the continent of Asia. We are even disposed to think, contrary to the general opinion, that the condition of property operated prior to the customs of war in the production of slavery. We are fortified in this opinion, by the example of Mexico and Peru in South America. In both of these empires, certainly the farthest advanced and most populous of the new world, " private property," says Dr. Robertson, "was perfectly understood, and established in its full extent." The most abject slavery existed in both these countries; and what still farther sustains our position, it very nearly, especially in Mexico, resembled that of the feudal ages. "The great body of the people was in a most humiliating state. A considerable number, known by the name of *Mayeques*, nearly resembling the condition of those peasants who, under various denominations, were considered, during the prevalence of the feudal system, as instruments of labor attached to the soil. Others were reduced to the lowest form of subjection, that of domestic servitude, and felt the utmost rigor of that wretched state."*

* Robertson's America, pp. 105, 107.

Now, slavery in both these countries, must have arisen from the state of property, for the laws of war are entirely too cruel to admit of captives among the Mexicans. "They fought," says Dr. Robertson, "to gratify their vengeance, by shedding the blood of their enemies—no captive was ever ransomed or spared."* And the Peruvians, though much milder in war, seem not to have made slaves of their captives, though we must confess that there is great difficulty in explaining their great comparative clemency to prisoners in war, unless by supposing they were made slaves.† We have no doubt, likewise, if we could obtain sufficient insight into the past history and condition of Africa, that slavery would be found to have arisen in many of those countries, rather from the state of property than the laws of war; for even to this day, many of the African princes are too cruel and sanguinary in war to forego the barbarous pleasure of murdering the captives, and yet slavery exists in their dominions to its full extent.

We will not here pause to examine into the justice or injustice of that species of slavery, which is sure to arise from a faulty distribution of property, because it is the inevitable result of the great *law of necessity*, which itself has no law, and, consequently, about which it is utterly useless to argue. We will, therefore, proceed at once to the third cause assigned for slavery—*bargain and sale*.

3. *Cause of Slavery, Bargain and Sale.*—This source of slavery might easily be reduced to that which depends on the

---

* Robertson's America, vol. 2, p. 114.

† We are sorry we have not the means of satisfactorily investigating this subject. If slavery was established among them from the laws of war, it would be one of the most triumphant examples which history affords of the effect of slavery, in mitigating the cruelties of war; for it is a singular fact, that the Peruvians were the only people in the new world who did not murder their prisoners.

state of property, but for the sake of perspicuity, we prefer keeping them apart. Adam Smith has well observed, that there is a strong propensity in man "to truck, barter, and exchange, one thing for another," and both the parties generally intend to derive an advantage from the exchange. This disposition seems to extend to every thing susceptible of being impressed with the character of property or exchangeable value, or from which any great or signal advantage may be derived—it has been made to extend, at times, to life and liberty. Generals, in time of war, have pledged their lives for the performance of their contracts. At the conclusion of peace, semi-barbarous nations have been in the habit of interchanging hostages—generally the sons of princes and noblemen—for the mutual observance of treaties, whose lives were forfeited by a violation of the plighted faith; and in all ages, where the practice has not been interdicted by law, individuals have occasionally sold their own liberty, or that of others dependent on them. We have already seen how the small allodial possessors, during the feudal ages, were obliged to surrender their lands and liberty to some powerful baron, for that protection which could be procured in no other manner. Throughout the whole ancient world, the sale of one's own liberty, and even that of his children, was common. The non-payment of debts, or failure to comply with contracts, frequently subjected the unfortunate offender to slavery, in both Greece and Rome. Instances of slavery from bargain and sale, occur in Scripture. Joseph was sold to the Ishmaelites for *twenty pieces* of silver, and carried down to Egypt in slavery. But this was a black and most unjustifiable act on the part of his envious brothers. There are other parts of Scripture, where the practice of buying and selling slaves seems to be justified. The Hebrew laws permitted the selling of even the Jews into slavery for six years. "If thou buy a Hebrew servant, six years he shall serve, and in the seventh he shall go out free for nothing." And if the servant chose, at the expiration of six years, to remain with his master as a slave, he might do so on having his ear bored through with an awl. It seems fathers could sell their children—thus: "And if a man sell his daughter to be a maid servant, she shall not go out as the men servants do."* An unlimited right to purchase slaves from among foreigners seems to have been granted, whether they had been slaves or not before the purchase; thus, in the twenty-fifth chapter of Leviticus, we find the following injunction: "Both thy bondmen and bondmaids which thou shalt have, *shall be* of the heathen that are round about you; of them *shall ye* buy bondmen and bondmaids. Moreover, of the children of strangers who sojourn among you, of them shall ye buy, and of the families that *are* with you, which they begat in your land; and they shall be your possession. And ye shall take them as an inheritance for your children after you, to inherit them for a possession; they shall be your *bondmen forever.*"† We may well suppose that few persons would ever be induced to sell themselves or children into slavery, unless under very severe pressure from *want*. Accordingly, we find the practice most prevalent among the most populous and the most savage nations, where the people are most frequently subjected to dearths and famines. Thus, in Hindostan and China, there is nothing more frequent than this practice of selling liberty. "Every year," said a Jesuit who resided in Hindostan, "we baptize a thousand children whom their parents can no longer feed, or who being likely to die, are sold to us by their mothers, in order to get rid of them." The great legislator of Hindostan. Menu, in his ordinances, which are described by Sir William Jones, justifies this practice in time of

* See 21st chapter of Exodus. † 44, 45, and 46 verses.

scarcity. "Ajigarta," says Menu, in one of his ordinances, "dying with hunger, was going to destroy his own son by selling him for some cattle; yet he was guilty of no crime, for he only sought a remedy against famishing." "In China," says Duhalde, "a man sometimes sells his son, and even himself and wife, at a very moderate price. The common mode is to mortgage themselves with a condition of redemption, and a great number of men and maid servants are thus bound in a family." There is no doubt but at this moment, in every densely populated country, hundreds would be willing to sell themselves into slavery if the laws would permit them, whenever they were pressed by famine. Ireland seems to be the country of modern Europe most subjected to these dreadful visitations. Suppose, then, we reverse the vision of the Kentucky Senator,* and imagine that Ireland could be severed during those periods of distress from the Britannic isle, and could float, like the fabled island of Delos, across the ocean, and be placed by our side, and our laws should inhumanely forbid a single son of Erin from entering our territory, unless as a slave, to be treated exactly like the African, is there any man, acquainted with the state of the Irish, in years of scarcity, who would doubt for a moment, but that thousands, much as this oppressed people are in love with liberty, would enter upon this hard condition, if they could find purchasers. Indeed, the melancholy fact has too often occurred in Ireland, of individuals committing crimes merely for the purpose of being thrown into the houses of correction, where they could obtain *bread and water!*

Among savages, famines are much more dreadful than among civilized nations, where they are provided against by previous accumulation and commerce. Dr. Robertson has given us a glowing, and no doubt, correct picture, of the

* Mr. Clay, in the debate on his resolutions on the tariff, 1832.

dreadful ravages of famine among the North American Indians, and on such occasions, we are informed by the " Lettres Edifiantes et Curieuse," that the ties of nature are no longer binding. A father will sell his son for a knife or hatchet.* But, unfortunately, among savages in the hunting state, scarcely any one can do more than maintain himself and one or two children, and therefore cannot afford to keep a slave.

If we turn to Africa, we shall find this cause of slavery frequently operating with all its power; and, accordingly, Parke has ranked *famine* as the second among the four causes which he assigns for slavery in Africa. "There are many instances of freemen," says he, "voluntarily surrendering up their liberty to save their lives. During a great scarcity, which lasted for three years, in the countries of the Gambia, great numbers of people became slaves in this manner. Dr. Laidley assured me, that at that time, many freemen came and begged with great earnestness, *to be put upon his slave chain*, to save them from perishing with hunger. Large families are very often exposed to absolute want, and as the parents have almost unlimited authority over their children, it frequently happens in all parts of Africa, that some of the latter are sold to purchase provisions for the rest of the family. When I was at Jarra, Damon Jumma pointed out to me three young slaves which he had purchased in this manner."† Bruce, in his travels in Africa, saw whole villages and districts of country depopulated by the famines which had visited them, and gives us a most appalling picture of the walking skeletons and lawless rapine which were every where exhibited during those frightful periods of distress. We cannot wonder, then, under these circumstances, that famine should be a

---
* Tom. 8.

† Parke's Travels in Africa, chap. 22, p. 216, N. Y. ed.

fruitful source of slavery, by giving rise to a sale of liberty for the preservation of life.

The remark of Judge Blackstone, as to this kind of slavery, is known to every one—that every sale implies a "*quid pro quo*"—but that, in the case of slavery, there can be no equivalent, no quid pro quo—for nothing is an equivalent for liberty; and even the purchase money, or the price, whatever it might be, would instantly belong to the master of the slave.* Upon this we would remark, that Blackstone seems to have his attention fixed exclusively on those countries where every man can easily maintain himself, and where, consequently, his life can never be in jeopardy from want. If there is any country in the world to which this argument will apply, that country is ours. We believe every man here may obtain a subsistence, either by his own exertions, or by the aid of the poor rates. But this is far from being the case with semi-barbarous or densely populated countries. Again: Blackstone alludes to that pure state of slavery, where a man's life, liberty, and property, are at the mercy of his master. That is far from being the condition of slavery now. In most parts of the world the slave is carefully protected in life, limb, and even in a moderate share of liberty, by the policy of the laws; and his nourishment and subsistence are positively enjoined. Where this is the case, we can imagine many instances in which *liberty* might have an *equivalent*. Who for a moment can doubt but that the abundant daily supplies of subsistence, consisting of wholesome *meat, bread*, and frequently vegetables and refreshing drinks besides, which are furnished to our slaves, are more than an equivalent for the liberty of the Chinese laborer, who exhausts himself with hard labor—feeds on his scanty and unseasoned rice—tastes no wholesome meat from the beginning to the end of the

* Tucker's Blackstone, vol. 2, p. 423.

toilsome year—sees his family frequently perishing before his eyes, or more cruel still, consents himself to be the executioner, in order that he may release them from the intolerable torments of unsatisfied wants, and who, even in seasons of ordinary supply, fishes up with eagerness the vilest garbage from the river or canal, and voraciously devours meat which, with us, would be left to be fed on by the vultures of the air. The fact is, the laborer in this hard condition is already a slave, or rather in a situation infinitely worse than slavery—he is subjected to all the hardships and degradation of the slave, and derives none of the advantages. In the case of famine, the *equivalent* seems to be *life* for *liberty ;* and when this is the case, although the *philosopher* may consider death as preferable to slavery, "yet," says Parke, "the poor negro, when fainting with hunger, thinks, like Esau of old, '*behold I am at the point to die, and what profit shall this birthright do to me?*'" The reason why persons do not more frequently sell themselves into slavery is, because they are forbidden by the laws, or can find no purchasers. So far from persons not selling their liberty because there is no equivalent, it is directly the contrary in most countries; the price or equivalent, consisting of continued support, protection, &c., is too great—more than can be afforded. The capitalist in Great Britain could not afford to purchase the operative, and treat him as we do the slave; the price paid, the *quid pro quo* of Blackstone, would be more than the liberty would be worth. We have no doubt, if the English laws were to allow of slavery, such as we have in this country, there would be many more persons wishing to sell their liberty than of those wishing to buy! But whether the remarks of Judge Blackstone are correct in theory or not, is a matter of no practical importance; for, in point of fact, as we have shown by undeniable testimony, *bargain and sale* have ever been a most fruitful source of slavery in ancient times, and among many people of the present day; and, consequently, we could not pretermit it in a general survey of the sources of slavery. We shall now proceed to a consideration of the last mentioned source of slavery.

4. *Crime.*—All governments, even those of the states of our confederacy, have ever been considered as perfectly justifiable in enslaving for crime. All our penitentiaries are erected upon this principle, and slavery in them, of the most abject and degrading character, endures for a certain number of months, years, or for life, according to the offence. In South America and Russia, the criminals are frequently sentenced to slavery in the mines, and in France and England, to the gallies and work-houses; but as it is principally with domestic slavery that we are concerned in this article, we shall not consider farther that which is of a public character.

Throughout the ancient world, domestic slavery, arising from crime, seems to have been very common. We have already spoken of the slavery which was inflicted frequently on insolvent debtors in both Greece and Rome. In Africa, too, we find *insolvency* a very frequent source of slavery. "Of all the offences," says Parke, "if *insolvency* may be so called, to which the laws of Africa have affixed the punishment of slavery, this is the most common. A negro trader commonly contracts debts on some mercantile speculation, either from his neighbors to purchase such articles as will sell to advantage in a distant market, or from the European traders on the coast—payment to be made in a given time. In both cases, the situation of the adventurer is exactly the same: if he succeeds, he may secure an independency; if he is unsuccessful, his person and services are at the disposal of another; for, in Africa, not only the effects of the insolvent, but the insolvent himself, is sold to satisfy the lawful demands of his creditors."* Insolvency, however, is, after all, rather a misfortune than a crime; and we rank it here as a crime, more in deference to the institutions of the ancients, and the customs of certain modern nations, than as an indication of our own sentiments—for we are decidedly of opinion, that slavery is much too high a penalty to be attached to what, in many cases, is sheer misfortune. But, besides insolvency, the laws of Africa affix slavery as a punishment to the crimes of *murder, adultery, and witchcraft.* In case of murder, the nearest relation of the murdered, after conviction, may either kill or sell into slavery, at his option. In adultery, the offended party may enslave or demand a ransom at pleasure; and as to witchcraft, Parke not having met with any trial for this offence, could only assure us that it was the source of slavery, though not common.† We have now surveyed the principal sources of slavery, and although we do not pretend to be minute and complete in the division which we have made, we hope we have said enough upon this branch to show that slavery is inevitable in the progress of society, from its first and most savage state, to the last and most refined. We started out with announcing the fact, *startling* to those who have never reflected upon the subject, that slavery existed throughout the whole of the ancient, and in a very large portion of the modern world. We have farther shown by the preceding reasoning, that this was no *accident, the mere result of chance,* but was a *necessary and inevitable* consequence of the principles of human nature and the state of property. We shall now proceed to inquire briefly into the advantages which have resulted to mankind from the institution of slavery.

Advantages which have resulted to the world from the in-

* Parke's Travels in Africa, p. 216.
† Parke's Travels, p. 217.

stitution of slavery.—When we turn our thoughts from this world "of imperfections" to the God of nature, we love to contemplate Him as perfect and immaculate, and amid all the divine attributes with which we delight to clothe Him, none stands more conspicuous than his *benevolence.* To look upon Him in this light, may be said to be almost the impulse of an instinct of our nature, and the most enlarged experience and perfect knowledge combine in fortifying and strengthening this belief. Accordingly, when we look abroad to the works of Omnipotence, when we contemplate the external, the physical world, and again, when we turn to the world of mind, we never find *evil* the sole object and end of creation. *Happiness* is always the main design; evil is merely incidental. All the laws of matter, every principle, and even passion of man, when rightly understood, demonstrate the general benevolence of the Deity, even in this world. "It is, perhaps," says Mr. Allison, "the most striking and the most luminous fact in the history of our intellectual nature, that that principle of curiosity which is the instinctive spring of all scientific inquiry into the phenomena of matter or mind, is never satisfied until it terminates in the discovery, not only of design, but of benevolent design." Well, then, might we have concluded, from the fact that slavery was the *necessary result of the laws of mind and matter, that it marked some benevolent design, and was intended by our Creator for some useful purpose.* Let us inquire, then, what that useful purpose is, and we have no hesitation in affirming that slavery has been, perhaps, the principal means for impelling forward the civilization of mankind. Without its agency, society must have remained sunk into that deplorable state of barbarism and wretchedness which characterized the inhabitants of the Western World, when first discovered by Columbus.

We have already spoken of the great advantage of slavery

in mitigating the horrors of savage warfare; but not only is this most desirable effect produced, but it has a farther tendency to check the frequency of war, and to destroy that migratory spirit in nations and tribes, so destructive to the peace and tranquillity of the world. Savages, living in the hunting state, must have an extensive range of country, for the supply of the wants of even a few persons. "Hence," says Dr. Robertson, "it is of the utmost importance to prevent neighboring tribes from destroying or disturbing the game in their hunting grounds, they guard this national property with a jealous attention. But as their territories are extensive, and the boundaries of them not exactly ascertained, innumerable subjects of disputes arise, which seldom terminate without bloodshed."* Uncertain boundaries, constant roaming through the forests, in search of game, and all the unchecked and furious passions of the savage, lead on to constant and exterminating wars among the tribes. What, then, let us ask, can alone prevent this constant scene of strife and massacre? Nothing but that which can bind them down to the soil, which can establish *homes and firesides*, which can change the wandering character of the savage, and make it his interest to cultivate peace instead of war. Slavery produces these effects. It necessarily leads on to the taming and rearing of numerous flocks, and to the cultivation of the soil. Hunting can never support slavery. Agriculture first suggests the notion of servitude, and, as often happens in the politico-economical world, the effect becomes, in turn, a powerfully operating cause. Slavery gradually fells the forest, and thereby destroys the haunts of the wild beasts; it gives rise to agricultural production, and thereby renders mankind less dependent on the precarious and diminishing production

* History of America, vol. 1, p. 192.

of the chase; it thus gradually destroys the roving and unquiet life of the savage; it furnishes a home, and binds him down to the soil; it converts the idler and the wanderer into the man of business and the agriculturist.

If we look to the condition of Africa, and compare it with that of the American Indians, we shall find a complete illustration of these remarks, and Africa, as we shall soon see, would enjoy a much greater exemption from war, if it were not for the slave trade, whose peculiar operation we shall presently notice.

But, secondly, the labor of the slave, when slavery is first introduced, is infinitely more productive than that of the freeman. Dr. Robertson, in his History of America, speaks of the acquisition of dominion over the inferior animals, as a step of capital importance in the progress of civilization. It may with truth be affirmed, that the *taming* of man and rendering him fit for labor, is more important than the taming and using the inferior animals, and nothing seems so well calculated to effect this as slavery. Savages have ever been found to be idle and unproductive, except in the chase. "The aborigines of North America resembled rather beasts of prey," says Dr. Robertson, "than animals formed for labor. They were not only averse from toil, but seemed at first entirely incapable of it. There is nothing which so completely proves the general indolence and inactivity of the Indian, as their very moderate appetites. Their constitutional temperance exceeded that of the most mortified hermits, and the appetites of the Spaniards (generally reckoned very temperate in Europe) appeared to the natives insatiably voracious, and they affirmed that one Spaniard devoured, in a day, more food than was enough for ten Indians.*

* Robertson's America, vol. 1, book 4.

The improvidence and utter recklessness of the savage are noticed, too, by all the historians. "They follow blindly," says Robertson, "the impulse of the appetite which they feel, but are entirely regardless of distant consequences, and even of those removed in the least degree from immediate apprehension. When, on the approach of evening, a Carabee feels himself disposed to go to rest, no consideration will tempt him to sell his hammock; but in the morning, when he is sallying out to the business or pastime of the day, he will part with it for the slightest toy that catches his fancy. At the close of winter, while the impression of what he has suffered from the rigor of the climate is fresh in the mind of the North American, he sets himself with vigor to prepare materials for erecting a comfortable hut, to protect him against the inclemency of the succeeding season; but as soon as the weather becomes mild, he forgets what is past, abandons his work, and never thinks of it more, until the return of cold compels him, when too late, to resume it."* There is nothing but slavery which can destroy those habits of indolence and sloth, and eradicate the character of improvidence and carelessness, which mark the independent savage. He may truly be compared to the wild beast of the forest—he must be broke and tamed, before he becomes fit for labor, and for the task of rearing and providing for a family. There is nothing but slavery that can effect this; the means may appear exceedingly harsh and cruel, and, as among wild beasts, many may die in the process of taming and subjugating, so among savages, many may not be able to stand the hardships of servitude; but, in the end, it leads on to a milder and infinitely better condition than that of savage independence, gives rise to greater production, increases the provisions in nature's

---

* History of America, vol. 1, pp. 170, 171.

great storehouse, and invites into existence a more numerous population, better fed and better provided, and thus gives rise to society, and, consequently, speeds on more rapidly the cause of civilization. But upon this great, this delicate and all-important subject, we wish to risk no vain theories, no unfounded conjectures—from beginning to end, we shall speak conscientiously, and never knowingly plant in our bosom a *thorn* which may *rankle* there. Let us, then, see whether the above assertions may not be satisfactorily proved, paradoxical as they may at first appear, by fact and experience. If we turn to the Western World, where an ample field is presented for the contemplation of man, in his first and rudest state, we find that slavery existed nowhere throughout the American continent, except in Peru and Mexico, and these were decidedly the most flourishing portions of this vast continent. "When compared," says Dr. Robertson, "with other parts of the New World, Mexico and Peru may be considered as polished states. Instead of small, independent, hostile tribes, struggling for subsistence amidst woods and marshes, strangers to industry and arts, unacquainted with subordination, and almost without the appearance of regular government, we find countries of great extent subjected to the dominion of one sovereign, the inhabitants collected together in cities, the wisdom and foresight of rulers employed in providing for the maintenance and security of the people, the empire of laws in some measure established, the authority of religion recognized, many of the arts essential to life brought to some degree of maturity, and the dawn of such as are ornamental beginning to appear."*

Again: In the Islands of the South Sea, Captain Cook was astonished at the populousness of Otaheite and the Society

* Robertson's America, vol. 2, page 101.

Islands. Slavery seems to have been established throughout these Islands, and compensated, no doubt, in part, for many of those abomidable practices which seem to have been prevalent among the natives.

Again: On turning to Africa, where we find the most abundant and complete exemplifications of every species of slavery, and its effects, and where, consequently, the philosophy of the subject may be most advantageously studied, we find most conclusive proof of our assertions. "It deserves *particular* notice, that the nations in this degrading condition (state of slavery) are the most numerous, the most powerful, and the most advanced in all the arts and improvements of life; that, if we except the human sacrifices to which blind veneration prompts them, they display even a disposition more amiable, manners more dignified and polished, and moral conduct more correct, than prevail among the citizens of the small free states, who are usually idle, turbulent, quarrelsome and licentious."* The Africans, too, display, in a remarkable degree, the *love of home*, and fondness for their native scenes—a mark of considerable advancement in civilization. "Few of them," says the author of the History of Africa just quoted, "are nomadic and wandering; they generally have native seats, to which they cling with strong feelings of local attachment. Even the tenants of the desert, who roam widely in quest of commerce and plunder, have their little watered valleys, or circuit of hills, in which they make their permanent abode."† Can any general facts more strikingly illustrate our position than those which we have just mentioned?

But there is other, and abundant testimony, on this subject;

---

* See Family Library, No. 16, page 237, Africa.
† Family Library, No. 16, page 228.

the difference between the negroes imported into the West Indies still farther substantiates all we have said. The negroes from Whida, or Fida, called in the West Indies *Papaws*, are the best disposed and most docile slaves. The reason seems to be, that the great majority of these people are in a state of *absolute slavery* in Africa; and "Bosman," says Bryan Edwards, "speaks with rapture of the improved state of their soil, the number of villages, and the industry, riches, and obliging manners of the natives."* So that slavery seems to be an incalculable advantage to them, both in the West Indies and in their own country.

The Koromantyn, or Gold Coast negro, is generally stubborn, intractable, and unfit for labor, at first. His habits, in his native country, are very similar to those of the North American Indian. He must be broke and tamed, before he is fit for labor. When they are thus tamed, however, they become the best laborers in the West Indies. "They sometimes," says Bryan Edwards, "take to labor with great promptitude and alacrity, and have constitutions well adapted to it." And he gives, as a reason for this, that "many of them have undoubtedly been slaves in Africa." Still, this country seems yet too barbarous for a regular system of slavery. Accordingly, the Koromantyns are described as among the most ferocious of the Africans in war, never sparing the life of an enemy, except to make him a slave, and that but rarely. Their whole education and philosophy, consequently, seem directed, as is the case with all savages, to prepare and steel them against the awful vicissitudes to which they are ever liable—they have their *yell* of war, and their *death songs* too. Nothing but slavery can civilize such beings, give them habits

* Edward's West Indies, vol. 2, pp. 278, 279.

of industry, and make them cling to life for its enjoyments.*

Strange as it may seem, we have little hesitation in declaring it as our opinion, that a much greater number of Indians, within the limits of the United States, would have been saved, had we rigidly persevered in enslaving them, than by our present policy. It is, perhaps, the most melancholy fact connected with the history of our young republic, that in proportion as the whites have been advancing, the Indians have been constantly and rapidly decreasing in numbers. When our ancestors first settled on this continent, the savages were around and among them, and were everywhere spread over this immense territory. Now, where are they? Where are the warlike tribes that went to battle under their chieftains? They have rapidly disappeared, as the pale faces have advanced. Their numbers have dwindled to insignificance. Within the limits of the original States, the primitive stock has been reduced to 16,000. Within the whole of the United States, east of the Mississippi, there are but 105,000; and on the whole of our territory, east and west of the Mississippi, extending over 24 derees of latitude and 58 of longitude, there are but 313,130!! Miserable remnant of the myriads of former days! And yet the government of our country has exhausted every means for their civilization, and

---

* This increasing love of life, as an effect of slavery, is exemplified in the following anecdote, related by Edwards: "A gentleman of Jamaica, visiting a valuable Koromantyn negro, that was sick, and perceiving that he was thoughtful and dejected, endeavored, by soothing and encouraging language, to raise his drooping spirits. 'Massa,' said the negro, in a tone of self-reproach and conscious degeneracy, 'since me come to white man's country, me lub (love) life too much.'" History of the West Indies, vol. 2, p. 275.

the philanthropist has not been idle in their behalf. Schools have been erected, both public and private, missionaries have been sent among them, and all in vain. The President of the United States now tells you that their removal farther West is necessary—that those who live on our borders, in spite of our efforts to civilize them, are rapidly deteriorating in character, and becoming every day more miserable and destitute. We agree with the President in this policy—to remove them is all we can now do for them. But, after all, the expedient is temporary, and the relief is short lived. Our population will again, and at no distant day, press upon their borders, their game will be destroyed, the intoxicating beverage will be furnished to them, they will engage in wars, and their total extermination will be the inevitable consequence. The *hand-writing* has indeed appeared on the *wall*. The mysterious decree of Providence has gone forth against the red man. His destiny is fixed, and final destruction is his inevitable fate. Slavery, we assert again, seems to be the only means that we know of, under heaven, by which the ferocity of the savage can be conquered, his wandering habits eradicated, his slothfulness and improvidence—by which, in fine, his nature can be changed. The Spaniards enslaved the Indians in South-America, and they were the most cruel and *relentless* of masters. Still, under their system of cruel and harsh discipline, an infinitely larger proportion of the aborigines were saved than with us, and will, no doubt, in the lapse of ages, mix and harmonize with the Europeans, and be, in all respects, their equals.*

---

* Humboldt, in his recapitulation of the population of New Spain, gives us the following table:

Indigenous, or Indians,		2,500,000
Whites, or Spaniards, { Creoles, 1,025.000 } { Europeans, 70,000 }		1,100,000

From their inhuman treatment of the Indians, at first, numbers died in the process of taming and subjugating; but, in the end, their system has proved more humane than ours, and demonstrates, beyond a doubt, that nothing is so fit as slavery, to change the nature of the savage.* "We observe," says Humboldt, "and the observation is consoling to humanity, that not only has the number of Indians in South America and Mexico been on the increase, for the last century, (he published his work in 1808,) but that the whole of the vast region which we designate by the general name of New Spain, is much better inhabited at present than it was before the arrival of the Europeans."† He gives a very remarkable instance of the effects of even unjust slavery, on the industry and agriculture of the country. He speaks of the *Alcaldias Mayores*, a sort of provincial magistrates and judges in Mexico, forcing the Indians to purchase cattle of them, and afterwards reducing them to slavery, for non-payment of the debts thus contracted. And he adds, upon the authority of Fray Antonio, Monk of St. Jerome, that "the individual happiness of these unfortunate wretches was not, certainly, increased by the sacrifice of their liberty, for a horse or a mule to work for their master's profit; *but yet, in this*

African negroes, - - - - - - - 6,100
Casts of mixed blood, - - - - - 1,231,000
[Humboldt's New Spain, N. Y. ed., vol. 2, p 246.

Again: The number of Indians in Peru is estimated at 600,000, nearly double of the whole Indian population of the United States.—[Vol. 1, p. 69.

* We shall soon see that there is not, in the annals of history, an instance of such rapid improvement in civilization, as that undergone by the negro slaves in our country, since the time they were first brought among us.

† Humboldt's New Spain, vol.1, p. 71.

state of things, brought on by abuses, agriculture and industry were seen to increase."

We beg our readers to bear in mind, that we are here merely discussing the effects of slavery, and not passing our opinions upon the justice or injustice of its origin. We shall now close our remarks upon this head, by the citation of an instance furnished by our own country, of the great advantage of slavery to masters—for, among savages, the benefit seems to extend to both master and slave. There is an able article in the 66th number of the North American Review, on the "Removal of the Indians," from the pen of Governor Cass, whom we have no hesitation, from the little we have seen of his productions, to pronounce one of the most philosophical and elegant writers in this country. In this article, after pointing out the true condition of the Indian tribes in the neighborhood of the whites, and proving, beyond a doubt, that they are injured, instead of benefitted, by their juxtaposition, he admits that the Cherokees constitute a solitary, and but a partial exception—that some individuals among them have acquired property, and, with it, more enlarged and just notions of the value of our institutions. He says that these salutary changes are confined principally to the *half breeds*, and their immediate connexions, and are not sufficiently numerous to overturn his reasoning, against the practicability of civilizing the Indians. Now, what are the causes of this dawn of civilization among the Cherokees? "The causes which have led to this state of things," says Governor Cass, " are too peculiar ever to produce an extensive result. . . . They have been operating for many years, and *among the most prominent of them, has been the introduction of slaves*, by which means, that *unconquerable* aver-

---

* Vol. 1, pp. 146, 147.

sion to labor, so characteristic of all savage tribes, can be indulged."*

We hope, now, we have said enough to convince even the most sceptical, of the powerful effects of slavery, in changing the habits peculiar to the Indian or savage, by converting him into the agriculturist, and changing his slothfulness and aversion to labor into industry and economy, thereby rendering his labor more productive, his means of subsistence more abundant and regular, and his happiness more secure and constant. We cannot close our remarks on the general effects of slavery on the progress of civilization, without pointing out the peculiar influence on that portion of the human race, which the civilized nations of modern times so much delight to honor and to cherish—*the fair sex.*

3. *Influence of slavery on the condition of the female sex.*—The bare name of this interesting half of the human family, is well calculated to awaken in the breast of the generous the feeling of tenderness and kindness. The wrongs and sufferings of meek, quiet, forbearing woman, awaken the generous sympathy of every noble heart. Man never suffers without murmuring, and never relinquishes his rights without a struggle. It is not always so with woman: her physical weakness incapacitates her for the combat; her sexual organization, and the part which she takes in bringing forth and nurturing the rising generation, render her necessarily domestic in her habits, and timid and patient in her sufferings. If man choose to exercise his power against woman, she is sure

* See North American Review, No. 66, article 3. The Spaniards, when they first conquered Mexico and Peru, were, as we have already said, the most cruel and relentless of masters. They are now the most humane and kind, and perhaps the Portuguese come next, who were equally cruel with the Spaniards, during the first century after their settlement in the New World.

to fall an easy prey to his oppression. Hence, we may always consider her progressing elevation in society as a mark of advancing civilization, and, more particularly, of the augmentation of disinterested and generous *virtue*. The lot of women, among savages, has always been found to be painful and degrading. Dr. Robertson says that, in America, their condition " is so peculiarly grievous, and their depression so complete, that servitude is a name too mild to describe their wretched state. A wife, among most tribes, is no better than a beast of burthen, destined to every office of labor and fatigue. While the men loiter out the day in sloth, or spend it in amusement, the women are condemned to excessive toil. Tasks are imposed on them without pity, and services are received without complacence or gratitude. Every circumstance reminds women of this mortifying inferiority. They must approach their lords with reverence. They must regard them as more exalted beings, and are not permitted to eat in their presence. There are districts in America where this dominion is so grievous, and so sensibly felt, that some women, in a wild emotion of maternal tenderness, have destroyed their female children in their infancy, in order to deliver them from that intolerable bondage to which they knew they were doomed."*

This harrowing description of woman's servitude and sufferings, among the aborigines of America, is applicable to all savage nations. In the Islands of Andaman, in Van Dieman's Land, in New Zealand,† and New Holland, the lot of woman is the same. The females carry, on their heads and bodies, the traces of the superiority of the males. Mr. Col-

---

* Robertson's America, vol. 1, p. 177.

† In New Zealand, agriculture has worked a most wonderful change in the lot of woman. She is now more respected and loved. See Library of Entertaining Knowledge, vol. 5, New Zealanders.

lins says, of the women of New South Wales, "Their condition is so wretched, that I have often, on seeing a female child borne on its mother's shoulders, anticipated the miseries to which it was born, and thought it would be mercy to destroy it." And thus it is that the most important of all connections, the marriage tie, is perverted, to the production of the degradation and misery of the one sex, and the arrogant assumption and unfeeling cruelty of the other. But the evil stops not with the sufferings of woman—her prolificness is in a measure destroyed. Unaided by the male in the rearing of her children, and being forced to bear them on their shoulders, when the huntsmen are roaming through the forest, many of their offspring must die, from the vicissitudes to which they are subjected at so tender an age. Moreover, "among wandering tribes," says Dr. Robertson, "the mother cannot attempt to rear a second child until the first has attained such a degree of vigor as to be in some measure independent of her care. . . . When twins are born, one of them is commonly abandoned, because the mother is not equal to the task of rearing both. When a mother dies while she is nursing a child, all hope of preserving its life fails, and it is buried, together with her, in the same grave."*

It is not necessary that we should continue farther this shocking picture; but let us proceed at once to inquire if the institution of slavery is not calculated to relieve the sufferings and wrongs of injured woman, and elevate her in the scale of existence? Slavery, we have just seen, changes the hunting to the shepherd and agricultural states,—gives rise to augmented productions, and, consequently, furnishes more abundant supplies for man. The labor of the slave thus becomes a substitute for that of the woman; man no longer wanders

* Robertson's America, vol. 1, p. 177.

through the forest, in quest of game; and woman, consequently, is relieved from following on his track, under the enervating and harassing burthen of her children. She is now surrounded by her domestics, and the abundance of their labor lightens the toil and hardships of the whole family. She ceases to be a mere "*beast of burthen;*" becomes the cheering and animating centre of the family circle—time is afforded for reflection and the cultivation of all those mild and fascinating virtues, which throw a charm and delight around our homes and firesides, and calm and tranquillize the harsher tempers and more restless propensities of the male: Man, too, relieved from that endless disquietude about subsistence for the morrow—relieved of the toil of wandering over the forest—more amply provided for by the productions of the soil—finds his habits changed, his temper moderated, his kindness and benevolence increased; he loses that savage and brutal feeling which he had before indulged towards all his unfortunate dependants; and, consequently, even the slave, in the agricultural, is happier than the free man in the hunting state.

In the very first remove from the most savage state, we behold the marked effects of slavery on the condition of woman—we find her at once elevated, clothed with all her charms, mingling with and directing the society to which she belongs, no longer the slave, but the equal and the idol of man. The Greeks and Trojans, at the siege of Troy, were in this state, and some of the most interesting and beautiful passages in the Iliad relate to scenes of social intercourse and conjugal affection, where woman, unawed and in all the pride of conscious equality, bears a most conspicuous part. Thus, Helen and Andromanche are frequently represented as appearing in company with the Trojan chiefs, and mingling freely in conversation with them. Attended only by one or two maid servants, they walk through the streets of Troy, as business or fancy directs: even the prudent Penelope, persecuted as she is by her suitors, does not scruple occasionally to appear among them; and scarcely more reserve seems to be imposed on virgins than married women. Mitford has well observed, that "Homer's elegant eulogiums and Hesiod's severe sarcasm, equally prove woman to have been in their days important members of society. The character of Penelope in the Odyssee, is the completest panegyric on the sex that ever was composed; and no language even give a more elegant or more highly colored picture of conjugal affection, than is displayed in the conversation of Hector and Andromanche, in the 6th book of the Iliad."*

The Teutonic races who inhabited the mountains and fastnesses of Germany, were similarly situated to the Greeks; and even before they left their homes to move down upon the Roman Empire, they were no more distinguished by their deeds in arms, than for devotion and attention to the weaker sex. So much were they characterized by this elevation of the female sex, that Gilbert Stuart does not hesitate to trace the institution of chivalry, whose origin has never yet been satisfactorily illustrated, to the German manners.†

Again: if we descend to modern times, we see much the largest portion of Africa existing in this second stage of civilization, and, consequently, we find woman in an infinitely better condition than we any where find her among the aborigines on the American continent. And thus is it a most singular and curious fact, that woman, whose sympathies are ever alive to the distress of others; whose heart is filled with benevolence and philanthropy, and whose fine feelings, un-

* See Mitford's Greece, vol. 1, pp. 166, 167, Bost. Ed
† See Stuart's View of Society, particularly book 1, chap. 2, sec. 4 and 5.

checked by considerations of interest or calculations of remote consequences, have ever prompted to embrace with eagerness even the wildest and most destructive schemes of emancipation, has been in a most peculiar and eminent degree indebted to slavery, for that very elevation in society which first raised her to an equality with man. We will not stop here to investigate the advantages resulting from the ameliorated condition of woman: her immense influence on the destiny of our race is acknowledged by all: upon her must ever devolve, in a peculiar degree, the duty of rearing into manhood a creature, in its infancy the frailest and feeblest which Heaven has made—of forming the plastic mind—of training the ignorance and imbecility of infancy into virtue and efficiency. There is, perhaps, no moral power, the magnitude of which swells so far beyond the grasp of calculation, as the influence of the female character on the virtues and happiness of mankind : it is so searching, so versatile, so multifarious, and so universal : it turns on us like the eye of a beautiful portrait, wherever we take our position ; it bears upon us in such an infinite variety of points, on our instincts, our passions, our vanity, our tastes, and our necessities ; above all, on the first impressions of education and the associations of infancy." The *rule* which woman should act in the great drama of life, is truly an important and an indispensable one; it must and will be acted, and that too, either for our weal or woe : all must wish then, that she should be guided by virtue, intelligence, and the purest affection ; which can only be secured by elevating, honoring, and loving *her*, in whose career we feel so deep an interest.

We have thus traced out the origin and progress of slavery, and pointed out its effects in promoting the civilization of mankind. We should next proceed to an investigation of those causes, of a general character, which have a tendency, in the progress of society, gradually to remove and extinguish slavery; but these we shall have such frequent opportunities of noticing in the sequel, while discussing various schemes of abolition that have been proposed, that we have determined to omit their separate consideration.

We shall now proceed to inquire into the origin of slavery in the United States.

It is well known to all, at all conversant with the history of our country, that negro slavery in the United States, the West India Islands, and South America, was originally derived from the African slave trade, by which the African negro was torn from his home, and transferred to the western hemisphere, to live out his days in bondage; we shall briefly advert—First, to the origin and progress of this trade—Secondly, to its effects on Africa; and lastly, to the consideration of the part which the United States have taken in this traffic, and the share of responsibility which must be laid at their door.

1. *Origin and Progress of the African Slave Trade.*— This trade, which seems so shocking to the feelings of mankind, dates its origin as far back as the year 1442: Antony Gonzales, a Portuguese mariner, while exploring the coast of Africa, in 1440, seized some Moors near *Cape Bojador*, and was subsequently forced by his king, the celebrated Prince Henry, of Portugal, to carry them back to Africa: he carried them to *Rio del Oro*, and received from the Moors in exchange, *ten blacks* and a quantity of gold dust, with which he returned to Lisbon; and this, which occurred in 1442, was the simple beginning of that extensive trade in human flesh, which has given so singular an aspect to the texture of our population, and which has and will continue to influence the character and destiny of the greatest portion of the inhabitants of the two Americas.

"The success of Gonzales not only awakened the admiration, but stimulated the avarice, of his countrymen, who, in the course of a few succeeding years, fitted out no less than thirty seven ships, in the pursuit of the same gainful traffic. So early as the year 1502, the Spaniards began to employ a few negroes in the mines of Hispaniola, and in the year 1517, the Emperor, Charles V., granted a patent to certain persons, for the exclusive supply of 4,000 negroes annually, to the islands of Hispaniola, Cuba, Jamaica, and Puerto Rico."*

African slaves were first imported into this country in 1620, more than a century after their introduction into the West Indies. It seems that, in the year 1620, the trade to Virginia was thrown open to all nations, and a Dutch vessel availing itself of the commercial liberty which prevailed, brought into James River twenty Africans, who were immediately purchased as slaves ; " and as that hardy race," says Robertson, " was found more capable of enduring fatigue under a sultry climate than Europeans, their number has been increased by continual importations."† Slavery was thus introduced into the New World, and its fertile soil and extensive territory its sparse population and warm climate, so congenial to the African constitution, soon gave a powerful stimulus to the trade, and drew towards it the mercantile enterprise of every commercial nation of Europe. England being the most commercial of European nations, naturally engrossed a large portion of the trade ; Bryant Edwards says, that from the year 1680 to 1786, there were imported into the British possessions alone, 2,130,000 slaves—making an average annual importation of more than 20,000.

The annual importation into the two Americas from all

* See Bryant Edward's West Indies, vol. 3, p. 238, and the sequel.

† See upon this subject 2d chapter of the first volume of Marshall's Life of Washington, and Robertson's Virginia.

quarters, has frequently transcended 100,000! But our limits will not allow us to enter more fully into this subject; and, therefore, we must content ourselves by calling the attention of the reader to the 9th section of *Walsh's Appeal* on the subject of negro slavery and the slave trade, in which he has brought together all the information upon this subject up to the time at which he wrote (1819.)

We will now proceed to consider, 2d—*The effects of the Slave Trade on the condition of Africa*—and first, will briefly advert to the supposed advantages. It is well known that almost the whole of Africa exists in a barbarous state—only one or two removes above the Indian of America. At the commencement of the slave trade, slavery, as we have already seen, was established throughout Africa, and had led on to great mitigation of the cruel practices of war; but still, in consequence of the limited demand for slaves under their very rude system of agriculture, the prisoner of war was frequently put to death.

So soon, however, as the slave trade was established, great care was taken in the preservation of the lives of prisoners, in consequence of the great demand for them occasioned by the slave traffic; so that, although an extension has been given to the system of slavery, many lives are supposed to have been saved by it.

Again: it has been contended that the slave trade, by giving a value to the African negro which would not otherwise have been attached to him, has produced much more mildness and kindness in the treatment of slaves in Africa; that the utmost care is now taken in the rearing of children, and, consequently, that although Africa has lost many of her inhabitants from this cause, yet a stimulus has thereby been given to population, which has in some measure made up the loss.

"Africa," says Malthus, "has been at all times the principal mart of slaves. The drains of its population in this way have been great and constant, particularly since their introduction into the European colonies; but, perhaps, as Doctor Franklin observes, it would be difficult to find the gap that has been made by a hundred years' exportation of negroes, which has blackened half America."* Lastly, it has been urged, and with great apparent justness, that the slave trade has contributed greatly to the civilization of a large portion of the African population; that, by transportation to the western world, they have been placed in contact with the civilized white, and have been greatly benefitted by the change; that the system of slavery throughout our continent and the islands, is much less cruel than in Africa; that there nowhere prevails in America, the horrid practice of sacrificing the slave on the death of his master, in order that he may be well attended in another world; a practice which all travellers in Africa assert to be extremely common in many nations; and finally, that the climate of our temperate and torrid zones, is much more suitable to the African constitution, than even their own climate; and, consequently, that the physical condition of the race has greatly improved by the transplantation.

There is certainly much truth in the above assertions; but still we cannot agree that the advantages of Africa from the slave trade, have preponderated over the disadvantages. Although wars have been made more mild by the trade, yet they have been made much more frequent: an additional and powerful motive for strife has been furnished. Countries have been overrun, and cities pillaged, mainly with a view of procuring slaves for the slave dealer. Brougham likens the

* See Malthus on population, vol. 1, page 179, Georgetown Edition.

operation of the slave trade in this respect, to the effect which the different menageries in the world and the consequent demand for wild beasts, have produced on the inferior animals of Africa. They are now taken alive, instead of being killed as formerly; but they are certainly more hunted and more harassed than if no foreign demand existed for them. The unsettled state of Africa, caused by the slave trade, is most undoubtedly unfavorable to the progress of civilization in that extensive region. In proof of the fatal effects of the slave trade on the peace, order, and civilization of Africa, Mr. Wilberforce asserted, and his assertion is upheld by the statements of all travellers who have penetrated far into the interior, that while in every region the sea coast and the banks of navigable rivers, those districts which, from their situation, had most intercourse with civilized nations, were found to be most civilized and cultivated; the effects of the slave trade had been such in Africa, that those parts of the coast which had been the seats of the longest and closest intercourse with European nations in carrying on a flourishing slave trade, were far inferior in civilization and knowledge to many tracts of the interior country, where the face of the white man had never been seen; and thus has the slave trade been able to reverse the ordinary effects of Christianity and Mahomedanism, and to cause the latter to be the instructor and enlightener of mankind, while the former left them under the undisturbed or rather increased influence of all their native superstitions.*

Again: the condition of the negro during what is called the *middle passage*, is allowed by all to be wretched in the extreme. The slave traders are too often tempted to take on

* It is proper to state here, that Parke ascribes the superior condition of the interior districts of Africa, principally to a more healthy climate.

board more slaves than can be conveniently carried; they are then stored away in much too narrow space, and left to all the horrors and privations incident to a voyage through tropical seas. The Edinburgh Review asserts, that about seventeen in a hundred died generally during the passage, and about thirty-three afterwards in the seasoning—making the loss of the negroes exported, rise to the frightful amount of 50 per cent. It has been further asserted, that the treatment of the negroes after importation, has been generally so cruel, as that the population has not, by its procreative energies, kept up its numbers in any of the West India islands; that it has been cheaper for the West Indian to *work out* his negroes, and trust to the slave trade for a supply, than to raise them in the islands where provisions are so dear. We believe the accounts of the ill treatment of slaves in the West Indies have been greatly exaggerated, and have no doubt that their condition has generally been better than in Africa; but still it is true, that breeding has been discouraged generally where the slave trade was in full operation; and children not being allowed full attention from the mother, have too frequently died from the want of care. And this is most probably a principal reason of the slow increase of the slaves in the West Indies, by procreation.* Upon the whole, then, we must come to the conclusion, that the slave trade has been disadvantageous to Africa; has caused a violation of the principles of humanity, and given rise to much suffering and to considerable destruction of human life.† Judging by its ef-

* Another cause of the difficulty of keeping up the slave population of the West Indies, is the great disproportion between the sexes among those imported—the males being greatly more numerous than the females.

† We do not by any means wish to be understood as contending that negro slavery in our hemisphere, has lessened the number of ne-

fects, we must condemn it, and consequently, agree that slavery in our hemisphere was based upon injustice in the first instance.

But we believe that there are many circumstances of an alleviating character, which form at least, a strong apology for the slave trade, thus: slavery exists throughout the whole of Africa; the slave must necessarily be looked upon in the light of property, and subject to bargain, sale, and removal, as all kinds of moveable property are. The *Adscripti Glebæ*, or slaves attached to the soil, and not suffered to be removed, fare the worst. When they multiply too greatly for the products of the soil on which they are situated, their subsistence is scanty, and their condition is miserable. When not in proportion to the extent of the soil, then they are sure to be overworked, as there is a deficiency of labor. It is certainly best, therefore, if slavery exists, at all, that buying and selling should be allowed, and upon this principle the *middle passage* certainly constitutes the greatest objection to the slave trade, when those alone are imported who were slaves in Africa.

But again: it is extremely difficult, in all questions of morality, to say, how far ignorance, conscientious opinions, and concomitant circumstances, may atone for acts extremely hurtful and improper in themselves; we all agree that these produce great modifications. The bigot who burns his religious enemy at the stake, and conscientiously believes that he has done his God a service, and the North American Indian, who torments with every refinement of cruelty the prisoner who has unfortunately fallen into his hands, and believes that

groes throughout the world. On the contrary, there is nothing more true, than that the number has greatly increased by it. We only allude to the destruction of life in the Middle Passage and the Seasoning.

the Great Spirit applauds him, and that the blood of his fathers calls for it, surely do not commit the same amount of sin as the perfectly enlightened statesman, who should do the same things from policy, *knowing them to be wrong.* In like manner, the slave trade, at its origin, can lay claim to the same sort of apology, from the condition of the world when it arose, and the peculiar circumstances which generated it. Slavery was then common throughout almost every country of Europe.

Indeed, the slaves under the appellation of *main mortables*,* in France, were never liberated until the revolution in 1789. The public law of Europe, too, justified the killing or enslaving of the prisoner, at the option of the captor. Under these circumstances, we are not to wonder that the slave trade, so far from exciting the horrors of mankind, as now, actually commanded the admiration of Europe. Gonzales, we have just seen, during the reign of the celebrated Prince Henry, in 1442, brought the first negro slaves into Lisbon, and the deed excited the admiration of all : again, three years afterwards, Dinis Fernandez, a citizen of Lisbon, and an Esquire to the King Don John, captured four negroes on the coast of Africa and brought them into Lisbon ; and the Portuguese historian, Barras, "eulogizes Dinis," says Walsh, in his notices of Brazil, "that he did not stop at the time, to make forays into the country, and capture more slaves on his own account, but brought those he had caught back to his master, who was *mightily pleased*, not only with the discoveries he had made, but with the people he had carried with him, which had not been delivered from the hands of the Moors like the other ne-

* It is a singular fact, that the slaves belonging to the Church were the last liberated—a striking illustration of the feeble effects of religion and philanthropy, when arrayed against interest.

groes, which had up to that time come into the kingdom, but had been *caught* on their own soil."

The famous Bartholomew de Las Casas, Bishop of Chiapi, who is said to have been the first to recommend the importation of Africans into the New World, was a man of the mildest and most philanthropic temper, yet he never doubted at all the right to enslave Africans, though he was the zealous advocate and protector of the Indian. "While he contended, says Robertson, "for the liberty of people born in one quarter of the globe, he labored to enslave the inhabitants of another region; and in the warmth of his zeal to save the Americans from the yoke, pronounced it to be lawful and expedient to impose one *still heavier* upon the Africans."*

We have already seen that Charles V. granted a commission to a company to supply his American possessions with 4,000 slaves per annum. Ferdinand and Isabella likewise had permitted the trade before him.

John Hawkins was the first Englishman who embarked in the trade, and he seems by his daring and enterprise in the business, to have greatly pleased his sovereign, Queen Elizabeth, who so far from disgracing him, conferred on him the honors of knighthood, and made him treasurer of the navy.† Elizabeth, James I., Charles I. and II., were all in the habit of chartering companies to carry on the trade. No scruples of conscience seem ever to have disturbed the quiet of these royal personages, or of the agents whom they employed. The last chartered company was called the Royal African company, and had among the subscribers, the King, (Charles II.) the Duke of York, his brother, and many other persons of high rank and quality.‡ In fact, women, the most virtuous and

* Robertson's America.
† See Edward's West Indies, vol. 8, page 242.
‡ Edward's West Indies, vol. 2, pp. 247–8.

humane, were often subscribers to this kind of stock, and seem never to have reflected upon the injustice and iniquity of the traffic, which has so long scandalized civilized Europe. It would indeed be a most difficult question in casuistry, to determine the amount of sin and wickedness committed by the various governments of Europe, in sanctioning a trade which the condition of Europe, Africa, and America, and all the habits and practices of the day, seemed so completely to justify.

We shall now proceed, 3dly, *to the consideration of the share of responsibility which attaches to the United States in the commission of the original sin by which slavery was first introduced into this country.*—The colonies, being under the control and guidance of another country, were of course responsible for no commercial acts and regulations in which they had no share whatever. The slave trade, on the part of Great Britain, commenced during the reign of Elizabeth, who, personally, took a share in it. *The colonies did not then exist.* It was encouraged in the successive reigns of Charles I. and II. and James II.; and William III. outdid them all: with Lord Sumers for his minister, he declared the slave trade *to be highly beneficial to the nation.* The colonies, all this time, took no share in it themselves, *merely purchasing* what the British merchants brought them, and doing therein what the British government invited them to do, by every means in their power. And now let us see who it was that first marked it with disapprobation, and sought to confine it within narrow bounds. The colonies began in 1760. South-Carolina, a British colony, passed an act to prohibit further importation ; but Great Britain rejected this act with indignation, and declared that the slave trade *was beneficial and necessary to the mother country.* The governors of the colonies had positive orders to sanction no law enacted against the slave trade. In Jamaica, in the year 1765, an attempt was made to abolish the trade to that island. The governor declared that his instructions would never allow him to sign the bill. It was tried again on the same island in 1774, but Great Britain, by the Earl of Dartmouth, president of the board, answered : "*We cannot allow the colonies to check or discourage in any degree a traffic so beneficial to the nation.*" The above historical account we have taken from a *British writer.* (Barnham's Observations on the Abolition of Negro Slavery.)

Among all the colonies, none seem to be more eager and more pressing for the abolition of the slave trade than Virginia—in which State the citizens, wonderful to relate, seem now more remorseful and conscience-stricken than any where else in the whole southern country. Judge Tucker, in his Notes on Blackstone's Commentaries, has collected a list of no less than twenty-three acts imposing duties on slaves, which occur in the compilation of Virginia laws. The first bears date as far back as 1699 ; and the real design of all of them was not revenue, but the repression of the importation. In 1772, most of the duties previously imposed were re-enacted, and the Assembly transmitted, at the same time, a petition to the throne, which, as Mr. Walsh most justly observes, speaks almost all that could be desired, for the *confusion* of our slanderers. The following are extracts : " We are encouraged to look up to the throne and implore your majesty's paternal assistance in averting a calamity of a most alarming nature." "The importation of slaves into the colonies from the coast of Africa, hath long been considered a trade of *great inhumanity*, and, under its present encouragement, we have too much reason to fear, will endanger the very existence of your Majesty's American dominions."

" Deeply impressed with these sentiments, we most humbly beseech your majesty to *remove all those restraints on your majesty's governors of this colony* which inhibit their assenting to such laws as might check so very pernicious a commerce." The petition, of course, was unavailing. The first Assembly which met in Virginia, after the adoption of her constitution, prohibited the traffic; and the "*inhuman use of the royal negative,*" against the action of the colony upon this subject, is enumerated in the first clause of the first Virginia constitution, as a reason of the separation from the mother country.

The action of the United States Government likewise upon the slave trade, seems to have been as deeply and efficient as could possibly have been expected from a government necessarily placed under great restraint and limitation.

Not being able to enter into the details, we quote, with great pleasure, the following remark of Mr. Walsh, who, with great indefatigable zeal and industry, has collected all the important information on the subject of the slave trade, and furnished the world with a complete and triumphant vindication of the United States, against the taunts and illiberal insinuations of British writers. "It is seen," says Mr. Walsh, "by the foregoing abstract, that federal America interdicted the trade from her ports, thirteen years before Great Britain; that she made it punishable as a crime seven years before; that she had fixed four years sooner the period of non-importation—which period was earlier than that determined upon by Great Britain for her colonies. We ought not to overlook the circumstance, that these measures were taken by a Legislature composed in considerable part of the *representatives of Slaveholding States; slaveholders* themselves, in whom, of course, according to the Edinburgh Review, 'conscience had suspended its functions,' and 'justice, gentleness and pity were extinguished.' In truth, the *representatives from our*

Southern States have been foremost in testifying their abhorrence of the traffic."* Are we not then fully justified, from a historical review of the part which the colonists took, before and after the independence, in relation to the slave trade, in asserting that slavery was forced upon them, and the slave trade continued contrary to their wishes? If ever a nation stood justified before heaven, in regard to an evil, which had become interwoven with her social system, is not that country ours? Are not our hands unpolluted with the original sin, and did we not wish them clean of the contagion the moment our independent existence was established? Where is the stain that rests upon our escutcheon? There is none! United America has done her duty, and Virginia has the honor of taking the lead of the abolition of the slave trade, whose example has been so tardily and reluctantly followed by the civilized nations of Europe. Virginia, therefore, especially, has nothing to reproach herself with—" the still small voice of conscience" can never disturb her quiet. She truly stands upon this subject, like the Chevalier Bayard—" *sans peur et sans reproche.*"

We have now finished the first principal division of our subject—in which we have treated, we hope satisfactorily, of the origin of slavery in ancient and modern times, and have closed with a consideration of the slave trade, by which slavery has been introduced into the United States. We hope that this preliminary discussion will not be considered inappropriate to our main subject. We have considered it indispensably necessary to point out the true sources of slavery, and the principles upon which it rests, in order that we might appreciate fully the value of those arguments based upon the principles that " all men are born equal"—that " slavery in the abstract is wrong"—that " the slave has a natural right to

* See Walsh's Appeal, 2d edition, page 323.

regain his liberty," &c. &c.—all of which doctrines were most pompously and ostentatiously put forth by some of the abolitionists in the Virginia Legislature. No set of legislators ever have, or ever can, legislate upon purely abstract principles, entirely independent of circumstances, without the ruin of the body politic, which should have the misfortune to be under the guidance of such quackery. Well and philosophically has Burke remarked, that circnmstances give in reality to every political principle its distinguishing color and discriminating effect. The circumstances are what render every political scheme beneficial or noxious to mankind, and we cannot stand forward and give praise or blame to anything which relates to human actions and human concerns, on a simple view of the object as it stands, stript of every relation, in all the nakedness and solitude of metaphysical abstraction. The historical view which we have given of the origin and progress of slavery, shows most conclusively that something else is requisite to convert slavery into freedom, than the mere enunciation of abstract truths, divested of all adventitious circumstances and relations. We shall now proceed to the second great division of our subject, and inquire seriously and fairly, whether there be any means by which we may get rid of slavery.

II. Plans for the Abolition of Negro Slavery.—Under this head we will examine first, those schemes which propose abolition and deportation; and secondly, those which contemplate emancipation without deportation.

1st. *Emancipation and Deportation.*—In the late Virginia Legislature, where the subject of slavery underwent the most thorough discussion, all seemed to be perfectly agreed in the necessity of removal in case of emancipation. Several members from the lower counties, which are deeply interested in this question, seemed to be sanguine in their anticipations of the final success of some project of emancipation and deportation to Africa, the original home of the negro. "Let us translate them," said one of the most respected and able members of the Legislature, (Gen. Broadnax,) "to those realms from which, in evil times, under inauspicious influences, their fathers were unfortunately abducted. Mr. Speaker, the idea of restoring these people to the region in which nature had planted them, and to whose climate she had fitted their constitutions—the idea of benefitting, not only our condition and their condition, by the removal, but making them the means of carrying back to a great continent, lost in the profoundest depths of savage barbarity, unconscious of the existence even of the God who created them, not only the arts and comforts, and multiplied advantages of civilized life, but what is of more value than all, a knowledge of true religion—intelligence of a Redeemer—is one of the grandest and noblest, one of the most expansive and glorious ideas which ever entered into the imagination of man. The conception, whether to the philosopher, the statesman, the philanthropist, or the christian, of rearing up a colony which is to be the nucleus around which future emigration will concentre, and open all Africa to civilization, and commerce, and science, and arts, and religion—when Ethiopia shall stretch out her hands, indeed, is one which warms the heart with delight." (*Speech of Gen. Broadnax, of Dinwiddie*, pp. 36 and 37.) We fear that this splendid vision, the creation of a brilliant imagination, influenced by the pure feelings of a philanthropic and generous heart, is destined to vanish at the severe touch of analysis. Fortunately for reason and common sense, all these projects of deportation may be subjected to the most rigid and accurate calculations, which are amply sufficient to dispel all doubt, even in the minds of the most sanguine, as to their practicability.

We take it for granted, that the right of the owner to his slave is to be respected, and, consequently, that he is not required to emancipate him, unless his full value is paid by the State. Let us, then, keeping this in view, proceed to the very simple calculation of the expense of emancipation and deportation in Virginia. The slaves, by the last census (1830,) amounted within a small fraction to 470,000; the average value of each one of these is, $200; consequently, the whole aggregate value of the slave population of Virginia, in 1830, was $94,000,000; and allowing for the increase since, we cannot err far in putting the present value at $100,000,000. The assessed value of all the houses and lands in the State, amounts to $206,000,000, and these constitute the material items in the wealth of the State, the whole personal property besides bearing but a very small proportion to the value of slaves, lands, and houses. Now, do not these very simple statistics speak volumes upon this subject? It is gravely recommended to the State of Virginia to give up a species of property which constitutes nearly one-third of the wealth of the whole State, and almost one-half of that of Lower Virginia, and with the remaining two-thirds to encounter the additional enormous expense of transportation and colonization on the coast of Africa. But the loss of $100,000,000 of property is scarcely the half of what Virginia would lose, if the immutable laws of nature could suffer (as fortunately they cannot) this tremendous scheme of colonization to be carried into full effect. Is it not population which makes our lands and houses valuable? Why are lots in Paris and London worth more than the silver dollars which it might take to cover them? Why are lands of equal fertility in England and France, worth more than those of our Nothern States, and those again worth more than Southern soils, and those in turn worth more than the soils of the distant West? It is the presence or absence of population which alone can explain the fact. It is, in truth, the slave labor in Virginia which gives value to her soil and her habitations; take away this, and you pull down the Atlas that upholds the whole system; eject from the State the whole slave population, and we risk nothing in the prediction, that on the day in which it shall be accomplished, the worn soils of Virginia would not bear the paltry price of the government lands in the West, and the Old Dominion will be a " waste howling wilderness;"—" the grass shall be seen growing in the streets, and the foxes peeping from their holes."

But the favorers of this scheme say they do not contend for the sudden emancipation and deportation of the whole black population; they would send off only the increase, and thereby keep down the population to its present amount, while the whites, increasing at their usual rate, would finally become relatively so numerous as to render the presence of the blacks among us for ever afterwards entirely harmless. This scheme, which at first, to the unreflecting, seems plausible, and much less wild than the project of sending off the whole, is nevertheless impracticable and visionary, as we think a few remarks will prove. It is computed that the annual increase of the slaves and free colored population of Virginia is about six thousand. Let us first, then, make a calculation of the expense of purchase and transportation. At $200 each, the six thousand will amount in value to $1,200,000. At $30 each, for transportation, which we shall soon see is too little, we have the whole expense of purchase and transportation $1,380,000, an expense to be annually incurred by Virginia to keep down her black population to its present amount. And let us ask, is there any one who can seriously argue that Virginia can incur such an annual expense as this for the next twenty-five or fifty years, until the whites have multipled so greatly upon the blacks, as, in the *opinion* of the *alarmists*, for ever to quiet the fears of the community ? Vain and delusive hope, if any were ever wild enough to entertain it ! Poor old Virginia ! the leader of the *poverty stricken team*, which have been for years so heavily dragging along under the intolerable burthen of the Federal Government, must inevitably be crushed, whenever this new weight is imposed on her, in comparison with which federal exactions are light and mild. We should as soon expect the *Chamois*, the hardy rover over Alpine regions, by his unassisted strength to hurl down the snowy mantle which for ages has clothed the lofty summit of Mount Blanc, as that Virginia will be ever able, by her own resources, to purchase and colonize on the coast of Africa six thousand slaves for any number of years in succession.

But this does not develope, to its full extent, the monstrous absurdity of this scheme. There is a view of it yet to be taken, which seems not to have struck very forcibly any of the speakers in the Virginia Legislature, but which appears to us, of itself perfectly conclusive against this whole project. We have made some efforts to obtain something like an accurate account of the number of negroes every year carried out of Virginia to the South and Southwest. We have not been enabled to succeed completely ; but from all the information we can obtain, we have no hesitation in saying, that upwards of 6,000 are yearly exported to other States. Virginia is, in fact, a *negro* raising State for other States ; she produces enough for her own supply, and six thousand for sale. Now, suppose the government of Virginia enters the slave market resolved to purchase six thousand for emancipation and deportation, is it not evident that it must overbid the Southern seeker, and thus take the very slaves who would have gone to the South ? The very first operation, then, of this scheme, provided slaves be treated as property, is to arrest the current which has been hitherto flowing to the South, and to accumulate the evil in the State. As sure as the moon in her transit over the meridian arrests the current which is gliding to the ocean, so sure will the action of the Virginia government, in an attempt to emancipate and send off 6,000 slaves, stop those who are annually going out of the State; and when 6,000 are sent off in one year, (which we never expect to see,) it will be found, on investigation, that they are those who would have been sent out of the State by the operation of our slave trade, and to the utter astonishment and confusion of our abolitionists, the black population will be found advancing with its usual rapidity—the only operation of the scheme being to substitute our government, *alias, ourselves*, as purchasers, instead of the planters of the South. This is a view which every legislator in the State should take. He should beware, lest in his zeal for action, this efflux, which is now so salutary to the State, and such an abundant source of wealth, be suddenly dried up, and all the evils of slavery be increased instead of diminished. If government really could enter with capital and zeal enough into the boundless project, we might even in a few years see the laws of nature reversed, and the tide of slavery flowing from the South in Virginia, to satisfy the philanthropic demand for colonization. The only means which the government could use to prevent the above described effect, would be either arbitrarily to fix the price of slaves below their market value, which would be a clear violation of the right of property, (which we shall presently notice,) or to excite a feeling of insecurity and apprehension as to this kind of property, and thus dispose the owner to part with it at less than its true value; but surely no statesman would openly avow such an object, although it must be confessed that some of the speakers, even, who contended that slaves should ever be treated as property, avowed sentiments which were calculated to produce such a result.

It is said, however, that the southern market will at all events be closed against us, and consequently, that the preceding argument falls to the ground. To this we answer, that as long as the demand to the south exists, the supply will be furnished in some way or other, if our government do not unwisely tamper with the subject. Bryant Edwards has said, that " an attempt to prevent the introduction of slaves into the West Indies would be like chaining the winds, or giving laws to the ocean." We may with truth affirm, that an attempt to prevent a circulation of this kind of property through the slave-holding States of our confederacy, would be equally if not more impracticable. But there is a most striking illustration of this now exhibiting before our eyes—the Southampton massacre produced great excitement and apprehension throughout the slave-holding States, and two of them, hitherto the largest purchasers of Virginia slaves, have interdicted their introduction under severe penalties. Many in our State looked forward to an immediate fall in the price of slaves from this cause; and what has been the result? Why, wonderful to relate, Virginia slaves are now higher than they have been for many years past; and this rise in price has no doubt been occasioned by the number of southern purchasers who have visited our State, under the belief that Virginians had been frightened into a determination to get clear of their slaves at all events ; " and from an artificial demand in the slave purchasing States, caused by an apprehension on the part of the farmers of those States, that the regular supply of slaves would speedily be discontinued by the operation of their non-importation regulations;"* and we are, consequently, at

---

* From Louisiana, many of the farmers themselves have come into

this moment exporting slaves more rapidly, through the operation of the internal slave trade, than for many years past.

Let us now examine a moment into the object proposed to be accomplished by this scheme. It is contended, that free labor is infinitely superior to slave labor in every point of view, and therefore it is highly desirable to exchange the latter for the former, and that this will be gradually accomplished by emancipation and deportation ; because the vacuum occasioned by the exportation of the slaves will be filled up by the influx of freemen from the north and other portions of the Union—and thus, for every slave we lose, it is contended that we shall receive in exchange a free laborer, much more productive and moral. If we are not greatly mistaken, this, on analysis, will be found to be a complete specimen of that arithmetical *school boy* reasoning, which has ever proved so deceptive in politics, and so ruinous in its practical consequences ;' and first, let us see whether anything will be gained in point of productiveness, by this exchange of slave labor for free, even upon the avowed principles of the abolitionists themselves. The great objections to slave labor seems to be—First, that it is unproductive, or at least, not as productive as free labor ; and secondly, that it is calculated to repel free labor from the sphere in which it is exercised. This latter effect has been briefly and more ingeniously urged by a writer in the Richmond Enquirer of the 3rd of March, 1832, over the signature of "York," than by any one, who is known

our State, for the purpose of purchasing their own slaves, and thereby evading the laws. There are, in fact, so many plans which will effectually defeat all these preventive regulations, that we may consider their rigid enforcement utterly impracticable ; and moreover, as the excitement produced by the late insurrection in Virginia, dies away, so will these laws be forgotten, and remain as dead letters upon the statute books.

to us, and we shall consequently introduce an extract from his essay.

"Society naturally resolves itself," says this writer, "into three classes. The first comprehends professional men, capitalists and large landed proprietors; the second embraces artisans and small proprietors; and the third is composed of common laborers. Now, we are a society placed in the anomalous predicament of being *totally without a laboring class;* for all our labor is performed by slaves, who constitute no part of that society, and who *quoad* that society, may be regarded as brutes or machines. This circumstance operates directly as a check upon the increase of white population. For, as some intelligence or property is required to enable a man to belong to either of the two first classes above enumerated, (and which I have remarked are the only classes which we have,) and so no one with ordinary self-respect can submit to sink below them, and become outcasts, the immediate tendency of the supernumerary members is to emigration." We will not, for the present, dispute the premises of the very intelligent and graceful writer, from whom we have copied the above extract; we have endeavored throughout the review, to show that our adversaries are not justified in their conclusions, even if we admit the truth of their premises. Now, what is the conclusion arrived at by our adversaries, from the premises just mentioned? That we must deport our slaves as fast as possible, and leave the vacuum to be filled by free labor. In the first place, then, we say upon their own principles even, they cannot expect free labor to take the place of slave, for every one acknowledges it utterly impossible to send away, at once, all our slaves—there is scarcely, we presume, a single abolitionist in Virginia, who has ever supposed that we can send away more than the annual increase. Now, then, we ask, how can any one reasonably expect that the taking away of two or three negroes from a body of one hundred, (and this is a much greater proportion than the abolitionists hope to colonize,) can destroy that prejudice against laboring with the blacks, which is represented, as preventing the whites from laboring, and as sending them in multitudes to the West. If we are too proud to work in a field with fifty negro men this year, we shall surely be no more disposed to do it next year, because one negro, the increase of fifty, has been sent to Liberia; and consequently the above reasoning, if it prove any thing, proves that we must prevent our laboring classes (the blacks) from increasing, because whites will not work with them—although the whites will be just as averse to working with them after you have checked their increase as before.

But let us suppose, that by some kind of logical *legerdemain*, it can be proven that free labor will supply the place of slave labor, which is deported to Africa—even then, we think, they will fail upon their other great principle, that free labor is better than slave, the truth of which principle, for the present, we are willing to allow—and their whole argument fails, for this plain and palpable reason, that free labor, by association with slave labor, must inevitably be brought down to its level, and even below it,—for the vices of the slave you may correct, by means of your authority over him, but those of the associate free laborer you cannot. Every farmer in Virginia, can testify to the truth of this assertion. He knows full well, that if he employs a white laborer to work with a black one, even at job work, where of course the inducement of labor is greatest—he will do no more than the negro, and perhaps, in a majority of cases, he will not do as much. What then might we expect of him, if he should enter the field with fifty fold his number of blacks, to work along with them regularly through the four seasons of the year? We hazard little in saying, he would be a more unproductive laborer than the black, for he would soon have all his idle propensities, without being subjected to the same salutary restraint.

It is a well known general fact, to all close observers of mankind, that if two different grades of labor as to productiveness be associated together in the same occupation, the higher has a tendency to descend to the level of the lower. Schmalz, in his Political Economy, says, that the indolence and carelessness of the serfs in the north of Europe, corrupt the free laborers who come in contact with them. Jones, in his volume on Rents, says, " a new road is at this time (1831) making, which is to connect Hamburg and the Elb with Berlin; it passes over the sterile sands, of which so much of the north of Germany consists, and the materials for it are supplied by those isolated blocks of granite, of which the presence on the surface of those sands forms a notorious geological puzzle. These blocks, transported to the line of road, are broken to the proper size by workmen, some of whom are Prussian free laborers, others Leibeigeners of the Mecklenburg territory, through a part of which the road passes. They are paid a stipulated sum for breaking *a certain* quantity, *and all are paid alike*. Yet the Leibeigeners could not at first be prevailed upon to break more than one-third of the quantity which formed the ordinary task of the Prussians. The men were mixed in the hope that the example and the gains of the more industrious would animate the sluggish. Now, mark the result. A contrary effect followed ; the Leibeigeners *did not improve*, but the exertions of other laborers *sensibly slackened*, and at the time my informant (the English Engineer who superintended the work) was speaking to me, the men were again at work in separate gangs, carefully kept asun der."* And thus do we find, by an investigation of this subject, that if we should introduce, by any means, free labor in the stead of slave labor deported to Africa, that it will be certain to deteriorate by association with slave labor, until it sinks down to and even below its level. So far, we have admitted the possibility of exchanging slave for free labor, and have endeavored to prove, upon the principles of the abolitionists, that nothing would be gained by it. We will endeavor to prove, and we think we can do it incontestibly, that the scheme of the abolition and deportation will not and cannot possibly effect this exchange of slave labor for free, even if it were desirable. And in order that we may examine the project fully in this point of view, we will endeavor—first, to trace out its operation on the slave population, and then on the white.

Since the publication of the celebrated work of Dr. Malthus, on the "principle of population," the knowledge of the causes which effect its condition and increase, is much more widely diffused. It is now well known to every student of political economy, that in the wide range of legislation, there is nothing more dangerous than too much tampering with the elastic and powerful spring of population.

The energies of government are for the most part feeble or impotent when arrayed against its action. It is this procreative power of human species either exerted or dormant, which so frequently brushes away *in reality* the visionary fabrics of the philanthropists, and mars the cherished plots and schemes of statesmen. Euler has endeavored to prove, by some calculations, that the human species, under the most favorable circumstances, is capable of doubling itself once in twelve years.

* See Jones's Political Economy, vol. 1, pp. 51, 52—London Edition.

In our Western country, the progress of population has, in many extensive districts, been so rapid as to show, in our opinion most conclusively, that it is capable of doubling itself once in fifteen years without the aid of emigration. The whole of our population, since the independence of the United States, has shown itself fully capable of duplication in periods of twenty-five years, without the accession from abroad.* In some portions of our country the population is stationary, in others but very slowly advancing. We will assume then for the two extremes in our country, the stationary condition on the one side, and such increase on the other as to give rise to a duplication every fifteen years. Now as throughout the whole range comprehended between these extremes, population is capable of exerting various degrees of energy, it is very evident that the statesman who wishes to increase or diminish population, must look cautiously to the effect of his measures on its spring, and see how this will be acted on. If, for example, his object be to lessen the number of slowly increasing population, he must be convinced that his plan does not stimulate the procreative energies of society to produce more than he is capable of taking away; or if his object be to increase the numbers, take heed lest this project deaden and paralyze the source of increase so much as to more than counterbalance any effort of his. Now looking at the texture of the Virginia population, the desideratum is to diminish the blacks and increase the whites. Let us see how the scheme of emancipation and deportation will act. We have already shown that the first operation of the plan, if slave property were rigidly respected and never taken without full compensation, would be to put a stop to the efflux from the State through other channels; but this would not be the only effect.

* The longest period of duplication has been about twenty-three

Government entering into the market with individuals, would elevate the price of slaves beyond their natural value, and consequently, the raising of them would become an object of primary importance throughout the whole State. We can readily imagine that the price of slaves might become so great that each master would do all in his power to encourage marriage among them—would allow the females almost entire exception from labor, that they might the better breed and nurse—and would so completely concentrate his efforts upon this object, as to neglect other schemes and less productive sources of wealth. Under these circumstances, the prolific African might, no doubt, be stimulated to press hard upon one of the limits above stated, doubling in numbers in fifteen years; and such is the tendency which our abolition schemes, if seriously engaged in, will most undoubtedly produce; they will be certain to stimulate the procreative powers of that very race which they are aiming to diminish; they will enlarge and invigorate the very monster which they are endeavoring to stifle, and realize the beautiful but melancholy fable of Sisyphus, by an eternal renovation of hope and disappointment. If it were possible for Virginia to purchase and send off annually for the next twenty-five or fifty years, 12,000 slaves, we should have very little hesitation in affirming, that the number of slaves in Virginia would not be at all lessened by the operation, and at the conclusion of the period such habits would be generated among our blacks, that for a long time after the cessation of the drain, population might advance so rapidly as to produce among us all the calamities and miseries of an over-crowded people.

We are not now detailing in mere conjecture; there is ample proof of the correctness of these anticipations in the years seven months, so that the addition of one year and five months more than compensate for the emigration.

history of own hemisphere. The West India Islands, as we have before seen, are supplied with slaves more cheaply by the African slave trader than they can raise them, and consequently the black population in the islands nowhere keeps up its numbers by natural increase. It appears by a statement of Mr. F. Buxton, recently published, that the total number of slaves in the British West Indies, in 1817, was 730,112. After the lapse of eleven years, in 1828, the numbers were reduced to 678,527, making a loss on the capital of 1817, in the short space of eleven years, of 51,585.* In the Mauritius, in the same space of time, the loss on the capital of 1817, amounting to but 76,774, was 10,767. Even in the Island of Cuba, where the negro slave is treated as humanely as any where on the globe, from 1804 to 1817, the blacks lost 4,461, upon the stock of 1804. "Prior to the annexation of Louisiana to the United States," says Mr. Clay in his Colonization Speech of 1830, "the slaves from Africa were abundant. The price of adults was generally about $100, a price less than the cost of raising an infant. Then it was believed that the climate of that province was unfavorable to the rearing of negro children, and comparatively few were raised. After the United States abolished the slave trade, the price of adults rose very considerably—greater attention was, consequently, bestowed on their children, and now nowhere is the African female more prolific than she is in Louisiana, and the climate of no one of the Southern States is supposed to be more favorable to the rearing of her offspring." For a similar reason

* Bryant Edwards attributes the decrease of the slaves in the West Indies principally to the disproportion of the sexes. But in the present instance, we are constrained to attribute it to another cause, for we find of the 730,112 slaves in the sugar islands in 1817, 369,577 were males, and 363,535 were females, being very nearly an equal division of the sexes.

now, the slaves in Virginia multiply more rapidly than in most of the Southern States; the Virginians can raise cheaper than they can buy; in fact, it is one of their greatest sources of profit. In many of the other slaveholding States, this is not the case, and consequently, the same care is not taken to encourage matrimony and the rearing of children.

For a similar reason, in ancient times, few slaves were reared in populous districts and large towns, these being supplied with slaves raised at a distance or taken in war, at a cheaper rate than they could be raised. "The comparison is shocking," says Mr. Hume, "between the management of human beings and that of cattle; but being extremely just when applied to the present subject, it may be proper to trace the consequences of it. At the capital, near all great cities, in all populous, rich, industrious provinces, few cattle are bred. Provisions, lodging, attendance, labor, are there dear, and men find their accounts better in buying the cattle after they come to a certain age, from the remote and cheaper countries. These are, consequently, the only breeding countries for cattle; and by parity of reason for men too, when the latter are put on the same footing with the former, as to buying and selling. To rear a child in London till he could be serviceable, would cost much dearer than to buy one of the same age from Scotland or Ireland, where he had been bred in a cottage, covered with rags, and fed on oatmeal and potatoes. Those who had slaves, therefore, (in ancient times,) in all the richer and more populous countries, would discourage the pregnancy of the females, and either prevent or destroy the birth.* . .

A perpetual recruit was, therefore, wanted from the poorer

---

* Such means as the last mentioned, will never be resorted to by any civilized nation of modern times, either in Europe or America; but others of a less objectionable character most certainly will be, whenever the rearing of slaves entails a great expense on the master and more desert provinces. . . . All ancient authors tell us that there was a perpetual flux of slaves to Italy from the remoter provinces, particularly Syria, Cilicia,* Cappadocia, and the lesser Asia, Thrace and Egypt. Yet the number of people did not increase in Italy."† It is thus we see everywhere, that the spring of population accommodates itself to the demand for human beings, and becomes inert or active in proportion to the value of the laborer and the small or great expense of rearing him.

It was upon this very principle that Mr. Pitt, in 1791, based the masterly and unanswerable argument contained in his splendid speech on the abolition of the slave trade ; in which he proved, upon data furnished by the West India planters themselves, that the moment an end was put to slave trade, the natural increase of negroes would commence, and more than keep up their numbers in the islands.

But our opponents, perhaps, may be disposed to answer, that this increase of slavery from the stimulus to the black population afforded by the colonization abroad, ought not to be objected to on our own principles, since each slave will be worth two hundred dollars or more. This answer would be correct enough if it were not that the increase of the blacks is effected at our expense, both as to wealth and numbers ; and to show this, we will now proceed to point out the operation of the scheme under consideration upon the white population. Malthus has clearly shown that population depends on the *means of subsistence,* and will, under ordinary circumstances, increase to a level with them. Now, by means of subsistence, we must not only comprehend the necessaries of life, such as

* " 10,000 slaves in a day have often been sold for the use of the Romans at Delos, in Cilicia."—Strabo, Lib. 14.

† See Hume's Essays, part 2d, essay 11th, on Populousness of Ancient Empires.

food, clothing, shelter, &c., but likewise such conveniences, comforts, and even luxuries, as the habits of the society may render it essential for all to enjoy. Whatever, then, has a tendency to destroy the wealth and diminish the aggregate capital of society, has the effect, as long as the *standard of comfort** remains the same, to check the progress of the population.

It is sure to discourage matrimony and cause children to be less carefully attended to, and to be less abundantly supplied. The heavy burthens which have hitherto been imposed on Virginia, through the operation of the federal exactions, together with the *high standard* of comfort prevalent throughout the whole State, (about which we shall, by and by, make a few observations,) have already imposed checks upon the progress of the white population of the State. If not one single individual were to emigrate from the State of Virginia, it would be found, so inert has become the principle of increase in the State, that the population would not advance with the average rapidity of the American people. Now, under these circumstances, an imposition of an additional burthen of $1,380,000 for the purpose of purchase and deportation of slaves, would add so much to the taxes of the citizens—would subtract so much from the capital of the State, and increase so greatly the embarrassments of the whole population, that fewer persons would be enabled to support families, and consequently to get married. This great tax, added to those we are already suffering under, would weigh like an incubus upon the whole State—it would operate like the blighting hand of Providence that should render our soil barren and our labor unproductive. It would

---

* By standard of comfort, we mean that amount of necessaries, conveniences, luxuries, which the habits of any people render essential to them.

diminish the value of the *fee simple* of Virginia, and not only check the natural increase of population within the Commonwealth, but would make every man desirous of quitting the scenes of his home and his infancy, and fleeing from the heavy burthen which would forever keep him and his children buried in the depths of poverty. His sale of negroes would partly enable him to emigrate ; and we have little doubt, that whenever this wild scheme shall be seriously commenced, it will be found that more whites than negroes will be banished by its operation from the State. And there will be this lamentable difference between those who are left behind: a powerful stimulus will be given to the procreative energies of the blacks, while those of the whites will be paralyzed and destroyed. Every emigrant from among the whites will create a *vacuum* not to be supplied—every removal of a black will stimulate the generation of another.

"Uno avulso non deficit alter."

The *poverty* stricken master would rejoice in the prolificness of his female slave, but pray Heaven in its kindness to strike with barrenness his own spouse, lest, in the plenitude of his misfortunes, brought on by the wild and quixotic philanthropy of his government, he might see around him a numerous offspring unprovided for, and destined to galling indigence.

It is almost useless to inquire whether this deportation of slaves to Africa would, as some seem most strangely to anticipate, invite the whites of other States into the Commonwealth. Who would be disposed to enter a State with worn out soil, and a black population mortgaged to the payment of millions *per annum*, for the purpose of emancipation and deportation, when in the West the most luxuriant soils, unincumbered with heavy exactions, could be purchased for the paltry sum of $1 25 per acre?

Where, then, is that multitude of whites to come from, which the glowing fancy of orators has sketched out as flowing into and filling up the *vacuum* created by the removal of slaves? The fact is, throughout the whole debate in the Virginia Legislature, the speakers seemed to consider the increase of population as a sort of fixed quantity, which would remain the same under the endless change of circumstance, and consequently that every man exported from among the blacks, lessened *pro tanto* exactly the black population, and that the whites, moving on with their usual speed, would fill the void; which certainly was an erroneous supposition, and manifested an almost unpardonable inattention to the wonderful *elasticity* of the powerful spring of population. The removal of inhabitants, accompanied with great loss of productive labor and capital, so far from leaving the residue in a better situation, and disposing them to increase and multiply, produces the directly opposite effect; it deteriorates the condition of society, and deadens the spring of population. It is curious to look to the history of the world, and see how completely this position is sustained by facts. Since the downfall of the Roman Empire, there have been three forced emigrations of very considerable extent, from three of the countries of Europe. The Moors were expelled from Spain, the Protestants from the Netherlands, and the Huguenots from France; each of these expulsions came well nigh ruining the country from which it took place. We are best acquainted with the effects of the expulsions of the Huguenots from France, because it happened nearer to our own times, during the reign of Louis XIV. In this case, only 500,000 are supposed to have left France, containing then a population of 20 or 25,000,000 of souls. The energies of this mighty country seemed at once paralyzed by this emigration, her prosperity was instantly arrested, her remaining population lost the vigor which characterised them as long as this *leaven* was among them, and to this day France has not recovered from the tremendous blow. Her inferiority to England in industry and all the useful arts, is in a great measure to be traced back to this stupid intolerance of her *great* monarch Louis XIV. The reason why these expulsions were so very injurious to the countries in question, was because the emigrants were the laboring classes of society, and their banishment consequently dried up the sources of production, and lessened the aggregate wealth and capital of the people. Now, these expulsions are *nothing* in comparison with that contemplated by our abolitionists. In France, only one in fifty of the population was expelled, and no expense was incurred in the deportation; but, in Virginia, the proportion to be expelled is much greater, and the exense is to devolve on the government.

When the emigration is accompanied with no loss of capital to the State, and no abstraction of *productive* labor, then the population will not be injuriously affected, but sometimes greatly benefitted. In the hunting state, the expulsion of half of the tribe would benefit the remainder in a politico-economical light, because they live on the game of the forest, which becomes more abundant as soon as the consumers diminish. Pastoral nations, for a like reason, are rarely injured by emigration, for they live on cattle, and the cattle live on the spontaneous produce of the earth, and when a colony is sent off, the remainder will generally be benefitted, since the consumption is relieved while the production is not diminished. And this satisfactorily explains the difficulty which has so much puzzled historians; how the North of Europe, which Gibbon, Hume, and Robertson, all maintain was in a pastoral state, and not nearly so thickly settled as at present, should nevertheless have been able for several centuries to furnish those terrible swarms of barbarians, who, "gathering fresh darkness and terror" as they rolled on upon the south, at length, with their congregated multitudes, "obscured the sun of Italy, and sunk the Roman world in night." This example of the barbarians in the north of Europe, sending so many hundreds of thousands of emigrants to the south, is a beautiful illustration of the capacity of population to counteract the effects of emigration, in all those cases where the spring of population is not weakened. As soon as new swarms left the country, the means of subsistence were more ample for the residue; the vigor of population soon supplied the deficiency; and then another swarm went forth and relieved again the national *hive.* Our purchase and deportation of slaves would produce a similar effect on our blacks, but it would be entirely at the expense of both the numbers and wealth of the whites, and would be, therefore, one of the most blighting curses that could scathe the land. Ireland, at present, is suffering heavy afflictions from an overcrowded population; but her government could not relieve her by sending off the paupers, and for the simple reason that it would require an expense on the part of Ireland, which would produce as great or even greater abstraction of capital than of unproductive mouths, and would, moreover, give more vigor to the spring of population. If other nations would incur the expense for her, then perhaps there might be for her a temporary benefit; but in a short time such a stimulus would be given to population, as would counteract all the vain efforts of man, and in the end, leave her in a worse condition than before. We doubt whether England, France, and Germany, by a steady concentration of all their financial resources upon the deportation and comfortable settlement and support of the superabundant population of Ireland, would, at the expiration of fifty years, be found to have lessened the numbers by one single individual. The effect would merely be, to pledge the resources of these three nations to the support of the Irish population, and to substitute the procreation of Irishmen for that of Englishmen, Frenchmen, and Germans ; and as soon as this support was withdrawn, the very habits which had been generated by it in Ireland, would be its greatest curse. The only effectual means of relieving Ireland, will be to raise the *standard of comfort* in that country, and to arrest the population by the preventive checks which would lessen the marriages. Until this be done, in some way or other, Ireland is doomed to suffer the heavy penalty.

We are now prepared to explain how it is that so many negroes have been exported from Africa by the slave trade, while the gap, says Franklin, is almost imperceptible. Gen. Broadnax, in his speech, computes the average number now annually sent out from Africa, by the operation of the slave trade, to be 100,000 ; and, he adds, if all this can be effected against so many risks and hazards, and in violation of the laws of God and man, shall it be said that the whole State of Virginia cannot export 6,000 to Africa in a year ? Yes, strange as it may seem, this is all true ; and the simple reason of the great difference is that Africa incurs no expense, but on the contrary, generally receives a full equivalent for the deported slave, which augments her means of subsistence, and stimulates the spring of population. The slave trade, which takes off 100,000 human beings from Africa, for the slave markets of the West Indies and South America, has, by its operation, quickened the procreative powers of society in Africa to such an extent, as not only to keep up her numbers, but to furnish besides 100,000 souls for exportation. Could we suppose it possible for this slave trade to be annihilated at a blow ; repugnant and shocking as it is to every feeling of humanity, it would be found that its sudden cessation would plunge the whole of Western Africa, for a season, into the most dreadful anarchy and appalling distress. It would be found that the habits of the people had been formed to suit the slave trade, and accordingly, would be much too favorable to the rapid increase of population without that trade—prisoners of war would be slaughtered, infants murdered, marriages discouraged, and swarms of redundant citizens sent forth to ravage neighboring countries; and all this would arise from the too rapid increase of population, for the means of subsistence, caused by the sudden stopping of the slave trade. It will be thus seen, that the 100,000 annually sent off from Africa, are a source of profit and not of expenditure. Saddle Africa with the whole of this burthen, and we are perfectly sure that the entire resources of that immense continent would not suffice to purchase up, send off, and colonize 5,000 per annum. There is the same difference between this exportation from Africa, and that proposed by the abolitionists from Virginia, that there is between the agriculturist who sends his produce to a foreign state or country, and receives back a full equivalent, and him who is condemned to send his abroad at his own expense, and to distribute it gratuitously. We imagine that no one who was acquainted with the condition of these two farmers would wonder that one should grow wealthy, and the other miserably poor. The 6,000 slaves which Virginia annually sends off to the South are a source of wealth to Virginia; but the 1,000 or 2,000 whites who probably go to the West, are a source of poverty; because, in the former case, we have an equivalent left in the place of the exported slave—in the latter, we lose both labor and capital, without an equivalent; and precisely such a result in a much more aggravated form, will spring from this mad colonization scheme, should it ever be carried into operation. If the governments of Europe were silly enough to appropriate their resources to the purchase of our slaves, at their full marketable value, for the purpose of deportation, they should, for aught that we could do, have every one that they could buy. An equivalent would thus be left for the deported slave, and however much others might suffer for their folly, we should escape.*

Against most of the great difficulties attendant on the plan of emancipation above examined, it was impossible for the abolitionists entirely to close their eyes ; and it is really curious to pause a moment and examine some of the reflections and schemes by which Virginia was to be reconciled to the plan. We have been told that it would not be necessary to purchase all the slaves sent away—that many would be surrendered by their owners without an equivalent. "There are a number of slaveholders," said one who has all the lofty feeling and devoted patriotism which have hitherto so proudly characterized Virginia, "at this very time, I do not speak from vain conjecture, but from what I know from the best information, and this number would continue to increase, who would voluntarily surrender their slaves, if the State would provide the means of colonizing them elsewhere. And there would be again another class, I have already heard of many, while they could not afford to sacrifice the entire value of their slaves, would cheerfully compromise with the State for half their value." In the first place, we would remark, that the gentleman's anticipation would certainly prove delusive—

* Perhaps one of the greatest blessings (if it could be reconciled to our conscience,) which could be conferred on the Southern portion of the Union, would arise from the total abolition of the African slave trade, and the opening of the West India and South American markets to our slaves. We do not believe that deportation to any other, or in any other way, can ever effect the slightest diminution.

the surrender of a very few slaves would enhance the importance and value of the residue, and make the owner much more reluctant to part with them. Let any farmer in Lower Virginia ask himself how many he can spare from his plantation—and he will be surprised to see how few can be dispensed with. If that intelligent gentleman, from the storehouse of his knowledge, would but call up the history of the past, he would see that *mere philanthropy*, with all her splendid boastings, has never yet accomplished one great scheme ; he would find the remark of that great judge of human nature, the illustrious author of the "Wealth of Nations," that no people had the generosity to liberate their slaves, until it became their interest to do so, but too true ; and the philosophic page of Hume, Robertson, Stuart, and Sismondi, would inform him that the serfs of Europe have been only gradually emancipated through the operation of *self-interest*, and not *philanthropy ;* and we shall soon see that it was fortunate for both parties that this was the case.

But it is strange, indeed, that gentlemen have never reflected, that the pecuniary loss to the State will be precisely the same, whether the negroes be purchased or gratuitously surrendered. In the latter case, the burthen is only shifted from the whole State to that portion where the surrender is made—thus, if we own $10,000 worth of this property, and surrender the whole to government, it is evident that we lose the amount of $10,000; and if the whole of Lower Virginia could at once be induced to give up all of this property, and it could be sent away, the only effect of this generosity and self-devotion would be to inflict the *blow* of *desolation* more exclusively on this portion of the State—the aggregate loss would be the same, the burthen would only be shifted from the whole to a part—the West would dodge the blow, and perhaps every candid citizen of Lower Virginia would confess that he is devoid of that refined incomprehensible patriotism which would call for self-immolation on the shrine of folly, and would most conscientiously advise the Eastern Virginians never to surrender their slaves to the government without a fair equivalent. Can it be genuine philanthropy to persuade them *alone* to step forward and bear the whole burden?

Again: some have attempted to evade the difficulties by seizing on the increase of the negroes after a certain time. Thus, Mr. Randolph's plan proposed that all born after the year 1840, should be raised by their masters to the age of eighteen for the female, and twenty-one for the male, and then hired out, until the neat sum arising therefrom amounted to enough to send them away. Scarcely any one in the Legislature—we believe not even the author himself—entirely approved of this plan.* It is obnoxious to the objections we have just been stating against voluntary surrender. It proposes to saddle the slaveholder with the whole burthen; it infringes directly the rights of property; it converts the fee simple possession of this kind of property into an estate for years; and it only puts off the great sacrifice required of the State to 1840, when most of the evils will occur that have already been described. In the meantime, it destroys the value of slaves, and with it all landed possessions—checks the productions of the State, imposes (when 1840 arrives) upon the master the intolerable and grievous burthen of raising his young slaves to the ages of eighteen and twenty-one, and then liberating them to be hired out under the superintendence of government, (the most miserable of all managers,) until the proceeds arising therefrom shall be sufficient to send

* The difficulty of falling upon any definite plan which can for a moment command the approbation of even a few of the most intelligent abolitionists, is an unerring symptom of the difficulty and impracticability of the whole.

them away. If any man, at all conversant with political economy, should ever anticipate the day when this shall happen, we can only say that his faith is great indeed, enough to remove mountains, and that he has studied in a totally different school from ourselves. Let us ask, in the language of one of Virginia's most cherished statesmen, who has stood by and defended with so much zeal and ability the interests of Lower Virginia—and who shone forth one of the brightest stars in that constellation of talent which met together in the Virginia Convention—" Is it supposed that any tyranny can subdue us to the patient endurance of such a state of things? Every prudent slaveholder in the slaveholding part of the State, would either migrate with his slaves to some State where his rights in slave property would be secured to him by the laws, or would surrender at once his rights in the parent stock as well as in their future increase, and seek some land where he may enjoy at least the earnings of his own industry. In the first case, the country would be deserted; in the other, it would be abandoned to the slaves, to be cultivated under the management of the State. The plan would result in a sacrifice, more probably an abandonment, of our *landed*, as well as the abolition of our *slave* property. Can any thing but force—can any force tame us to wrongs like these?"* Again; we entirely agree with the assertion of Mr. Brown, one of the ablest and most promising of Virginia's sons, that the ingenuity of man, if exerted for the purpose, could not devise a more efficient mode of producing discontent among our slaves, and thus endangering the peace of the community. There are born annually of this population about 20,000 children. Those which are born before the year 1840 are to be slaves; those which are born after that period to be free at a certain age. These two classes will be reared together;

* Letters of Appomattox to the people of Virginia, 1st letter, p. 13.

they will labor together, and commune together. It cannot escape the observation of him who is doomed to servitude, that although of the same color and born of the same parents, a far different destiny awaits his more fortunate brother—as his thoughts again and again revert to the subject, he begins to regard himself as the victim of injustice. Cheerfulness and contentment will flee from his bosom; and the most harmless and happy creature that lives on earth, will be transformed into a dark, designing and desperate rebel.—(*Brown's Speech*, pp. 8, 9.)

There are some again who exhaust their ingenuity in devising schemes for taking off the breeding portion of the slaves to Africa, or carrying away the sexes in such disproportions as will, in a measure, prevent those left behind from breeding. All of these plans merit nothing more than the appellation of *vain juggling legislative conceits*, unworthy of a statesman and a moral man. If our slaves are ever to be sent away in any systematic manner, humanity demands that they should be carried in families. The voice of the world would condemn Virginia if she sanctioned any plan of deportation by which the male and female, husband and wife, parent and child, were systematically and relentlessly separated. If we are to indulge in this kind of regulating vice, why not cure the ill at once, by following the counsel of Xenophon in his Economics, and the practice of old Cato the Censor? Let us keep the male and female separated* in *ergastula* or dungeons, if it be necessary, and then one generation will pass away, and the evil will be removed to the heart's content of our humane philanthropists! But all these puerile conceits

---

* See Hume's Essay on the Populousness of Ancient Nations, where he ascribes this practice of Cato and others, to prevent their slaves from breeding.

fall far short of surmounting the great difficulty which, like Memnon, is eternally present and cannot be removed.

"Sedet eternumque sedebit,"

There is slave property of the value of $100,000,000 in the State of Virginia, &c., and it matters but little how you destroy it, whether by the slow process of the cautious practitioner, or with the frightful despatch of the self-confident *quack;* when it is gone, no matter how, the deed will be done, and Virginia will be a desert.

We shall now proceed to examine briefly, the most dangerous of all the wild doctrines advanced by the abolitionists in the Virginia Legislature, and the one which, no doubt, will be finally acted upon, if ever this business of emancipation shall be seriously commenced. *It was contended that property is the creature of civil society, and is subject to action, even to destruction.* But lest we may misrepresent, we will give the language of the gentleman who first boldly and exultingly announced it. "My views are briefly these," said Mr. Faulkner; "they go to the foundation upon which the social edifice rests—property is the creature of civil society. So long as that property is not dangerous to the good order of society, it may and will be tolerated. But, sir, so soon as it is ascertained to jeopardize the peace, the happiness, the good order, nay the very existence of society, from that moment the right by which they hold their property is gone, society ceases to give its consent, the condition upon which they are permitted to hold it is violated, their right ceases. Why, sir, it is ever a rule of municipal law, and we use this merely as an illustration of the great principles of society, *sic utere tuo ut alienum non lædas.* So hold your property as not to injure the property, still less the lives and happiness, of your neighbors. And the moment, even in the best regulated communities, there is in practice a departure from this principle, you may abate the nuisance. It may cause loss, but it is what our black letter gentlemen term *damnum absexue injuria*, a loss of which the law affords no remedy." Now, for the application of these principles: " Sir, to contend that full value shall be paid for the slaves by the commonwealth, now, or at any future period of their emancipation, is to deny all right of action upon this subject whatsoever. It is not within the financial ability of a State to purchase them. We have not the means—the utmost extremity of taxation would fall short of an adequate treasury. What then shall be done? We must endeavor to ascertain some middle ground of compromise between the rights of the community and the rights of individuals, some scheme which, while it responds to the demands of the people for the extermination of the alarming evils, will not in its operations disconcert the settled institutions of society, or evolve the slaveholder in pecuniary ruin and embarrassment." (*Faulkner's Speech, pp.* 14, 15, 16.)

To these doctrines we call the serious attention of the whole slaveholding population of our Union, for all alike are concerned. It is time, indeed, for Achilles to rise from his inglorious repose and buckle on his armor, when the enemy are about to set fire to the fleet. This doctrine, absurd as it may seem, in the practical application made by the speaker, will be sure to become the most popular with those abolitionists in Virginia, who have no slave property to sacrifice. It is the remark of Hobbes, that men might easily be brought to deny that "things equal to the same are equal to each other," if their fancied interests were opposed in any way to the admission of the axiom. We find that the highly obnoxious doctrine just spoken of, was not entertained by the gentleman from Berkeley alone, but was urged to an equally offensive extent by Mr. M'Dowell, who is supposed by his friends to have made the most able and eloquent speech in favor of abolition. He says, "when it (property) loses its utility, when it no longer contributes to the personal benefits and wants of its holders in any equal degree with the expense or the risk, or the danger of keeping it, much more when it jeopards the security of the public,—when this is the case, then the original purpose for which it is authorized is lost, its character of property in the just and beneficial sense of it is gone, and it may be regulated without private injustice, in any manner which the general good of the community, by whose laws it was licensed, may require." (*M'Dowell's Speech, see Richmond Whig, 24th March,* 1832.) It is thus, if we may borrow the justly indignant language of Mr. Goode's eloquent and forcible speech, that "our property has been compared to a nuisance which the commonwealth may abate at pleasure. A nation of souls to be abated by the mere effort of the will of the General Assembly. A nation of freemen to hold their property by the precarious tenure of the precarious will of the General Assembly! and to reconcile us to our condition, we are assured by the gentleman from Berkeley, that the General Assembly, in the abundance of its liberality, is ready to enter into a compromise, by which we shall be permitted to hold our own property *twenty-eight years!* on condition that we then surrender it absolutely and unconditionally. Sir, I cannot but admire the frankness with which these gentlemen have treated this subject. They have exhibited themselves in the fullness of their intentions; given us warning of their designs; and we now see in all its nakedness the vanity of all hope of compensation." (*Goode's Speech, p.* 29.)

The doctrine of these gentlemen, so far from being true in

its application, is not true in theory. The great object of government is the protection of property;—from the days of the patriarchs down to the present time, the great desideratum has been to find out the most efficient mode of protecting property. There is not a government at this moment in Christendom, whose peculiar practical character is not the result of the state of property.

No government can exist which does not conform to the state of property; it cannot make the latter conform entirely to the government; an attempt to do it would and ought to revolutionize any state. The great difficulty in forming the government of any country arises almost universally from the state of property, and the necessity of making it to conform to that state; and it was the state of property in Virginia which really constituted the whole difficulty in the late Convention. There is a right which these gentlemen seem likewise to have had in their minds, which writers on the law of nations call the right of eminent or *transcendental domain;* that right by which, in an exigency, the government or its agents may seize on persons or property, to be used for the general weal. Now, upon this there are two suggestions which at once present themselves. First, that this right only occurs in cases of real exigency;* and secondly, that the writers on the national law—and the constitution of the United States expressly sanctions the principle—say, that no property can be thus taken without full and fair compensation.†

---

* It is, then, the right of necessity, and may be defined that right which authorizes the performance of an act absolutely necessary for the discharge of an indisputable duty. But private property must always be paid for.

† The Congress of the United States, in the case of Marigny d'Auterive, placed slave property upon precisely the same footing, in this respect, with all other kinds.

These gentlemen, we hope to prove conclusively before finishing, have failed to show the exigency; and even if they have proved that, they deny the right of compensation, and upon what principle? why, that the whole State is not competent to afford it, and may therefore justly abate the nuisance. And is it possible that a burthen, in this Christian land, is most unfeelingly and remorselessly to be imposed upon a portion of the State, which, by the very confession of the gentlemen who urge it, could not be borne by the whole without inevitable ruin? But it was the main object of their speeches to show, that slave property is valueless, that it is a burthen, a nuisance to the owner; and they seemed most anxious to enlighten the poor ignorant farmers on this point, who hold on with such pertinacity to this kind of property, which is inflicting its bitterest sting upon them. Now, is it not enough for the slaveholder to reply, that the circumstance of the slave bearing the price of two hundred dollars in the market, is an evidence of his value with every one acquainted with the elements of political economy; that, generally speaking, the market value of the slave is even less than his real value; for no one would like to own and manage slaves unless equally or more profitable than other kinds of investments in the same community; and, if this or that owner may be pointed out as ruined by this species of property, might we not point to merchants, mechanics, lawyers, doctors, and divines, all of whom have been ruined by their several pursuits; and must all these employments be abated as *nuisances* to satisfy the crude, undigested theories of tampering legislators! "It is remarkable," we quote the language of the author of the Letters of Appomattox, "that this 'nuisance' is more offensive in a direct ratio to its distance from the complaining party, and in an inverse ratio to the quantity of offending matter in his neighborhood; that a 'magazine of gun-powder' in the town of Norfolk is a 'nuisance' to the county of Berkeley, and to all the people of the West! The people of the West, in which there are comparatively few slaves, in which there never can be any great increase of that kind of property, because their agriculture does not require it, and because in a great part of their country the negro race cannot be acclimated—the people of the West find our slave property in *our planting country*, where it is valuable, a 'nuisance' to them. This reverses the proverb, that men bear the ills of others better than their own. I have known men to sell their slave property and vest the proceeds in the stocks, and become zealous for the abolition of slavery. And it would be a matter of curiosity to ascertain (if it could be done) the aggregate number of slaves, held by all the orators and all the printers who are so willing to abate the nuisance of slave property held by other people. I suspect the census would be very short." *Letters of Appomattox to the people of Virginia.*

The fact is, it is always a most delicate and dangerous task for one set of people to legislate for another, without any community of interest. It is sure to destroy the great principle of responsibility, and in the end to lay the weaker interest at the mercy of the stronger. It subverts the very end for which all governments are established, and becomes intolerable, and consequently against the fundamental rights of man, whether prohibited by the constitution or not.

If a convention of the whole State of Virginia were called, and in due form the right of slave property were abolished by the votes of Western Virginia alone, does any one think that Eastern Virginia would be bound to yield to the decree? Certainly not. The strong and unjust man in a state of nature robs the weaker, and you establish government to prevent this oppression. Now, only sanction the doctrine of Virginia orators, let one interest in the government (the West) rob another at pleasure (the East); and is there any man who can fail to see that government is systematically producing that very oppression for which it is intended to remedy, and for which alone it is established? In forming the late Constitution of Virginia, the East objected to the "white basis principle," upon the very grounds that it would enable Western to oppress Eastern Virginia, through the medium of slave property. The most solemn asseverations of a total unwillingness, on the part of the West, to meddle with or touch the slave population, beyond the rightful and equitable demands of revenue, were repeatedly made by their orators. And now, what has the lapse of two short years developed? Why, that the West, unmindful of former professions, and regardless of the eternal principles of justice, is urging on an invasion and final abolition of that kind of property which it was solemnly pledged to protect! Is it possible that gentlemen can have reflected upon the consequences which even the avowal of such doctrines are calculated to produce? Are they conciliatory? Can they be taken kindly by the East? Is it not degrading for freemen to stand quailing with the fear of losing that property which they have been accumulating for ages, to stand waiting in fearful anxiety for the capricious edict of the West, which may say to one man, "Sir, you must give up your property, although you have amassed it under the guarantee of the laws and constitution of your State and of the United States;" and to another, who is near him, and has an equal amount of property of a different description, and has no more virtue and no more conscience than the slaveholder, "you may hold yours, because we do not yet consider it a 'nuisance'?" This is language which cannot fail to awaken the people to a sense of their danger. These doctrines, whenever announced in debate, have a tendency to disorganize and unhinge the condition of society, and to produce uncertainty and alarm ;* to create revulsions of capital ; to cause the land of Old Virginia, and real source of wealth, to be abandoned; and her white wealthy population to flee the State, and seek an asylum in a land where they will be protected in the enjoyment of the fruits of their industry. In fine, we would say, these doctrines are 'nuisances,' and if we were disposed to retaliate, would add that they ought to be 'abated.' We will close our remarks on this dangerous doctrine, by calling upon Western Virginia and the non-slaveholders of Eastern Virginia, not to be allured by the syren song. It is as delusive as it may appear fascinating ; all the sources of wealth and departments of industry, all the great interests of society, are really interwoven with one another—they form an indissoluble chain ; a blow at any part quickly vibrates through the whole length—the destruction of one interest involves another. Destroy agriculture, destroy tillage, and the ruin of the farmer will draw down ruin upon the mechanic, the merchant, the sailor and the manufacturer—they must all flee together from the land of desolation.

We hope we have now satisfactorily proved the impracticability of sending off the whole of our slave population, or even the annual increase ; and we think we have been enabled to do this, by pointing out only one-half the difficulties which attend the scheme. We have so far confined our attention to the expense and difficulty of purchasing the slaves, and sending them across the ocean. We have now to look a little to the recipient or territory to which the blacks are to be sent ;

* We look upon these doctrines as calculated to produce precisely the same results as are produced by the government of Turkey, which, by rendering property insecure, has been able to arrest, and permanently to repress, the prosperity of the fairest and most fertile portions of the globe.

and if we know any thing of the history and nature of colonization, we shall be completely upheld in the assertion, that the difficulties on this score are just as great and insurmountable as those which we have shown to be attendant on the purchase and deportation. We shall be enabled to prove, if we may use the expression, *a double impracticability* attendant on all these schemes.

The Impossibility of Colonizing the Blacks.—The whole subject of colonization is much more difficult and intricate than is generally imagined, and the difficulties are often very different from what would, on slight reflection, be anticipated. They are of three kinds—physical, moral, and national. The former embraces unhealthy climate or want of proper seasoning; a difficulty of procuring subsistence and the conveniences of life; ignorance of the adaptations and character of the soils; want of habitations, and the necessity of living together in multitudes for the purposes of defence, whilst purposes of agriculture require that they should live as dispersed as possible. The moral difficulties arise from a want of adaptation on the part of the new colonists to their new situation, want of conformity in habits, manners, tempers, and dispositions, producing a heterogeneous mass of population, uncemented and unharmonizing. Lastly, the difficulties of a national character embrace all the causes of altercation and rupture between the colonists and neighboring tribes or nations; all these dangers, difficulties and hardships, are much greater than generally believed. Every new colony requires the most constant attention, the most cautious and judicious management, in both the number and character of the emigrants, a liberal supply of both capital and provisions, together with a most watchful and paternal government on the part of the mother country, which may defend it against the incursions and depredations of warlike or savage neighbors. Hence, the very slow progress made by all colonies in the first settlements.

The history of colonization is well calculated of itself to dissipate all the splendid visions which our chimerical philanthropists have indulged, in regard to its efficacy in draining off a redundant or noxious population. The rage for emigration to the New World, discovered by Columbus, was at first very considerable; the brilliant prospects which were presented to the view of the Spaniards, of realizing fortunes in the abundant mines, and on the rich soils of the islands and the continent, enticed many at first to leave their homes in search of wealth, happiness, and distinction; and what was the consequence? "The numerous hardships with which the members of infant colonies have to struggle," says Robertson, "the diseases of unwholesome climates, fatal to the constitutions of Europeans; the difficulty of bringing a country covered with forests into culture; the want of hands necessary for labor in some provinces, and the slow reward of industry in all, unless where the accidental discovery of mines enriched a few fortunate adventurers, were evils immensely felt and magnified. Discouraged by the view of these, the spirit of migration was so much damped, that sixty years after the discovery of the New World, the number of Spaniards in all its provinces is computed not to have exceeded 15,000!"* Even these few were settled at an expense of life, both to the emigrants and the natives, which is really shocking to the feelings of humanity; and we cannot peruse the accounts of the conquests of Mexico and Peru, without feeling that the race destroyed was equal, in moral worth at least, to their destroyers.

In the settlement of Virginia, begun by Sir Walter Raleigh,

* Robertson's America, vol. 2, p. 151.

and established by Lord Delaware, three attempts completely failed; nearly half of the first colony was destroyed by the savages, and the rest, consumed and worn down by fatigue and famine, deserted the country and returned home in despair. The second colony was cut off to a man, in a manner unknown; but they were supposed to have been destroyed by the Indians. The third experienced the same dismal fate; and the remains of the fourth, after it had been reduced by famine and disease, in the course of six months, from five hundred to sixty persons, were returning in a famished and desperate condition to England, when they were met in the mouth of the Chesapeake, by Lord Delaware, with a squadron loaded with provisions, and every thing for their relief and defence.* The first puritans and settlers, in like manner, suffered "woes unnumbered,"—nearly half perished by want, scurvy, and the severity of the climate.

The attempts to settle New Holland, have presented a melancholy and affecting picture of the extreme hardships which infant colonies have to struggle with, before their produce is even equal to the support of the colonists. The establishment of colonies, too, in the eastern part of the Russian dominions, has been attended with precisely the same difficulties and hardships.

After this very brief general review of the history of modern colonization, we will now proceed to examine into the prospects of colonizing our blacks on the coast of Africa, in such numbers as to lessen those left behind. And in the first place we will remark, that almost all countries, especially those in southern and tropical latitudes, are extremely unfavorable to life when first cleared and cultivated. Almost the whole territory of the United States and South America, offer

* Malthus on population, given upon the authority of both Burke's and Robertson's Virginia.

a conclusive illustration of this fact. We are daily witnessing, in the progress of tillage, in our country, the visitation of diseases of the most destructive kind, over regions hitherto entirely exempt; our bilious fevers, for example, seem to travel, in a great measure, with the progress of opening, clearing, and draining of the country. Now, when we turn our attention to Africa, on which continent all agree that we must colonize, if at all, we find almost the whole continent possessing an insalubrious climate, under the most favorable circumstances; and, consequently, we may expect this evil will be enhanced during the incipient stages of society at any given point, while the progress of clearing, draining, and tilling is going forward. All the travellers through Africa agree in their descriptions of the general insalubrity of the climate. Park and Buffon agree in stating, that longevity is very rare among the negroes. At forty they are described as wrinkled and gray haired, and few of them survive the age of fifty-five or sixty. A Shangalla woman, says Bruce, at twenty-two, is more wrinkled and deformed by age, than a European at sixty. This short duration of life is attributable to the climate; for in looking over the returns of the census in our country, we find a much larger proportional number of cases of longevity among the blacks than the whites. "If accurate registers of mortality," says Malthus, (and no one is more indefatigable in his researches or more capable of drawing accurate conclusions,) "were kept among those nations, (African,) I have little doubt that, including the mortality of wars, one in seventeen or eighteen, at least, dies annually, instead of one in thirty-four or thirty-six, as in the generality of European states."* The sea coast is described as being generally much more unhealthy than the interior. "Perhaps it is on this account chiefly," says Park, "that the interior countries

* See Malthus on Population, Book 1, 1. 8.

abound more with inhabitants than the maritime districts."*
The deleterious effects of African climate, are of course much
greater upon those accustomed to different latitudes and not
yet acclimated. It is melancholy, indeed, to peruse the dreadful hardships and unexampled mortality attendant upon those
companies which have, from time to time, actuated by the
most praiseworthy views, penetrated into the interior of
Africa.

It is difficult to say, which has presented the most obstacles
to the inquisitive traveller, the suspicion and barbarity of the
natives, or the dreadful insalubrity of the climate. Now, it is
to this continent, the original home of our blacks, to this destructive climate, we propose to send the slave of our country,
after the lapse of ages has completely inured him to our colder
and more salubrious continent. It is true, that a territory
has already been secured for the Colonization Society of this
country, which is said to enjoy an unusually healthful climate.
Granting that this may be the case, still when we come to
examine into the capacity of the purchased territory for the
reception of emigrants, we find that it only amounts to about
10,000 square miles, not a seventh of the superfices of Virginia. When other sites are fixed upon, we may not, and cannot expect to be so fortunate; are not the most healthy districts in Africa the most populous, according to Park and all
travellers? Will not these comparatively powerful nations, in
all probability, relinquish their territory with great reluctance?
Will not our lot be consequently cast on barren sands or amid
the pestilential atmosphere; and then what exaggerated tales
and false statements must be made, if we would reconcile the
poor blacks to a change of country pregnant with their
fate?

* See Park's Travels in Africa, p. 193, New York Edition.

But we believe that the very laudable zeal of many conscientious philanthropists has excited an overweening desire to make our colony in Liberia, in every point of view, appear greatly superior to what it is. We know the disposition of all travellers to exaggerate; we know the benevolent feelings of the human heart, which prompts us to gratify and minister to the desires and sympathies of those around us, and we know that philanthropic schemes, emancipation and colonization societies, now occupy the public mind, and receive the largest share of public applause. Under these circumstances we are not to wonder if coloring should sometimes impair the statements of those who have visited the colony; for ourselves, we may be too sceptical, but are rather disposed to judge from facts which are acknowledged by all, than from general statements from officers and interested agents. In 1819, two agents were sent to Africa to survey the coast and make a selection of a suitable situation for a colony; in their passage home in 1820, one died. In the same year, 1820, the Elizabeth was chartered and sent out with three agents and eighty emigrants. All three of the agents and twenty of the emigrants died, a proportional mortality greater than in the *middle passage*, which has so justly shocked the human feelings of mankind, and much greater than that occasioned by that dreadful plague (the Cholera) which is now clothing our land in mourning and causing our citizens to flee in every direction to avoid impending destruction. In the spring of 1821, four new agents were sent out, of whom one returned sick, one died in August, one in September, and we know not what became of the fourth.* It is agreed on all hands, that there is a seasoning necessary, and

* These facts we have stated upon the authority of Mr. Carey, of Philadelphia, who has given us an interesting, but I fear too flattering account of the colony, in a series of letters addressed to the Hon. Charles F. Mercer.

a formidable fever to be encountered, before the colonies can enjoy tolerable health. Mr. Ashmun, who afterwards fell a victim to the climate, insisted that the night air of Liberia was free from all noxious effects; and yet we find that the emigrants carried by the Valador to Liberia, a year or two since, are said to have fared well, losing only two, in consequence of every precaution having been taken against the night air, while the most dreadful mortality destroyed those of the Carolinian, which went out nearly cotemporaneously with the Valador. The letter of Mr. Reyrolds, marked G, at the conclusion of the Fifteenth Annual Report of the American Colonization Society, instructs us in the proper method of preserving health on the coast of Africa, and in spite of the flattering accounts and assurances of agents and philanthropists, we should be disposed to take warning from these salutary hints. The following are some of them:

"1st. On no account to suffer any of the crew to be out of the ship *at* sunset."

"2d. To have a sail stretched on the windward *side* of the vessel; and an awning was also provided, which extended over the poop and the whole main deck, *to defend the crew from the night air.*

"3d. The night watch was encouraged to smoke tobacco.

"4th. To distribute French brandy to the crew whilst in port, in lieu of rum. (The editor of the report modestly recommends strong coffee.) The crew, on rising, were served with a liberal allowance of strong coffee, before commencing their day's work.

"The result was, that the ships on each side of the Cambridge lost the *greater* part of their crew; and not one man of her crew were seriously unwell." (*Fifteenth Annual Report*, p. 54, *published in Georgetown*, 1832.)

We have said enough to show that the contiguance of Africa, and its coasts particularly, are extremely unhealthy—that the natives themselves are not long lived—and that unacclimated foreigners are in most imminent danger- That there may be some healthy points on the sea shore, and salubrious districts in the interior, and that Liberia may be fortunately one of them, we are even willing to admit—but then we know that generally the most insalubrious portion will fall into our possession, because those of an opposite character are already too densely populated to be deserted by the natives— and consequently, let us view the subject as we please, we have this mighty evil of unhealthy climate to overcome. We have seen already, in the past history of our colony, that the slightest blunder, in landing on an unhealthy coast, in exposure to a deadly night air, or in neglecting the necessary precautions during the period of acclimating, has proved most frightfully fatal to both black and whites. Suppose now, that instead of the one or two hundred sent by the Colonization Society, Virginia should actually send out six thousand—or if we extend our views to the whole United States, that sixty thousand should be annually exported, accompanied of course by some hundreds of whites, what an awful fatality might we not occasionally expect? The chance for blundering would be infinitely increased, and if some ships might fortunately distribute their cargoes with the loss of a few lives, others again might lose all their whites and a fourth or more of the blacks, as we know has already happened; and although this fatality might arise from blunder or accident, yet would it strike the imagination of men—and that which may be kept comparatively concealed now, would, when the number of emigrants swelled to such multitudes, produce alarm and consternation. We look confidently to the day, if this wild scheme should be persevered in for a few years, when the poor African slave, on bended knee, might implore a remission of that fatal sentence which would send him to the land of his forefathers.

But the fact is, that all climates will prove fatal to emigrants who come out in too great crowds, whether they are naturally unhealthy or not. One of the greatest attempts at colonization in modern times, was the effort of the French to plant at once 12,000 emigrants on the coast of Guiana. The consequence was, that in a very short time 10,000 of them lost their lives in all the horrors of despair, 2,000 returned to France, the scheme failed, and 25,000,000 of francs, says Raynal, were totally lost. Seventy-five thousand christians, says Mr. Eaton in his account of the Turkish empire, were expelled by Russia from the Crimea, and forced to inhabit the country deserted by the Nogai Tartars, and in a few years only 7,000 of them remained. In like manner, if 6,000, or much more, if 60,000 negroes, with careless and filthy habits, were annually sent to Africa, we could not calculate, for the first one or two years, upon less than the death of one-half or perhaps three-fourths: and, repugnant as the assertion may be to the feelings of benevolence, we have no hesitation in saying, that nothing but a most unparalleled mortality among the emigrants would enable us to support the colony for even a year or two. Aristotle was of opinion, that the keeping of 5,000 soldiers in idleness would ruin an empire. If the brilliant anticipations of our colonization friends shall be realized, and the day actually arrives, when 60,000, or even 6,000 blacks can be annually landed in health upon the cost of Africa, then will the United States, or broken down Virginia, be obliged to support an *empire* in idleness. "The first establishment of a new colony," says Malthus, "generally presents an instance of a country peopled considerably beyond its actual produce: and the natural consequence seems to be, that this population, if not amply supplied by the mother country, should, at the commencement, be diminished to the level of the first scanty productions, and not begin permanently to increase till the remaining numbers had so far cultivated the soil as to make it yield a quantity of food more than sufficient for their own support, and which consequently they could divide with a family. The frequent failures of new colonies tend strongly to show the order of precedence between food and population."* It is for this reason the colonies so slowly advance at first, and it becomes necessary to *feed* (if we may so express ourselves) with extreme caution, and with limited numbers, in the beginning. But a few additional mouths will render support from the mother country necessary. If this state of things continues for a short time, you make the colony a great pauper establishment, and generate all those habits of idleness and worthlessness which will ever characterize a people dependent on the bounty of others for their subsistence. If Virginia should send out 6,000 emigrants to Africa, and much more, if the United States should send out 60,000, the whole colony would inevitably perish, if the wealth of the mother country was not exhausted for their supply. Suppose a member in Congress should propose to send out an army of 60,000 troops, and maintain them on the coast of Africa; would not every sensible man see at once that the thing would be impracticable, if even the existence of our country depended upon it?—it would ruin the greatest empire on the globe—and yet, strange to tell, the philanthropists of Virginia are seriously urging her to attempt that which would every year impose upon her a burthen proportionally greater than this!

If any man will for a moment revert to the history of Liberia, which has been as flourishing or even more flourishing than similar colonies, there will be seen at once enough to convince the sceptical of the truth of this assertion. What says Mr. Ashmun, perhaps the most intelligent and most judicious of colonial

* Malthus on Population, vol. 2, pp. 140, 141.

agents? "If rice grew spontaneously," said he, "and covered the country, yet it is possible by sending few or none able to reap and clean it, to starve 10,000 helpless children and infirm old people in the midst of plenty. Rice does not grow spontaneously, however; nor can any thing necessary for the subsistence of the human species be procured here without the sweat of the brow. Clothing, tools, and building materials are much dearer here than in America. But send out emigrants, laboring men and their families only, or laborious men and their families, accompanied only with their natural proportion of inefficients; and *with the ordinary blessings of God*, you may depend on their causing you a *light expense* in Liberia," &c. Again, "if such persons, (those who cannot work,) are to be supported by American funds, *why not keep them in America*, where they can do something by picking cotton and stemming tobacco, towards supporting themselves? I know that nothing is effectually done in colonizing this country, till the colony's own resources can sustain *its own*, and *a considerable annual increase of population*." Here then are statements from one of the most zealous and enthusiastic in the cause of colonization, one who has sacrificed his life in the business, which clearly show, that the Colonization Society, with its very limited means, has ever supplied the colony with emigrants. What then might not be expected from the tremendous action of the State and General Government on this subject? they would raise up a pauper establishment, which, we conscientiously believe, would require the disposable wealth of the rest of the world to support, and the thousands of emigrants who would be sent, so far from being laborious men, would be the most idle and worthless of a race, who only desire liberty because they regard it as an exemption from labor and toil. Every man, too, at all conversant with the subject, knows that such alone are the slaves which a kind master will ever consent to sell, to be carried to a distant land. Sixty thousand emigrants per annum to the United States, would even now sink the wages of labor, and embarrass the whole of our industrious classes, although we have at this moment lands capable of supporting millions more when gradually added to our population.

The Irish emigrants to Great Britain, have already begun to produce disastrous effects. "I am firmly persuaded," says Mr. McCulloch, "that nothing so deeply injurious to the character and habits of our people, has ever occurred, as the late extraordinary influx of Irish laborers. If another bias be not given to the current of emigration, Great Britain will necessarily continue to be a grand outlet for the pauper population of Ireland, nor will the tide of beggary and degradation cease to flow, until the plague of poverty has spread its ravages over both divisions of empire."* Where, then, in the wide world, can we find a fulcrum upon which to place our mighty lever of colonization? nowhere! we repeat it, *nowhere!* unless we condemn emigrants to absolute starvation. Sir Josiah Childe, who lived in an age of comparative ignorance, could well have instructed our modern philanthropists in the true principles of colonization. "*Such as our employment is,*" says he, "*so will our people be;* and if we should imagine we have in England employment but for one hundred people, and we have born and bred (or he might have added brought) amongst us one hundred and fifty—fifty must flee away from us, or starve, or be hanged to prevent it."† And so say we in regard to our colonization; if our new colony cannot absorb readily more than one or two hundred per annum, and we send them 6,000 or 60,000, the surplus "must either flee away, or starve, or be

* McCulloch's Wealth of Nations, 4th vol. pp. 154, 55. Edinburgh Edition.
† Sir Josiah Childe's Discourse on Trade.

hanged," or be fed by the mother country, (which is impossible.)

So far we have been attending principally to the difficulties of procuring subsistence; but the habits and moral character of our slaves prevent others of equal importance and magnitude. Dr. Franklin says that one of the reasons why we see so many fruitless attempts to settle colonies at an immense public and private expense by several of the powers of Europe, is that moral and mechanical habits adapted to the mother country, are frequently not so to the new settled one, and to external events, many of which are unforeseen; that it is to be remarked that none of the English colonies became any way considerable, till the necessary manners were born and grew up in the country. Now with what peculiar and overwhelming force does this remark apply to our colonization of liberated blacks! We are to send out thousands of these, taken from a state of slavery and ignorance, unaccustomed to guide and direct themselves, void of all the attributes of free agents, with dangerous notions of liberty and idleness, to elevate them at once to the condition of freemen, and invest them with the power of governing an empire, which will require more wisdom, more prudence, and at the same time more firmness, than ever government required before. We are enabled to support our position by a quotation from an eloquent supporter of the American colonization scheme. "Indeed," said the Rev. Mr. Bacon, at the last meeting of the American Colonization Society, "it is something auspicious, that in the earlier stages of our undertaking, there has been a general rush of emigration to the colony. In *any single year* since Cape Montserado was purchased, the influx of *a thousand emigrants* might have been fatal to our enterprise. The new-comers into any community must always be a *minority*, else every arrival is a *revolution;* they must be a *decided minority*, easily absorbed in the system and mingled with the mass, else the community is constantly liable to convulsion. Let 10,000 *foreigners, rude and ignorant*, be landed at once in this district (of Columbia), and what would be the result? Why you must have an armed force here to keep the peace—so *one thousand* now landing *at once* in our colony, might be its ruin."*

The fact is, the *true* and *enlightened* friends of colonization must reprobate all those chimerical schemes proposing to deport anything like the increase of one State, and more particularly of the whole United States. The difficulty just explained, has already been severely felt in Liberia, though hitherto supplied very scantily with emigrants, and those generally the most exemplary of the free blacks ; thus, in 1828, it was the decided opinion of Mr. Ashmun, "that for at least two years to come, a much more discriminating selection of settlers must be made, than ever has been—even in the first and second expeditions by the Elizabeth and Nautilus, in 1820 and '21, or that the prosperity of the colony will *inevitably* and *rapidly decline*." Now, when to all these difficulties we add the prospect of frequent wars with the natives of Africa,† the great expense we must incur to support the colony, and the anomolous position of Virginia, an *imperium in imperio*, holding an empire abroad, we do not see how the whole scheme can be pronounced anything less than a *stupendous piece of folly*.

The progress of the British colony at Sierra Leone is well calculated to illustrate the great difficulties of colonizing negroes on the coast of Africa: and we shall at once present our readers with a brief history of this colony, given by one who seems to be a warm advocate of colonization, and, consequently, disposed to present the fact in the most favorable aspect.

---

* See Fifteenth Annual Report of American Colonization Society, p. 10.

† The colony has already had one conflict with the natives, in which it had liked to be overwhelmed.

On the 8th of April, 1787, 400 negroes and 60 Europeans sailed from England, supplied with provisions for six or eight months, for Sierra Leone. Now mark the consequences:—
"The result was unfortunate and even discouraging. The *crowded* condition of the transports, the *unfavorable* season at which they arrived on the coast, and the *intemperance* and *imprudence* of the emigrants, brought on a mortality which reduced their numbers nearly *one-half* during the *first* year. Others *deserted* soon after landing, until *forty* individuals only remained. In 1788, Mr. Sharp sent out 39 more, and then a number of the deserters returned, and the settlement *gradually* gained strength. But during the next year, a *controversy* with a *neighboring native chief*, ended in *wholly* dispersing the colony; and some time elapsed before the remnants could be again collected. A charter of incorporation was obtained in 1791. Not long afterwards, about 1,200 new emigrants were introduced, being originally refugees from *this* country, (U. States,) who had placed themselves under British protection. Still, affairs were *very badly* managed. *One-tenth* of the Nova Scotians, and *half* of the Europeans, died during *one* season, as much from *want of provisions* as any other cause. Two years afterwards, a store-ship belonging to the company, which had been made the receptacle of African produce, was lost by fire, with a cargo valued at £15,000. Then INSURRECTIONS arose among the blacks! *Worst of all*, in 1794, a large French squadron, wholly without provisions, *attacked* the settlement, and although the colors were immediately struck, proceeded to an *indiscriminate pillage.** . . . (Some years) afterwards, a large number of the worst part of

---

* We would beg leave most respectfully to ask our Virginia abolitionists, how an insult of this character offered to any colony which we might establish in Africa, would be resented? Would the Nation of Virginia declare war on the aggressor? and if she did, where would be her navy, her sailors, her soldiers, and the constitutionality of the act?

the settlers, chiefly the Nova Scotians, *rebelled* against the Colonial Government. The Governor called in the assistance of the *neighboring African tribes,* and matters were on the eve of a battle, when a transport arrived in the harbor, bringing 550 Maroons from Jamaica. Lots of land were given to these men; they proved regular and industrious, and the insurgents laid down their arms. *Wars* next ensued with the *natives,* which were not finally concluded until 1807. On the first January, 1808, all the rights and possessions of the company were surrendered to the British Crown; and in this situation they have ever since remained." [*See* 76*th No. of the North American Review, pp.* 120 *and* 121.] The progress of the colony since 1808, has been as little flattering as before that period; and even Mr. Everett, before the Colonization Society in Washington, has been forced to acknowledge its failure. [*See Mr. Everett's Speech,* 15*th Annual Report.*]

Thus this negro colony at Sierra Leone illustrates, most fully, the fearful and tremendous difficulties which must ever attend every infant colony formed on the coast of Africa. During the brief period of its existence, it has been visited by all the plagues that colonial establishments "are heir to." It has been cursed with the intemperance, imprudence, and desertion of the colonists, with want of homogeneous character, and consequent dissentions, civil wars and insurrections. It has experienced famines, and suffered insult and pillage. Its numbers have been thinned by the blighting climate of Africa. Its government has been wretched, and it has been almost continually engaged in war with the neighboring African tribes.*

* Perhaps it may be said, that all these things may be avoided in our colonies, by wise management and proper caution. To this we answer, that in speculating upon the destiny of multitudes or nations, we must embrace within our calculation all the elements as they ac-

Some have supposed that the circumstance of the Africans being removed a stage or two above the savages of North America, will render the colonization of Africa much easier than that of America. We draw directly the opposite conclusion. The Indians of North America had nowhere taken possession of the soil; they were wanderers over the face of the country; their titles could be extinguished for slight considerations; and it is ever melancholy to reflect that their habits of improvidence and of intoxication, and even their cruel practices in war, have all been (such has been for them the woful march of events) favorable to the rapid increase of the whites, who have thus been enabled to exterminate the *red men*, and take their places.

The natives of Africa exist in the rude agricultural state, much more numerously than the natives of America. Their titles to land will be extinguished with much more difficulty and expense. The very first contact with our colony will carry to them the whole art and implement of war.* As our

---

tually exist, civil, political, moral and physical, and our deductions to be true, must be taken not from the beau ideal which a vivid imagination may sketch out, but from the average of concomitant circumstances. It would be a poor apology which a statesman could offer, for the failure of a certain campaign which he had planned, to say that he had calculated that every officer in the army was a Napoleon or a Cæsar, and that every regiment was equal to Cæsar's 10th Legion or the Imperial Guard of Napoleon. The physicians say there is not much danger to be apprehended from Cholera, when due caution and prudence are exercised. Yet, we apprehend it would be a very unfair conclusion if we were to assert, that when the Cholera breaks out in Charleston there will not be one single death; and yet we have just as much right to make this assertion, as to say that our colony in Africa will be free from all the accidents, plagues and calamities, to which all such establishments have ever been subjected.

* Powder and fire arms formed material items in the purchase of Liberia.

colonists spread and press upon them, border wars will arise; and in vain will the attempt be made to extirpate the African nations, as we have the Indian tribes: every inhabitant of Liberia who is taken prisoner by his enemy, will be consigned according to the universal practice of Africa, to the most wretched slavery, either in Africa or the West-Indies. And what will our colony do? Must they murder, while their enemies enslave? Oh, no, it is too cruel, and will produce barbarizing and exterminating wars? Will they spare the prisoners of war? No! There does not and never will exist a people on earth, who would tamely look on and see their wives, mothers, brothers and sisters, ignominiously enslaved, and not resent the insult. What, then, will be done? Why, they will be certain to enslave too; and if domestic slavery should be interdicted in the colony, it would be certain to encourage the slave trade;* and if we could ever look forward to the time when the slave trade should be destroyed, then the throwing back of this immense current upon Africa would inundate all the countries of that region. It would be like the checking of the emigration from the northern hives upon the Roman world. The northern nations, in consequence of this check, soon experienced all the evils of a redundant population, and broke forth with their redundant numbers in another quarter; both England and France were overrun, and the repose of all Europe was again disturbed. So, would a sudden check to the African slave trade, cause the redundant population of Africa to break in, like the Normans and the Danes, on the abodes of civilization situated in their neighborhood. Let, then, the real philanthropist ponder over these things, and tremble for the fate of colonies which may be imprudently

* We fear our colony at Liberia is not entirely free from this stain even now; it is well known that the British colony at Sierra Leone has frequently aided the slave trade.

planted on the African soil. The history of the world has too conclusively shown, that two races, differing in manners, customs, language, and civilization, can never harmonize upon a footing of equality. One must rule the other, or exterminating wars must be waged. In the case of the savages of North America, we have been successful in exterminating them; but in the case of African nations, we do think, from a view of the whole subject, that our colonists will most probably be the victims; but the alternative is almost equally shocking, should this not be the case. They must then be the exterminators or enslavers of all the nations of Africa with which they come in contact. The whole history of colonization, indeed, presents one of the most gloomy and horrific pictures to the imagination of the genuine philanthropist, which can possibly be conceived. The many Indians who have been murdered, or driven in despair from the haunts and hunting grounds of their fathers—the heathen driven from his heritage, or hurried into the presence of his God in the full blossom of all his heathenish sins—the cruel slaughter of Ashantees—the murder of Burmese—all, *all* but too eloquently tell the misery and despair portended by the advance of civilization to the savage and the pagan, whether in America, Africa or Asia. In the very few cases where the work of desolation ceased, and a commingling of races ensued, it has been found that the civilized man has sunk down to the level of barbarism, and there has ended the mighty work of civilization! Such are the melancholy pictures which sober reason is constrained to draw of the future destinies of our colony in Africa. And what, then, will become of that grand and glorious idea of carrying religion, intelligence, industry, and the arts, to the already wronged and injured African? It is destined to vanish, and prove worse than mere delusion. The rainbow of promise will be swept away, and we shall awake at last to all the sad realities of savage warfare and increasing barbarism. We have thus stated some of the principal difficulties and dangers accompanying a scheme of colonization, upon a scale as large as proposed in the Virginia Legislature. We have said enough to show, that if we ever send off 6,000 per annum, we must incur an expense far beyond the purchase money.

The expense of deportation to Africa we have estimated at thirty dollars; but when there is taken into the calculation the further expense of collecting in Virginia,* of feeding, pro-

* Even supposing the number of blacks to be annually deported should ever be fixed by the State, the difficulty of settling upon a proper plan of purchase and collection will be infinitely greater than any man would be willing to admit, who has not seriously reflected on the subject, and the apple of discord will be thrown into the Virginia Legislature the moment it shall ever come to discuss the details. Suppose, for example, six thousand are to be sent off annually; will you send negro buyers through the country to buy up slaves wherever they can be bought, until six thousand are purchased! If you do, you will inevitably gather together the very dregs of creation, the most vicious, the most worthless, and the most idle, for these alone will be sold!—a frightful population, whose multitudes, when gathered together and poured upon the infant settlements in Africa, will be far more destructive than the lava flood from the volcano. Again, some portions of the State might sell cheaper than others, and an undue proportion of slaves would be purchased from these quarters, and cause the system to operate unequally. Will you divide the State into sections, and purchase from each according to black population? Then, what miserable sectional controversies should we have in the State? What dreadful grumbling in the west? Moreover, the same relative numbers abstracted from a very dense and very sparse population, will produce a very different effect on the labor market. Thus, we will suppose along the margin of the James River, from Richmond to Norfolk, the blacks are twenty for one white, and that in some country beyond the Blue Ridge, this proportion is reversed. Suppose, further, that a twentieth of the blacks are to be bought up and sent off, this demand will have but a slight effect on the labor market in the country beyond the Ridge, because it calls for only one in four hundred of the population; whereas the effect should

tecting, &c., in Africa, the amount swells beyond all calculation. Mr. Tazewell, in his able report on the colonization of free people on the African coast, represents this expense as certainly amounting to one hundred dollars; and, judging from actual experience, was disposed to think two hundred dollars would fall below the fair estimate. If the Virginia scheme shall ever be adopted, we have no doubt that both these estimates will fall below the real expense. The annual cost of removing six thousand, instead of being $1,380,000, will swell beyond $2,400,000,—an expense sufficient to destroy the entire value of the whole property of Virginia. Voltaire, in his Philosophical Dictionary, has said, that such is the inherent and preservative vigor of nations, that governments cannot possibly ruin them; that almost all governments which have been established in the world had made the attempt, but had failed. If the sage of France had lived in our days, he would have had a receipt furnished by some of our philanthropists, by which this work might have been accomplished! We read in Holy Writ of one great emigration from the land of Egypt, and the concomitant circumstances should bid us well beware of an imitation, unless assisted by the constant presence of Jehovah. Ten plagues were sent upon the land of Egypt before Pharaoh would consent to part with the Israelites, the productive laborers of his kingdom. But a short time convinced him of the heavy loss which he sustained by

be great along the James River, as it would take away one in twenty-one of the population. The slaves, in every section, would command a different price, and we would be obliged to establish our Octroi and Douanier, and tax or prevent the migration of negroes from one section to another. But we will not pursue further the examination of mere details, which do not fall within our original design. It will be discovered from even a slight analysis, that every single branch of this gigantic scheme of folly, like the teeth of the fabled dragon, will bring you forth an armed man to arrest your progress.

their removal, and he gave pursuit; but God was present with the Israelites. He parted the waters of the Red Sea for *their* passage, and closed them over the Egyptians. He led on his chosen people through the wilderness, testifying his presence in a pillar of fire by night, and a cloud of smoke by day. He supplied them with manna in their long journey, sending a sufficiency on the sixth for that and the seventh day. When they were thirsty, the rocks poured forth waters, and when they finally arrived in the land of promise, after the loss of a generation, the mysterious will of heaven had doomed the tribes of Canaan to destruction; fear and apprehension confounded all their counsels; their battlements sunk down at the trumpet's sound; the native hosts, under heaven's command, were all slaughtered; and the children of Israel took possession of the habitations and property of the slaughtered inhabitants. The whole history of this emigration beautifully illustrates the great difficulties and hardships of removal to foreign lands of multitudes of people. And as a citizen of Virginia, we can never consent to so grand a scheme of colonization on the coast of Africa, until it is sanctioned by a *decree* of heaven, made known by signs, far more intelligible than an *eclipse* and *greenness* of the sun—till *manna* shall be rained down for the subsistence of our black emigrants—till seas shall be parted, and waters flow from rocks for their accommodation—till we shall have a leader like Moses, who, in the full confidence of all his piety and religion, can, in the midst of all the appalling difficulties and calamities by which he may be surrounded, speak forth to his murmuring people, in the language of comfort, "Fear ye not, stand still, and see the salvation of the Lord, which he will shew to you to-day."

But, say some, if Virginia cannot accomplish this work, let us call upon the General Government for aid—let Hercules be requested to put his shoulders to the wheels, and roll us through the formidable *quagmire* of our difficulties. Delusive prospect! Corrupting scheme! We will throw all constitutional difficulties out of view, and ask if the Federal Government can be requested to undertake the expense for Virginia, without encountering it for the whole slaveholding population? And then, whence can be drawn the funds to purchase more than 2,000,000 of slaves, worth at the lowest calculation $400,000,000; or if the increase alone be sent off, can Congress undertake annually to purchase at least 60,000 slaves, at an expense of $12,000,000, and deport and colonize them at an expense of twelve or fifteen millions more?* But the fabled hydra would be more than realized in this project. We have no doubt that if the United States in good faith should enter into the slave markets of the country, determined to purchase up the whole annual increase of our slaves, so unwise a project, by its artificial demand, would immediately produce a rise in this property, throughout the whole southern country, of at least $33\frac{1}{3}$ per cent. It would stimulate and invigorate the *spring* of black population, which, by its tremendous action, would set at nought the puny efforts of man, and, like the Grecian matron, unweave in the night what had been woven in the day. We might well calculate upon an annual increase of at least four and a half per cent. upon our two millions of slaves, if ever the United States should create the artificial demand which we have just spoken of; and then, instead of an increase of 60,000, there will be 90,000, bearing the average price of $300 each, making the enormous annual expense of purchase alone $27,000,000! and difficulties, too, on the side of the colony, would more than enlarge with the increase

* We must recollect, that the expense of colonizing increases much more rapidly than in proportion to the simple increase of the number of emigrants.

of the evil at home. Our Colonization Society has been more than fifteen years at work; it has purchased, according to its funds, a district of country as congenial to the constitution of the black as any in Africa; it has, as we have seen, frequently over-supplied the colony with emigrants; and mark the result, for it is worthy of all observation, there now are not more than 2000 or 2500 inhabitants in Liberia! And these are alarmed lest the Southampton insurrection may cause such an emigration as to inundate the colony. When, then, in the lapse of time, can we ever expect to build up a colony which can receive sixty or ninety thousand slaves per annum? And if this should ever arrive, what guarantee could be furnished us that their ports would always be open to our emigrants? Would law or compact answer? Oh, no! Some legislator, in the plenitude of his wisdom, might arise, who could easily and truly persuade his countrymen that these annual importations of blacks were *nuisances*, and the laws of God, whatever might be those of men, would justify their abatement. And the drama would be wound up in this land of promise and expectation, by turning the cannon's mouth against the liberated emigrant and deluded philanthropist. The scheme of colonizing our blacks on the coast of Africa, or anywhere else, by the United States, is thus seen to be more stupendously absurd than even the Virginia project. King Canute, the Dane, seated on the sea shore, and ordering the rising flood to recede from his royal feet, was not guilty of more vanity and presumption than the Government of the United States would manifest, in the vain effort of removing and colonizing the annual increase of our blacks. So far from being able to remove the whole annual increase every year, we shall not be enabled to send off a number sufficiently great to check even the *geometrical rate of increase.* Our black population is now producing 60,000 per annum, and next year we must add to this sum 1,800, which the increment alone is capable of producing, and the year after, the increment upon the increment, &c. Now, let us throw out of view, for a moment, the idea of grappling with the whole annual increase, and see whether by colonization we can expect to turn this geometrical increase into an arithmetical one. We will then take the annual increase, 60,000, as our capital, and it will be necessary to send off the increase upon this 1800, to prevent the geometrical increase of the whole black population. Let us, then, for a moment, inquire whether the abolitionists can expect to realize this *petty advantage*.

Mr. Bacon admits, that 1,000 emigrants now thrown on Liberia, would ruin it. We believe that every reflecting sober member of the Colonization Society will acknowledge that 500 annually, are fully as many as the colony can now receive. We will assume this number, though no doubt greatly beyond the truth; and we will admit further, (what we could easily demonstrate to be much too liberal a concession,) that the capacity of the colony for the reception of emigrants may be made to enlarge in a geometrical ratio, equal to that of the rate of increase of the blacks in the United States. Now, with these very liberal concessions on our part, let us examine into the effect of the colonization scheme. At the end of the first year, we shall have for the amount of the 60,000, increasing at the rate of three and a half per cent., 61,800; and subtracting 500, we shall begin the second year with the number of 61,300, which, increasing at the rate of three and a half per centum, gives 63,139 for the amount at the end of the second year. Proceeding thus, we obtain, at the end of twenty-five years, for the amount of the 60,000, 101,208. The number taken away, that is the sum of $500 + 500 \times 1,003 + 500 \times 1,003$, &c., will be 18,197. It is thus seen, that in spite of the efforts of the colonization scheme, the bare annual increase of our slaves will produce 41,208 more than can be sent off; which number, of course, must be added to the capital of 60,000; and long, *very long*, before the colony in Africa, upon our system of calculation, even could receive the increase upon this accumulating capital, its capacity as a recipient would be checked by the limitation of territory, and the rapid filling up of the population, both by emigration and natural increase. And thus, by a simple arithmetical calculation, we may be convinced that the effort to check even the geometrical rate of increase, by sending off the increment upon the annual increase of our slaves, is greatly more than we can accomplish, and must inevitably terminate in disappointment—more than realizing the fable of the frog and the ox; for in this case we should have the frog *swelling*, not for the purpose of rivalling the ox in *size*, but to *swallow him down, horns and all!*

Seeing, then, that the effort to send away the increase, on even the present increase of our slaves, must be vain and fruitless, how stupendously absurd must be the project, proposing to send off the whole increase, so as to keep down the negro population at its present amount! There are some things which man, arrayed in all his "brief authority," cannot accomplish, and this is one of them. Colonization schemers, big and busy in the management of all their *little machinery*, and gravely proposing it as an *engine* by which our black population may be sent to the now uncongenial home of their ancestors, across an ocean of thousands of miles in width, but too strongly remind us of the vain man who, in all the pomp and circumstance of power, ordered his servile attendants to stop the rise of ocean's tide, by carrying off its accumulating waters. Emigration has rarely checked the increase of population, by directly lessening its number; it can only do it by the abstraction of capital, and by paralyzing the spring of population, and then it blights and withers the prosperity of the land. The population of Europe has not been thinned by emigration to the new world—the province of Andalusia, in Spain, which sent out the greatest number of emigrants to the Islands, and to Mexico and Peru, has been precisely the district in Spain which has increased its population most rapidly. Ireland now sends forth a greater number of emigrants than any other country in the world, and yet the population of Ireland is now increasing faster than any other population of Europe!

We hope we have now said enough of these colonization schemes to show that we can never expect to send off our black population, by their means—and we cannot conclude without addressing a word of caution to the generous sons of the Old Dominion. It behooves them well to beware with what intent they look to the Federal Government for aid in the accomplishment of these delusive—these *impracticable* projects. The guileful tempter of our original parents seduced them with the offer of an *apple*, which proved their heaviest curse, drove them from the garden of Eden, and destroyed for ever their state of innocence and purity. Let Virginia beware, then, that she be not tempted by the apple, to descend from that lofty eminence which she has hitherto occupied in our confederacy, and sacrifice upon the altar of misconceived interests those pure political principles by which she has hitherto been so proudly characterized. This whole question of emancipation and deportation is but too well calculated to furnish the political *lever*, by which Virginia is to be prised out of her natural and honorable position in the Union, and made to sacrifice her noble political creed. We have witnessed with feelings of no common kind, the almost suppliant look cast towards the General Government, by some of the orators in the Virginia debate. It has pained us to read speeches, and pamphlets, and newspaper essays, suggesting changes in the constitution, or at once boldly imploring, without such changes, the action of the Federal Government. Unless the sturdy patriots of Virginia stand forth, we fear, indeed, that her noble principles will be swept away by the tide of corruption. The agitation of the slave question in the last Virginia Legislature, has already begun the work, and the consent of Virginia to receive Federal aid in the scheme of emancipation and deportation would complete it. As long as a State relies upon its own resources, and looks to no foreign quarter for aid or support, so long does she place herself without the sphere of temptation, and preserve her political virtue. This is one principal reason why Virginia has produced so many disinterested patriots. We will go further still; the generous, disinterested and noble character of southern politicians generally, is, in a great measure, attributable to this very cause. The South has hitherto had nothing to ask of the Federal Government—she has been no dependant, no expectant at the door of the Federal Treasury—she has never, therefore, betrayed the interest of the Union, for some paltry benefit to herself. But let her once consent to supplicate the aid of the General Government on this slave question—and that moment will she sacrifice her high political principles, and become a dependant on that government. When Virginia shall consent to receive this boon, her hands will be tied for ever, the *emancipating* interest will be added to the *internal improvement* and *tariff* interests, and Virginia can no more array herself against the torrent of Federal oppression. Hitched to the car of the Federal Government, she will be so ignominiously dragged forward, a conscience-stricken partner in the unholy alliance for oppression; and in that day, the genuine patriot may well cast a longing, lingering look back to the days of purer principles, and "sigh for the loss of Eden." And in this melancholy, saddening retrospect, he will not have the poor consolation left, of seeing his noble State reap the paltry reward, which had so fatally tempted her to an abandonment of her principles. Can any reflecting man, for a moment, believe that the North and West, forming the majority of our Confederacy, would ever *seriously* consent to that enormous expenditure which would be necessary to carry into effect this gigantic colonization scheme—a scheme whose direct operation would be, to take away that *very labor*, which now bears the burthen of federal exactions —a scheme whose operation would be to dry up the sources of that *very revenue*, upon which its success entirely depends! Vain and delusive hope! Not one negro slave will ever be sent away from this country by federal funds—and heaven forbid that they should; and yet we fear the longing, lingering hope, will corrupt the pure principles of many a deluded patriot.

We have thus examined fully this scheme of emancipation and deportation, and trust we have satisfactorily shown, that the whole plan is utterly impracticable, requiring an expense and sacrifice of property far beyond the entire resources of the State and Federal Governments. We shall now proceed to inquire, whether we can emancipate our slaves with permission that they remain among us.

Emancipation without Deportation.—We candidly confess, that we look upon this last mentioned scheme as much more practicable, and likely to be forced upon us, than the former. We consider it, at the same time, so fraught with danger and mischief both to the whites and blacks—so utterly subversive of the welfare of the slaveholding country, in both an economical and moral point of view, that we cannot, upon any principle of right or expediency, give it our sanction. Almost all the speakers in the Virginia Legislature seemed to think there ought to be no emancipation without deportation. Mr. Clay, too, in his celebrated colonization speech of 1830, says, "if the question were submitted whether there should be immediate or gradual emancipation of all the slaves in the United States, without their removal or colonization, painful as it is to express the opinion, I have no doubt that it would be unwise to emancipate them. I believe that the aggregate of evils which would be engendered in society, upon the supposition of general emancipation, and of the liberated slaves remaining principally among us, would be greater than all the evils of slavery. great as they unquestionably are." Even the northern philanthropists themselves admit, generally, that there should be no emancipation without removal. Perhaps, then, under these circumstances, we might have been justified in closing our review with a consideration of the colonization scheme; but as we are anxious to survey this subject fully in all its aspects, and to demonstrate upon every ground the complete justification of the whole southern country in a further continuance of that system of slavery which has been originated by no fault of theirs, and continued and increased contrary to their most earnest desires and petitions, we have determined briefly to examine this scheme likewise. As we believe the scheme of deportation utterly impracticable, we have come to the conclusion that in the present great question, the real and decisive line of conduct is either abolition without removal, or a steady perseverance in the system now established. "Paltry and timid minds," says the present Lord Chancellor of England on this very subject, "shudder at the thought of mere activity, as cowardly troops tremble at the idea of calmly waiting for the enemy's approach. Both the one and the other hasten their fate by relentless and foolish movements."

The ground upon which we shall rest our argument on this subject is, *that the slaves, in both an economical and moral point of view, are entirely unfit for a state of freedom among the whites;* and we shall produce such proofs and illustrations of our position, as seem to us perfectly conclusive. That condition of our species from which the most important consequences flow, says Mr. Mill, the Utilitarian, is the necessity of labor for the supply of the fund of our necessaries and conveniences. It is this which influences, perhaps more than any other, even our moral and religious character, and determines more than everything else besides, the social and political state of man. It must enter into the calculations of not only the political economist, but even of the metaphysician, the moralist, the theologian, and politician.

We shall, therefore, proceed at once to inquire what effect would be produced upon the slaves of the South in an economical point of view, by emancipation with permission to remain—whether the voluntary labor of the freed-man would be as great as the involuntary labor of the slave? Fortunately for us, this question has been so frequently and fairly subjected to the test of experience, that we are no longer left to vain and fruitless conjecture. Much was said in the Legislature of Virginia about superiority of free labor over slave, and perhaps, under certain circumstances, this might be true; but, in the present instance, the question is between *the relative amounts of labor which may be obtained from slaves before and after their emancipation.* Let us, then, first commence with our country, where, it is well known to everybody, that slave labor is vastly more efficient and productive than the labor of free blacks.

Taken as a whole class, the latter must be considered the most worthless and indolent of the citizens of the United States. It is well known that throughout the whole extent of our Union, they are looked upon as the very *drones* and *pests* of society. Nor does this character arise from the disabilities and disfranchisement by which the law attempts to guard against them. In the non-slaveholding States, where they have been more elevated by law, this kind of population is in a worse condition, and much more troublesome to society, than in the slaveholding, and especially in the planting States. Ohio, some years ago, formed a sort of land of promise for this deluded class, to which many have repaired from the slaveholding States,—and what has been the consequence? They have been most harshly expelled from that State, and forced to take refuge in a foreign land. Look through the Northern States, and mark the class upon whom the eye of the police is most steadily and constantly kept—see with what vigilance and care they are hunted down from place to place—and you cannot fail to see that idleness and improvidence are at the root of all their misfortunes. Not only does the experience of our own country illustrate this great fact, but others furnish abundant testimony.

"The free negroes," says Brougham, "in the West Indies are, with a very few exceptions, chiefly in the Spanish and Portuguese settlements, equally averse to all sorts of labor which do not contribute to the supply of their immediate and most urgent wants. Improvident and careless of the future, they are not actuated by that principle which inclines more civilized men to equalize their exertions at all times, and to work after the necessaries of the day have been procured, in order to make up for the possible deficiencies of the morrow; nor has their intercourse with the whites taught them to consider any gratification as worth obtaining, which cannot be produced by slight exertion of desultory and capricious industry."*

In the report of the Committee of the Privy Council in Great Britain, in 1788, the most ample proof of this assertion

* Brougham's Colonial Policy, Book IV., Sec. 1.

is brought forward. In Jamaica and Barbadoes, it was stated, that free negroes were never known to work for hire, and they have all the vices of the slave. Mr. Braithwait, the agent for Barbadoes, affirmed, that if the slaves in that island were offered their freedom on condition of working for themselves, not one-tenth of them would accept it. In all the other colonies the statements agree most accurately with those collected by the Committee of the Privy Council. "M. Malouet, who bore a special commission from the present government to examine the character and habits of the Maroons in Dutch Guiana, and to determine whether or not they were adapted to become hired laborers, informs us that they will only work one day in the week, which they find abundantly sufficient, in the fertile soil and genial climate of the new world, to supply all the wants that they have yet learnt to feel. The rest of their time is spent in absolute indolence and sloth. '*Le repos*,' says he, '*et l'oisivete sont devenus dans leur etat social leur unique passion?*' He gives the very same description of the free negroes in the French colonies, although many of them possessed lands and slaves. The spectacle, he tells us, was never yet exhibited of a free negro supporting his family by the culture of his little property. All other authors agree in giving the same description of free negroes in the British, French and Dutch colonies, by whatever denomination they may be distinguished, whether Maroons, Caraibes, free blacks, or fugitive slaves. The Abbe Raynald, with all his ridiculous fondness for savages, cannot, in the present instance, so far twist the facts according to his fancies and feelings, as to give a favorable portrait of this degraded race."*

From these facts, it would require no great sagacity to come to the conclusion, that slave cannot be converted into free labor without imminent danger to the prosperity and wealth

* Brougham's Colonial Policy.

of the country where the change takes place—and in this particular it matters not what may be the color of the slave. In the commencement of the reign of Charles V., the representations of Las Casas determined Cardinal Ximenes, the prime minister of Charles, to make an experiment of the conversion of slave labor into free, and for this purpose pious commissioners were sent out, attended by Las Casas himself, for the purpose of liberating the Indian slaves in the new world. Now mark the result. These commissioners, chosen from the cloister, and big with real philanthropy, repaired to the Western world intent upon the great work of emancipation. "Their ears," says Robertson, "were open to information from every quarter—they compared the different accounts which they received—and after a *mature* consideration of the whole, they were fully satisfied that the state of the colony rendered it *impossible* to adopt the plan proposed by Las Casas, and recommended by the Cardinal. They plainly perceived that no allurement was so powerful as to surmount the natural aversion of the Indians to any laborious effort, and that nothing but the authority of a master could compel them to work; and if they were not kept constantly under the eye and discipline of a superior, so great were their natural listlessness and indifference, that they would neither attend to religious instruction, nor observe those rights of Christianity which they had been already taught. Upon all these accounts the superintendents found it *necessary* to tolerate *repartimientos*, and to suffer the Indians to remain under subjection to their Spanish masters."* In the latter part of his reign, Charles, with most imprudent and fatal decision, proclaimed the immediate and universal emancipation of all the Indians—and precisely what any man of reflection might have anticipated, resulted. Their industry and freedom were found entirely incompatible. The

* Robertson's America, vol. 1, p. 123.

alarm was instantaneously spread over the whole Spanish colonies. Peru, for a time lost to the monarchy, was only restored by the repeal of the obnoxious law; and in New Spain, quiet was only preserved by a combination of the governor and subjects to suspend its execution. During the mad career of the French revolution, the slaves in the French colonies were, for a time, liberated; and even in Cayenne, where the experiment succeeded best in consequence of the paucity of slaves, it completely demonstrated the superiority of slave over free black labor; and generally the re-establishment of slavery was attended with the most happy consequences, and even courted by the negroes themselves, who became heartily tired of their short-lived liberty. Of the great experiment which has been recently made in Colombia and Guatemala, we shall presently speak. We believe it has completely proved the same well established fact—the great superiority of slave over free negro labor.

Mr. Clarkson, in his pamphlet on slavery, has alluded in terms of high commendation to an experiment made in Barbadoes, on Mr. Steele's plantation, which, he contends, has proved the safety and facility of the transition from slave to free labor. It seems Mr. Steele parcelled out his land among his negroes, and paid them wages for their labor. Now, we invite particularly the attention of our readers to the following extracts from the letter of Mr. Sealy, a neighbor of Mr. Steele, which will not only serve to establish our position, but afford an illustration of the melancholy fact, that the best of men cannot be relied on when under the influence of prejudice and passion. "It so happened," says Mr. Sealy, "that I resided on the nearest adjoining estate to Mr. Steele, and superintended the management of it myself for many years; I had, therefore, a better opportunity of forming an opinion than Mr. Clarkson can have—he has read Mr. Steele's account—*I wit-*

nessed the operations and effects of his plans. He possesses one of the largest and most seasonable plantations, in a delightful part of the island ; with all these advantages, his estate was never in as good order as those in the same neighborhood, and the crops were neither adequate to the size and resources of the estate, nor in proportion to those of other estates in the same part of the island. Finally, after an experiment of thirty years under Mr. Steele, and his executor, Mr. T. Bell, Mr. Steele's debts remained unpaid, and the plantation was sold by a decree of the Court of Chancery. After the debts and costs of suit were paid, very little remained out of 45,000*l.* to go to the residuary legatees.

"It was very well known that the negroes rejoiced when the change took place, and thanked their God that they were relieved from the copyhold system. Such was the final result and success that attended this system, which has been so much eulogized by Mr. Clarkson. After the estate was sold and the system changed, I had equally an opportunity of observing the management, and certainly the manifest improvement was strong evidence in favor of the change. Fields, which had been covered with bushes for a series of years, were brought into cultivation, and the number of pounds of sugar was in some years more than doubled under the new management: the provision crops also were abundant; consequently, the negroes and stock were amply provided for." Again: the Attorney-General of Barbadoes corroborates the statements of Mr. Sealy in the most positive terms. He says, "I was surprised to see it asserted lately in print, that his,— Steele's plantation,—succeeded well under the management. *I know it to be false.* It failed considerably; and had he lived a few years longer, he would have died not worth a farthing. Upon his death, they reverted to the old system, to which the slaves readily and willingly returned; the plantation now succeeds, and the slaves are contented and happy, and think themselves much better off than under the copyhold system, for their wages would not afford them many comforts which they have now."* (Upon this subject see No. LX. *London Quarterly.* ART — *West India Colonies.*) But a short time since, a highly respectable, and one of the most intelligent farmers of Virginia, informed us that he had actually tried, upon a much smaller scale, a similar experiment, and that it entirely failed; the negroes, devoid of judgment and good management, became lazy and improvident, and every time one was so unfortunate as to fall sick, it immediately became necessary to support him. The whole plan soon disgusted the master, and proved that the free labor system would not answer for the best of our negroes; for those he tried were his best. Now these experiments were the more conclusive, because the master reserved the right of re-imposing slavery upon them in case the experiment should not meet his approbation: every stimulus was thus offered, in case their freedom was really desirable, to work hard, but their natural

* If it were not that the experiment would be too dangerous and costly, we would have no objection to see our slaves gratified with the enjoyment of freedom for a short time. There is no doubt but that they, like the Poles, Livonians, &c., and the negroes of Mr. Steele, would soon sigh again for a master's control, and a master's support and protection. It is a well known fact that upon the borders of the free States, our slaves are not so much disposed to elope, as those who are situated further off; and the reason is, they are near enough to witness the condition of the free black laborer, and they know it is far more wretched than their own. A citizen of the West, who is as well acquainted with this whole subject as any other in the State or in the United States, informed us, a short time since, that the slaves of Botetourt and Montgomery were much more disposed to elope and settle in Ohio, than those of Cabel and Mason, situated on the borders—because the former are not so well acquainted with the real condition of the free blacks as the latter.

indolence and carelessness triumphed over love of liberty, and demonstrated the fact, that free labor, made out of slaves, is the worst in the world.

So far we have adduced instances from among mixed populations alone. Some have imagined that the indolence of liberated blacks in these cases, has arisen entirely from the presence of the whites, acknowledged to be the superior race both by law and custom ; that, consequently, if the blacks could be freed from the degrading influence exerted by the mere pressure of the whites, they would quickly manifest more desire to accumulate and acquire all the industrious habits of the English operative or New England laborer, Although this is foreign to our immediate object, which is to prove the inefficacy of free black labor in our country, where, of course, whites must always be present, we will, nevertheless, examine this opinion, because it has been urged in favor of that grand scheme of colonization recommended by some of the orators in the Virginia Legislature. Our own opinion is, that the presence of the whites ought rather to be an incentive and encouragement to labor. Habits of industry are more easily acquired when all are busy and active around us. A man feels a spirit of industry and activity stir within him, from moving amongst such societies as those of Marseilles, Liverpool, and New York, where the din of business and bustle assails his ears at every turn, whereas, he soon becomes indolent and listless at Bath or Saratoga. Why, then, are our colored free men so generally indolent and worthless among the industrious and enterprising citizens of even our Northern and New England States ? It is because there is an inherent and intrinsic cause at work, which will produce its effect under all circumstances. In the free black, the principle of idleness and dissipation triumphs over that of accumulation and the desire to better our condition ; the animal part of the man gains the victory over the moral, and he, consequently, prefers sinking down into the listless, inglorious repose of the brute creation, to rising to that energetic activity which can only be generated amid the multiplied, refined, and artificial wants of civilized society. The very conception which nine slaves in ten have of liberty, is that of idleness and sloth with the enjoyment of plenty; and we are not to wonder that they should hasten to practice upon their theory so soon as liberated. But the experiment has been sufficiently tried to prove most conclusively that the free black will work nowhere except by compulsion.

St. Domingo is often spoken of by philanthropists and schemers; the trial has there been made upon a scale sufficiently grand to test our opinions, and we are perfectly willing to abide the result of the experiment.

The main purpose of the mission of Consul-General McKenzie, to Hayti, by the British Government, was to clear up this very question. We have made every exertion to procure the very valuable notes of that gentleman, on Hayti, but have failed; we are, therefore, obliged to rely upon the eighty-ninth numbers of the London Quarterly, in one article of which mention is made of the result of M'Kenzie's observations. "By all candid persons," says the Review, "the deliberate opinion which that able man has formed from careful observation, and the whole tenor of the evidence he has furnished, will be thought conclusive. Such invincible repugnance do the free negroes of that Island feel to labor, that the system of the code rural of 1826, about the genuineness of which so much doubt was entertained a few years ago, is described as falling little short of the compulsion to which the slaves had been subjected previous to their emancipation. 'The consequences of delinquincy,' he says, 'are heavy fine and imprisonment, and the provisions of the law are as despotic as can well be conceived.' He afterwards subjoins :—Such have been the various modes for inducing or compelling labor for nearly forty years. It is next necessary to ascertain, as far as it is practicable, the degree of success which has attended each; and the only mode with which I am acquainted, is to give the returns of the exported agricultural produce during the same period, marking, where it can be done, any accidental circumstance that may have had an influence.' He then quotes the returns at length, and observes—' There is one decided inference from the whole of these six returns, viz: the positive decrease of cane cultivation, in all its branches— the diminution of other branches of industry, though not equally well marked, is no less certain, than the articles of spontaneous growth maintain, if not exceed, their former amount.' We may further add, that even the light labor required for trimming the planting coffee trees, has been so much neglected, that the export of coffee in 1830, falls short of that of 1829, by no less than 10,000,000 lbs." (*See London Quarterly Review, No. 89, Art. West India Question.*)

We subjoin here, to exhibit the facts asserted by Mr. M'Kenzie in a more striking manner, a tabular view of some of the principle exports from St. Domingo, during her subjection to France, and during the best years of the reigns of Toussaint, Dessalines, and Boyer,* upon the authority of James Franklin, on the present state of Hayti.

Produce.	French.	Toussaint.	Dessalines.	Boyer.
	1791.	1802.	1804.	1822.†
	lbs.	lbs.	lbs.	lbs.
Sugar,	163,405,220	53,400,000	47,600,000	652,541
Coffee,	68,151,180	34,370,000	31,000,000	35,117,834
Cotton,	6,286,126	4,050,000	3,000,000	891,950

* It is known that under Boyer there was a union of the Island under one government.

† The other years give the returns of the French part of the Island;

There has been a gradual diminution of the amount of the products of Hayti, since 1822. In 1825, the whole value of exports was about $8,000,000, more than $1,000,000 less than in 1822, and the revenue of the Island was not equal to the public expenditure. Is not this fair experiment for forty years, under more favorable circumstances than any reasonable man had a right to anticipate, sufficient to convince and overwhelm the most sceptical as to the unproductiveness of slave labor converted into free labor!

But the British colony at Sierra Leone is another case in point, to establish the same position. Evidence was taken in 1830, before a committee of the House of Commons. Capt. Bullen, R. N., stated that at Sierra Leone, they gave the blacks a portion of land to cultivate, and they cultivate just as much as will keep them, and not an inch more. Mr. Jackson, one of the Judges of the mixed Commission Court, being asked—"Taking into consideration the situation of Sierra Leone, and the attention paid by government to promote their comfort, what progress have they made towards civilization or the comforts of civilized life?" makes this answer—"I should say very inadequate to the efforts which have been made to promote their comfort and civilization." Capt. Spence, being asked a similar question, replies—"I have formed a very different opinion as to their progress of industry. I have not been able to observe that they seem inclined to cultivate the country farther than vegetables and things of that kind. They do not seem inclined to cultivate for exportation. Their wants are very few, and they are very wild; and their wants are supplied by the little exertion they make. They have sufficient to maintain them in clothing and food, and these are all their wants."

this for the Spanish and French, ought therefore, to be proportionably greater.

Our own colony, upon the coast of Africa proves, too, the same fact. It has been fed slowly and cautiously, with emigrants, and yet Mr. Ashmun's entreaties to colonization friends in the United States, to recollect that rice did not grow spontaneously in Africa, to send out laboring men, of good character, &c., but too conclusively show, in spite of the colored and exaggerated statements of prejudiced friends, the great difficulty of making the negroes work even in Liberia;* and we have no doubt, that if 6,000 or 60,000 could be colonized annually in Africa, there would not be a more worthless and indolent race of people upon the face of the globe, than our African colonies would exhibit.

We have now, we think, proved our position, that slave labor, in an economical point of view, is far superior to free negro labor; and have no doubt that if an immediate emancipation of negroes were to take place, the whole southern country would be visited with an immediate general famine, from which the productive resources of all the other States of the Union could not deliver them.

It is now easy for us to demonstrate the second point in our argument—that the slave is not only *economically* but *morally* unfit for freedom. And first, idleness and consequent want are, of themselves, sufficient to generate a catalogue of vices of the most mischievous and destructive character. Look to the penal prosecution of every country, and mark the situation

* We understand, from most undoubted authority, that Mr. Barbour, a negro gentleman from Liberia, who lately visited the Virginia Springs, for the purpose of re-establishing his health, which had given way under the deleterious influence of an African climate, bears most unequivocal testimony to the idleness of the blacks in Liberia—thinks that the statement which has been generally given of the colony greatly exaggerated—considers it a partial failure at least; and laughs at the idea of its being made a recipient for the immense and rapidly increasing mass of our whole black population.

of those who fall victims to the laws. And what a frightful proportion do we find among the indigent and idle classes of society! Idleness generates want, want gives rise to temptation, and strong temptation makes the villain. The most appropriate prayer for frail, imperfect man, is "lead us not into temptation." Mr. Archer, of Virginia, well observed in his speech, before the Colonization Society, that "the free blacks were destined by an insurmountable barrier—to the want of occupation—thence to the want of food—thence to the distresses which ensue from that want—thence to the settled deprivation which grows out of those distresses, and is nursed at their bosoms; and this condition *was not casualty, but fate.* The evidence was not speculation in political economy—it was geometrical demonstration."

We are not to wonder that this class of citizens should be so depraved and immoral. An idle population will always be worthless; and it is a mistake to think that they are only worthless in the Southern States, where it is erroneously supposed the slavery of a portion of their race depress them below their condition in the free States; on the contrary, we are disposed rather to think their condition better in the slave than the free States. Mr. Everett, in a speech before the Colonization Society, during the present year, says: "they (the free blacks) form, in Massachusetts, about one seventy-fifth part of the population; *one-sixth of the convicts in our prisons are of this class.*" The average number of annual convictions in the State of Virginia, estimated by the late Governor Giles, from the penitentiary reports, up to 1829, is seventy-one for the whole population—making one in every sixteen-thousand of the white population, one in every twenty-two thousand of the slaves, and one for every five thousand of the free colored people. Thus, it will be seen, that crimes among the free blacks are more than three times as numerous as among the whites, and four and a half times more numerous than among the slaves. But, although the free blacks have thus much the largest proportion of crime to answer for, yet the proportion is not so great in Virginia as in Massachusetts. Although they are relatively to the other classes more numerous, making the one-thirtieth of the population of the State, not one-eighth of the whole number of convicts are from among them in Virginia, while in Massachusetts there is one-sixth. We may infer, then, they are not so degraded and vicious in Virginia, a slaveholding State, as in Massachusetts, a non slaveholding State. But there is one fact to which we invite particularly the attention of those philanthropists who have the elevation of Southern slaves so much at heart—*that the slaves in Virginia furnish a much smaller annual proportion of convicts than the whites, and among the latter a very large proportion of convicts consist of foreigners or citizens of other States.*

There is one disadvantage attendant upon free blacks, in the slaveholding States, which is not felt in the non-slaveholding. In the former, they corrupt the slaves, encourage them to steal from their masters by purchasing from them, and they are, too, a sort of moral conductor by which the slaves can better organize and concert plans of mischief among themselves.

So far we have been speaking of the evils resulting from mere idleness; but there are other circumstances which must not be omitted in an enumeration of the obstacles to emancipation. The blacks have now all the habits and feelings of slaves, the whites have those of masters; the prejudices are formed, and mere legislation cannot improve them. "Give me," said a wise man, "the formation of the habits and manners of a people, and I care not who makes the laws." Declare the negroes of the South free to-morrow, and vain will be your decree, until you have prepared them for it; you depress, instead of elevating. The law would, in every point of view, be one of the most cruel and inhuman which could possibly be passed. The law would make them freemen, and custom or prejudice, we care not which you call it, would degrade them to the condition of slaves; and soon should we see, that "it is happened unto them, according to the true proverb, the dog is turned to his own vomit again, and the sow that has been washed, to her wallowing in the mire." "*Ne quid nimis*" should be our maxim; and we must never endeavor to elevate beyond what circumstances will allow. It is better that each one should remain in society in the condition in which he has been born and trained, and not to mount too fast without preparation. If a Virginia or South-Carolina farmer wished to make his *overseer* perfectly miserable, he could not better do it, than by persuading him that he was not only a freeman, but a polished gentleman likewise, and consequently, induce him to enter his drawing room. He would soon sigh for the fields, and less polished but more suitable companions. Hence, in the Southern States, the condition of the free blacks is better than in the Northern; in the latter, he is told, that he is a freeman and entirely equal to the white, and prejudice assigns to him a degraded station—light is furnished him by which to view the interior of the fairy palace which is fitted up for him, and custom expels him from it, after the law has told him it was his. He, consequently, leads a life of endless mortification and disappointment. Tantalus like, he has frequently the cup to his lips, and imperious custom dashes it untasted from him. In the Southern States, law and custom more generally coincide: the former makes no profession which the latter does not sanction, and consequently, the free black has nothing to grieve and disappoint him.

We have already said, in the course of this review, that if we were to liberate the slaves, we could not, in fact, alter their condition—they would still be virtually slaves; talent, habit, and wealth, would make the white the master still, and the emancipation would only have the tendency to deprive him of those sympathies and kind feelings for the black which now characterize him. Liberty has been the heaviest curse to the slave, when given too soon; we have already spoken of the eagerness and joy with which the negroes of Mr. Steele, in Barbadoes, returned to a state of slavery. The east of Europe affords hundreds of similar instances. 1791, Stanislaus Augustus, preparing a hopeless resistance to the threatened attack of Russia, in concert with the states, gave to Poland a constitution which established the complete personal freedom of the peasantry. The boon has never been recalled, and what was the consequence? " Finding (says Jones, in his volume on Rents) their dependence on their proprietors for subsistence remained undiminished, the peasants showed no very grateful sense of the boon bestowed upon them; they feared they should now be deprived of all claim upon the proprietors for assistance, when calamity or infirmity overtook them. It is only since they have discovered that the *connection* between them and the owners of the estates on which they reside *is little altered in practice*, and that their old masters very generally *continue*, from expediency or humanity, the occasional aid they formerly lent them, that they have become *reconciled* to their new character of freemen." " The Polish boors are, therefore, in *fact* still *slaves*," says Burnett, in his 'View of the present state of Poland' "and relatively to their political existence, absolutely subject to the will of their lord as in all the barbarism of the feudal times." " I was once on a short journey with a nobleman, when we stopped to bait at a farm-house of a village. The peasants got intelligence of the presence of their lord, and assembled in a body of twenty or thirty, to prefer a petition to him. I was never more struck with the appearance of these poor wretches, and the *contrast* of their condition with that of their master: I stood at a distance, and perceived that he did not yield to their supplication. When he dismissed them, I had the curiosity to inquire the object of their petition, and he replied, that they had begged for an increased allowance of land, on the plea that what they had was insufficient for their support. He added, 'I did not grant it them because their present allotments is the usual quantity, and as it has sufficed hitherto, so I know it will in time to come. 'Besides,' said he, 'if I give them more, I well know that it will not in *reality* better their circumstances.' Poland does not furnish a man of more humanity than the one who rejected this apparently reasonable petition; but it must be allowed that he had reasons for what he did. Those degraded and wretched beings, instead of hoarding the small surplus of their absolute necessaries, are almost universally *accustomed to expend* it in that abominable spirit, which they call *schnaps*. It is incredible what quantities of this pernicious liquor are drunk by the peasant men and women. The first time I saw any of these withered creatures was at Dantzic. I was prepared by printed accounts, to expect a sight of singular wretchedness; but I shrunk involuntarily from the sight of the reality. Some involuntary exclamation of surprise, mixed with compassion, escaped me; a thoughtless and a feelingless person (which are about the same thing) was standing by—'Oh, sir,' says he, 'you will find plenty of such people as these in Poland; and you may strike them, and kick them, or do what you please with them, and they will never resist you: they dare not.' Far be it from me to ascribe the feelings of this man to the more cultivated and humanized Poles; but each such incidental and thoughtless expressions betray too sensibly the general state of the feeling which exists in regard to these oppressed men." The traveller will now look in vain, throughout our slaveholding country, for such misery as is here depicted; and in spite of all the tales told by gossipping travellers, he will find no master so relentless as the Polish proprietor, and no young man so "thoughtless" and "feelingless" as the young Pole above mentioned. But liberate our slaves, and in a very few years we shall have all these horrors and reproaches added unto us.

In Livonia, likewise, the serfs were permaturely liberated; and mark the consequences. Von Helen, who travelled through Livonia in 1819, observes: "Along the high road through Livonia are found, at short distances, filthy public houses, called in the country *Rhatcharuas*, before the doors of which are usually seen a multitude of wretched carts and sledges belonging to the peasants, who are so addicted to brandy and strong liquors,* that they spend whole hours in those places. Nothing proves so much the state of barbarism in which those men are sunk, as the manner in which they received the decree issued about this time. These savages, unwilling to depend upon their own exertions for support, *made all the resistance in their power* to that decree, the execution of which was at length *entrusted to an armed force*." The Livonian peasants, therefore, received their new privileges yet more ungraciously than the Poles, though accompanied with the gift of property and secure means of subsistence, if they *chose to exert themselves*. By an edict of Maria Theresa, called by the Hungarians the *ubarium*, personal slavery and attachment to the soil were abolished, and the peasants declared to be "*hominus liberæ transmigrationis*;" and yet, says Jones, " the

---
* We believe, in case of an emancipation of our blacks, that drunkenness would be among them like the destroying angel.

authority of the owners of the soil over the persons and property of their tenantry has been very imperfectly abrogated; the necessities of the peasants oblige them frequently to resort to their landlords for loans of food; they become laden with heavy debts, to be discharged by labor.* The proprietors retain the right of employing them at pleasure, paying them, in lieu of subsistence, about one-third of the actual value of their labor; and lastly, the administration of justice is still in the hands of the nobles; and one of the first sights which strikes a foreigner, on approaching their mansions, is a sort of low-frame work of posts, to which a serf is tied when it is thought proper to administer the discipline of the whip, for offences which do not seem grave enough to demand a formal trial."

Let us for a moment revert to the black republic of Hayti, and we shall see that the negroes have gained nothing by their bloody revolution. Mr. Franklin, who derives his information from personal inspection, gives the following account of the present state of the island: " Oppressed with the weight of an overwhelming debt, contracted without an equivalent, with an empty treasury, and destitute of the ways and means for supplying it; the soil almost neglected, or at least very partially tilled; without commerce or credit. Such is the present state of the republic; and it seems almost impossible that, under the system which is now pursued, there should be any amelioration of its condition, or that it can arrive at

* Almost all our free negroes will run in debt to the full amount of their credit. "I never knew a free negro (says an intelligent correspondent in a late letter) who would not contract debts, if allowed, to a greater amount than he could pay; and those whom I have suffered to reside on my land, although good mechanics, have been generally so indolent and impoverished as to be in my debt at the end of the year, for provisions, brandy, &c., when I would allow it."

any very high state of improvement. Hence, there appears every reason to apprehend that it will *recede into irrecoverable insignificance, poverty, and disorder.*'' (p. 265.) And the great mass of the Haytiens are virtually in a state of as abject slavery as when the island was under the French dominion. The government soon found it absolutely necessary to establish a system of compulsion in all respects as bad, and more intolerable than, when slavery existed. The Code Henri prescribed the most mortifying regulations, to be obeyed by the laborers of the island; *work was to commence at day-light and continue uninterruptedly till eight o'clock; one hour was then allowed to the laborer to breakfast on the spot; at nine, work commenced again, and continued until twelve, when two hours repose was given to the laborer; at two, he commenced again and worked until night.* All these regulations were enforced by severe penal enactments. Even Toussaint l'Ouverture, who is supposed to have had the welfare of the negroes as much at heart as any other ruler in St. Domingo, in one of his proclamations in the ninth year of the French Republic, peremptorily directs—" all *free laborers*, men and women, now in a state of idleness, and living in towns, villages, and on other plantations than those to which they belong, with the intention to evade work, even those of both sexes who had not been employed in field labor since the revolution, *are required to return immediately* to their respective plantations." And in article seven, he directs, that the " overseers and drivers of every plantation shall make it their business to inform the commanding officer of the district in regard to the conduct of the laborers *under their management*, as well as those who shall absent themselves from their plantations without a pass, and of those who, residing on the plantations, shall refuse to work; they shall be forced to go to labor in the field, and if they prove obstinate, they shall be arrested and carried before the military commandant, in order to suffer the punishment above prescribed, according to the exigence of the case, the punishment being fine and imprisonment." And here is the boasted freedom of the negroes of St. Domingo: the appalling vocabulary of "overseer," "driver," "pass," &c., is not even abolished. Slavery to the government and its military officers is substituted for private slavery; the black master has stepped into the shoes of the white; and we all know that he is the most cruel of masters, and more dreaded by the negro than any of the ten plagues of Egypt. We are well convinced that there is not a single negro in the commonwealth of Virginia, who would accept such *freedom ;* and yet the happiest of the human race are constantly invited to sigh for such freedom, and to sacrifice all their happiness in the vain wish. But, it is not necessary further to multiply examples; enough has already been said, we hope, to convince the most sceptical of the great disadvantage to the slave himself, of freedom, when he is not prepared for it. It is unfortunate, indeed, that prejudiced and misguided philanthropists so often assert as *facts*, what, on investigation, turns out not only false, but even hostile to the very theories which they are attempting to support by them. We have already given one example of this kind of deception, in relation to Mr. Steele. We will now give another.

"In the year 1760, the Chancellor Zamoyski," says Burnett, "enfranchised six villages in the Palatinate of Masovia. This experiment has been much vaunted by Mr. Coxe, as having been attended with all the good effects desired; and he asserts that the Chancellor had, in consequence, enfranchised the peasants on all his estates. *Both of these assertions are false.* I inquired particularly of the son of the present Count Zamoyski, respecting these six villages, and was grieved to learn, that the experiment had completely failed. The

Count said, that within a few years, he had sold the estate; and added, I was glad to get rid of it, from the trouble the peasants gave me. These degraded beings, on receiving their freedom, were overjoyed at they knew not what, having no distinct comprehension of what freedom meant; but merely a rude notion that they may now do what they like.* They ran into every species of excess and extravagance which their circumstances admitted. Drunkenness, instead of being occasional, became almost perpetual; riot and disorder usurped the place of quietness and industry; the necessary labor suspended, the lands were worse cultivated than before; the small rents required of them they were often unable to pay." (*Burnett's View of Poland*, p. 105.) Indeed, it is a calamity to mankind, that zealous and overheated philanthropists will not suffer the truth to circulate, when believed hostile to their visionary schemes. Such examples as the foregoing ought to be known and attended to. They would prevent a great deal of that impatient silly action which has drawn down such incalculable misery, so frequently, upon the human family. "There is a time for all things," and nothing in this world should be done before its time. An emancipation of our slaves would check at once that progress of improvement which is now so manifest among them. The whites would either gradually withdraw, and leave whole districts or settlements in their possession, in which case they would sink rapidly in the scale of civilization; or, the blacks, by closer intercourse, would bring the whites down to their level. In the contact between the civilized and uncivilized man, all history and experience show, that the former will be sure to sink to the level of the latter. In these cases, it is always easier to

---

* Precisely such a notion as that entertained by the slaves of this country and the West Indies.

descend than ascend, and nothing will prevent the *facilis descensus* but slavery.

The great evil, however, of these schemes of emancipation, remains yet to be told. They are admirably calculated to excite plots, murders and insurrections; whether gradual or rapid in their operation, this is the inevitable tendency. In the former case, you disturb the quiet and contentment of the slave who is left unemancipated; and he becomes the midnight murderer to gain that fatal freedom whose blessings he does not comprehend. In the latter case, want and invidious distinction will prompt to revenge. Two totally different races, as we have before seen, cannot easily harmonize together, and although we have no idea that any organized plan of insurrection or rebellion can ever secure for the black the superiority, even when free,* yet his idleness will produce want and worthlessness, and his very worthlessness and degradation will stimulate him to deeds of rapine and vengeance; he will oftener engage in plots and massacres, and thereby draw down on his devoted head, the vengeance of the provoked whites. But one limited massacre is recorded in Virginia history; let her liberate her slaves, and every year you would hear of insurrections and plots, and every day would perhaps record a murder; the melancholy tale of Southampton would not alone blacken the page of our history, and make the tender mother shed the tear of horror over her babe as she clasped it to her bosom; others of a deeper dye would thicken upon us; those regions where the brightness of polished life has dawned and brightened into full day, would relapse into darkness, thick and full of horrors, and in those dark and dismal hours, we might well exclaim, in the shuddering language of the poet:

* Power can never be dislodged from the hands of the intelligent, the wealthy, and the courageous, by any plans that can be formed by the poor, the ignorant, and the habitually subservient; history scarce furnishes such an example.

"Nox atra cava circumvolat umbra
Quis cladem illius noctis, quis funera fando
Explicit?   *   *   *
Urbs antiqua ruit, multos dominata per annos
Plurima perque vias sternunter inertia passim
Corpora per que domos, et religiosa deorum
Limina.   *   *   Crudelis ubique
Luctus ubique pavor, et plurima mortis imago."

Colombia and Guatemala have tried the dangerous experiment of emancipation, and we invite the attention of the reader to the following dismal picture of the city of Guatemala, drawn by the graphic pencil of Mr. Dunn: " With lazaroni in rags and filth, a *colored population drunken and revengeful*, her females licentious, and her males shameless, she ranks as a true child of that accursed city, which still remains as a living monument of the fulfilment of prophecy, and the forbearance of God, the hole of every foul spirit, the cage of every unclean and hateful bird. The pure and simple sweets of domestic life, with its thousand tendernesses and its gentle affections are here exchanged for the feverish joys of a dissipated hour; and the peaceful home of love is converted into a theatre of mutual accusations and recriminations. This leads to violent excesses; men carry a large knife in a belt, *women one fastened in the garter. Not a day passes without murder;* on fast days and on Sundays, the average number killed is from four to five. From the number admitted into the hospital of St. Juan de Dios, it appears that in the year 1827, near fifteen hundred were stabbed, of whom from three to four hundred died."* Thank Heaven, no such scenes as these have yet been witnessed in our country. From the day of the arrival of the negro slaves upon our coast in the Dutch vessel, up to the present hour, a period of more than two hundred years,

* See Dunn's Sketches of Guatemala, in 1827 and 1828, pp. 95, 96, and 97.

there have not perished in the whole southern country, by the hands of slaves, a number of whites equal to the average annual stabbings in the city of Guatemala, containing a population of 30,000 souls! "Nor is the freed African," says Dunn, "one degree raised in the scale—*under fewer restraints, his vices display themselves more disgustingly; insolent and proud, indolent and a liar,* he imitates only the vices of his superiors, and to the catalogue of his former crimes adds drunkenness and theft." Do not all these appalling examples but too eloquently tell the consequences of emancipation, and bid us well beware how we enter on any system which will be almost certain to bring down ruin and degradation both on the whites and the blacks.

But in despite of all the reasoning and illustrations which can be urged, the example of the northern States of our confederacy and the west of Europe afford, it is thought by some, conclusive evidence of the facility of changing the slave into the freeman. As to the former, it is enough to say that paucity of numbers,* uncongenial climate, and the state of agriculture to the North, together with the great demand of slaves to the South, alone accomplished the business. In reference to the west of Europe, it was the rise of the towns, the springing up of a middle class, and a change of agriculture, which gradually and silently effected the emancipation of the slaves, in a great measure through the operation of the selfish principle itself. Commerce and manufactures arose in the western countries, and with them sprang up a middle class of freemen, in the cities and the country too, which gradually and imperceptibly absorbed into its body all the slaves. But for this middle class, which acted as the *absorbent,* the slaves

---

* "There are more free negroes and mulattoes (said Judge Tucker in 1803) in Virginia alone, than are to be found in the four New England States, and Vermont in addition to them."—(Tucker's Blackstone, vol. 1, part 2d, p. 66, foot note.)

could not have been liberated with safety or advantage to either party. Now, in our southern country, there is no body of this kind to become *the absorbent*, nor are we likely to have such a body, unless we look into the vista of the future, and imagine a time when the south shall be to the north, what England now is to Ireland, and will consequently be *overrun* with northern laborers, underbidding *the means of subsistence* which will be furnished to the negro: then, *perhaps*, such a laboring class, devoid of all pride and habits of lofty bearing, *may* become a proper *recipient* or *absorbent* for emancipated slaves. But even then, we fear the effects of difference of color. The slave of Italy or France could be emancipated or escape to the city, and soon all records of his former state would perish, and he would gradually sink into the mass of freemen around him. But, unfortunately, the emancipated black carries a mark which no time can erase; he forever wears the indelible symbol of his inferior condition; *the Ethiopian cannot change his skin, nor the leopard his spots.*

In Greece and Rome—and we imagine it was so during the feudal ages—the domestic slaves were frequently among the most learned, virtuous, and intelligent members of society. Terrence, Phædrus, Æsop, and Epicetus, were all slaves. They were frequently taught all the arts and sciences, in order that they might be more valuable to their masters. "Seneca relates," says Wallace, in his Numbers of Mankind, "that Calvisius Labinus had many Anagnosæ slaves, or such as were learned and could read to their masters, and that none of them were purchased under 807*l*. 5*s*. 10*d*. According to Pliny, Daphnis, the grammarian, cost 5651*l*. 10*s*. 10*d*. Roscius, the actor, would gain yearly 4036*l*. 9*s*. 2*d*. A morio, or fool, was sold for 161*l*. 9*s*. 2*d*." (*Wallace, on the Numbers of Mankind, page* 142.) There was no obstacle, therefore, to the emancipation of such men as these, (except as to the fool,) either on the score of color, intelligence, habits, or anything else—the *body* of freemen could readily and without difficulty or danger absorb them. Not so now—nor will it be in all time to come, with our blacks. With these remarks, we shall close our examination of the plans by which it has been or may be proposed to get rid of slavery. If our arguments are sound, and reasonings conclusive, we have shown they are all wild and visionary, calculated to involve the south in ruin and degradation; and we now most solemnly call upon the statesman and the patriot, the editor and the philanthropist, to pause, and consider well, before they move in this dangerous and delicate business. But a few hasty and fatal steps in advance, and the work may be irretrievable. For Heaven's sake, then, let us pause, and recollect, that on this subject, so pregnant with the safety, happiness, and prosperity of millions, we shall be doomed to realize the fearful motto, " nulla vestigia retrorsum."

There are some who, in the plenitude of their folly and recklessness, have likened the cause of the blacks to Poland and France, and have *darkly hinted* that the same aspirations which the generous heart breathes for the cause of bleeding, suffering Poland and revolutionary France, must be indulged for the *insurrectionary blacks*. And has it come at last to this: that the hellish plots and massacres of Dessalines, Gabriel and Nat Turner, are to be compared to the noble deeds and devoted patriotism of Lafayette, Kosciusko, and Schrynecki? and we suppose the same logic would elevate Lundy and Garrison to niches in the Temple of Fame, by the side of Locke and Rousseau. There is an absurdity in this conception, which so outrages reason and the most common feelings of humanity, as to render it unworthy of serious, patient refutation. But we will, nevertheless, for a moment examine it, and shall find, on their own principles, if such reasoners have any principles, that their conception is entirely fallacious. The true theory of the right of revolution we conceive to be the following: no men, or set of men, are justifiable in attempting a revolution which must *certainly* fail; or if successful, must produce *necessarily a much worse state* of things than the pre-existent order. We have not the right to plunge the dagger into the monarch's bosom, merely because he is a monarch—we must be sure it is the *only means* of dethroning a tyrant and giving peace and happiness to an aggrieved and suffering people. Brutus would have had no right to kill Cæsar, if he could have foreseen the consequences. If France and Poland had been peopled with a race of serfs and degraded citizens, totally unfit for freedom and self-government, and Lafayette and Kosciusko could have known it, they would have been *parricides*, instead of *patriots*, to have roused such ignorant and unhappy wretches to engage in a revolution, whose object they could not comprehend, and which would inevitably involve them in all the horrors of relentless carnage and massacre. No man has ever yet contended that the blacks could gain their liberty and an ascendancy over the whites by wild insurrections; no one has ever imagined that they could do more than bring down, by their rash and barbarous achievements, the vengeance of the infuriated whites upon their devoted heads. Where, then, is the analogy to Poland and to France,—lands of generous achievement, of learning, and of high and noble purposes, and with people capable of self-government? We shall conclude this branch of our subject with the following splendid extract from a speech of Mr. Canning, which should at least make the rash legislator more distrustful of his specifics:

"In dealing with a negro, we must remember that we are dealing with a being possessing the form and strength of a man, but the intellect only of a child. To turn him loose in the manhood of his physical passions, but in the infancy of his uninstructed reason, would be to raise up a creature resembling the splendid fiction of a recent romance; the hero of which constructs a human form with all the physical capabilities of man, and with the thews and sinews of a giant, but being unable to impart to the work of his hands a perception of right and wrong, he finds too late that he has only created a more than mortal power of doing mischief, and himself recoils from the monster which he has made. What is it we have to deal with? is it an evil of yesterday's origin? with a thing which has grown up in our time? of which we have watched the growth—measured the extent—and which we have ascertained the means of correcting or controlling? No, we have to deal with an evil which is the growth of centuries; which is almost coeval with the deluge; which has existed under different modifications since man was man. Do gentlemen, in their passion for legislation, think, that after only thirty years discussion, they can now at once manage as they will, the most unmanageable, perhaps, of all subjects? Or do we forget, sir, that in fact not more than thirty years have elapsed since we first presumed to approach even the outworks of this great question. Do we, in the ardor of our nascent reformation, forget that during the ages which this system has existed, no preceding generation of legislators has ventured to touch it with a reforming hand; and have we the vanity to flatter ourselves that we can annihilate it at a blow? No, sir,

o! If we are to do good, it is not to be done by sudden and violent measures." Let the warning language of Mr. Canning be attended to in our legislative halls, and all rash and intemperate legislation avoided. We will now proceed to the last division of our subject, and examine a little into the injustice and evils of slavery, with the view of ascertaining if we are really exposed to those dangers and horrors which many seem to anticipate in the current of time.

III. Injustice and Evils of Slavery.—1st. It is said slavery is wrong, in the *abstract* at least, and contrary to the spirit of Christianity. To this we answer as before, that any question must be determined by its circumstances, and if, as really is the case, we cannot get rid of slavery without producing a greater injury to both the masters and slaves, there is no rule of conscience or revealed law of God which *can* condemn us. The physician will not order the spreading cancer to be extirpated, although it will eventually cause the death of his patient, because he would thereby hasten the fatal issue. So, if slavery had commenced even contrary to the laws of God and man, and the sin of its introduction rested upon our heads, and it was even carrying forward the nation by slow degrees to final ruin—yet, if it were *certain* that an attempt to remove it would only hasten and heighten the final catastrophe—that it was, in fact, a "vulnus immedicabile" on the body politic which no legislation could safely remove, then we would not only not be found to attempt the extirpation, but we would stand guilty of a high offence in the sight of both God and man, if we should rashly make the effort. But the original sin of introduction rest not on our heads, and we shall soon see that all those dreadful calamities which the false prophets of our day are pointing to, will never, in all probability, occur. With regard to the assertion that slavery is against the spirit of Christianity, we are ready to admit the general assertion, but deny most positively, that there is any thing in the Old or New Testament, which would go to show that slavery, when once introduced, ought at all events to be abrogated, or that the master commits any offence in holding slaves. The children of Israel themselves were slaveholders, and were not condemned for it. All the patriarchs themselves were slaveholders; Abraham had more than three hundred; Isaac had a "great store"* of them; and even the patient and meek Job himself had "*a very great household.*" When the children of Israel conquered the land of Canaan, they made one whole tribe "hewers of wood and drawers of water," and they were at that very time under the special guidance of Jehovah; they were permitted expressly to purchase slaves of the heathen, and keep them as an inheritance for their posterity; and even the children of Israel might be enslaved for six years. When we turn to the New Testament, we find not one single passage at all calculated to disturb the conscience of an honest slaveholder. No one can read it without seeing and admiring that the meek and humble Saviour of the world in no instance meddled with the established institutions of mankind; he came to save a fallen world, and not to excite the black passions of men, and array them in deadly hostility against each other. From no one did he turn away; his plan was offered alike to all—to the monarch and the subject, the rich and the poor, the master and the slave. He was born in the Roman world—a world in which the most galling slavery existed, a thousand times more cruel than the slavery in our own country; and yet he no where encourages insurrection; he no where fosters discontent; but exhorts *always* to implicit obedience and fidelity. What a rebuke does the practice of the Redeemer of mankind imply upon the conduct of some of his nominal disciples of the day, who seek to destroy the contentment of the slaves, to rouse their most deadly passions, to break up the deep foundations of society, and to lead on to a night of darkness and confusion! "Let every man [says Paul] abide in the same calling wherein he is called. Art thou called *being* a servant? care not for it; but if thou mayest be made

---

* And the man (Isaac) waxed great and went forward, and grew until he became very great; for he had possession of flocks, and possession of herds, and great store of servants.—(Genesis chap, 26.)

free, use *it* rather."—(1 *Corinth.* vii. 20, 21.) Again: "Let as many servants as are under the yoke, count their own masters worthy of all honor, that the name of God and his doctrines be not blasphemed; and they that have believing masters, let them not despise *them*, because they are brethren, but rather do them service, because they are faithful and beloved partakers of the benefit. These things teach and exhort."—(1 *Tim.* vi. 1, 2.) Servants are even commanded in Scripture to be faithful and obedient to unkind masters. "Servants," (says Peter,) "be subject to your masters with all fear; not only to the good and gentle, but to the froward. For what glory is it if when ye shall be buffeted for your faults ye take it patiently; but if when ye do well and suffer for it, ye take it patiently, this is acceptable with God."—(1 *Peter,* ii. 18, 20.) These and many other passages in the New Testament, most convincingly prove, that slavery in the Roman world was no where charged as a fault or crime upon the holder, and every where is the most implicit obedience enjoined. *

We beg leave, before quitting this topic, to address a few remarks to those who have conscientious scruples about the holding of slaves, and therefore consider themselves under an obligation to break all the ties of friendship and kindred—dissolve all the associations of happier days, to flee to a land where this evil does not exist. We cannot condemn the conscientious actions of mankind, but we must be permitted to say, that if the assumption even of these pious gentlemen be correct, we do consider their conduct as very unphilosophical; and we will go further still: we look upon it as even immoral upon their own principles. Let us admit that slavery is an evil, and what then? Why, it has been entailed upon us by no fault of ours, and must we shrink from the charge which

* See Ephesians, vi. 5, Titus ii. 9, 10. Philemon, Colossians, iii. 22, and iv. 1.

devolves upon us, and throw the slave in consequence into the hands of those who have no scruples of conscience—those who will not perhaps treat him so kindly? No! this is not philosophy, it is not morality; we must recollect that the unprofitable man was thrown into utter darkness. To the slaveholder has truly been entrusted the five talents. Let him but recollect the exhortation of the Apostle—"Masters, give unto your servants that which is just and equal; knowing that ye also have a master in heaven;" and in the final day he shall have nothing on this score with which his conscience need be smitten, and he may expect the welcome plaudit—"Well done thou good and faithful servant, thou hast been faithful over a few things, I will make thee ruler over many things; enter thou into the joy of thy Lord." Hallam, in his History of the Middle Ages, says, that the greatest moral evil flowing from monastic establishments, consisted in withdrawing the good and religious from society, and leaving the remainder unchecked and unrestrained in the pursuit of their vicious practices. Would not such principles as those just mentioned lead to a similar result? We cannot, therefore, but consider them as *whining* and *sickly*, and highly unphilosophical and detrimental to society.

2dly. *But it is further said that the moral effects of slavery are of the most deleterious and hurtful kind;* and as Mr. Jefferson has given the sanction of his great name to this charge, we shall proceed to examine it with all that respectful deference to which every sentiment of so pure and philanthropic a heart is justly entitled.

"The whole commerce between master and slave," says he, "is a perpetual exercise of the most boisterous passions; the most unremitting despotism on the one part, and degrading submission on the other. Our children see this, and learn to imitate it, for man is an imitative animal—this quality is the germ of education in him. From his cradle to his grave, he is learning what he sees others do. If a parent had no other motive, either in his own philanthropy or self-love, for restraining the intemperance of passion towards his slave, it should always be a sufficient one that his child is present. But generally it is not sufficient. The parent storms, the child looks on, catches the lineaments of wrath, puts on the same airs in the circle of smaller slaves, gives a loose to his worst of passions, and thus nursed, educated, and daily exercised in the worst of tyranny, cannot but be stamped by it with odious peculiarities."* Now we boldly assert that the fact does not bear Mr. Jefferson out in his conclusions. He has supposed the master in a continual passion—in the constant exercise of the most odious tyranny, and the child, a creature of imitation, looking on and learning. But is not this master sometimes kind and indulgent to his slaves? Does he not mete out to them, for faithful service, the reward of his cordial approbation? Is it not his interest to do it? and when thus acting humanely, and speaking kindly, where is the child, the creature of imitation, that he does not look on and learn? We may rest assured, in this intercourse between a good master and his servant, more good than evil *may* be taught the child; the exalted principles of morality and religion may thereby be sometimes indelibly inculcated upon his mind, and instead of being reared a selfish contracted being, with nought but self to look to—he acquires a more exalted benevolence, a greater generosity and elevation of soul, and embraces for the sphere of his generous actions a much wider field. Look to the slaveholding population of our country, and you every where find them characterized by noble and elevated sentiments, by humane and virtuous feelings. We do not find among them that cold, contracted, calculating *selfishness*, which

* Jefferson's Notes on Virginia.

withers and repels every thing around it, and lessens or destroys all the multiplied enjoyments of social intercourse. Go into our national councils, and ask for the most generous, the most disinterested, the most conscientious, and the least unjust and oppressive in their principles, and see whether the slaveholder will be past by in the selection. Edwards says that slavery in the West Indies seems to awaken the laudable propensities of our nature, such as, " frankness, sociability, benevolence and generosity. In no part of the globe is the virtue of hospitality more prevalent than in the British sugar islands. The gates of the planter are always open to the reception of his guests—to be a stranger is of itself a sufficient introduction."

Is it not a fact, known to every man in the south, that the most cruel master are those who have been unaccustomed to slavery. It is well known that northern gentlemen who marry southern heiresses, are much severer masters than southern gentlemen.* And yet, if Mr. Jefferson's reasoning were correct, they ought to be milder: in fact, it follows from his reasoning, that the authority which the father is called on to exercise over his children, must be seriously detrimental; and yet we know that this is not the case; that on the contrary, there is nothing which so much humanizes and softens the heart, as this *very authority ;* and there are none, even among those who have no children themselves, so disposed to pardon the follies and indiscretion of youth, as those who have seen most of them, and suffered greatest annoyance. There may be many cruel masters, and there are unkind and cruel fathers too; but both the one and the other make all those around

---

* A similar remark is made by Ramsay, and confirmed by Bryant Edwards, in regard to the West Indies. Adventurers from Europe are universally more cruel and morose towards the slaves, than the Creole or native West Indian. (Hist. of W. I. Book 4, Chap. I.)

them shudder with horror. We are disposed to think that their example in society tends rather to strengthen than weaken the principle of benevolence and humanity.

Let us now look a moment to the slave, and contemplate his position. Mr. Jefferson has described him as hating, rather than loving his master, and as losing, too, all that *amor patriæ* which characterizes the true patriot. We assert again, that Mr. Jefferson is not borne out by the fact. We are well convinced that there is nothing but the mere relations of husband and wife, parent and child, brother and sister, which produce a closer tie, than the relation of master and servant.* We have no hesitation in affirming, that throughout the whole slaveholding country, the slaves of a good master are his warmest, most constant, and most devoted friends; they have been accustomed to look up to him as their supporter, director and defender. Every one acquainted with southern slaves, knows that the slave rejoices in the elevation and prosperity of his master; and the heart of no one is more gladdened at the successful debut of young master or miss on the great theatre of the world, than that of either the young slave who has grown up with them, and shared in all their sports, and even partaken of all their delicacies—or the aged one who has looked on and watched them from birth to manhood, with the kindest and most affectionate solicitude, and has ever met from them all the kind treatment and generous sympathies of feeling, tender hearts. Judge Smith, in his able speech on Foote's Resolutions, in the Senate, said, in an emergency, he would rely upon his own slaves for his defence—he would put arms into their hands, and he had no doubt they would defend him faithfully. In the late Southampton insurrection, we know

---

* There are hundreds of slaves in the southern country who will desert parents, wives or husbands, brothers and sisters, to follow a kind master—so strong is the tie of master and slave.

that many actually convened their slaves and armed them for defence, although slaves were here the cause of the evil which was to be repelled. We have often heard slaveholders affirm that they would sooner rely upon their slaves' fidelity and attachment in the hour of danger and severe trial, than on any other equal number of individuals; and we all know, that the son or daughter, who has been long absent from the parental roof, on returning to the scenes of infancy never fails to be greeted with the kindest welcome and the most sincere and heartfelt congratulations from those slaves among whom he has been reared to manhood.

Gilbert Stuart, in his History of Society, says that the time when the vassals of the feudal ages was most faithful, most obedient, and most interested in the welfare of his master, was precisely when his dependence was most complete, and when, consequently, he relied upon his lord for everything. When the feudal tenure was gradually changing, and the law was interposing between landlord and tenant, the close tie between them began to dissolve, and with it, the kindness on one side, and the affection and gratitude on the other, waned and vanished. From all this, we are forced to draw one important inference—that it is dangerous to the happiness and well-being of the slave, for either the imprudent philanthropist to attempt to interpose too often, or the rash legislator to obtrude his regulating edicts, between master and slave. They only serve to render the slave more intractable and unhappy, and the master more cruel and unrelenting. The British West India Islands form at this moment a most striking illustration of this remark; the law has interposed between master and servant, and the slave has been made idle and insolent, and consequently worthless; a vague and irrational idea of liberty has been infused into his mind; he has become restless and unhappy; and the planters are deserting the islands, because the very law itself is corrupting and ruining the slave. The price of slaves, it is said, since the passage of those laws, has fallen fifty per cent., and the rapid declension of the number of slaves, proves that their condition has been greatly injured, instead of benefited. This instance is fraught with deep instruction to the legislator, and should make him pause. And we call upon the reverend clergy, whose examples should be pure, and whose precepts should be fraught with wisdom and prudence, to beware, lest in their zeal for the black, they suffer too much of the passion and prejudice of the human heart to meddle with those pure principles by which they should be governed. Let them beware of "what spirit they are of." "No sound," says Burke, "ought to be heard in the church, but the healing voice of christian charity. Those who quit their proper character, to assume what does not belong to them, are for the most part ignorant of the character they assume, and of the character they leave off. Wholly unacquainted with the world in which they are so fond of meddling, and inexperienced in all its affairs, on which they pronounce with so much confidence, they have nothing of politics but the *passions* they excite. Surely the church is a place where one day's truce ought to be allowed to the dissensions and animosities of mankind."

In the debate in the Virginia Legislature, no speaker *insinuated even*, we believe, that the slaves in Virginia were not treated kindly; and all, too, agree that they were most abundantly fed; and we have no doubt but that they form the happiest portion of our society. A merrier being does not exist on the face of the globe, than the negro slave of the U. States. Even Captain Hall himself, with his thick "crust of prejudice," is obliged to allow that they are happy and contented, and the master much less cruel than is generally imagined. Why, then, since the slave is happy, and happiness is the great object of all animated creation, should we endeavor to disturb his contentment by infusing into his mind a vain and indefinite desire for liberty—a something which he cannot comprehend, and which must inevitably dry up the very sources of his happiness.

The fact is that all of us, and the great author of the Declaration of Independence is like us in this respect, are too prone to judge of the happiness of others by ourselves—we make *self* the standard, and endeavor to draw down every one to its dimensions—not recollecting that the benevolence of the Omnipotent has made the mind of man pliant and susceptible of happiness in almost every situation and employment. We might rather die than be the obscure slave that waits at our back—our education and our habits generate an ambition that makes us aspire at something loftier—and disposes us to look upon the slave as unsusceptible of happiness in his humble sphere, when he may indeed be much happier than we are, and have his ambition too; but his ambition is to excel all his other slaves in the performance of his servile duties—to please and to gratify his master—and to command the praise of all who witness his exertions. Let the wily philanthropist but come and whisper into the ears of such a slave that his situation is degrading and his lot a miserable one—let him but light up the dungeon in which he persuades the slave that he is caged—and that moment, like the serpent that entered the garden of Eden, he destroys his happiness and his usefulness. We cannot, therefore, agree with Mr. Jefferson, in the opinion that slavery makes the unfeeling tyrant and ungrateful dependant; and in regard to Virginia especially, we are almost disposed, judging from the official returns of crimes and convictions, to assert, with a statesman who has descended to his tomb, (Mr. Giles,) " that the whole population of Virginia, consisting of three *castes*—of free white, free colored, and slave colored population, is the soundest and most moral of any other, according to numbers, in the whole world, as far as is known to me."

3dly. *It has been contended that slavery is unfavorable to a republican spirit;* but the whole history of the world proves that this is far from being the case. In the ancient republics of Greece and Rome, where the spirit of liberty glowed with most intensity, the slaves were more numerous than the freemen. Aristotle, and the great men of antiquity, believed slavery necessary to keep alive the spirit of freedom. In Sparta, the freemen were even forbidden to perform the offices of slaves, lest he might lose the spirit of independence. In modern times, too, liberty has always been more ardently desired by slaveholding communities. "Such " says Burke, " were our Gothic ancestors ; such, in our days, were the Poles ; and such will be all masters of slaves who are not slaves themselves." "These people of the southern (American) colonies are much more strongly, and with a higher and more stubborn spirit, attached to liberty, than those of the northward." And from the time of Burke down to the present day, the Southern States have always borne the same honorable distinction. Burke says, " it is because freedom is to them not only an enjoyment, but a kind of rank and privilege." Another, and perhaps more efficient cause of this, is the perfect spirit of equality so prevalent among the whites of all the slaveholding States. Jack Cade, the English reformer, wished all mankind to be brought to one common level. We believe slavery in the U. States has accomplished this, in regard to the whites, as nearly as can be expected or even desired in this world. The menial and low offices being all performed by the blacks, there is at once taken away the greatest cause of distinction and separation of the ranks of society. The man to the north will not shake hands familiarly with his servant, and converse, and laugh and dine with him, no matter how honest and respectable he may be. But go to the south, and you will find that no white man feels such inferiority of rank as to be unworthy of association with those around him. Color alone is here the badge of distinction, the true mark of aristocracy, and all who are white are equal in spite of the variety of occupation. The same thing is observed in the West Indies. "Of the character common to the white resident of the West Indies, it appears to me," says Edwards, "that the leading feature is an independent spirit, and a display of *conscious equality* throughout all ranks and conditions. The poorest white person seems to consider himself nearly on a level with the richest; and emboldened by this idea, approaches his employer with extended hand, and a freedom which, in the countries of Europe, is seldom displayed by men in the lower orders of life towards their superiors." And it is this spirit of equality which is both the generator and preserver of the genuine spirit of liberty.

4thly. *Insecurity of the whites, arising from plots, insurrections, &c., among the blacks.* This is the evil, after all, let us say what we will, which really operates most powerfully upon the schemers and emancipating philanthropists of those sections where slaves constitute the principal property. Now, if we have shown, as we trust we have, that the scheme of deportation is utterly impracticable, and that emancipation, with permission to remain, will produce all these horrors in *still greater degree*, it follows that this evil of slavery, allowing it to exist in all its latitude, would be no argument for legislative action, and therefore we might well rest contented with this issue; but as we are anxious to exhibit this whole subject in its true bearings, and as we do believe that this evil has been most strangely and causelessly exaggerated, we have determined to examine it a moment, and point out its true extent. It seems to us that those who insist most upon it, commit the enormous error of looking upon every slave in the whole slave-holding country as actuated by the most deadly enmity to the whites, and possessing all that reckless, fiendish temper, which would lead him to murder and assassinate the moment the opportunity occurs. This is far from being true; the slave, as we have already said, generally loves the master and his family ;* and few indeed there are, who can coldly plot the murder of men, women and children ; and if they do, there are fewer still who can have the villany to execute. We can sit down and imagine that all the negroes in the south have conspired to rise on a certain night, and murder all the whites in their respective families ; we may suppose the secret to be kept, and that they have the physical power to exterminate, and yet we may say the whole is morally impossible. No insurrection of this kind can ever occur where the blacks are as much civilized as they are in the United States. Savages and Koromantyn slaves can commit such deeds, because their whole life and education have prepared them; and they glory in the achievement; but the negro of the United States has imbibed the principles, the sentiments, and feelings of the white ; in one word, he is civilized—at least, comparatively ; his whole education and course of life are at war with such fell deeds. Nothing, then, but the most subtle and poisonous principles, sedulously infused into his mind, can break his allegiance, and transform him into the midnight murderer. Any man who will attend to the history of the Southampton massacre, must at once see, that the cause of even the partial success of the insurrectionists, was the very circumstance that there was no extensive plot, and that Nat, a demented fanatic, was under the impression that heaven had enjoined him to

* We scarcely know a single family, in which the slaves, especially the domestics, do not manifest the most unfeigned grief at the deaths which occur among the whites.

liberate the blacks, and had made its manifestations by loud noises in the air, an eclipse, and by the greenness of the sun. It was these signs which determined *him*, and ignorance and superstition, together with implicit confidence in Nat, determined a few others, and thus the bloody work began. So fearfully and reluctantly did they proceed to the execution, that we have no doubt that if Travis, the first attacked, could have waked whilst they were getting into his house, or could have shot down Nat or Bill, the rest would have fled, and the affair would have terminated *in limine*.

We have read with great attention the history of the insurrections in St. Domingo, and have no hesitation in affirming, that to the reflecting mind, that whole history affords the most complete evidence of the difficulty and almost impossibility of succeeding in these plots, even under the most favorable circumstances. It would almost have been a moral miracle, if that revolution had not succeeded. The French revolution had kindled a blaze throughout the world. The society of the *Amis des Noirs*, (the friends of the blacks,) in Paris, had educated and disciplined many of the mulattoes, who were almost as numerous as the whites in the island. The National Assembly, in its mad career, declared these mulattoes to be equal in all respects to the whites, and gave them the same privileges and immunities as the whites. During the ten years, too, immediately preceding the revolution, more than 200,000 negroes were imported into the island from Africa. It is a well known fact, that newly imported negroes are always greatly more dangerous than those born among us; and of those importations a very large proportion consisted of Koromantyn slaves, from the Gold Coast, who have all the savage ferocity of the North American Indian.* And lastly, the whites themselves,

---

* It was the Koromantyns who brought about the insurrection in Jamaica, in 1760. They are a very hardy race, and the Dutch, who are

disunited and strangely inharmonious, would nevertheless have suppressed the insurrections, although the blacks and mulattoes were nearly *fifteen-fold* their numbers, if it had not been for the constant and too fatal interference of France. The great sin of that revolution rests on the National Assembly, and should be an awful warning to every legislature to beware of too much tampering with so delicate and difficult a subject, as an alteration of the fundamental relations of society.

But there is another cause which will render the success of the blacks forever impossible in the South, as long as slavery exists. It is, that in modern times, especially, wealth and talent must ever rule over mere physical force. During the feudal ages, the vassals never made a settled concerted attempt to throw off the yoke of the lord or landed proprietor, and the true reason was, they had neither property nor talent, and consequently the power, under these circumstances, could be placed no where else than in the hands of the lords; but so soon as the *tiers etat* arose, with commerce and manufactures, there was something to struggle for, and *le crise des revolutions*, (the crisis of revolutions,) was the consequence. No connected, persevering, and well concerted movement, ever takes place, in modern times, unless for the sake of property. Now, the property, talent, concert, and we may add, habit, are all with the whites, and render their continued superiority absolutely certain, if they are not meddled with, no matter what may be the disproportion of numbers. We look upon these insurrections in the same light that we do the murders and robberies which occur in society, and in a slave-

---

a calculating, money-making people, and withal the most cruel masters in the world, have generally preferred these slaves, because they might be forced to do most work; but the consequence of their avarice has been that they have been more cursed with insurrections than any other people in the West Indies.

holding State,—they are a sort of substitute for the latter; the robbers and murderers in what are called free States, are generally the poor and needy, who rob for money; negro slaves rarely murder or rob for this purpose; they have no inducement to do it—the fact is, the whole capital of the South is pledged for their maintenance. The present Chief Magistrate of Virginia has informed us that he has never known of but one single case in Virginia where negroes murdered for the sake of money. Now, there is no doubt, but that the common robberies and murders for money, take off, in the aggregate, more men, and destroy more property, than insurrections among the slaves; the former are the result of fixed causes eternally at work, the latter of occasional causes which are rarely, *very rarely*, in action. Accordingly, if we should look to the whole of our southern population, and compare the average number of deaths, by the hands of assassins, with the numbers elsewhere, we would be astonished to find them perhaps as few, or fewer, than in any other population of equal amount on the globe. In the city of London there is, upon an average, a murder, or a house-breaking and robbery, every night in the year, which is greater than the amount of deaths by murders, insurrections, &c., in our whole southern country; and yet the inhabitant of London walks the streets, and sleeps in perfect confidence, and why should not we, who are in fact in much less danger?* These calamities in London very properly give rise to the establishment of a

---

* We wish that accurate accounts could be published of all the deaths which had occurred from insurrections in the United States, West Indies, and South America, since the establishment of slavery; and that these could be compared to the whole population that have lived since that epoch, and the number of deaths which occur in other equal amounts of population from popular sedition, robberies, &c., and we would be astonished to see what little cause we have for the slightest apprehension on this score.

police, and the adoption of precautionary measures; and so they should in our country, and every where else. And if the Virginia Legislature had turned its attention more to this subject during its last session, we think, with all due deference, it would have redounded much more to the advantage of the State than the intemperate discussion which was gotten up.

But it is agreed on almost all hands, that the danger of insurrection now is not very great; but a time must arrive, it is supposed by many, when the dangers will infinitely increase, and either the one or the other race must necessarily be exterminated. "I do believe," said one in the Virginia Legislature, "and such must be the judgment of every reflecting man, that unless something is done in time to obviate it, the day must arrive when scenes of inconceivable horror must inevitably occur, and one of these two races of human beings will have their throats cut by the other." Another gentleman anticipates the dark day when a negro Legislature would be in session in the capital of the Old Dominion! Mr. Clay, too, seems to be full of gloomy anticipations of the future. In his colonization speech of 1830, he says, "Already the slaves may be estimated at two millions, and the free population at ten; the former being in the proportion of one to five of the latter. Their respective numbers will probably double in periods of thirty-three. In the year 1863, the number of the whites will probably be twenty, and of the blacks four millions. In 1896, forty and eight; and in the year 1929, about a century, eighty and sixteen millions. What mind is sufficiently extensive in its reach—what nerve sufficiently strong—to contemplate this vast and progressive augmentation, without an awful foreboding of the tremendous consequences." If these anticipations are true, then may we in despair sit quietly down by the waters of Babylon, and weep over our lot, for we can never remove the blacks—"*Hæret lateri lethalis arundo.*"

But we have none of these awful forebodings. We do not look to the time when the throats of one race must be cut by the other; on the contrary, we have no hesitation in affirming, and we think we can prove it, too, that in 1929, taking Mr. Clay's own statistics, we shall be much more secure from plots and insurrections than we are at this moment. It is an undeniable fact that, in the increase of population, the power and security of the dominant party always increases much more than in proportion to the relative augmentation of their numbers. One hundred men can much more easily keep an equal number in subjection than fifty, and a million would rule a million more certainly and securely than any lesser number. The dominant can only be overturned by concert and harmony among the subject party, and the greater the relative numbers on both sides, the more impossible does this concert on the part of the subjected become. A police, too, of the same relative numbers, is much more efficient amid a numerous population than a sparse one. We will illustrate by example, which cannot fail to strike even the most sceptical. Mr. Gibbon supposes that the hundredth man in any community is as much as the people can afford to keep in pay for the purposes of a police. Now suppose the community be only one hundred, then one man alone is the police. Is it not evident that the ninety-nine will be able at any moment to destroy him, and throw off all restraint? Suppose the community one thousand, then ten will form the police, which would have rather a better chance of keeping up order among the nine hundred and ninety, than the one in the one hundred—but still this would be insufficient. Let your community swell to one million, and ten thousand would then form the police, and ten thousand troops will strike terror in any city on the face of the globe. Lord Wellington lately asserted in the British Parliament, that Paris, containing a population of a million of souls, (the most boisterous and ungovernable,) never required, before the reign of Louis Philippe, more than forty-five hundred troops to keep it in the most perfect subjection. It is this very principle which explains the fact so frequently noticed, that revolutions are effected much more readily in small states than in large ones. The little republics of Greece underwent revolution almost every month; the dominant party was never safe for a moment. The little states of modern Italy have undergone more changes and revolutions than all the rest of Europe together, and if foreign influence were withdrawn, almost every ship from Europe, even now, would bring the news of some new revolution in those states. If the standing army will remain firm to the government, a successful revolution in most large empires, as France, Germany, and Russia, is almost impossible. The two revolutions in France have been successful, in consequence of the disaffection of the troops, who have joined the popular party.

Let us apply these principles to our own case; and for the sake of simplicity, we will take a county of a mixed population of twenty thousand, viz, blacks ten thousand, and whites as many:—the patrol which they can keep out, would, according to our rule, be two hundred; double both sides, and the patrol would be four hundred; quadruple, and it would be eight hundred—now, a patrol of eight hundred would be much more efficient than the two hundred, though they were, relatively to the numbers kept in order, exactly the same; and the same principle is applicable to the progress of population in the whole slaveholding country. In 1929, our police would be much more efficient than now, if the two castes preserve anything like the same relative numbers. We believe it would be better for the whites that the negro population should double, if they added only one-half more to their numbers, than that they should remain stationary on both sides. Hence, an insuperable objection to all these deporting schemes—they cannot diminish the relative proportion of the blacks to the whites, but on the contrary increase it, while they check the augmentation of the population as a whole, and consequently lessen the security of the dominant party. We do not fear the increase of the blacks, for that very increase adds to the wealth of society, and enables it to keep up the police. This is the true secret of the security of the West Indies and Brazil. In Jamaica, the blacks are eight-fold the whites; throughout the extensive empire of Brazil they are three to one. Political prophets have been prophesying for fifty years past, that the day would speedily arrive, when all the West Indies would be in possession of the negroes; and the danger is no greater now than it was at the commencement. We sincerely believe the blacks never will get possession, unless through the mad interference of the mother countries, and even then we are doubtful whether they can conquer the whites. Now, we have nowhere in the United States the immense disproportion between the two races observed in Brazil and the West Indies, and we are not like to have it in all time to come. We have no data, therefore, upon which to anticipate that dreadful crisis, which so torments the imagination of some. The little islands of the West Indies, if such crisis were fated frequently to arrive, ought to exhibit one continued series of massacres and insurrections, for their blacks are relatively much more numerous than with us, and a small extent of territory is, upon the principle just explained, much more favorable to successful revolution than a large one. Are we not, then, most unphilosophically and needlessly tormenting ourselves with the idea of *insurrection*—seeing that the West India Islands, even so much worse off than ourselves, are, nevertheless, but rarely disturbed? It is well known that where the range is sufficiently extensive, and the elements sufficiently numerous, the calculation of chances may be reduced to almost a mathematical certainty; thus, although you cannot say what will be the profit or loss of a particular gambling house in Paris on any one night, yet you may, with great accuracy, calculate upon the profits for a whole year, and with still greater accuracy, for any longer period, as ten, twenty, or one hundred years. Upon the same principle we speculate with much greater certainty upon masses of individuals, than upon single persons. Hence, bills of mortality, registers of births, marriages, crimes, &c., become very important statistics, when calculated upon large masses of population, although they prove nothing in families or among individuals. Proceeding upon this principle, we cannot fail to derive the greatest consolation from the fact, that although slavery has existed in our country for the last two hundred years, there have been but three attempts at insurrection—one in Virginia, one in South-Carolina, and, we believe, one in Louisiana—and the loss of lives from this cause has not amounted to one hundred persons in all. We may then calculate in the next two hundred years, upon a similar result, which is incomparably smaller than the number which will be taken off in free States by murders for the sake of money.

But our population returns have been looked to, and it has been affirmed that they show a steady increase of blacks, which will finally carry them in all proportion beyond the whites, and that this will be particularly the case in Eastern Virginia. We have no fears on this score either; even if it were true, the danger would not be very great. With the increase of the blacks, we can afford to enlarge the police;

and we will venture to say, that with the hundredth man at our disposal, and faithful to us, we would keep down insurrection in any large country on the face of the globe. But the speakers in the Virginia Legislature, in our humble opinion, made most unwarrantable inferences from the census returns. They took a period between 1790 and 1830, and judged exclusively from the aggregate results of the whole time. Mr. Brown pointed out their fallacy, and showed that there was but a small portion of the period in which the blacks had rapidly gained upon the whites, but during the residue they were most rapidly losing their high relative increase, and would, perhaps, in 1840, exhibit an augmentation less than the whites. But let us go a little back. In 1740, the slaves in South-Carolina, says Marshall, were three times the whites; the danger from them was greater then than it ever has been since, or ever will be again. There was an insurrection in that year, which was put down with the utmost ease, although instigated and aided by the Spaniards. The slaves in Virginia, at the same period, were much more numerous than the whites. Now, suppose some of those *peepers* into futurity could have been present, would they not have predicted the speedy arrival of the time when the blacks, running ahead of the whites in numbers, would have destroyed their security? In 1763, the black population of Virginia was 100,000, and the white 70,000. In South-Carolina, the blacks were 90,000, and the whites 40,000. Comparing these with the returns of 1740, our prophets, could they have lived so long, might have found some consolation in the greater relative increase of the whites. Again, when we see in 1830, that the blacks in both States have fallen in numbers below the whites, our prophets, were they alive, might truly be pronounced *false*. (See *Holmes' Annals and Marshall's Life of Washington*, on this subject.)

But we will now proceed to examine more closely the melancholy inference which has been drawn from the relative advances of the white and black populations in Virginia, during the last forty years, and to show upon principles of an undeniable character, that it is wholly gratuitous, without any well founded data from which to deduce it. During the whole period of forty years, Virginia has been pouring forth emigrants more rapidly to the West than any other State in the Union; she has indeed been "the fruitful mother of empires." This emigration has been caused by the cheap, fertile, and unoccupied lands of the West, and by the oppressive action of the Federal Government on the southern agricultural States. This emigration has operated most injuriously upon Virginia interests, and has had a powerful tendency to check the increase of the whites, without producing anything like an equal effect on the blacks.

As this is a subject of very great importance, we shall endeavor briefly to explain it. We have already said in the progress of this discussion, that the emigration of a class of society will not injure the community, or check materially the increase of population, where a full equivalent is left in the stead of the emigrant. The largest portion of slaves sent out of Virginia, is sent through the operation of our internal slave trade; a full equivalent being thus left in place of the slave, this emigration becomes an advantage to the State, and does not check the black population as much as at first we should imagine, because it furnishes every inducement to the master to attend to his negroes, to encourage marriage, and to cause the greatest possible number to be raised, and thus it affords a powerful stimulus to the *spring* of black population, which, in a great measure, counteracts the emigration. But when we come to examine into the efflux of the white population from our State to the West, we find a totally different case presented to our view. The emigration of the white man not only takes a laborer from the State, but capital likewise; so far, therefore, in this case, from the State gaining an equivalent for the emigrant, she not only loses him, but his capital also, and thus she is impoverished, or at least advances more slowly in the acquisition of wealth, from a double cause— from the loss of both persons and capital.

Let us examine a little more fully, the whole extent of the loss which the State thus suffers, and we shall find it immeasurably beyond our hasty conceptions. In the first place, we cannot properly estimate the loss of *labor* by the number of emigrants, for we must recollect the majority of emigrants from among the whites consists of males, who form decidedly the more productive sex; and these males are generally between eighteen and thirty, precisely that period of life at which the laborer is most productive, and has ceased to be a mere consumer. Up to this period, we are generally an expense to those who rear us, and when we leave the State at this time, it loses not only the individuals, but all the capital, together with interest on that capital, which have been spent in rearing and educating. Thus a father has been for years spending the whole profits of his estate in educating his sons, and so soon as that education is completed they roam off to the West. The society of Virginia then loses both the individuals and the capital which had been spent upon them, without an equivalent. Perhaps a young man, thus educated, if he were to remain among us, could make, by the exercise of his talents, two or three thousand dollars per annum. This is more than ten field laborers could make by their labor, and consequently the loss of one such man as above described, is equal to the loss of ten common laborers in a politico-economical view, and perhaps to more than one hundred in a moral point of view. We have made some exertion to ascertain the average annual emigration of whites from the State, but without success. Supposing the number to be three thousand, and we have no doubt that it is far less less than the true amount, we would err but little in saying that these three thousand would be at least equal to twelve thousand taken from among *mere laborers.*

Now, what is the effect of this great abstraction from Virginia, of productive citizens and capital? Why, most assuredly, to prevent the accumulation of wealth, and the increase of white population. You will find, on examination, that this emigration robs the land of its fair proportion of capital and labor, and thus injures our agriculture, and entirely prevents all improvements of our lands; it sweeps off from the State the circulating capital as soon as formed, and leaves scarcely any thing of value behind, but *lands, negroes and houses.* All this has a tendency to check the increase of the whites, not only by the direct lessening of the population by emigration, but much more by paralyzing the spring of white population. The increase of the blacks, under these circumstances, becomes much more rapid, and has served in part to counteract the deleterious effects springing from the emigration of whites. In this point of view, the augmentation of our black population should be a source of consolation, instead of alarm and despondency. Let us now see whether this state of things is forever to be continued, or whether there be not some cheering signs in the political horizon, portending a better and a brighter day for the Old Dominion, in the vista of the future. There are two causes evidently calculated to check this emigration of capital and citizens from Virginia, and to insure a more rapid increase of her white population, and augmentation of her wealth. These are, first, the filling up of our vacant territory of population; and second, the completion of such a system of internal improvement in Virginia, as will administer to the multiplied wants of her people, and take off the surplus produce of the interior of the State to the great market of the world—the first dependent on *time*, and the second on the energy and enterprise of the State.

1st. It is very evident, that as population advances and overflows our Western territory, all the good lands will be gradually occupied; a longer and a longer barrier of cultivated and populous region will be interposed between Virginia and cheap Western lands, and with this onward march of population and civilization, emigration from the old States must gradually cease. The whole population of the Union is now 13,000,000; in less than fifty years from this time, (a short period in the history of nations,) we shall have fifty millions of souls—our people will then cease to be migratory, and assume that stability every where witnessed in the older countries of the World; and this result will be greatly accelerated, if the southern country shall, in the meantime, be relieved from the blighting oppression of federal exactions, As this state of things arrives, the whites in Virginia will be found to increase more rapidly than the blacks; and thus, that most alarming inference drawn from disproportionate increase of the two castes, for the last forty years, will be shown, in the lapse of time, to be a false vision, engendered by *fear*, and unsupported by *philosophy* and *fact*. We already perceive that the whites, in the ratio of their increase, have been, for the last twenty years, gradually gaining on the blacks; thus, in 1790, east of the Blue Ridge, the whites were 314,523, and the slaves 277,449—in 1830, the proportions were, in the same district, whites, 375,935; slaves, 418,529; gain of the blacks on the whites, 77,398. "But when did this gain take place?" Between 1800 and 1810, the rate of increase of the whites was only seven-tenths of one per cent., while that of the slaves was eleven per cent. From 1810 to

1820, the ratio of the increase of whites was three per cent., and that of slaves was six per cent. From 1820 to 1830, the ratio of increase of the whites was near eight per cent., and that of the slaves not quite nine per cent.; and when we take into consideration the whole population of our State, east and west of the Blue Ridge, we find that the whites have been gaining at the rate of fifteen per cent. for the last ten years, while the slaves have been increasing at the rate of ten per cent. only—and thus is it we find that those very statistics which are adduced by the abolitionists, to alarm the timid, and operate on the imagination of the unreflecting, turn out, upon closer scrutiny, to be of the most cheering and consolatory character, clearly demonstrating, upon the very principle of calculation assumed by the abolitionists themselves, that the condition of the whites is rapidly altering for the better, with the lapse of time.

We will now proceed to point out the operation of the second cause, above mentioned—a judicious system of internal improvement in checking emigration to the West. It is well known, that in proportion to the facilities which are offered to commerce, and the ease and cheapness with which the products of land may be conveyed to market, so do the profits of agriculture rise, and with them, a general prosperity is diffused over the whole country—new products are raised upon the soil—new occupations springing up—old ones are enlarged and rendered more productive—a wider field is opened for the display of the energies of both mind and body, and the rising generation are bound down to the scenes of their infancy, and the homes of their fathers; not by the tie of affection and association alone, but by the still stronger ligament of *interest*. Sons who have spent in their education all the profits which a kind father has earned by hard industry on the soil, will not now be disposed to wring from his kindness the small patrimony which he may possess, and move off with the proceeds to the West; but general prosperity will induce them to remain in the land which gave them birth, to add to the wealth and the population of the State, and to be a comfort and a solace to their aged parents in the decline of their days. We do, indeed, consider internal improvement in Virginia, the great *panacea* by which most of the ills which now weigh down the State may be removed, and health and activity communicated to every department of industry.

We are happy to see that the Legislature of Virginia, during the last session, incorporated a company to complete the James River and Kanawha improvements, and that the city of Richmond has so liberally contributed by her subscriptions, as to render the project almost certain of success. It is this great improvement which is destined to revolutionize the financial condition of the Old Dominion, and speed her on more rapidly in wealth and numbers, than she has ever advanced before; the snail pace at which she has hitherto been crawling, is destined to be converted into the giant's stride, and this very circumstance, of itself, will defeat all the gloomy predictions about the blacks. The first effect of the improvement will be to raise up larger towns in the eastern portion of the State.* Besides other manifold advantages which

* Dr. Cooper, of Columbia, whose capacious mind has explored every department of knowledge, and whose ample experience through a long life, has furnished him with the most luminous illustrations and facts, has most admirably pointed out in the 25th chapter of his Political Economy, the great advantages of large towns, and we have no doubt but that the absence of large towns in Virginia, has been one cause of the inferiority of Virginia to some of the Northern States, in energy and industry. We are sorry that our limits will not allow us to insert a portion of the chapter on the advantages of large towns, just referred to, and that we must content ourselves with a warm recommendation of its perusal.

these towns will diffuse, they will have a tendency to draw into them the capital and free laborers of the North, and in this way to destroy the proportion of the blacks. Baltimore is now an exemplification of the fact, which, by its mighty agency, is fast making Maryland a non-slaveholding State. Again, the rise of cities in the lower part of Virginia, and increased density of population, will render the division of labor more complete, break down the large farms into small ones, and substitute, in a great measure, the garden for the plantation cultivation; consequently, less slave, and more free labor will be requisite, and in due time the abolitionists will find this most lucrative system working to their heart's content, increasing the prosperity of Virginia, and diminishing the evils of slavery, without those impoverishing effects which all other schemes must necessarily have.

Upon the West, *particularly*, the beneficial effects of a judicious system of improvement, will be almost incalculable, At this moment, the emigration from the western and middle counties of Virginia, is almost as great as from the eastern. The western portion of Virginia, in consequence of its great distance from market, and the wretched condition of the various communications leading through the State, is necessarily a grazing country. A grazing country requires but a very sparse population, and consequently, but small additions to our western population renders it redurdant, and there is an immediate tendency in the supernumeraries to emigration. A gentleman from the West lately informed us, that in his immediate neighborhood he knew of seventy persons who had moved off, and many others were exceedingly anxious to go, but were detained because they could not dispose of their lands. The remedy for all this is as glaring as the light of the mid-day sun. Give to this portion of the State the communications which they require. Let our great central improvement be completed, and immediately the grazing system will be converted into the grain growing, and the very first effect of sticking the plough into the soil, which has hitherto grown grass alone, will be an increased demand for labor, which will at once check the tide of emigration, so rapidly flowing on to the distant West—and agricultural profits will rise at once 50 or 100 per cent. One of the most closely observant citizens of the West has informed us, that he can most conclusively show, that if flour would command $3 a barrel, on the farms in his neighborhood, the profits of raising grain would be double those of the grazing system. Here, then, is the *true ground* for *unity* of *action*, between the eastern and western portion of Virginia; let them steadily unite in pushing forward a vigorous system of internal improvement. Under what a miserably short-sighted and suicidal policy must the West act, then, if it seriously urges the emancipation of our slaves. The very first effect of it will be, to stop forever the great central improvement. Where is the State to get the money from, to cut canals and railroads through her territory, and send out thousands besides to Africa ? The very agitation of this most romantic and impracticable scheme is calculated to *nip in the bud* our whole system of internal improvements ; and we can but hope that the intelligence of the West will soon discover how very hostile this whole abolition scheme is to all its true interests, and will curb in their wild career, by the right of instruction, those who would uproot the very foundations of society, if their schemes should ever be carried out to their full extent. We venture to predict, that, if these abolition schemes shall ever be seriously studied in Virginia, that there will be but one voice—but one opinion concerning them, throughout the State—that they are at war with the true interests of Virginia, in every quarter—in the West as well as the East. We hope then, most sincerely, that those gentlemen who have been so perseveringly engaged in urging forward this great scheme of improvement, will not falter until the work is accomplished. We are well convinced that they are the true benefactors of the State—and they deserve well of the republic—and at some day, not very distant, they will have the consolation of seeing that the moral effects of this system will be no less salutary than the physical. We hope, then, we have shown, upon principles which cannot be controverted, that the experience of the last forty years in Virginia, need not fill us with apprehensions for the future. Time and internal improvement will cure all our ills, and speed on the Old Dominion more rapidly in wealth and prosperity.

Many are most willing to allow the force of the preceding reasoning, and to admit that there is no real danger to be apprehended either now, or in future, from our blacks; and yet, they say there is a feeling of insecurity throughout the slaveholding country, and this sense of insecurity destroys our happiness. Now, we are most willing to admit that, after such an insurrection as that in Southampton, the public mind will be disturbed, and alarm and apprehension will pervade the community. But the fact proves, that all this is of short, *very short* duration. We believe that there was not a single citizen in Virginia, who felt any alarm from the negroes, previous to the Southampton tragedy, and we believe at this moment there are very few who feel the slightest apprehension. We have no doubt, paradoxical as it may seem to some, but that the population of our slaveholding country enjoys as much or more conscious security, than any other people on the face of the globe! You will find throughout the whole slaveholding portion of Virginia, and we believe it is the same in the southern States, generally, that the houses are scarcely ever fastened at night, so as to be completely inaccessible to those without, except in towns. This simple fact is *demonstration complete* of the conscious security of our citizens, and their great confidence in the fidelity of the blacks. There is no *bas peuple*, no *lower class*, on the globe, among whom the life of a man is so secure as among the slaves of America, for they rarely murder, as we have already seen, for the sake of money. A negro will rob your hen-roost or your stye, but it is rare indeed, that he can ever be induced to murder you. Upon this subject we speak from experience. We have sojourned in some of the best regulated countries of Europe, and we know that every where the man of property dares not close his eyes before every window and door are barred against intruders from without. And, we believe, even in our northern States, these precautions are adopted to a much greater extent than with us; and, consequently, mark a much greater sense of insecurity than exists among us.

5thly, and lastly. *Slave labor is unproductive, and the distressed condition of Virginia and the whole South is owing to this cause.* Our limits will not allow us to investigate fully this assertion, but a very partial analysis will enable us to show that the truth of the general proposition upon which the conclusion is based, depends on circumstances, and that those circumstances do not apply to our southern country. The ground assumed by Smith and Storch, who are the most able supporters of the doctrine of the superior productiveness of free labor, is that each one is actuated by a desire to accumulate when free, and this desire produces much more efficient and constant exertions than can possibly be expected from the feeble operation of fear upon the slave. We are, in the main, converts to this doctrine, but must be permitted to limit it by some considerations. It is very evident, when we look to the various countries in which there is free labor alone, that a vast difference in its productiveness is manifested. The English operative we are disposed to consider the most productive laborer in the world, and the Irish laborer, in his immediate neighborhood, is not more than equal to the southern slave—the Spanish and even Italian laborers are inferior. Now, how are we to account for this great difference? It will be found *mainly* to depend upon the operation of two great principles, and *secondarily* upon attendant circumstances. These two principles are the desire to accumulate and better our condition, and a desire to indulge in idleness and inactivity.

We have already seen that the principle of idleness triumphed over the desire for accumulation among the savages of North and South America, among the African nations, among the blacks of St. Domingo, &c., and nothing but the strong arm of authority could overcome its operation. In southern countries idleness is very apt to predominate, even under the most favorable circumstances, over the desire to accumulate, and slave labor, consequently, in such countries, is most productive. Again, staple growing States are *cœteris paribus*, more favorable to slave labor than manufacturing States. Slaves in such countries may be worked by bodies under the eye of a superintendent, and made to perform more labor than freemen. There is no instance of the successful cultivation of the sugar cane by free labor. St. Domingo, once the greatest sugar growing island in the world, makes now scarcely enough for her own supply. We very much doubt even whether slave labor be not best for all southern agricultural countries. Humboldt, in his New Spain, says he doubts whether there be a plant on the globe so productive as the banana, and yet these banana districts, strange to tell, are the poorest and most miserable in all South America, because the people only labor a little to support themselves, and spend the rest of their time in idleness. There is no doubt but slave labor would be the most productive kind in these districts. We doubt whether the extreme south of the United States, and the West India Islands, would ever have been cultivated to the same degree of perfection as now, by any other than slave labor. The history of colonization furnishes no example whatever, of the transplantation of whites to very warm or tropical latitudes without signal deterioration of character, attended with an unconquerable aversion to labor. And it would seem, that nothing but slavery can remedy this otherwise inevitable tendency. The fact, that to the North, negro slavery has every where disappeared, whilst to the South it has maintained its ground triumphantly against free labor, is of itself conclusive of the superior productiveness of slave labor in southern latitudes. We believe that Virginia and Maryland are too far North for slave labor, but all the States to the South of these are, perhaps, better adapted to slave labor than free.

But it is said, with the increasing density of population, free labor becomes cheaper than slave, and finally extinguishes it, as has actually happened in the west of Europe; this, we are ready to admit, but think it was owing to a change in the tillage, and rise of manufactures and commerce, to which free labor alone is adapted. As a proof of this, we can cite the populous empire of China, and the Eastern nations, generally, where slave labor has stood its ground against free labor, although the population is denser, and the proportional means of subsistence more scanty than any where else on the face of the globe. How is this to be accounted for, let us ask? Does it not prove, that under some circumstances, slave labor is as productive as free? We would as soon look to China to test this principle, as any other nation on earth. The slave districts in China, according to the report of travellers, are determined by latitude and agricultural products. The wheat growing districts have no slaves, but the rice, cotton, and sugar-growing districts, situated in warm climates, have all of them slaves, affording a perfect exemplification of the remarks above made. Again, looking to the nations of antiquity, if the Scriptural accounts are to be relied on, the number of inhabitants of Palestine must have been more than 6,000,000; at which rate, Palestine was at least, when taking into consideration her limited territory, five times as populous as England.* Now, we know the tribes of Judah and Israel both used slave labor, and it must have been exceedingly productive; for, we find the two Kings of Judah and Israel bringing into the field no less than 1,200,000 chosen men;† and Jehosaphat, the son of Asa, had an army consisting of 1,160,000;‡ and what a prodigious force must he have commanded, had he been sovereign of all the tribes. Nothing but the most productive labor could ever have supported the immense armies which were then led into the field.

Wallace thinks that ancient Egypt must have been thrice as populous as England; and yet so valuable was slave labor, that ten of the most dreadful plagues that ever affected mankind, could not dispose the selfish heart of Pharoah to part with his Israelitish slaves; and when he lost them, Egypt sunk, never to rise to her pristine grandeur again. Ancient Italy, too, not to mention Greece, was exceedingly populous, and perhaps Rome was a larger city than any of modern times; and yet slave labor supported these dense populations, and even rooted out free labor. All these examples prove sufficiently, that under certain circumstances, slave is as productive, and even more productive, than free labor.

But the Southern States, and particularly Virginia, have been compared with the non-slaveholding States, and pronounc-

* See Wallace on the Numbers of Mankind, p. 52, Edin. edition.
† 2d. Chron. xiii. 3.
‡ 2d. Chron. xvii.

ed far behind them in the general increase of wealth and population; and this, it is said, is a decisive proof of the inferiority of slave labor in this country. We are sorry that we have not space for a thorough investigation of this assertion, but we have no doubt of its fallacy. Look to the progress of the colonies before the establishment of the Federal Government, and you find that the slaveholding were the most prosperous and the most wealthy. The North dreaded the formation of the confederated government, *precisely* because of its *poverty*. This is an historical fact. It stood to the South, as Scotland did to England at the period of the Union; and feared lest the South, by its superior wealth, supported by this very *slave labor*, all *of a sudden*, has become so unproductive, should abstract the little wealth which it possessed. Again, look to the exports at the present time of the whole confederacy, and what do we see? Why, that one-third of the States, and those *slaveholding*, too, furnish two-thirds of the whole exports! But although this is now the case, we are still not prosperous. Let us ask, then, two simple questions: 1st. How came the South, for two hundred years, to prosper with her slave labor, if so very unproductive and ruinous? And 2dly. How does it happen, that her exports are so great, even now, and that her prosperity is, nevertheless, on the decline? Painful as the accusation may be to the heart of the true patriot, we are forced to assert, that the unequal operation of the Federal Government has principally achieved it. The North has found that it could not compete with the South in agriculture, and has had recourse to the system on duties, for the purpose of raising up the business of manufactures. This is a business in which the slave labor cannot compete with northern, and in order to carry this system through, a coalition has been formed with the West, by which a large portion of the Federal funds are to be spent in that quarter for internal improvements. These duties act as a discouragement to southern industry, which furnishes the exports by which the imports are purchased, and a bounty to northern labor, and the partial disbursements of the funds, increase the pressure on the South to a still greater degree. It is not slave labor, then, which has produced our depression, but it is the action of the Federal Government which is ruining slave labor.

There is, at this moment, an exemplification of the destructive influence of government agency in the West Indies. The British West India Islands are now in a more depressed condition than any others, and both the Edinburgh and London Quarterly Reviews charge their depression upon the regulations, taxing sugar, coffee, &c., and preventing them, at the same time, from purchasing bread stuffs, &c., from the United States, which can be furnished by them cheaper than from any other quarter. Some of the philanthropists of Great Britain cry out it is slavery which has done it, and the slaves must be liberated; but they are at once refuted by the fact, that never has an island flourished more rapidly than Cuba, in their immediate neighborhood. And Cuba flourishes because she enjoys free trade, and has procured, of late, plenty of slaves. It is curious that the population of this island has, for the last thirty years, kept pace with that of Pennsylvania, one of the most flourishing of the States of the confederacy, and her wealth has increased in a still greater ratio.* Look again to Brazil, perhaps at this moment the most prosperous state of South America, and we find her slaves three times more numerous than the freemen. Mr. Brougham, in his Colonial Policy, says that Cayenne never flourished as long as she was scantily supplied with slaves, but her prosperity commenced the moment she was supplied with an abundance of

* See some interesting statistics concerning this island in Mr. Poinsett's Notes on Mexico.

this *unproductive* labor. Now we must earnestly ask an explanation of these phenomena, upon the principle that slave labor is unproductive.

There are other causes, too, which have operated in concert with the Federal Government, to depress the South. The climate is unhealthy, and upon average, perhaps one-tenth of the labor is suspended during the sickly months. There is a great deal of travelling, too, from this cause to the North, which abstracts the capital from the South, and spreads it over the North. The emigration from the South to the West, as we have before seen, is very great and very injurious; and added to all this, the *standard of comfort* is much higher in the slaveholding than the non-slaveholding States.* All these circumstances together, are sufficient to account for the depressed condition of the South, without asserting that slave labor is valueless.

---

* In the Virginia debate, it was said that the slow progress of the Virginia population was a most unerring symptom of her want of prosperity, and the inefficacy of slave labor. Now we protest against this criterion, unless very cautiously applied. Ireland suffers more from want and famine than any other country in Europe, and yet her population advances almost as rapidly as ours, and it is this very increase which curses the country with the plague or famine. In the Highlands of Scotland, they have a very sparse population, scarcely increasing at all; and yet they are much better fed, clothed, &c., than in Ireland. Malthus has proved, that there are two species of checks which repress redundant populations—positive and preventive. It is the latter which keeps down the Scotch population; while the former, always accompanied with misery, keeps down the Irish. We believe, at this time, the preventive checks are in full operation in Virginia. The people of this State live much better than the same classes to the North, and they will not get married unless there is a prospect of maintaining their families in the same style they have been accustomed to live in. We believe the preventive checks may commence their operation too soon for the wealth of a State, but they always mark a high degree of civilization—so that the slow progress of population in Virginia turns out be her highest eulogy.

But we believe all other causes as "dust in the balance," when compared with the operation of the Federal Government.

How does it happen that Louisiana, with a greater proportional numbers of slaves than any other State in the Union, with the most insalubrious climate, with one-fourth of her white population spread over the more northern States in the sickly season, and with a higher *standard of comfort* than perhaps any other State in the Union, is nevertheless one of the most rapidly flourishing in the whole southern country? The true answer is, she has been so fortunately situated as to be able to reap the fruits of Federal protection. "Midas's wand" has touched her, and she has reaped the golden harvest. There is no complaint there of the unproductiveness of slave labor.

But it is time to bring this long article to a close; it is upon a subject which we have most reluctantly discussed; but, as we have already said, the example was set from a higher quarter; the seal has been broken, and we therefore determined to enter fully into the discussion. If our positions be true, and it does seem to us they may be sustained by reasoning almost as conclusive as the demonstrations of the mathematician, it follows, that the time for emancipation has not yet arrived, and perhaps it never will. We hope, sincerely, that the intelligent sons of Virginia will ponder before they move—before they enter into a scheme which will destroy more than half Virginia's wealth, and drag her down from her proud and elevated station among the mean things of the earth,—and when, Sampson-like, she shall, by this ruinous scheme, be shorn of all her power and all her glory, the passing stranger may at some future day exclaim,

> The Niobe of nations—there she stands,
> "¶Friendless and helpless in her voiceless woe."

Once more, then, do we call upon our statesmen to pause, ere they engage in this ruinous scheme. The power of man has limits, and he should never attempt impossibilities. We do believe it is beyond the power of man to separate the elements of our population, even if it were desirable. The deep and solid foundations of society cannot be broken up by the vain *fiat* of the legislator. We must recollect that the *laws* of Lycurgus were promulgated, the sublime eloquence of Demosthenes and Cicero was heard, and the glorious achievements of Epaminondas and Scipio were witnessed, in countries where slavery existed—without *for one moment* loosening the tie between master and slave. We must recollect, too, that Poland has been desolated; that Kosciusko, Sobieski, Scrynecki, have fought and bled for the cause of liberty in that country; that one of her monarchs annulled, *in words*, the tie between master and slave, and yet the *order of nature* has, in the end, vindicated itself, and the dependence between master and slave has scarcely for a moment ceased. We must recollect, in fine, that our own country has waded through two dangerous wars—that the thrilling eloquence of the Demosthenes of our land has been heard with rapture, exhorting to death, rather than slavery,—that the most liberal principles have ever been promulgated and sustained, in our deliberate bodies, and before our judicial tribunals—and the whole has passed by without breaking or tearing asunder the elements of our social fabric. Let us reflect on these things, and learn wisdom from experience; and know that the relations of society, generated by the *lapse of ages*, cannot be altered in a *day*.